T0165691

POWDER RIVER!
A HISTORY OF THE
91ST INFANTRY DIVISION
IN WWII

by Roy Livengood

TURNER PUBLISHING COMPANY
Paducah, Kentucky

TURNER PUBLISHING COMPANY

The Front Line of Military History Books
412 Broadway, P.O. Box 3101
Paducah, KY 42002-3101
(502) 443-0121

Author: Roy Livengood

Library of Congress
Catalog Card No. 94-60146
ISBN: 156311-135-7

Printed in the United States of America
Limited Edition

Additional books may be purchased directly
from the publisher

Also by Roy Livengood:
Thunder in the Apennines

TABLE OF CONTENTS

INTRODUCTION

This book is dedicated to all those men, living and dead, who wore the Fir Tree shoulder patch.

"War is a malignant disease, an idiocy, a prison, and the pain it causes is beyond telling or imagining; but war was our condition and our history, the place we had to live in."

...Martha Gellhorn

This is the story of an infantry division, an organization of 15,000 civilians who were drafted into the United States Army to help defeat the forces of Nazism and Fascism in the years 1942-45. The World War II Army consisted of ninety divisions: infantry, armor and airborne. The story of each division is similar in that they were activated, trained and sent overseas. Men from all forty-eight states served in each division so they were all remarkably alike, yet somehow different. Sometimes it was the commander who set a unit apart, especially if that commander was a colorful General George S. Patton; sometimes it was geography, for every division has its own regional heritage and shoulder patch and comes from a particular state. The red keystone of Pennsylvania is the patch of the 28th Division; the letters O-H-I-O form the patch of the 83rd Division; the Kansas National Guard's 35th Division wears the insignia of the old Santa Fe Railroad. The 29th Division from Virginia and Maryland is represented by a circle of half blue and half gray, both the Confederacy and the Union.

The 91st Division was activated at Camp Lewis, Washington in September, 1917. Its members came from the far western states of California, Idaho, Montana, Oregon, Washington and Wyoming, so these men chose a Douglas fir tree as their symbol. During the seventy-seven years since activation, the division has become steeped in western lore and tradition; however, it's not the shoulder patch, the traditions or the cavalry background that makes the 91st unique, but a casual cry uttered by a man from Wyoming on a rainy morning at Camp Lewis. According to the story, several hundred men were assembling for reveille. A first sergeant was calling off the names of the recruits. He paused for a moment, then hollered, "Where do you boys hail from?"

From the rear ranks, a cowboy still clad in civvies, yelled out:

"From Wyoming! Powder River! Let 'er buck!"

The expression goes back many years and no doubt has been used as both an expletive and epithet. During those long months in Italy the phrase was shortened to a simple, "Powder River!" It was sounded out when one tripped over a log, or at the end of a long hike or when an artillery barrage went on and on and on. In his story of the river, Struthers Burt tells us:

"The most famous river in Wyoming? The Powder is the most famous river in the Northwest. Famous now all over the country, its name familiar to thousands who haven't the faintest idea where the river is, or whether it's an actual river or merely an exclamation. A river spoken of with contempt by all who first saw it, whose name has become a battle cry. A shout of encouragement. A cry of derision. A password to a secret society. And above all a symbol of an American way of living which, despite all the varied drama of American life, took hold of the American imagination, and still holds it, as an epitome of perhaps the deepest and most universal expression of this continent's wish."

These two words, "Powder River!", Burt writes, are short, sharp and shrill, like the cowboy yell, which is the Confederate yell brought up the Texas trail with the longhorns, with the echo of the coyote added.

The famous cry has sounded out over the battlefields of France and has echoed through the mountains of Italy and is now woven into the history of American valor and endurance.

Though I served with the 91st Division throughout its long period of combat it is not my intent to glorify the actions of the division. Its battle record, in both World Wars, speaks for itself and those of us who were there know what we had to endure and there was nothing glorious about it.

So the purpose of this book is to tell what happened to the men of one division of the United States Army in the Italian Campaign of the Second World War and to tell it simply and honestly.

Unlike the division history published in 1947 I do not follow each regiment through its many actions since this would be repetitive, but have tried to give a general description of the division in combat, along with personalities and eye-witness reports and have chosen those narratives which I consider an accurate portrayal of the war as it actually was. I realize some will argue with the eye-witness accounts of a few men, but those of us who were there know a battle is a confusing thing, sometimes chaotic, and in the tangle of events men of a single squad will sometimes see the battle very differently. Over the years I've researched the 91st Division after-action reports rather thoroughly in both the National Archives and the Eisenhower Library at Abilene, Kansas. During the time I was writing *Thunder in the Apennines* I read the entire regimental records of the 361st Infantry. As a veteran of the 363rd Infantry, I've researched the wartime documents of that regiment. My biggest disappointment in writing this book was my failure to locate sufficient material on the 362nd Infantry. I've used very little of my previous research while putting together *Powder River!* but have relied almost solely on the personal narratives of those veterans who fought with the Division. For my research into the Fifth Army actions I've used the nine volumes of the original history which were privately published in Italy and the United States instead of the condensed volume written by professor Chester G. Starr.

To some members there may seem to be far more detailed actions written about one company than another. This is not because the author preferred writing about one unit over another unit, it is a matter of a lack of records, particularly in the case of the 362nd Infantry. In World War II an infantry regiment consisted of nine rifle companies and during the tne months the 91st Division was in combat these companies were in many battles. The performance of some may have been more brilliant than others, but one action is seldom the basis for a military reputation. In the lengthy struggle to win the Italian Campaign one infantry regiment was no more gallant than another, nor were the men of one regiment more courageous than the men of another, at least not over the long haul. Like the regiments of the other Fifth Army divisions, the men of the 91st did what they had to do and there were good days and bad. As Bill Mauldin said, "When 15,000 men from 48 states are put together in an outfit their thinking and their actions are going to be pretty much like those of any other 15,000. Their efficiency and their accomplishments are altered to a certaom extent by the abilities of their commanders, but the guys themselves are pretty much the same."

PREFACE

Fifty years ago, Highway 65 was the main route between the Tuscan city of Florence and the Emilian city of Bologna, a distance of some seventy-five kilometers. Today, this highway has given way to the four lane Autostrada del Sole (Highway of the Sun) which runs west of the old road and catches the expressway to Milan at the Bologna suburb of Casalecchio. During the late summer and autumn of 1944, the 91st Infantry Division, accompanied by three other U.S. Army divisions, the 34th, 85th and 88th, fought directly up Sixty-five and through the mountainous terrain of the region. After a series of ferocious battles that lasted nearly two months these troops were stopped by the German Fourteenth Army just nine miles short of the flat, fertile fields of the valley of the Po. At times, the mountain fighting was the most fierce of the entire campaign.

For seven long months, from the fall of Rome, 4 June, 1944 until the beginning of 1945, these four infantry divisions bore the brunt of Fifth Army operations in Italy.

Now, driving along the highway south of Bologna, the tourist will travel through the towns of Pianoro, Livergnano, Loiano and Monghidoro, then top the peak of Raticosa Pass, the very tip of the roof of the Northern Apennines. The highway drops fast to Passo della Futa, which was the most heavily fortified of the German defenses, rising and falling, twisting and turning, until it levels out near the village of Vaglia and leads to the Arno River valley and the city of Florence.

The autumn 1944 war that was fought along this secondary road has been all but forgotten by American historians and that sad campaign has been relegated to the dark corridors of history. Even a generation of Italians cannot remember the ravaged regions that were Tuscany and Emilia-Romagna when the fighting ended. Not a town, not a village, not a house, or a hill or a mountain escaped the onslaught that swept through the Northern Apennines. Pianoro was pulverized; Livergnano was totally destroyed and Loiano was left in ruins. The only thing to survive in Monghidoro was the church steeple with its round-faced clock. The pass at Futa was scarred by a three mile long anti-tank ditch and Vaglia was nothing but a cold heap of rubble. But today, due to the perseverance and hard work of the Italian people and the restorative power of nature, the mountain sides are once again covered with dense shrubbery and the forty-five year old pine trees grow thick, tall and green. The towns have been rebuilt and their houses are bright, fresh and new.

The first troops of the 91st Division went into action near Anzio one hundred and eighty-five miles south of Florence; however, the advance to the Arno River was so swift that most veterans have only fleeting memories of the towns and the terrain of that region of Italy, but the memories of the villages and people north of the Renaissance city are vivid and lasting because the division spent the long bitter months of the Winter Line in the Highway 65 sector.

For the United States Army, the Italian Campaign was the longest sustained campaign of the Second World War. It began 9 September, 1943 and ended 2 May, 1945 in the foothills of the Alps. During those twenty months of combat the American Fifth Army suffered 188,746 battle casualties, more than the total casualties of the entire war in the Pacific from the bombing of Pearl Harbor to the nuclear blast at Hiroshima.

Until D-Day, 6 June, 1944, the press covered the events in Italy rather thoroughly, but once the beaches of Normandy were invaded all news shifted to the European Theatre of Operations and the Italian Campaign became a forgotten front. Never again would the war in Italy gain front page headlines though the fighting became even more furious as the Allies attempted to break out of the last range of mountains.

From the beginning to the bitter end, the war was a mountain campaign fought by regular infantry divisions. In early 1945 a specialized division of mountain trained troops was sent to the front and for a brief period took part in the fight; however, its arrival did not preclude the infantry units from having to fight in the mountains the best way they could as they had been doing for sixteen months. From the initial landing at Salerno to the heights overlooking Bologna, the standard infantry divisions conquered hundreds of miles of mountainous terrain. So it was the common infantryman who did the bulk of the mountain fighting in Italy.

The campaign was fraught with controversies. It began with a covert attempt to force the capitulation of the Italian Army and ended with secret negotiations for a separate surrender of the German Army in Italy. In between, there was a long series of disputatious operations: the bloody defeat at the Rapido River, the debacle at Anzio, the questionable destruction of the Monte Cassino abbey, the near disaster at Salerno and the irresolute offensive in the Northern Apennines. Yet, in spite of all the difficulties, the American soldier fought and won a long and arduous battle against a stubborn foe, the snows and ice of winter, the rain and mud of autumn and the dust and heat of summer; and above all, in some of the most formidable terrain in the history of warfare.

91st Division Insignia. Fort Baker, California.

POWDER RIVER!

by A.L. Kirby

Have you heard the tale of valor
That is whispered here and there?
How a horde of Western hombres
Made the Germans take the air.
How they faced the slug-fed Mausers
Which they never learned to duck;
With the war-cry of the plainsman,
"Powder River! Let 'er buck!"

In my mind I see them wading
Through the gaping maws of Hell
Through the hail of flying bullets
Mortar thuds and bursting shell;
Now again I hear the challenge,
That old cry of Western pluck,
High above the noise of battle,
"Powder River! Let 'er buck!"

Once a Royal Irish Lancer
Who had watched them in the fight
From the first grey streak of dawning
'Til the hush of falling night,
Said in awe and admiration
To a listening Cannuck,
"Faith, they went through hell a yellin'
"Powder River! Let 'er buck!"

Spectre Death rode there beside them
On his grim, ill-favored steed,
Gazing on each mangled body
With a grin of ghoulish greed.
But they faced the apparition,
There amid the mud and muck,
Laughed and hollered, "Ride'em, Cowboy,
Powder River! Let 'er buck!"

Listen, soldier, here's a moral,
Which is worth your while to keep,
'Tis the bunch that won the struggle
Over there across the deep.
If the cards seem stacked against you
Do not whine or curse your luck,
Be a soldier, grin and tell them,
"Powder River! Let 'er buck!"

COMPOSITION OF THE 91ST INFANTRY DIVISION IN WORLD WAR II

DIVISION HEADQUARTERS AND SPECIAL TROOPS

Headquarters Company

91st Reconnaissance Troop

91st Signal Company

91st Quartermaster Company

791st Ordnance (LM) Company

91st Military Police Platoon

DIVISION ARTILLERY	Brig. Gen Ralph Hospital
916th F.A. Bn	Lt. Col. James E. Shaw, Jr.
346th F.A. Bn	Lt. Col. Calvin E. Berry
347th F.A. Bn	Lt. Col. Woodrow L. Lynn
348th F.A. Bn	Lt. Col. Robert B. Collier

361ST INFANTRY REGIMENT	Colonel Rudolph W. Broedlow
362ND INFANTRY REGIMENT	Colonel John W. Cotton
363RD INFANTRY REGIMENT	Colonel W. Fulton Magill, Jr.
316TH MEDICAL BATTALION	Lt. Col. Paul W. Brecher
316TH ENGINEER BATTALION	Lt. Col. Willialm B. Holley

2nd Platoon, Company B, 363rd Infantry. Camp Adair, Oregon. 1943.

CHAPTER ONE — OREGON DAYS

"Make no mistake about it, however, each man's war is separate and personal unto himself and not exactly like that of any other. It is fought first within his own heart and soul, and the outcome is buried with his bones."

Charles R. Cawthon . . .OTHER CLAY[1]

I

The legendary Powder River is not much of a river and some might not even call it a river. A brackish, yellowish little stream, three hundred miles in length, it meanders from the Rattlesnake range in central Wyoming northward through endless groves of cottonwoods, between banks of sand and mud, and on through the whistle-stop hamlets of Powder River, Sussex and Arvada. Then, it crosses the border into Montana just east of the Custer National Forest and winds its way through the town of Broadus, curving up through Powderville and Mizpah and mysteriously disappearing somewhere east of Miles City. On its way north it passes through the huge Powder River Basin which, years ago, was one of the great cattle countries of the nation. Now, trains out of Wyoming that once hauled bawling cattle to market, pull gondola cars full of another precious commodity; coal; for under the ground of the once disputed rangeland lies billions of tons of the black fuel. The town of Gillette booms with migrant workers flocking in to work the mines: the Caballo, the Rawhide, the Wyodak and the Black Thunder. In the after-hour bars the raucous revelry that issues forth from the miners, drinking inside the numerous taverns and nightly haunts, harks back to the frontier towns of more than one hundred years ago. Places like the prefabricated and lusterless Wright, Wyoming, have sprung up over night, not with houses, but with mobile home after mobile home. Such is the continuing heritage of the famous Powder River.

Forty miles west of Gillette, in the shadows of the Bighorns Mountains, is Johnson county, home of the warring Crow and Sioux and the site of the vicious wars of the cattleman and sheepman. Further south, rising up from the sagebrush covered hills, is Teapot Rock. Here the 1922 scandal involving the Mammoth Oil Company ruined the presidency of Warren G. Harding. Northwest of the chalky Teapot is one of the most famous hideouts in Western history, the Hole-in-the-Wall, which housed that gang of rowdies, Butch Cassidy, Harvey Logan and other assorted scoundrels and cut-throats that made up the Wild Bunch. In this region roamed the great warrior chiefs: Red Cloud, Sitting Bull, Crazy Horse and the greatest of them all,

The Meuse-Argonne Front. September 1918.

Soldiers of Co. B, 364th Infantry, 91st Div. Vauquois, France. September, 1918.

Chief Joseph. All were eventually subdued by the U.S. Cavalry whose 5th, 7th, 8th and 12th Regiments are part of the history of the 91st Division.

By the end of the nineteenth century the frontier was gone and so were the Indians, sent to their respective reservations by their conqueror and betrayer, the white man. The Wild West was tamed and the guns were silenced.

Fifteen years into the twentieth century on 28 June, 1914, the Archduke Ferdinand, heir to the throne of Austria-Hungary, was assassinated in Sarajevo, Bosnia. The actions of the assassin, Princip, would eventually kill ten million men. In less than a month, Europe was engulfed in what was to become known as the First World War. For nearly three, long bloody years the armies of the Allies and the Central Powers see-sawed back and forth along the Western Front. In early 1917, Germany announced the inauguration of unrestricted submarine warfare against the United States which made war between the two countries all but inevitable. On 2 April, President Woodrow Wilson sent before Congress and told his countrymen:

"It is a fearful thing to lead this great, peaceful country into war, into the most terrible and disastrous of all wars, civilization itself seeming to be in the balance. But right is more precious than peace, and we shall fight for the things which we have always carried nearest to our hearts—for democracy...To such a task we dedicate our lives and fortunes everything that we are and everything that we have . . . God helping us, we can do no other."

The divisions of the National Guard were mobilized in July, followed in late summer by the divisions of the National Army. Camp Lewis, Washington, the cantonment for the 91st Division, was the only one situated on the Pacific Coast. Three quarters of a century later it is still there, but now known as Fort Lewis.[2]

The advance detachment of the 91st sailed out of Brooklyn on 28 June, 1918 and arrived at various ports in England and Scotland and Brest, France. By 6 September the division was in the Sorcy-sur-Meuse area training and awaiting orders.

On the night of 19-20 September the 91st began the relief of several French units between the Meuse river and the Argonne Forest and attacked on the morning of the 26th. The heaviest fighting was not in the famous Argonne but in two valleys east of the forest. This was territory the French and Germans had fought over time and again. It was a wasteland of pock-marked mud, barbed wire, rotting bodies and thousands of shell holes.

For nearly two weeks the division moved over this embattled terrain driving the enemy from the strong points of Very, Epininville, Gesnes, Eclisfontaine and Tronsol Farm. At midnight 3 October, the 32nd U.S. Division relieved the weary men of the "Wild West" Division, the new name for the 91st.

On 7 October the division again went into the line.

By the middle of the month the Allies had made considerable progress in the great battle of the Argonne Forest; however, on the Eastern Front, in the vicinity of Ypres, the advance had not been so rapid and General

13

John J. Pershing, commander of American forces, received an urgent call from Marshal Foch for two United States divisions to help the French 6th Army. In answer to the call, the 37th and 91st Divisions were promptly sent north and on 30 October took up the fight. They methodically broke down the German resistance and were relieved 4 November.

The 91st remained in reserve until it moved forward for an attack on 10 November. All during the day and night the division gained ground. At 1 a.m., 11 November, Company E, 363rd Infantry took over the town of Boucle-Saint-Blaise from a French patrol. It was to be the last combat action by a division unit. At 11:15 a.m. orders were issued directing that all hostilities would cease at 11 a.m.

So, at the eleventh hour on the eleventh day of the eleventh month, 1918, the First World War came to an end.

During the days after the Armistice the division patrolled the Franco-Belgian border, then on 2 January, 1919 the first troops sailed from Brest to the United States. The last elements of the division arrived in New York on 29 April.

The war had cost the 91st Division 6,108 battle casualties: 1,454 killed in action and died of wounds and 4,654 wounded in action.

Twenty-three short years would pass from the end of the First Great War to the

General John J. Pershing confers with the 91st Division CO, Maj. Gen. William Johnston.

The Argonne

beginning of the Second and those years would be some of the most traumatic in the history of the United States. The prosperous decade of the Roaring Twenties came to a halt Thursday, 24 October, 1929 when the speculation of the stock market ended in disaster and the country was plummeted into the Great Depression. Many of the veterans of the 91st Division who had returned so triumphantly from France just eleven years before now found themselves without a job and with a very dim future. By the spring of 1930 over four million Americans were out of work and the entire forty-eight states were in despair. The decade of the 30s was to be a tough one indeed.

"Saddling Up"

Shortly after the end of the war, Congress had voted to pay bonuses to all those men who fought to "make the world safe for democracy". The bonuses were to be paid by 1945; however, in May, 1932, in Portland, Oregon, some veterans of the 91st, along with other veterans, decided they should receive the bonuses immediately since many of them were living hand to mouth with a few actually going hungry. They formed the BEF—Bonus Expeditionary Force and took their cause to Washington. By the time the men had arrived at the U.S. Capitol their number had grown to more than 1,000 and they set up camp in a place called Anacostia Flats. What followed during the next two months was to become one of the most shameful

Escort Wagon.

incidents in American history. On 17 June, the Bonus Bill came to a vote and was defeated. Upon hearing the news, the veterans rioted. The Hoover administration immediately called in the Army to drive the veterans from the city. On the afternoon of 28 July, Army Chief of Staff Douglas MacArthur, astride a white horse and accompanied by his aide, Major Dwight Eisenhower, led four troops of cavalry, six tanks and a company of infantry against the men. The camp was set afire and the BEF routed. Another American soldier who later became famous also participated in the attack upon the unarmed veterans: George S. Patton. These three officers, who would later become renowned generals, would never live down the shame of Anacostia Flats.

The routing of the BEF was only the beginning of the Great Depression. Next came Mussolini and the Fascists, then Franklin D. Roosevelt, the WPA, the CCC, NRA, then Adolf Hitler, followed by the swastika, hobo jungles, the dust bowl, the Grapes of Wrath, the invasion of Austria, Neville Chamberlin and "peace in our time", and finally, the rape of Poland. Ten years after the crash of the stock market the world was once again at war.

II

April 12, 1942 was just another weekend for the troops of the First Cavalry Division stationed at Fort Bliss. On this peaceful Sunday the camp was quiet and restful and the weather pleasant. The winter had been cold and bitter but now there was a promise of spring in the air. At the entrance to the headquarters of the 5th Regiment, the rectangle of rocks that surrounded the huge letters, 5-T-H C-A-V-A-L-R-Y, shone white in the sun. A few cars were parked near the entrance but they were empty. Beyond the fort, the grey hills of southwestern Texas rose abruptly from the plains. The 5th had had a long and colorful history. Its first commander was Robert E. Lee who took over the reins when the Civil War broke out. It was also at

Appomattox to watch the surrender. It had roamed the ranges of the Bighorn mountains and pursued the Cheyenne, Arapaho, Apache and Sioux; when those years ended, it shipped to Hawaii for four years. The regiment was now commanded by Colonel Lucian K. Truscott.

The troopers of the 5th had been issued their canteen checks on Friday. The checks were a cavalry holdover from the days of the War between the States and provided the men with PX chits for tobacco, toilet articles and watered down beer. Some of these chits went to smokers and provided them with sacks of Bull Durham, Golden Grain or Brown's Mule, a chewing tobacco. Those were the days of roll your own.

Poker and dice games had flourished all during the weekend with a fast exchange of chits. Over in the Special Weapons Troop, the dayroom was occupied by a handful of men playing a weird game called bridge. These characters were considered a bit strange by the older cavalrymen who played only one game: poker, black jack and five card stud. Pearl Harbor had not dramatically changed life at Bliss. The war seemed remote and far away. Three days before, 10,000 Americans had surrendered to the Japanese at a place called Bataan. One of the prisoners was a former officer of the 5th, Jonathan Wainwright; other than that, the event had little meaning for the men of the regiment. Some of the bridge players were college educated one-year draftees who had gone into the Army singing, "Goodbye, dear! I'll be back in a year!", but December Seventh had changed that tune.

Like his fellows soldiers, Trooper James E. Bell was taking life easy that lazy Sunday afternoon but in his mind there was always the thought of his Monday detail. As the troop saddler, Bell hung out in the saddle shop, working with leather gear, canvas and pack saddles. In addition to those chores he was required to drive the open "escort wagon" to the manure dump, usually two trips daily. He was not looking forward to the task.[3]

Monday morning came soon enough and Bell was on his first trip to the dump, located two miles from the fort. The wagon was pulled by a team set up with four lines. They were ordinary pack horses and did not take kindly to harness; occasionally they could get downright nasty. The dump consisted of several acres of mounds up to eight feet high and the wagons needed a full gallop to reach the top. As the team slowly walked, Bell used a 14 inch fork to spread the manure as evenly as possible. If it wasn't even sometimes a chicken dump sergeant would send the saddler back and make him repeat his efforts. Bell didn't want that. Finally, he was finished and he headed back home for another load.

It was late in the afternoon when Bell drove to the stables to secure his team, harness and wagon. He sensed something strange was going on for the stables were deserted. The horses lacked hay and there was no grain in the feed bins, so Bell fed his team then walked toward the troop tent row to shower, wash his clothes and get ready for chow. On the way he met the stable sergeant.

Into the Sunset

A shirtless trio. ADC Brigadier General Percy W. Clarkson, CO Major General Charles H. Gerhardt and Brigadier General Edward S. Ott, Division Artillery Commander.

"What the hell is going on?" Bell asked him.

"A lot of today's stable cop detail just became non-coms," said the sergeant. "I let 'em all go. They're leaving and so are you."

Since the sergeant was known to hit the bottle frequently Bell figured it was one of those days and disregarded the comment. Arriving at his tent he noticed the upper area near the orderly room was alive with people. Some new USO shows, he thought. He then walked down to the latrine, showered, washed his clothing on the shower floor, cleaned his brogans and returned to his tent where he found the troop clerk waiting for him.

"Where have you been?" asked the clerk. "I've been looking all over hell for you."

"The dump," said Bell. "Where else? What's for chow?"

"Forget chow," the clerk told him. "Get your butt up to the orderly room. The First Sergeant wants to see you. Immediately."

Bell dressed in his work fatigues and made his way to the orderly room. First Sergeant Juan Roybal was at his desk.

"Bell," Roybal said quietly, "you've just been prompted to sergeant. Turn in all your personal troop equipment and get ready to join the 91st Infantry Division at Camp White, Oregon. Here are your orders, your service record folder and your travel money. You're now on a 30 day delay route out to Oregon. Good luck. Any questions?"

Bell stood there dumbfounded, then he took the sergeant's pen and signed his payroll signature. He thanked Roybal and walked out of the room thinking, I've made my last trip to the manure dump.

The same thing was happening in all the orderly rooms of all the regiments, the 5th, 7th, 8th and 12th. The war had finally caught up with the First Cavalry Division. Those men who left Fort Bliss for Camp White, Oregon had traded the Cavalry yellow hat cord for the blue of the infantry and though few realized it then, it was the end of an era. Within a few months all the horses would be gone from the Texas fort. In February 1943, the First Cavalry Division became a dismounted unit and the horse soldier passed into history. Never again would those riders in campaign hats carry the fluttering guidons over the hills and plains.

III

In 1940 the WPA's Oregon Writer's Project completed its guide to the state and titled it **OREGON. The End of the Trail.** It is a 549 page book and, like the histories that were written about the other 48 states, it was sponsored by the government to help depression-ridden writers and to give the people a look at their home land. Most of the town and cities of Oregon are listed in detail and there is a general description of each region as it appeared some 53 years ago. In the 1930s, the book tells us, Medford was a town of 11,000 population nestled in the Rogue River Valley. It was a summer resort and a lumber center, a place encompassed by endless orchards and surrounding mountains. Firs, pines and oak climbed those mountainsides. The valleys were filled with an abundance of apple, pear and peach trees. In the autumn, grapes and almonds were harvested. The bus station was located at the Jackson Hotel at 614 S. Central Street. The Municipal Airport was three miles northwest of town and the taxi fare was one dollar and twenty-five cents; inside the city limits, the fare was two bits. To play 18 holes of golf at the Rogue River Valley Golf Association one forked over a dollar bill; Sundays, it was a buck and a half. There was a sawmill that could turn out 250,000 board feet every day. The city had a candy factory and a flour mill and a plate glass works, a catsup plant and 21 fruit packing plants. It was, indeed, a small paradise where one could live off the fat of the land.

Forced smiles come from the faces of Powder Rivermen as they near the end of the famous 91 miles march.

Headquarters Company, 2nd Battalion, 362nd Infantry. Camp White. January, 1943.

However, in the Preface of the book the authors expressed concern about Oregon's future and wrote an uncanny prophecy:

"Oregon today is still the most unspoiled and uncluttered spot in America. Soon, perhaps, it will be changed by the coming of Power, the inrolling of immigration from the Dust Bowl, the devastation of timber-cutting and forest fires, and the boosting activities of chambers of commerce. It may be regrettable to see this peaceful and beautiful land transferred into a network of highways, clogged with cars and defaced by hot dog stands, the groves littered with tin cans and papers, the hills pockmarked with stumps, and the cities cursed with the slums that seem to accompany industrial progress.

"The sons of Oregon today are tall and sturdy, and the complexion of the daughters is faintly like that of the native rose—a hue gained from living outdoors. Will the sons of the impending industrial age be shorter and shrewder, and the daughters dependent for their beauty upon commodities sold in drug-stores; and will Oregonians become less appreciative of nature and rooted living and more avid and neurotic in the pursuit of wealth? These are some of the questions and misgivings in the mind of native Oregonians, including some of those who wrought the Oregon Guide."[4]

On a warm day in August, 1942 the 91st Infantry Division came to this land of milk and honey. At the newly constructed Camp White, a few miles northeast of Medford, the colors of the division were again unfurled after being dormant for twenty-four years. The 91st had been a silent member of the Army's Organized Reserve Corps. Orders for the activation was General Order 45 issued from the Headquarters of the 9th Service Command at Fort Douglas, Utah. Attending the ceremonies was a crowd of 10,0000, including 529 division officers and 1,279 enlisted men, headed by the new commander Major General Charles H. Gerhardt. The colors were presented by Major A.B. Richeson, a veteran of the World War One division. The first German rifle captured by the 91st in France was given to General Gerhardt by the former First Sergeant of Company I, 362nd Infantry, Floyd K. Dover, who told the crowd:

"We fought and many died that the world might be free, and that our country might be free and we are ready to fight again."

General Gerhardt accepted the rifle and colors and stepped up to speak a few sentences of inflated rhetoric:

"I have every respect for the traditions and achievements of our predecessors in this division. We have shown you the glory of the military profession here this morning, but now we shall begin training to transfer these gentlemen soldiers into savage killers on the field of battle. In less than one year, many of us will be dead, either victims of drowning on our way to fight, or we will be battle casualties. We of the armed forces stand ready to make these sacrifices and we ask you to make whatever sacrifices you must make to help us, and now, so that Berlin can hear us, at your command, "POWDER RIVER, LET 'ER BUCK!"[5]

A sixty foot fir tree was planted in front of division headquarters; a demonstration of military drill was given by the 361st Infantry; a demonstration of jujitsu was given by the 362nd Infantry and an anti-tank demonstration was given by the 363rd Infantry. The dedication closed with the Salvation Army handing out coffee and doughnuts, to civilians and soldiers alike, just as it had done in France in 1918.

So, the 91st Infantry Division began its long hike into the history of the Second World War.

General Gerhardt told his men they would learn how to **march, shoot and obey,** the latter by all means. Not too many days would pass until the division members would also learn about the word **march.** A salty, colorful individual, the general had been born in Lebanon, Tennessee in 1895 and entered West Point in 1913. He became a cadet hero when he quarter-backed the football team to a 30-10 win over Notre Dame. He had served in the 89th Division during World War One and spent a few of the post war years playing polo in Europe, then was given command of the 2nd Brigade of the First Cavalry Division. He was later to say that the most stirring event in his life was watching a full pack mounted parade review and inspection of the entire First Cavalry. His long service in the cavalry had earned him the nickname, "Hitchin' Charlie". At the end of the first week of September the division began its famous 91 mile march, an occasion that would earn the general a few more choice nicknames. The march was conducted over the back roads and twisting trails of the Cascade Mountains. The men carried a full pack, 90 rounds of ammunition and full canteens and covered the distance in twenty-eight and three-quarters of actual marching time. There were also other marches given on orders from the general, a seven mile forced march in two hours and a five mile march in one hour which required the men to walk 100 yards, then doubled time 100 yards. These usually separated the men from the boys. By the end of December, 1942 the division had grown to 734 officers, and 14,771 enlisted men.6

General Gerhardt rode herd on his men astride a bay gelding. He galloped from regiment to regiment at breakneck speed, accompanied by his aide, who would sometimes be overrun when the general made a quick stop. One of the first orders issued was that the uniform of the day would be khaki trousers, fatigue hats, field brogans and no shirts. Bare chests were the order of the day until the cool mornings of October forced them to be covered. One division member described Gerhardt as "go-go-go...do-it-now...it's already—too-late."[7] When asked why he drove his division so relentlessly, the general told his critics, "We are trying to guarantee every man that, by God, when his platoon leader takes him into action, he'll have a chance of getting back alive."

General Charles Bolte, who would later command the 34th Division in Italy, was assistant division commander during the early days of 1943. He said later of his experience with Charlie Gerhardt, "And that was an experience, a separate experience, I can assure you!"[8]

When one of the division officers arrived at Camp White, General Gerhardt asked him, "Are you ready to take the Division Commander's test? Everyone who joins the division takes the test, private or general."

"What is it?" asked the officer.

There were five questions:

What are the essentials of a combat order.

Describe stack arms.

Describe "change step, march".

Describe the resuscitation of a man drowning.

The officer couldn't remember the other one.

"It was all pretty crazy," he said. "I think I got four out of five. I don't remember. I just remember my surprise that, as a general officer, I was asked to take the test."[9]

A Time magazine article called General Gerhardt the toughest trainer in the U.S. Army and a "wiry little man who carries a full pack and a rifle while marching his troops across stony Oregon desert and who expects his staff officers to be as taut-bellied as the hardiest private." The article also stated the general broke in his new men "gently" by sleeping them in pup tents in the rain and making them swim icy rivers.[10]

In spite of all the opposition to Hitchin' Charlie's rigorous training program, there's little doubt it later paid dividends during combat operations in Italy.

For nine long months the training continued and on 20 June the entire division moved out to maneuver in the "D" series which were held north of the camp.

In early July, General Gerhardt received orders sending him to England where he was to take over the 29th Infantry Division. Replacing him as division commander was Major General William G. Livesay who had recently returned from Puerto Rico where he commanded U.S. Army troops in the Caribbean. A career officer, he had moved up through the ranks and had commanded a battalion in the 28th Infantry in World War One. On 26 October, 1942 he was promoted to major general. A quiet-spoken man, Livesay's personality was in complete contrast to Gerhardt's. During his stateside duty with the 91st General Livesay built such a solid, close-knit staff that all but two key officers who accompanied the Division overseas remained with it throughout its many days of battle.

On 3 September, 1943 the 91st moved into the central Oregon desert to participate in the IV Corps maneuvers along with the 96th and 104th Infantry Divisions. A month later it left Camp White and moved north to Camp Adair near the town of Corvallis. Here it rested and received replacements. Everyone knew what was coming next. On 20 January, 1944 a secret teletype message was sent to General Livesay:

ASSUME RESPONSIBILITIES AND EXECUTE FUNCTIONS OF SENIOR TACTICAL COMMANDER...READINESS DATE OF 1 MARCH 1944 HAS BEEN ASSIGNED THE 91ST INFANTRY DIVISION.

Of course, since the division was situated on the western coast of the United States, all troops assumed their destination would be the South Pacific, but there's the right way, the wrong way and the Army way and on 24 March the first troop trains headed east. Destination: Camp Patrick Henry, Virginia.

Endnotes for Chapter 1

1. Reprinted from Other Clay: A Remembrance of the World War II Infantry by Charles R. Cawthon (University Press of Colorado, 1991), by permission of the publisher.
2. Source material for the actions of the 91st Division in World War One comes from the 52 page booklet 91st Division Summary of Operation in the World War prepared by the American Battle Monuments Commission in 1944.
3. Personal narrative written by James E. Bell, March 20, 1993.
4. Workers of the Writer's Program. WPA. OREGON. End of the Trail. Metropolitan Press. Portland, Oregon. 1940. Taken from the Preface.
5. Hamilton, Eva. N. "Powder River! Echoes Again". Medford, **Oregon Journal,** August 16, 1942
6. Charles Gerhardt papers: "Memoirs," Eisenhower Library, Abilene, Kansas.
7. Lydick, Jesse with Paula Ruth Moore. One Man's Word. Nightjar Press. Las Cruces, New Mexico. 1990. Page 91.
8. Charles L. Bolte papers: (Burg Interview). Eisenhower Library, Abilene, Kansas.
9. Ibid.
10. December 14, 1942

CHAPTER TWO —
OPERATION VENDETTA

"The Germans were concerned about the threat of an Allied invasion in the south of France, but that concern was based on other, weightier, less melodramatic exploits—for example, the comings and goings at Oran of the assault-trained U.S. 91st Infantry Division."

Anthony Cave Brown...BODYGUARD OF LIES[1]

I

The troop trains that were to take the division to Virginia were formed in the rail yards of Camp Adair during the early hours of 21 March. Before daylight, they headed towards Seattle on the first leg of the long journey eastward. The long caravan of Pullman cars left in total darkness and slowly chugged out of Oregon through the great lumber country of the Northwest and into Washington. Upon reaching Puget Sound, they kept a northward course and made their way through the vast agricultural region west of Mt. Rainier. Along the waters of the Sound, gulls swarmed over the berry and vegetable gardens and out in the bay porpoises moved out to sea; farther out, ships bound for the Pacific war, lay at anchor. At the city of Everett, the trains turned eastward and began the long climb into the great range of the Cascade Mountains.

Eastward, ever eastward. Through the railroad town of Skyomish, through Spokane and into Idaho, through the Big Sky country of Montana and over the Continental Divide. Occasionally, the troops stopped for a short session of calisthenics, then moved on. Meals were served while the trains were in motion and consisted mostly of baked navy beans, canned stewed tomatoes, pork sausages, cookies, two slices of bread and half a dozen cherries. Volume-wise hardly enough to satisfy a hungry soldier, one GI remarked, but "calorie-wise sufficient."[2]

The town of Gillette, Wyoming passed and ahead lay the sagebrush covered hills of southwestern South Dakota and the immense farmland of Nebraska. The rolling Platte River was crossed, and then the wide Missouri: Iowa, Chicago, Indiana, Cincinnati, then the Ohio River. The trains sped on, over the Appalachian Mountains, the Blue Ridge Mountains and into Virginia. On the night of the 25th the division had reached its destination: Camp Patrick Henry and the port of Norfolk.

II

Camp Patrick Henry, Virginia was the staging area for troops destined for the Mediterranean Theatre of Operations. It had been built in a low lying area near Chesapeake Bay. Its dispirited inhabitants mockingly used the word "Swamp" instead of "Camp". It was a collection of dreary buildings that sat in the middle of a forest of scraggly pine trees. The place was so muddy and damp that duck boards were used as sidewalks. The barracks smelled of new timber and antiseptic and had double bunks and pot-bellied stoves. It was not a camp to raise the morale of men getting ready to sail into an anonymous future. One division wag observed that had Patrick Henry served at the camp his "give me liberty or give me death" speech may have been worded differently.

Fortunately, the stay at the port was a short one. The time was spent learning how to board ships and how to abandon them should a German torpedo find its mark. A few men chose the role of the fugitive rather than face the perils of the unknown, and went AWOL. A few were hospitalized. All these men had to be replaced to bring the division up to full T/O strength. The overseas movement was to be in four echelons: the advance party, the first half of the Division, the remainder of the Division, less the 2nd Battalion, 363rd Infantry. This regiment would be the last to leave the States. On April 1 the first units moved to Hampton Roads Port of Embarkation and sailed two days later.

III

Any veteran of the Second World War who crossed the Atlantic in a convoy of ships is going to tell a strikingly similar story about his trip over the waves, stories of stifling holds, endless chow lines, storms at sea, frustrating PT on cold iron decks, lifeboats drills, salt water showers, atabrine tablets, Mae West belts, crowded latrines, seasickness, destroyer escorts and German submarines. These were all part of life aboard the convoys. There was little to do to break the monotony but the one thing that did help to stir up a bit of excitement were the shithouse rumors that cropped up constantly and which never, ever, came true. A guy in the 1st Battalion knew a guy in Division headquarters who had a friend in the CIC detachment who had read a cable that the 91st was headed for the Panama Canal...the

Division was going the "southern route". Someone had it on "good authority" that the convoy was on its way to England going the "northern route". The Division would never see combat but would be broken up as soon as it hit shore and the regiments turned into service units. It was to be converted to armor and would train in the desert under the command of General George Patton. Each day there were newer and wilder rumors and they swept over each ship in a matter of minutes.

Some troops made the voyages in converted luxury liners, but the entire 91st Division traveled on Liberty ships, many dating back to the First War and even before that. The creaky old tubs moaned and groaned all the way over, shuddering and shaking in the heavy seas and straining to pull out of each swell. They were manned by merchant seamen and all were named after mysterious individuals whose names nobody had ever heard of: *SS Warren B. Giles, SS George H. Davis, SS William Floyd, SS John Cropper, SS Thaddeus Kowisly, SS Marshall Elliot* and *SS William Few*. They were slow moving and the journey seemed an infinite one.

General Livesay, accompanied by Chief of Staff Colonel Joseph Donnovin and Aide-de-Camp Captain Frederick Lash, had left Washington on 5 April and had flown to Algiers to attend a meeting with the commanders of the North African Theatre of Operations, then went on to Naples on 10 April for another conference where plans for the 91st were changed. From Naples, they flew to Oran, the Allied base in Algeria, to wait for the Division to arrive. It was all very top-secret.[3]

The first troops landed at Oran on Paul Revere's Day, 18 April, and bivouacked near Port-aux-Poules where the Division headquarters were set up. The 91st officially closed in North Africa on 10 May after fifty-four days and 7,500 miles!

Major General William G. Livesay. 1895-1979. Commanding General, 91st Infantry Division. World War II.

The Great Adventure.

There's nothing like a guitar to give you that old homesick feeling. Headquarters Company. 316th Engineers. North Africa. (Official U.S. Army Photograph)

IV

On 1 May, 1944, the Supreme Command in London issued a brief message to all Allied Commands. It read simply: "Word is Vendetta." This cryptic phrase set in motion a series of operations that were designed to keep the maximum number of German troops in the south of France and away from the beaches of Normandy where the invasion was only weeks away. The amphibious training of the Division at Port-aux-Poules was part of Vendetta. The 91st's mission was to confuse the Germans into thinking there would be a simultaneous invasion on the western coast of France and one on the coast of the French Riviera. The latter, Operation Anvil, was already planned but at a later date. German spies were rampant in North Africa and in Spain and so were Allied rumors. The strongest one was that the 91st Division would spearhead a huge invasion force in the south of France.[4] Allied agents made certain that this rumor was passed along in the cafes, bars and hotels of Oran and throughout Algeria. A request went out to the Spanish government asking for the use of the port of Barcelona for the "evacuation of casualties in impending operations." The Germans quickly learned of the request and of the actions of the 91st Division and concluded it would be best for them to keep their panzer divisions and their Army of the Riviera in the south.

From 18 April until mid-June when the last of the Division left for Italy, men of all three regiments, the artillery battalions, engineers and service units got a taste of the invasion training. There was little doubt in the minds of the men that they were headed for something big but no one had the foggiest idea of what it was. They were bivouacked in the desert and sparse vineyards a few miles outside of Oran and their first days were spent on long hikes which began in the morning and lasted well into the afternoon, with long columns of infantry weaving in and out of the small villages and up and down the ancient roads. North Africa was a strange land of mosques, squalid and dirty streets, camels, horses, donkeys, palm trees, fig trees, the French Foreign Legion and a red hot sun.

After being assigned to Major General Alexander Patch's Seventh Army, the 91st's deceptive amphibious training began in earnest. The troops left the desert and boarded LCI's (Landing Craft, Infantry) as guests of the United States Navy. They lived on the little vessels for days on end, packed together like peas in a can.

On 2 May, the Division began a series of operations which consisted of training individuals and small groups in the techniques of amphibious warfare: organization of boat teams, wire breaching, debarkation by cargo nets, demolition teams and flame thrower teams. Most of the exercises were practiced on the beaches of Arzew where the Rangers landed in November, 1942.

Third Platoon, Company A, 316th Engineers. North Africa. April, 1944. (Photo from Vito Valone.)

The fishing and resort village of Port-aux-Poules, Algeria where the 91st Division received amphibious training. (Offical Army Photograph)

The first lesson was learning to board LCVPs (Landing Craft, Vehicle and Personnel). Early morning found the troops out in the Mediterranean going through maneuvers, trying to climb down the cargo nets and into the waiting boats that rocked to and fro on the water. It could be a risky experience, especially if the sea was rough, as it often was. The trick was to reach the craft at the exact moment the LCVP rose up to meet the net. If a soldier missed, he had to wait for the next wave to again lift the boat, all the while wearing a full field pack and carrying a rifle, plus a Mae West life preserver. After the boats were loaded they headed out to sea. Here began the most sickening phase of the African training. The landing craft circled around and around and around, waiting to hit the beaches. Every landing was timed to the minute. With each circling, some men became queasier and queasier and some violently nauseous. Even though the exercises were "dry runs" in that there was no hostile fire, live bangalore torpedoes were used on the strands of barbed wire and the artillery was live. The coxswains who manned the boats were all very young and inexperienced and were reluctant to steer their boats too close to the shore, consequently some of the teams were dumped off into three or four feet of water and they had to slosh and struggle to make the beach.

From the beach the troops moved into the hills and the problem was ended a few miles inland.

On 1 June, **Operation Tarheel** was put into action. Two hundred and fifteen ships were to take part in an invasion of the Arzew landing area. The sector was heavily fortified with concertina wire, pillboxes and anti-tank traps. The embarkment began late at night and moved out of the Oran harbor and ten miles out to sea. The men crawled down the cargo nets and into the boats and headed for the beaches under the "protection" of the Navy's five inch guns. Live ammunition was used throughout the maneuver and to add to the excitement a heavy sea swelled up during the night and high winds blew the 363rd Infantry off course, forcing it to land far from its initial landing zone. The assault was made in fourteen waves and was considered a success in spite of the rough weather. A few days later the Division GIs again boarded the LCIs and steamed out of Oran and into the Mediterranean. So ended **Operation Vendetta.**

Operation Anvil, the actual landings in southern France, finally occurred on 14 August and was largely unopposed. The invasion had been so easy that it later became known as the "Champagne Campaign."

Endnotes for Chapter 2

1 . Brown, Anthony C. *Bodyguard of Lies.* New York: Harper and Row, 1975.
2 . Williams, West. "Across the Nation on a Troop Train." *The Powder River Journal.* December, 1987.
3 . Robbins, Robert A. *The 91st Infantry Division in World War II.* Washington, 1947. Page 15.
4 . Breuer, William B. *Hoodwinking Hitler.* Westport, Connecticut: Praeger, 1993.

CHAPTER THREE — ITALY

> "Open my heart and you will see
> Graved inside of it, 'Italy'."
>
> Robert Browning..."De Gustibus".

I

From the initial landings at Salerno, 9 September, 1943 through the first eight months of the Italian Campaign the Allied offensive had met with near disaster. The invasion in the Gulf of Salerno came within a whisker of being thrown back into the sea.[1] The advance against the Winter Line during the waning months of 1943 was a devastating affair of pushing forward, yard by yard, with the Germans contesting every inch of ground. The fall rains in late November flooded the streams and the men and vehicles mired down deep in the mud. The rain was endless and the leaden skies never cleared. In December, the bitter winds of winter swept over the southern Apennines. By the time the Fifth Army had worked its way through the Winter Line it had sustained 28,083 battle casualties. These were horrifying numbers. Things were not to get better. In mid-January the American army was confronted by the Gustav Line. The fight for this line of defense in the words of a battalion commander "would become a blood bath".[2] On 22 January the US VI Corps landed at

After the battle. The town of Cisterna, 1 June, 1944. (Official U.S. Army Photograph)

Anzio as part of a general offensive to seize Rome. An amphibious landing on the enemy flank hoped to cut off the German troops and, with a coordinated frontal assault, this would drive the Germans north of the last barrier in the approach to Rome. But it wasn't to be. The enemy reacted furiously and the Anzio beach head followed the pattern of all the other operations in Italy. It became one of the most murderous battles of World War II. Anzio, one respected historian wrote, "was a prime example of the horror of war."[3]

It wasn't until 11 May that the Allies were ready for a final offensive against the Gustav Line. At 2300 the guns roared into action. Progress was slow and bloody. On 13 May the French Expeditionary Corps broke through the Line, the Poles took Cassino and on the 19th the US II Corps captured Itri. Six days later a junction was made with the forces at Anzio and the US VI Corps broke through at Cisterna....everywhere the Fifth Army was on the offensive.

Because of the uncertainty of Operation Vendetta and the German reaction to it, the 91st Division was destined to be sent into combat by regiments and not as a complete division. On 15 May, the 361st Infantry completed its training and left North Africa for detached service with the Fifth Army in Italy. The regiment was joined by Company A, 316th Engineers, Company A, 316th Medical Battalion and the 916th Field Artillery Battalion. These units comprised the 361st RCT or Regimental Combat Team.[4] The troops boarded British vessels in the port of Mes-el-Kebir and sailed directly for Naples where they bivouacked near the Peninsular Base Section at Bagnoli. From the staging area above Naples, the men could see the blue waters of the Golfo di Napoli and the gently curving shoreline, the docks and the ships and the palm-lined avenues and, far below, Castel Nuovo jutted out into the sea. Across the bay, a thick, black plume of smoke drifted up from the mouth of Mount Vesuvius which had erupted in March.

Naples had fallen to the Allies on the first of October, 1943. The great port, second largest in Italy, had been totally destroyed. The Germans scuttled ships at the pier, sank others in the harbor, and systematically wrecked the unloading machinery. The Allied bombings and German demolitions had left the docks a mass of fire-twisted steel. Upon entering Naples, Fifth Army troops found the city in complete chaos. There was no electricity, not even candles. There were no street cars running, no taxis, no buses or funiculars, in this city on the side of a mountain. The main water distribution system had been smashed and water was so scarce many people were actually suffering from thirst. There were no hospitals open, no banks, no schools and no police. The enemy had opened the doors of all twelve prisons and criminals, many of them insane, roamed the back alleys and side streets. Food was not obtainable and people were starving; filth and garbage lay in the gutters; bodies of slain Partisans killed fighting the Germans during the four-day uprising lay rotting in the streets in the warm sunshine. The University of Naples Library and the thousand year old national Archives had been burned to the ground. It was a city paralyzed by war and in utter despair.

Now, more than eight months later, all facilities had been restored and the giant port was struggling towards normalcy. It had been a long winter and a serious outbreak of typhus had blanketed the bay area but was finally conquered by the Allies' skillful use of DDT, sprayed down the trousers and up the skirts of the citizens of Naples.[5]

While the 361st was moving to Italy, Colonel Rudolph W. Broedlow, regimental commander, and the regimental S-3, Major David F. Hawkinson, had visited the front lines and on 30 May the colonel gathered his flock near Bagnoli and gave them a pep talk along with some unwanted criticism.

He told them, "Men, the boys at the front are tired, dirty and unshaven, but they have clear eyes and clear heads." The infantrymen, gunners and medics had cut loose when they hit Naples and there had been a considerable amount of horseplay, wine drinking and merry making as they explored the city. Broedlow's statement meant he was highly displeased with such actions. The men knew it was all the colonel would have to say on the subject. And it was enough.

Colonel Broedlow was one of the shortest men in the regiment and one of the most solemn. A trooper called on the carpet for any infraction or violation was certain to leave regimental headquarters properly chastised. Broedlow not only expected, but demanded, that his men follow the rules...at all times. That was how the game was played. Their best was not good enough, they had to give their very best and more and then, perhaps, a little more. To offset his lack of stature, Broedlow wore a Colt .45 strapped over his right shoulder and with his perpetual worried-frown he was an authoritative figure in spite of his inadequate height.

Shortly after the colonel's gentle but castigating speech, the troops of the 361st Regimental Combat Team marched out of the bivouac area and down to the docks of the bay to board ships which would take them to the Anzio beach head. The men hiked through streets that were strangely silent. At an intersection a group of Army nurses bid the men goodbye with an occasional "good luck" and "so long". Not a single whistle, cat call or smart remark was made by any of the GIs. Things were getting serious now. As he walked along, Sergeant Bill Keith, a machine gunner in Company H, remembered it was a Memorial Day. He had been faithful in attending the ceremonies held at his home town cemetery during those long ago years before the war. He could only wonder how many of his comrades would die before the next holiday and how they would be honored.[6]

Darkness was fast approaching as the LSTs transporting the Combat Team left the little port of Nisidia and made their way north toward the war. By midnight, they were cutting furrows through the Golfo di Gaeta, hugging the shoreline past Terracina, swinging around the nose of San Felice, past Saubaudia and into the shambles that was Anzio. By 0930 the entire regiment was ashore. All weapons were checked and rechecked and unnecessary equipment was stored to make the 361st as mobile as possible. At 1030 the next morning, the troops assembled in a large field to hear an address by General Mark Clark the commander of US Fifth Army. The general pulled his lean, lanky frame up on the bed of a six-by truck and spoke into a sound microphone. He told the men the reputation of the division rested on the shoulders of the regiment since it was the first 91st unit to see combat. He expressed confidence in the 361st and wished the men well. It was a short speech. Clark then jumped down from the truck, got into his jeep and his driver whisked him away in a cloud of dust. "I'm sure he had made that same oration before," one soldier remarked. "He was like a politician addressing a group of voters."[7]

Colonel Rudolph W. Broedlow. CO, 361st Infantry.

Assigned to the 36th Division, the 361st began marching toward Velletri to occupy positions on a ridge four miles northeast of the town. Velletri lay atop a high hill along Highway 7 twenty miles south of the heart of the Eternal City of Rome and had been captured by the 141st Infantry that very afternoon after bitter fighting. The road to Velletri was dusty and dirty and littered with knocked-out enemy vehicles. Cisterna, the first town the regiment passed through, had been leveled flat. In the town square there was a statue of a woman high up on a pedestal. Her head had been blown off but one of her arms was still raised in defiance. "It was as if she didn't want us to move through her town," one infantryman said.

As the troops came to the southern outskirts of Velletri there was a heavy odor of sweet smelling flowers from the nearby fields but a little further on this smell was cut out by an even stronger odor of burning manure.

One member of the Second Battalion later described his passage through Velletri:

"At Velletri, just before going into first combat, we crossed several railroad tracks through lanes that were marked by white tape. In the darkness, before moonrise, the town appeared quite gruesome. Most buildings were heaps of rubble. Those left standing were shell torn and presented a spooky, scary contrast. Burning buildings cast flickering shadows. We picked up the pace and began marching rapidly with a feeling we couldn't get out of town fast enough. The deep stench of death from oxen, horses and men filled the air. Carrying humps (full field packs and fixed bayonets) we hurriedly filed up the steep, winding narrow mountain road. We were hot, sweaty and marching fast. I could hardly stand the smell. It was breathtaking, sickening, gagging. Artillery fire from the valley behind us boomed with a steady swish and whine. From the side of the mountain I could see a burning field of wheat and Jerry trucks moving in convoy in a ghostly apparition. The entire mountain seemed to be on fire."[8]

During the early hours of 3 June the 141st Infantry, 36th Division was relieved by the 361st and the regiment began moving up the Via del Laghi toward the town of Marino which sits on the shores of Lake Albano, the site of the summer residence of the pope. After a lively firefight near a wooded area along the highway, the Second Battalion routed the Germans and kept advancing northward. At 0715 the next morning it was resting some ten miles south of the outskirts of Rome.

II

No other event in the long Italian Campaign was celebrated with such wild anticipation and outright rejoicing as was the liberation of Rome. By the morning of 3 June the troops of Fifth Army were pouring down Highway 7 hell bent for the Eternal City. The agony of Anzio was over and in a frenzied burst of freedom that only men who have been confined for months can understand, the veterans of the beach head raced to be first into Rome. At 0800 4 June, elements of the 88th Reconnaissance Troop, 88th Infantry Division swept past a ROMA sign near the suburbs and earned the honor of being the leading Allied unit into the city. The streets of the capital city of the Roman Empire overflowed with cheering, hysterical citizens who lavished their liberators with wine, flowers and kisses. It was a great day to be alive and it was an occurrence never forgotten by those who were there. However, the party was a short one. By dusk of 5 June the noise of battle had rolled far beyond Rome as the weary men of the Fifth continued to pursue the retreating enemy.

Soon, the supporting units of Fifth Army would move up from the south and occupy the finer hotels and other first class buildings and the hometown of Romulus and Remus would belong to the hated rear echelon.

For one brief, glorious day the war in Italy had grabbed the headlines of all the major newspapers throughout the United States, then on 6 June, Allied forces crossed the English Channel and landed on the Normandy beaches. From that day on, the Italian Campaign of the Second World War became known as the "forgotten front".

III

The western coast of the Tyrrhenian Sea runs from Rome northward until it meets the arm of the Ligurian Sea near the city of Leghorn then continues on to the great Ligurian port of Genoa. During the month of June the 361st Infantry followed the coastal route to the island city of Orbetello, then the regiment swung inland and drove toward Siena capturing the towns of Montiano, Isita, Batignano, Roccastrada, Montieri, Radicondoli and Casole D'Elsa. By the end of the month it had pushed approximately 150 miles north of the Anzio beachhead. Veterans of the regiment remember those early days and the towns they fought through.[9]

"Company I crossed the Ombrone River around noon. We moved up over a powder dam. It was hot, dry and dusty and the fighting was mostly squad skirmishes in thickly wooded terrain. We sneaked into the

361st Infantrymen pass through newly liberated Rome to join the drive north, 5 June, 1944.

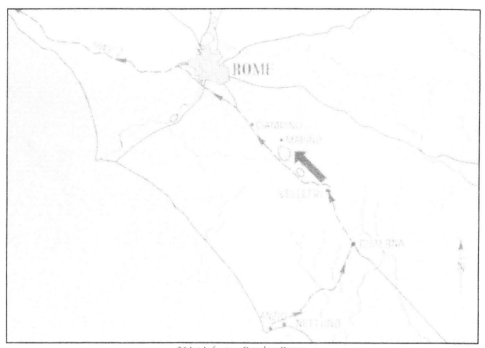

361st Infantry. Road to Rome.

Captain Edmund J. Carberry. CO Company E, 363rd Infantry.

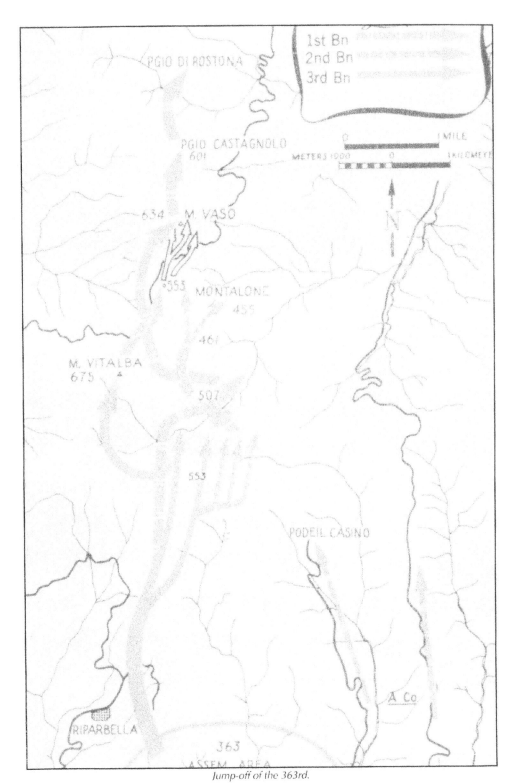

1st Bn
2nd Bn
3rd Bn

PGIO DI ROSTONA

PGIO CASTAGNOLO
601

0   1 MILE

METERS 1000   0   1 KILOMETER

N

634   M. VASO

553   MONTALONE
455

461

M. VITALBA
675

507

553

PODEIL CASINO

A Co

RIPARBELLA

363

ASSEM AREA

Jump-off of the 363rd.

town by a side road and ran into a buzz saw. It was an old village with stone houses and we moved from building to building cutting out and cutting up the Jerries. God! GI's and Germans all mixed together! We moved fast through the town with the enemy retreating rapidly. From one spot during the fighting I could see and count twenty German dead all sprawled in the square."

"Company K crossed the power dam about three o clock in the afternoon. The Germans had left in haste, so fast, they had abandoned five 88 guns and an anti-tank gun on the south bank of the Ombrone. There were orchards at the entrance to the town and many dead Jerries lay in among the trees. I noticed some of them were without shoes. I suppose the Italians stole them. Why not? All's fair in love and war."

"Company I followed the two other companies and crossed the Ombrone River dam just after nightfall. We wound our way slowly through the dark, shadowy power plant and climbed to an upper floor and across a porch, then through a window and then down again. One boy said it was like the old carnival spook houses back home. Once across the river we dug in in a wheat field and the other platoons were near some hay stacks and in an olive vineyard. We had just gotten some new replacements that very day and they were nervous as cats, but they did all right."

"I remember the town of Batignano hung crazily over the side of a mountain. For two days we tried to move into the damned place, but each time we were met by the very hottest kind of machinegun fire. It seemed like nothing could survive the shells the 916th threw into that village, but every time we went in we were hit hard. We finally took the town but we didn't take much. It was a wreck. I don't suppose it was much to look at even before the war came to it, but it was a mess when we got done with it."

"The village of Roccastrada was a town high above the wheat fields and fruit orchards and vineyards. It stood on top of a high hill, outlined against the blue sky, like castles with old weathered gray looking walls, too steep for anyone to climb. It was a beautiful place. We rode First Armored tanks up to the town and dismounted alongside a cliff. We fought all day in the boiling sun and were short of water and downright miserable. I'm told Roccastrada means 'Rock fortress or Rock road'. Either one fits."

"Casole D'Elsa? It was an old town that sat up on a mountaintop like all the ancient villages of Italy, and, of course, topped by the steeple of a church. We went in early in the morning over a narrow oxen trail. There weren't many Germans in the town but it was heavily booby-trapped. They were well concealed over doors, in furniture and hooked up to relics and ornaments. Bait for the souvenir hunters and hell for those boys who took the bait. I know a guy who has a hook for a left arm now because he was curious. It was cherry season and there was a cherry tree loaded with ripe, red cherries and under the tree sprawled a dead Jerry. When one of our men tried to remove him, a booby trap blew both of them all to hell. On the north side of the town the walls appeared to drop down a hundred feet into the hilly, rugged terrain. We couldn't get any supplies from the rear because a bridge had been destroyed across the river. In a cellar of one of the houses we found some of the best wine I ever drank. It sure went well with my rations!"

"For nearly a month, the regiment had been assigned to follow the German retreat and Company K was in on all the battles. It was an awesome task and this type of action gave the enemy an excellent opportunity to hit first, inflict casualties on us and to make things downright nasty for us all. The Germans made all their moves at night for fear of our air action against them during the day. On the evening of 29 June we decided to make a night maneuver to cut them off. For the first few weeks of the month we had been under the command of the 36th Division and had worked our way up the coast north of Rome, but as of this date, we were attached to the First Armored Division on an inland route toward the Arno River.

"On the morning of the 30th we had wound our way into the middle of the enemy escape route. As a result we were under a continuous barrage of close-in mortar and small arms fire, coming mostly from machine pistols. As members of the machinegun section, we were usually assigned to the forward rifle platoons in order to set up quickly for return fire. On this day we were unable to do so as we were on the slope of a mountain in the middle of heavy brush covered terrain. Frankly speaking, we were pinned down. Sergeant Garner of our section was the first one hit. He had a serious bullet wound in the groin and the cry of 'Medics!' started coming from all directions. It was soon evident that our only way out was to move ahead standing up, or crouching and firing from the hip in the direction of the incoming fire. We soon routed the Germans and worked our way out of this trap and continued the advance. Because they had knowledge of the terrain, the enemy took this advantage to pull back and continue the retreat. There's no doubt we had inflicted some pretty serious casualties on them. After taking care of our wounded we moved on winding our way along the hilly slopes, using whatever cover we could.

"The weather during the month of June had been extremely hot and humid with occasional thunder and lightning storms and the evenings cool. We took a small hamlet and some prisoners, then crossed a shallow river under sporadic enemy fire. As most of our foreward movements were "Indian style"; single file, it's difficult to say what the other elements of the company were experiencing. We started to bunch up as the day progressed, then we started to receive some direct fire from some 88's. It was the boom-bang! type of rounds we were getting. You heard the boom of the gun, then the bang of the shell landing, then the explosion right in front of you. I don't remember the name of the town that was our next objective, but we could see the unmistakable spire of a church in the distance. Just like one of many that we had liberated the past month.

"It was about four o'clock when I found myself lying in a prone position in a dried out creek bed surrounded by prickly foliage on all sides. Part of the platoon had been ushered into this spot to avoid the flying shrapnel from the 88s. Staff Sergeant Albin Kraus, our section sergeant, had picked out the spot. It seemed like a good place. I lay flat with my nose to the ground with the brim of my steel helmet pushed up with the back of it covering my head. I had a feeling something was coming in and I heard two reports, then there was a terrific explosion directly in front of me. I reached around to get my helmet which had been blown off, and as I did, I saw Sergeant Kraus die instantly from a big piece of shrapnel which had gone through his chest. He had been sitting to my left, helmet on his lap, wiping his forehead, and the blood gushed from his nose and mouth and into my helmet. Sergeant Howie Watts was to my right, and as he stood up holding his arm, I could see that it had been blown completely off. He was in a state of shock from the concussion. Behind me, Private Arnold Weigand was trying to hold his left arm in place as it had been nearly ripped off. Behind him, Sergeant John Matusik lay dead and Private Archie Williams and several others lay wounded. First Lieutenant Jack Sherman had been lying in the flat to the left of me and he was also wounded. Private Dick Flanders was hit and in bad shape. The Germans continued to traverse their fire which was now coming hot and heavy. Cries of "Medics!" were heard all along the line. I soon noticed that I had been hit in the left forearm, upper arm and shoulder. I made a sling with my field jackets and within a matter of second my wounds had instantly coagulated. A medic gave us all a shot of morphine to ease the pain then we all got together to assist each other and to size up the situation. Sergeant Rich was at hand and decided that those of us who were ambulatory should take off in the direction of the nearest aid station. I knew where the main road was and we proceeded in that direction. There were five of us and we poked our way along the edge of the main road under occasional shell fire and as we looked back we could see the rest of the company was taking one hell of a beating. The 88s were still exploding among the men. We finally reached a blown bridge and sneaked under it and to my great surprise we ran into none other than Colonel Broedlow who was

The 361st Infantry Monument. Florence Cemetery.

Col. W. Fulton Magill, CO, 363rd Infantry.

taking shelter. He asked about the situation of Company K, then told us to get aboard his jeep. The rest of the wounded were put on another jeep. We gave the colonel a run down on the day's action and shortly arrived at a First Armored Division aid station. It was under intense artillery fire, but I was treated and bandaged with the others and we were taken by ambulance back to the 94th Evacuation Hospital. I recovered quickly and rejoined the company.

"That day, 30 June was a bloody, deadly one. Company K alone had twenty casualties. At that rate a company would be wiped out in ten days."[10]

By 1 July the 361st Infantry had driven west of Siena and was headed for the Cecina River, and beyond that river was the famous Arno. In its first month of combat the regiment had suffered 681 battle casualties.

IV

After the fall of Rome the shattered German Fourteenth Army began retreating rapidly back to its new defense line in the Northern Apennines, there to lick its wounds and to rebuilt its badly splintered units. From the Gustav Line jump off to 4 June the German Army had lost more than 1,500 vehicles, 110 artillery pieces, 122 tanks and 15,000 prisoners of war. The exact number of battle casualties were unknown but they ran into the thousands and thousands. The Army was also given a new commander Lt. Gen. Joachim Lemelsen, who ordered his troops to bitterly oppose the swiftly advancing Americans who were gaining ground at the rate of 15 miles a day. Though this speed was heady stuff to the US Fifth Army commander, General Mark Clark, it also meant that his supply and communication lines were becoming longer and longer and more difficult to sustain. And there were other problems. One day the 11th Evacuation Hospital went into position 15 miles behind the front; 24 hours later the combat elements were 30 miles ahead! The advance was so swift that Signal Corps companies were unable to include the hospitals in its telephone network.

The German tactics were generally the hit and run type; however, some groups of infantry and tanks would give bitter resistance and the terrain was as much an obstacle as Lemelsen's army. The Germans destroyed every bridge and every culvert and the weary engineers worked night and day to repair them. Service troops were hard pressed to keep up with the advancing units and ordnance companies were overtaxed because the planned invasion by Seventh Army and the other theatres had priority over Italy in parts and equipment as well as personnel.

To help stem the Allied drive toward the Arno River and the important city of Leghorn, the German command moved the 16th SS Panzer Grenadier Division from Hungary to the Fourteenth Army front. This division, along with a number of other units, gradually slowed the drive north. The enemy evacuated Siena 2 July and the next day the 34th Division, in the toughest fighting since the liberation of Rome, ran into the 16th SS Panzers at the Cecina River. The town was captured after heavy casualties to the 133rd Infantry. The Germans defense was stiffening.

The movement of the 91st Division to Italy had begun on 15 June. On 20 June the division was assigned to the Fifth Army and the division command post was established on 2 July, at 0800, near Montalto di Castro. The next day the 363rd Infantry was attached to the 34th Division to assist in the drive north of the Cecina River. The Combat Team, consisting of the 347th Field Artillery Battalion, Company C, 316th Engineers, Company C, 316th Medic and the 363rd Infantry arrived at the port of Civitavecchia. The troops carried their equipment from the landing craft through the surf to the beaches, for the port had been destroyed, and climbed aboard waiting sixby trucks. Earlier, Colonel Fulton Magill, the regimental commander, had reported to the advance CP of Fifth Army and had arrived in the assembly area at 0200, 3 July.

The Combat Team took the coastal road for a number of miles then turned inland and drove through the rubbled city of Grossetto, then back onto the highway to Cecina where the men disembarked and started out on foot. The secondary roads had been churned into dust and it hung in clouds over the countryside. To the east were the Chianti Hills and the vast vineyards of central Italy and, further on, the great wine centers of San Gimignano and Poggibonsi. Artillery pieces were dug in along the roads and camouflage nets covered everything: company kitchens, service units, trucks, trailers, and even houses. The terrain was becoming more rugged and the going a bit more strenuous. Like an endless snake, the long columns of the 363rd Infantry moved up and over the hills.

As the 3rd Platoon, Company E, marched along, a rifleman in the 3rd Squad remarked that back home on the Fourth of July, he drank at least a gallon of beer in the patriotic picnics in the park. A killjoy in the 2nd Squad replied, "Well, this is the third of July and this is Italy and you ain't got no beer." And another soldier replied, "And this ain't exactly the city park neither."[11]

Combat Team 363 was now operating as Task Force Ramey attached to the 34th Infantry Division and was under the command of Brig. Gen. Rufus A. Ramey. Shedding all equipment except rifles, ammunition and packs the men of the regiment jumped off with the 3rd Battalion in the lead. Th objective was the high ground overlooking the town of Chianni 200 yards to the east. After moving forward several miles, the leading elements ran into enemy small arms fire and artillery began falling among the troops. The 363rd Infantry was in combat.

It is impossible to define the term "in combat". When an infantryman first enters the private hell of battle he is likely to be hit with an artillery or mortar barrage. There is no defense against shelling except a very deep foxhole and then one has to hope whoever pulled the lanyard, miles away, miscalculated and the shell will fall on somebody else's hole or slit trench. The soldier has to suffer through it—and suffering it is! There is always the shriek, wham and crash of artillery. One division veteran described the sound of small arms fire as "keen crack! zing! ping!" Something akin to being among a swarm of angry bees. It's another story with mortars. A mortar round whispers. Unlike an artillery shell, it doesn't seem to be in any hurry to kill you. Mortar rounds are fired in a high arc over the battle field and take their time coming down to earth. They are the silent killers.

During the first two days of combat the 363rd advanced nearly six miles through the thickly wooded and rugged mountainous region north of the Cecina River.

Late in the afternoon 6 July, the 3rd Battalion, led by Company L, continued the advance. Ahead of the troops lay the infamous Monte Vaso. The battle for this cone-shaped mountain would prove to be one of the most bitter of the entire campaign. The plan of the battalion commander, Lt. Col. Glen C. Long, was to move Companies L and I along the left side of Hill 553 and through a draw, then approach Mt. Vaso from the southwest. As it had done since early Oregon days, the 347th Field Artillery Battalion would continue to fire its rounds just in front of the leading platoons. No sooner had Captain Tom Draney, the Company L commander, ordered his men forward, then the Germans launched a fierce counterattack. The guns of the 347th were ordered to cease lobbing shells while Draney's men scrambled up the rough slopes firing as they climbed. In the bloody melee that followed, Company L was shattered but managed to reach the crest of

Private Larry Ayers.

the mountain. Company I, which had followed, was in equally bad shape. The men began digging in, trying to hack through the rocky soil. Company L was now down to 50 men. The 1st Platoon had 18 left; the 2nd, 24 men left. The 3rd Platoon had disappeared and its whereabouts were unknown. The Weapons Platoon was down to 8 able-bodied machinegunners and mortarmen. The two company commanders, Draney and Captain Willie Kriel of Company I, established outposts and listening posts on the forward slopes of the mountain while the remaining men of both companies formed a perimeter defense on the reverse slope.

Private Larry Ayers was one of the survivors of Mt. Vaso:

"I was 1st Scout, 3rd Squad, 3rd Platoon, Company L and it was my duty to keep contact between our Platoon and the 2nd Platoon. At one point during the advance, we were held up for a long time and our Platoon Sergeant kept calling to me in a low voice, 'Are they moving out yet?' 'Ayers, are you still awake?' Somehow during the confusion of battle, we lost communication with the 2nd and when we finally reached the crest of Mt. Vaso I found myself with Lt. Steve Eyherabide and took cover near one of the enemy's abandoned concrete-lined dugouts. I stayed there for awhile, then at dusk I rejoined my platoon and was delighted to see my old buddy Duke had also survived the assault. We discussed the events of the day and Duke was pretty solemn and told me he almost knew he'd never make it home. Some time later his premonition proved to be correct.

"We were ordered to dig in, but the soil was so rocky we were forced to improvise and we piled rocks around us to form makeshift slit trenches. They didn't offer us much defense but they were better than nothing. By now we were completely exhausted and sleep came easily.

"I was awakened around 0300, this was on the 7th, and told to relieve our outpost which was located some 75 to 100 yards away on the forwards slope of Vaso. I approached the outpost with extreme caution. We were all pretty tense and I had no desire to be shot by our own nervous lookout. Soon I was challenged, gave the password and was relieved to hear the correct response. The exchange was made and I watched my comrade disappear into the darkness. After settling down for my four hour watch, a feeling of loneliness swept over me. I thought, how many yards away is the enemy? I wonder what my buddies are doing now. I wonder what this day will bring? God knows, these thoughts did little to help my morale.

"There are few experiences in life as terrifying as night guard duty in a forward infantry emplacement, especially if the sentinel is green to combat. One is utterly and absolutely alone. There is nothing between the outpost and the enemy except the veil of darkness that shrouds no-man's-land and in the North Apennine mountains after dusk, darkness is complete.

"As I watched the sun rise on this beautiful July morning in the mountains, I was thankful my watch had been uneventful and was prepared to be relieved. By 0800 my relief had not arrived. I was notified to stay in place until relieved. Occasionally I could hear some small arms fire behind me and calls for medics. All the action seemed to be in back of the company. I felt pretty insecure and continued to watch and to listen to the incoming and outgoing 'mail' passing over me.

"At about 0900 I changed my position and propped up my legs on the rock that I had been sitting on and lit a cigarette. This was to prove my undoing. The sounds of the shells passing over me suddenly changed as the incoming rounds began kicking up dust in front of me. I felt the rush of air from one round before it hit and exploded, but the next round gave me no advance warning as it exploded. I immediately felt a searing pain in my right ankle. A piece of half inch shrapnel had entered my leg and lodged in my boot just above my heel—shattering my ankle.

"After the barrage ended, the cries of 'Medic! 'Medic!' began. Several minutes later two of my buddies came to my aid and carried me back to the CP because all the medics were busy. 1st Sgt. Weldon cut away my boot, applied sulfa powder and bandaged my wound. He gently patted my head and tenderly said, 'You'll be OK, Ayers.' This tall, broad-shouldered, square jowled man from Texas, who was equipped with a deep, resounding voice of authority was truly a credit to the Army and to Company L.

"As time passed, I wondered where the medics were and if they would be able to give me something for my pain. Sgt. Weldon soon passed the word down, 'If you can walk, move out. If you can't walk, we'll be back for you later.'

"The thought of staying there in my almost helpless condition distressed me to no end, but then I looked up and standing over me was one of the biggest men in my squad, BAR man Joe Riserbate. He said, 'I can't leave you here.' Despite a bloody flesh wound in his shoulder, Joe managed to stand me up on my left foot and we moved out. As we stumbled down the mountainside, I placed some weight on my right foot causing a compound fracture as a sharp bone splinter protruded through the flesh on the inside of my leg, a few inches above the ankle. The pain was excruciating and I asked my buddy to put me down and go on without me. He gently helped me down to the ground and reluctantly said goodbye.

"I have no ample way of describing the feeling of being left alone. The thought that I was so helpless and that the enemy might soon reclaim the area was frightening. Then out of nowhere, only a few hundred feet to my left, I saw a soldier moving rapidly down a narrow trail with his rifle in front of him, ready for action. Then I recognized him. It was Jesse. What a relief! He was alive and on his way off the mountain. He was the last Company L man I was to see on Mt. Vaso. I did run into him later at the 6th General Hospital in Rome.

I had been without food or water for nearly two days and by mid-afternoon, the combination of thirst and pain became unbearable. Still clearly capable of considering my options, I made the decision to quickly end my ordeal with the help from my M-1. But then I realized I had left it back where I was wounded! As I lay there contemplating a slow death, I summoned up the necessary strength to write a 'final note' to my mother—telling her of my desperate situation and the decision to take my own life.

"I stuffed the note into my pants pocket and wondered if she would have the opportunity to read it some day. Somehow I managed to crawl about 200 feet down the trail and spotted a trickle of water seeping slowly from the cliff above me. The water had puddled up the cow tracks and I was able to drink from them.

"I felt greatly refreshed and began my slow, painful journey down the trail. I decided to stay in place for the night. I had used my shirt and undershirt for a tourniquet and was naked from the waist up. Surprisingly, I spent a reasonable comfortable night, trying to walk from time to time, releasing the tourniquet now and then and taking a drink of the precious water by my side.

The 363rd Infantry Monument. Florence Cemetery.

"At dawn I crawled up to a small rise on the trail and from there I could see some men moving about 200 yards down the slope. I let out a yell and started crawling and rolling towards that area. Two medics soon came to my aid and moved me to a protected in a draw. They removed my tourniquet, administered morphine and redressed my wound. They told me they were from the 34th Infantry Division. An ambulance was scheduled to arrive at 1600, but I was later informed that the road had not been cleared of mines, thus no ambulance.

"A mule train came shortly after dark and the wounded men who were able to ride were advised they could ride back. I decided to give it a try. After the supplies were unloaded, I was assisted on to the back of one of those durable animals and instantly knew I shouldn't be sitting in the position I was in as the blood rushed to my injured ankle. I became dizzy and my leg felt like it might explode. The thought of remaining on the mountainside did not appeal to me and I decided to stay on the mules' back and hang on.

"A short time later, the Italian leading the mule I was riding lost contact with the mule train. My handler started wandering around shouting, 'Paisan! Paisan! The sergeant in charge told the Italian we were in sniper territory and to keep his —— mouth shut! The balance of my mounted trip was without incident. By dawn we had arrived at a very busy supply area where I was helped off the mule and placed on a stretcher which in turn was mounted on the hood of a jeep. After going several miles I was transferred to an ambulance for what seemed the longest and most jolting ride of my life.

"We arrived at a field hospital at dusk and I was examined by a doctor who frankly told me he did not think he could save my leg so I was prepared for the worst. After I woke up from surgery, I was relieved to see I still had my two legs. Then I was moved to the 6th General Hospital in Rome where the news about my leg varied from day to day. 'Your leg appears to be infected.' 'Your foot will probably have to be removed.' 'We will not have to amputate, but your ankle will always be impaired. A small piece of shrapnel is still lodged in your ankle and it will be safer to leave it there rather than risk damaging the nerves in the area.'

"My doctor's prognosis proved to be correct and while working in the construction business for 45 years, the pain in my right leg has acted as a constant reminder of my personal ordeal on Mt. Vaso."[12]

Meanwhile, the same afternoon of the attacks by Companies L and I, Captain Paul J. Maloney, 2nd Battalion Surgeon, anticipating heavy casualties in all companies, put together a number of packboards of blood plasm and other necessities and along with two of his aid men, braved the German fire to establish an aid station in an empty farmhouse on an open hill near Mt. Vaso. After the attacks began, and casualties mounted, Maloney and his men worked 70 continuous hours treating 96 wounded. The only source for water was a well in the farmyard and the medics made trip after trip to the well, drawing down heavy mortar fire. During the three days of bitter fighting Maloney often went up the mountain to care for the severely injured. Such acts of bravery were common at Mt. Vaso.

As the actions continued, it became increasingly difficult to supply the forward elements. Roads were almost non-existent and regimental vehicles could haul the provisions and munitions only so far forward, then man took over: stragglers, cooks, replacements, mail clerks, members of the Anti-Tank Company, anyone with a strong back or not so strong. These men were divided into guards and carriers and moved out at dark, struggling over the rugged mountain paths burdened down with bandoleers, machinegun belts, mortar rounds, jerricans of water, C and K rations, radios and batteries and communication wire. Even in time of peace it would have been exhausting labor, but these single files of sweating infantrymen were hit constantly by artillery and mortar fire that searched the draws and hillsides. No more than ten per cent of the supplies made it to the foxholes, so successful were the Germans in covering the sector south of Mt. Vaso.

The men of the 363rd Infantry who were with the regiment during those first few, awful days of combat will always remember Mt. Vaso. There were other mountains and hills, of course: Mt. Vitalba, Hills 553, 601, 509, 550, 506 and Ridge 461 but none of them could compare to Vaso and the sheer ferociousness of the German defense of it. The enemy knew he was facing an American division new to battle and he fully intended to try that division to the utmost and to test the courage of the troops to the limit. Robert K. Palassou, a rifleman in Company L, would later write:

"Out initial battle, the battle to seize Mt. Vaso, proved to be one of our toughest. Three times after a bad fight, Company L pulled back with apparently less than 30 men accounted for. This scared me, but each time it turned out that many of our missing men had been temporarily lost or separated. For example, after we took Vaso, our company commander Captain Draney, was the only officer left. Our 1st Sergeant, the only non-com and only nine other enlisted men could be located. At the time we thought we were the only survivors and each one of us felt so distressed, we broke down and cried. This would have been a terrible experience for veterans but experiencing this on our third day on the line was simply devastating. Any rifleman coming off the lines after a few days of combat looks like hell and I don't believe anything else can affect a man's body as quickly as time on the front lines. Yet, we endured and some of us were still alive ten months later when the war ended. It says something about the tenacity of the human spirit."[13]

How can those who were there ever forget that first week of July in the mountains of central Tuscany? The hot, sweltering weather and the lack of water. Every man carried two canteens and their contents were more precious than food. The heat was stifling and the dry-mouth, leg deadening ascent up the rugged trails soaked their ODs and the fear made their lungs ache. It was a stomach-turning fear that left a knot in the pit of the gut and for some men it was absolute terror, this fear of the unknown that seldom was as terrifying as the mind made it. Still, some were consumed by it and broke down completely and refused to go on. A few went out of their minds. But the rest persevered and kept going.

And there was the enemy. The German infantryman was a sinister-looking soldier with his coal-bucket helmet, grey uniform and high boots, and when he suddenly appeared, even at a distance, lugging his rifle and running with that strange lope most of them had, he could instill a great deal of anxiety in the heart of a soldier new to combat.

And there was always the dead. A veteran of the 2nd Battalion would write of Mt. Vaso:

"The next morning after the battle, we marched down the slope and around and up another mountain.

The dead of the 3rd Battalion lay everywhere. Some in bunches, killed by a single shell. Some alone and far off from their buddies, and some lay in pairs, all of them with their faces in the dirt. Scattered equipment was all over: helmets, smashed machineguns and mortars that had caught a direct hit and were torn apart by the blasts, K rations, letters fluttering in the breeze, medical kits, bloody bandages, torn shelter-halves, khaki-colored ammo boxes and empty bandoleers. By some of the bodies were upright M-1s, their bayonets sticking into the rocky soil and on some of the rifles were tied OD handkerchiefs which rustled in the wind. It was awful to leave those men like that but I knew the Graves Registration companies would come later and strap the bodies on the pack saddles of the mules for the final trip out of the mountains.[14]

By 0530 Friday morning, 7 July, Company K, commanded by Raymond H. Stewart, had worked its way to the reverse slope of Mt Vaso[15] and Lieutenant Eugene Milewski's 2nd Platoon was tied in with Company I for flank protection. No sooner was the company settled than the Germans made their move. The regimental history tells what happened:

"At this time artillery and mortar fire began to fall at the rate of six or seven rounds per minute. The enemy had excellent observation from the front and both flanks; several enemy tanks in turret defilade to the northwest were shelling the hill with direct observed fire. After two and a half hours of this steady, the positions were subject to a brief concentration of heavy fire which soon lifted and was followed by an enemy counterattack at 0800. After a half hour of bitter fighting Company L, aided by fire from the 347th Field Artillery, drove back the counterattack but at the cost of 35 casualties. The sector was subjected to a second enemy artillery and mortar barrage which lasted ten minutes and further reduced the strength of Company L. The remaining men, exhausted and battle-worn, found they were running short of ammunition. They replenished their supply from the bodies and weapons of the casualties, realizing no more could be brought up to them because no supplies, food or ammunition had gotten through during the night.

"At this moment of mounting difficulty, a force of about 200 Germans came sweeping up the hill in a second counterattack. As the foremost of the enemy approached through the dense foliage, the outposts fired. Meanwhile, the company mortars and machineguns began throwing down the final protective line fires while the rest of Company L ran toward the forward slope and better firing positions. By 0830 the full force of the counterattack was felt. Both friendly and enemy concentrations of mortar and artillery were placed so close together it was impossible to tell them apart. S/Sgt. Alexander M. Greig, Company L, at the conclusion of the first counterattack had gathered together eight or nine men to protect the right flank of the company position. As the Germans charged up the slope shouting "Heil Hitler!" several of the hastily formed squads began to waver and there was danger that the line would break. One man started to fall back. Greig jumped up from his firing position and faced his men. "Don't let the sons of bitches bluff you! Let's get 'em!" he shouted and turned and charged into the advancing enemy.

"So inspired were his courage and determination that four men, among them Pvt. Stanley M. Curtiss, Pvt. Walter Osenbaugh and Pfc Louis T. Bacciglieri followed him in his charge. The rest of the squad, taking positions of vantage, reopened fire. The crisis had been met and there was no question of the lines breaking. Curtiss had his shirt collar shot away by an enemy machine pistol. In the face of the assault, the enemy began to flee. Of the men who made the heroic charge only Curtiss and Osenbaugh came back. The others were later found lying in a group surrounded by a score of dead enemy soldiers.

"S/Sgt. Greig was awarded the Distinguished Service Cross."[16]

On the regimental maps, Monte Vaso was shown as Hill 634. It controlled the valleys and the ridge line and from it the Germans, as always during the Italian Campaign, could direct artillery, self-propelled 88 fire and machinegun and mortar barrages on the unlucky people below them. There was a macadam road between Vaso and Hill 675 and this route was little more than a shooting gallery for the enemy who had plenty of ammunition and good firing positions. Movement up the road during daylight hours was suicide.

Shortly after Sergeant Greig's selfless act, T/5 William A. Montooth, Company L, volunteered to act as a company observer. Back in the States Montooth was an extra cook, barber and all around handyman. He had replaced the company rocket-launcher man, and was given an observation post over on the left flank. It was unprotected and Montooth was ordered to hold the fort until reinforcements could be brought up to help him out. During his watch, he noticed the Germans had strung a communications line some distance down the hill. He cut the wire and tied it to a bush near his foxhole.

Montooth stood his ground for hours and during the first counterattack picked off 12 of the enemy with his M1. When he ran out of ammunition he took a rifle from a wounded comrade and shot five more.

Unfortunately, when the reinforcements reached him they totaled exactly one rifleman and a machinegunner!

It was to be a bloody day for Companies I and L. Around 1000 Sgt. Don Leath, manning one of the outposts, noticed several Germans sneaking along the side of the mountain in an obvious attempt to flank

Company L. "The Jerries are coming!" he yelled. The men, dug in along the outposts, took up the cry: "The Jerries are coming! The Jerries are coming!" Almost immediately 150 to 200 German infantrymen came scrambling over the summit of the hill, firing wildly. The two companies were hit hard but they fought back gallantly. During the fighting one of Company I's machinegun crews was hit, wounding every man but leaving the gun unharmed. Pfc Rex Jewkes picked up the gun, tagged a man to go along with him, and moved over the crest of Monte Vaso, set up the gun and began firing. He was so far forward that a friendly BAR ripped up a clump of grass no more than a foot from him. Jewkes valor helped drive back the Germans who finally withdrew after an hour of fierce fighting. At 1130 Captain Tom Draney radioed the battalion commander, Lt. Col. Glen Long, and told him the situation in the Company L sector. The company was shot to pieces, disorganized, exhausted and had ran out of ammunition. Colonel Long ordered Captain Draney to withdraw.

Sergeant James E. Bell was with Company A:

"After the 3rd Battalion and several other rifle companies in the regiment had executed many valiant and repeated actions, all involving bloody and extremely costly fighting, Monte Vaso was taken only after every heavy gun in the regiment and all the available 91st Division artillery, including some even heavier Corps support field pieces, had rained tons of red-hot steel on the mountain for nearly four hours. This was approximately from 0800 to 1200, Saturday, July 10, 1944. This awesome display of fire power was one of the few times, in the history of the regiment, that such a massive array of heavy artillery had opened up, all at once, on a single limited target. For those who had a ringside seat there was little doubt the will of God and the Field Artillery was a deciding factor in favor of the infantrymen of the 363rd.

"The regiment had entered combat with its own 347th Field Artillery Battalion but some of the batteries were hung up in a massive traffic jam at the Cecina River crossing. This left what guns did get across...the Regimental Cannon Company, commanded by Captain Ernie Land, and some artillery units of the 34th Division backing the 363rd. Because of the terrain and the lack of good forward observation, the mortar companies were unable to deliver the necessary support.

"Armed combat is, by its very nature, quite often a scene of confusion bordering on utter chaos. Some situations may be worse than others but the assault on Monte Vaso by the 363rd had this element...and more. Vaso was fought with what the forward rifle companies carried in with them. These supplies soon ran out and resupply was all but impossible for the Germans had maneuvered behind the leading companies. The exhausting see-saw back and forth for the company objectives clearly established the courage and endurance of the American citizen soldier. Inexperienced though they were, these men were a credit to themselves, their regiment, their division and their country. There were many awards for individual valor at Vaso. They were commonplace and they established an individual fighting standard for the 363rd. These men had entered combat not really angry at their enemy and they were easily imposed on. This was not unusual or abnormal for troops being brought under fire for the first time. It was a normal human reaction. Man's unused and untried instincts for survival take time to adjust in any combat situation. So it was on Monte Vaso.

"By the end of that July day each man had lost his "meekness" and was fighting mad. It was an anger in earnest and not a displayed condition of bravado for everyone had lost a friend and buddy on those bullets and shell-riddled mountain slopes. For those men who had survived the title "combat veteran" was well deserved.

"I remember the day before entry into battle our combat packs were again emptied and re-inspected for anything that might reveal the regiment's identity. M1 rifle ammunition clips were again individually inspected. The fresh, new looking machinegun ammo boxes were again opened and the belts carefully repacked with the loving tenderness of hand one would show toward a small child. BAR gunners reinspected their own twenty round clips and those of the ammo bearers. Rifle stocks plainly showed the fresh, small indents from repeated tapping the clips bullet ends against the wood to settle the clip. Grenade handles were rechecked. They had been taped with the black tape that came from the carton. This was passed on to us from the vets of the 34th Division. Bending the key ring was not recommended! Neither was it recommended to hang the grenade John Wayne fashion. What in the hell did John Wayne know about a grenade? These were all minor things, of course, but it was busy work. And it did help break the tension.

"Now, Company A sat idle in the open trucks waiting for the colossal traffic jam to end. It was highly likely the enemy knew much more about us than we did about them. Troops new to combat never need blazing neon signs to announce their arrival. First Sergeant Harley Franklin gave last minute instructions to the NCOs. I had known Franklin when we were cavalrymen at Fort Bliss. He told me, "Bell, you know what? It's like they used to say a long time ago. It's time to stop sweatin the mule and load the wagon!" In less than twenty-four hours Sergeant Franklin was dead. He was killed while leading a group of men to a better defensive position. So were many of the NCOs he addressed.

"Company A was to suffer the same fate that befell most of the American units during their initial combat days. The Germans let the lead elements pass, then opened up with all they had on the main platoons. Within a few minutes an infantry company could become leaderless, disorganized and nearly ineffective as a fighting force. During those first few days the weather was bright and clear and the German observation was so good he could afford to pick and choose his targets.

"Anyway, there we were in a bivouac area on the evening of July third. The next day would be it! There was an open stone shed near the area and there were a number of dead from the 34th Division who were carefully laid out in perfect formation, just a few feet away. They all wore the Red Bull patch. If this display was accidental, or had been put there for our benefit, I do not know. It didn't matter. The message struck home!

"After dark I reported to the CP and was told I was to accompany a small group from the 2nd Platoon headed by Lieutenant Young. We had three medium tanks with us and one 105 self-propelled gun from the 776th TD Battalion. We were to offer infantry support for these guys. An artillery OP was set up in the upper story of a farmhouse to be used as a combined observation post and company CP. At 0830 the next morning we moved into position as ordered. This was the Fourth of July. The rest of Company A moved along a cart trail about 1500 yards across a high, thick, brush-covered draw. The company was to take up positions on their objective, the high ground, beyond a small creek that ran north and south and bisected the route of march. Contact was to be established between the two groups and the 34th Division. A firm main line of resistance

Men of the 363rd Infantry move toward combat. July 4, 1944.

would be maintained to protect the balance of the regiment in its planned assault on the first of a series of main objectives and ultimately Monte Vaso. A reasonable and easily understood plan on paper. The Germans, however, had other ideas. We were told the 34th Division contact on our flank was already in position so passwords and counter signs were given. Our small support party lacked the men to invest in anything but its main mission so no scout parties were sent out. It's a pity these restricted areas were not better scouted out in advance. In combat of course, it's easy to be critical after the fact. The Fifth Army brass was flushed with the victory of Rome and the enemy was rapidly retreating back toward the Arno River. Why would he make a stand here? Or at Mount Vaso? Somewhere along the way we took a prisoner who confirmed that a large force of German infantry had moved parallel across our front. They were concealed by a rise in the terrain. It was this enemy group that would take Company A out of action just a short time later. This German force was not discovered until 1030. The news was relayed back and the radio operator told us they were moving forward with no enemy contact. Our small party continued on accompanied by a medium tank. We moved several hundred yards to a ridge to our front and attempted to set up a forward OP but before we could accomplish this we were hit by a tremendous concentration of small arms fire and rolling artillery. We pulled off the ridge. To try and stay there would have been foolish. The farmhouse OP was quick in bringing fire in the enemy's direction but these undirected fires had little real effect. We were pounded by artillery until around noon.

"Our BAR gunner had crawled up into a small tree so he could get a better field of fire and he chugged away at the ridge line we had just been driven from. He was joined by a light machinegun that had set up in an upper CP window. Both guns fired until they ran out of ammo.

"It now seemed clear from the Germans' sudden appearance that they had probably occupied the restricted fire area on our right flank and were prompted into action by our presence. No doubt the tanks concerned them. We certainly made enough noise moving in. We decided to give up on making contact with the 34th Division. We later learned they, too, were heavily engaged.

"Now we could hear small arms and mortar fire over in the Company A sector. It seemed to last just a short time. We tried but failed to contact the company on the radio. We called 1st Battalion who told us they had no better results than we did. We were then ordered to try and find out just what the hell the situation was. I volunteered to take a patrol of three men and attempt to cross the brush-covered draw. We preceded with little difficulty and no problems. At about 1530 hours we came upon an appalling scene. A real tragedy. Wounded and dead were scattered all over the area. I called battalion and asked for immediate assistance. I couldn't locate Lieutenant Young on the radio so I talked to a wounded officer whom I did not know. I told him the purpose of our patrol and he suggested I send a man back across the draw and have Lieutenant Young come over and assume command of the company. He then ordered me to organize a larger patrol of any men available and go forward across the creek and set up a defensive position. A few men began appearing up out of the foxholes. Three of them with a light machinegun told me they would help. The wounded officer also told me there were many men who had been hit several yards above the creek and this area needed to be scouted for dead and wounded. I gathered what few men there were, including the machinegun crew and went forward, dropping off the machinegun in a good spot.

"These guys were in one hell of a shape. I could tell some of them were still in shock. I thought about telling them to go to the rear but I knew they were needed desperately. Before I could ask them to stay one man smiled faintly and said in a voice barely above a whisper, 'We can handle it.'

"So we moved forward most carefully, following a ridge line with good cover. There were just a handful of us. I could tell some of the men were now recovering from their shock. In an open clearing we found the body of Sergeant Franklin and several others and a few walking wounded. I talked to one and got the picture. Company A had walked straight into an ambush. They had stopped, surprised at seeing no enemy, then were rained on by mortar and many snipers. Things went downhill fast.

"We moved on about a fourth of a mile but found no additional men. At about this time we had run out of ridge line cover and could not move further without scouting the area. We dug in. The next morning I was again ordered to take a patrol forward. We found one more injured man. He had heard us the previous evening but thought we were Germans and had remained silent. He was badly hit. What may have helped save him from serious infection were the large clusters of maggots that were now quite busy in the injured area. His wounds were very clean and was quickly doused with sulfa powder, bandaged, and taken away on a litter, maggots and all. I would see this several times in very hot weather. They could form in a matter of hours.

"That afternoon 7 July, I was attached to the 3rd Battalion and would work the Monte Vaso area with a forward observer officer, Captain Mel Cotton with Battery C, 347th. Vaso was not over. Heavy fighting continued in the assault companies of the Third. Other than being in and out of the area until the final artillery barrage on 10 July, this story is better told by those who were there. As a regular Army NCO I was very impressed and very proud of these men. On their first day of combat they had been flung at the enemy and suffered death and wounds in some of the heaviest fighting of the campaign. It was not the last time I would be proud of them."[17]

Earlier Company F moved up to Hill 553 without meeting much resistance. Shortly after they dug in the Germans threw in a tremendous barrage of artillery. This was a common tactic, to make green troops welcome; a ruse to terrify. Within 30 minutes over 100 rounds fell over the 300 yards that was the company area. Pfc. Haskel M. Reels, an aid man, bravely climbed out of his foxhole and hurried to tend to the wounded. Time and time again company medics risked their lives for their stricken comrades....these angels of the battle field. Reels continued his work until he was hit twice by close shell bursts. He was cut on the head and arm, then the next round broke his arm. This didn't stop him. He kept at his work until he no longer had the strength to carry on.

Since the jump-off from Mt. Vitalba on 5 July all regimental troops had been unable to resupply themselves, not only because of the heavy fighting but because the rugged country was almost impassable and because they were under complete observation. There could be no movement of the mule trains in daylight, or by any other means.

During the first seven hours of 7 July Company I had 31 men wounded and 33 killed. No litter squads had been able to reach the scene of battle so two company aid men, Pfc. Millard Grimes and Pfc. Charles Knight, walked the field braving the fire to administer to the wounded, giving morphine shots, bandaging and applying tourniquets.

At his outpost, T/5 Montooth kept his vigil and covered the withdrawal of Company L by firing every rifle he could find. When he had fired his last shot, he then began carrying the wounded over the reverse slope of the hill. Eventually, he became so exhausted he could carry on no longer. He had been fighting for three days and nights with little water and even less food. He was awarded the Distinguished Service Cross.

The withdrawal of the 3rd Battalion took all day. By midnight Friday, 7 July Captain Kriel and 14 men were all that was left of Company I and they had tied in with Company F on their right. Because there was not enough wire to stretch the hundred yards between the companies telephone communication was impossible.

While the men of Colonel Long's battalion were enduring their predicament, Company E had moved up the slopes of Montalone, set up their machineguns and mortars and prepared to defend the right half of the regimental sector. Montalone gave excellent flank protection because one could look out across the valley to the east and observe any movements by the enemy. The men of the company, commanded by Captain Thomas K. Franks, did not have to wait very long.

Lieutenant Edmund J. Carberry was the weapons platoon leader:

"We could see tanks moving on the road to our right. Evidently Jerry didn't know we were on Montalone. All at once we spotted three columns of Germans coming our way across the valley. There was about a company in each of the columns and they were well spread out. One column walked right down the axis of our machinegun barrels. Rifle fire, air bursts, mortar fire, everything, hit them as they crossed the open fields. It looked to me as if they left hundreds of dead when they pulled what was left back over the road where the ground dropped off and they were out of the fire."[18]

Nor had Lt. Col. Ralph N. Woods' 1st Battalion been idle. It was still without Company A which had not returned from the 776th TD Battalion area. By early morning of the 7th it was moving up the trail towards Hill 553 when Company B became involved in a vicious firefight with enemy guns located in a farmhouse and in a heavily wooded area to its right. All afternoon the shooting continued with neither the Germans nor the boys of Company B and Company C, who had joined the fight, giving ground. Only darkness brought a pause to the exchange of fire. The two companies were in a mess. The communications wire had been torn up, ammo, water and rations were low and the companies were not where they thought they were. They were not on Hill 553 but Ridge 461, a thousand yards south.

It wasn't until noon of the next day that the two companies were able to assemble and move out. By early afternoon they had finally reached the macadam road and began to work their way through the heavy undergrowth and dense brush of Hill 553; here they were observed by the Germans, who for the third time, had infiltrated back onto the hill and were hidden in the thick bushes and small timber along the trail. This firefight continued over five hours and well into the night. Finally, Companies F and I were able to disperse the enemy and end the resistance.

Colonel W. Fulton Magill was now faced with three woefully crippled and weary companies...Companies A, L and I. What could he do now? There were many men in the 363rd Infantry who considered the colonel far too old to be a combat commander. Magill was a rather tall, pudgy man with ruddy facial features. His hair was totally white and he looked older than he was. Monte Vaso was only one of many difficult battles he was to endure as regimental commander. In spite of Vaso and future problems Magill would hold on to the command of the 363rd until the end of the war.

Colonel Magill planned an all-out attack on the mountain for 9 July. He attached Company K to the 1st Battalion and Company A to the 3rd. On the morning of the 9th, a Sunday, the entire 91st Division Artillery came to the support of the 363rd: the 346th, 347th, 348th and 916th. At 0800 the division batteries opened fire. At 1100, so did the three battalions of infantry. By mid-afternoon the worn out infantrymen were on the top of Monte Vaso. The Germans had given up another mountain and the Americans again had paid a price. For the next ten months there was always one more mountain facing the troops of the 91st Division, and yet another one and another one.

Following the capture of Vaso, the regiment made good gains through the unbelievably rugged, almost uninhabited countryside. The slow moving, sweat-soaked columns moved like ants down one ravine and up the next, crossing fast moving streams, filling their canteens, and floundering onward, climbing the next hill, then down and up again.

Chianni, the regimental objective was taken 13 July. Company I, or what was left of it, entered the town at 1700. Several hundred Germans had evacuated the village early that morning. There was no resistance nor were there any enemy inside Chianni. Bagni was occupied the next day and at 0300 the 363rd Infantry went into Division reserve. The badly mauled regiment had its first relaxation in two weeks, its first hot meals and, more importantly, the weary troops were able to bathe. Bagni was eight miles east of the large seaport of Leghorn. It was the next objective.

The 363rd Infantry had seen its first baptism of fire in one of the most fierce, and costly, battles of the Arno River campaign. It bent, but it did not break. Two months later, to the day, the 363rd's action would bring it the highest award given a unit of the United States Army: the Presidential Unit Citation.

Endnotes for Chapter 3

1 . One of the finest accounts of the actions at Salerno is British historian Eric Morris' book, *Salerno: A Military Disaster*. New York. Stein and Day. 1984.
2 . Lt. Col. Willis Jackson. CO, 1st Battalion, 338th Infantry. Letter to the Author.
3 . D'Este, Carlo. *Fatal Decision*. New York. Harper Collins. Page v.
4 . A history of the 361st Infantry Regiment, *Thunder in the Apennines*, was written by the author and published in 1981. Fully documented with chapter notes, it's a very detailed look at the action of the regiment throughout its period of combat.
5 . "The Capture of Leghorn and Pisa". *The Powder River Journal*. June, 1988. Page 41. Written by the author. This magazine is published twice a year by the 91st Infantry Division Association.
6 . Letter to the author.
7 . Quoted in the Regimental history. June, 1944
8 . This description of Velletri is among the 361st records for June, 1944. There are other descriptions of various villages as they appeared when the infantry first entered them. On the first page an officer had scribbled, "Simon. Here is Bn Journal and some more notes. Sherman".
9 . The northward drive of the 361st is covered in Chapter Two of *Thunder in the Apennines*.
10 . The latter narrative was sent to the author by John Moehlenbrock, Company K. The others are unidentified.
11 . "The Powder River Journal". June, 1988. Page 42.
12 . "Echoes of the Past". Ibid. June, 1990. Pages 3-5
13 . Letter to the author.
14 . "The Powder River Journal". June, 1988. Page 43
15 . Forty-two years after the battle, Monte Vaso was once again in the news. Early in 1986 an inhabitant of Rosignano Marittimo was searching the mountainside for mushrooms and came upon the bones of several men whose bodies had somehow been left behind. Recent rains had washed away the soil revealing the bodies. Also discovered were rusty M1s, American and German helmets, several dogtags and a number of ammo boxes. The Italian press immediately published several stories in a number of Tuscany newspapers. According to these accounts the place where the bodies were found was "inaccessible and isolated". Within days, the event was international news. A friend of the author, Fernando Gemignani of Florence, became so intrigued with the story that he drove to Rosignano Marittimo to try and locate the man who first made the discovery. The following is his letter of 13 April, 1986:

"This strange vicissitude of Monte Vaso has excited me to such a point that I decided to meet personally Mr. Coppi, the man who first found the evidences of the bloody passage of war in that area. I wrote him. Then we spoke to each other on the phone, and the day set, I left for Rosignano Marittimo. That morning the sky was gloomy and it rained abundantly. Having arrived in the small town I asked some passerby where Mr. Coppi lived. He tells me that he's known by the name Coppino the grave digger. He's the custodian of the cemetery. I was told that Coppino, in his spare time, works at a bar in the pizza. I direct myself quickly to that locale. The owner tells me he had gone to Florence that very day.

"'Coppino in Florence?' I asked incredulously. 'Impossible! I am from Florence and I have an appointment with him here at Rosignano!'

"The man at the bar looked at me fixedly. He was taken by a suspicion. After having thought a bit, he tells me to wait. He goes out. After several minutes, he re-enters from the rear of the locale followed by Coppino. After a quick introduction, Coppino invites me to follow him. On the way he tells me that at his house there is an American journalist, before anything else he must finish his talk with him. The glass door of his old house opens directly on the street. We go in. Another glass door admits us to the kitchen, modestly furnished. An elderly woman comes to meet me with knitting needles and a ball of yarn in her hands. She is Coppino's mother. She hurries to prepare me a cup of coffee. Soon, Coppino and the journalist are back from having a 'look-over' on Monte Vaso. Their clothes are soaked and muddy. While the two speak I gaze around the room and noticed it is strewn with material recovered from Monte Vaso. I walked to the kitchen and noticed a series of helmets lined up on a shelf. On a table were cartridge cases, fuses, shell casings and artillery and mortar rounds. And there was more; machinegun belts, bullets, magazines, munition boxes, canteens and other things belonging to both the Germans and the Americans.

"When we were left alone, Coppino told me he was a simple working man for the Comune of Rosignano and had become in a short while a personality of whom the press and television spoke. His case had become the object of journalists and curious people. There was even the Italian and German television. Afterwards, from the USA, had come the television cameras of NBC News and the International Courier. All had taken photographs of him surrounded by his relics. Coppino laments to himself that he hadn't been more shrewd. He could have made a great profit from this event by getting paid for the news and the material which he had every time given away. 'But from today on,' he told me in a decided tone, making his face serious and slamming a hand down on the table. 'I won't say or do anything more for free!' In sum, his services must be for pay.

"He shows me many received letters. They are requests for military objects and information. Most want to acquire, some directly ask him to sell them war surplus. He pulls out of a small case an envelope containing the articles that he has cut out of various journals. I take from my pocket my clippings which I have brought with me. He has me read a warning come to him from the owner of the land on Monte Vaso. This says, 'Mr. Fausto Coppi must not dig any more nor do any type of searching on the possessions of Azienda Agricola Murri, on pain of denouncement to jurisdictional authority.'

Coppino shrugs his shoulders telling me that he doesn't care at all about such threats. He voluntarily risks arrest but he wants to return to dig on Monte Vaso when he feels like it.

"The news of the recovery of war items and other things, which had occurred on Monte Vaso, went out in the latter part of December, 1985 but Mr. Coppi had already made his discovery several months before. Only after the recovery of human bones had he made the thing public, denouncing the fact to the carbineri of Chianni. The man has me understand his difficulties that he has every time in his search. From Rosignano Marittimo he must go by car as far as Monte Vaso, then on foot, he must walk and climb in a very wild and rough zone. With a voice subdued by that thought, he tells me of the view of the earth stationed by spots of rust and copper, of human remains and hand grenades. In saying this, he caresses those inefficient grenades which he has lined up on the washing machine and had carried down from the mountain with much exhaustion, keeping them closed in the small American backpack which he had found in his house after the war and which was very heavy.

"But the news on the findings on the famous Monte Vaso had made many people rush there, people interested in or impassioned of military objects. Coppino tells me he often meets men and boy, furnished with hoe and spade, intent on digging. Here, he becomes full of anger. He's angry because among his equipment is a metal detector he paid dearly for. After a moment of silence he begins to speak again. 'Up there are things buried that no one can imagine. I know the place where they are and I will bring them to light!' In conclusion he alludes to the finding of six dogtags belonging to soldiers of the 5th American Army. I think these surely must belongs to your 91st Division men. Coppino doesn't respond to my request to show them to me. He quickly changes the subject. In showing me a helmet of the US Army with evident signs of age and rust, crushed on top and with a large hole in the back, he confides in me, 'Under the ground where I found the helmet there are still objects to be brought up.'

"Coppino then sits down and writes some numbers. I agree to pay the amount and I ask him to take me up to Monte Vaso. He tightens up his thin shoulders, fixed his black eyes on me, then lowers his gaze making a gesture of 'No' with his head. He quickly changes the subject. 'I', he says, 'am opposed to the confiscation of these things which I gathered with much sweat, difficulty and hard work. I managed to save them after having promised to declare them to the police. That's my right. I found them!' He gestures for me to wait and hurriedly goes out of the house and returns shortly with a large bundle which he put on the floor and unwraps. He shows me military material. I agree that they are interesting but they are far too expensive.

"I decide to put an end to our meeting. I greet his mother and we got out. As soon as we are outside the house he draws near me and says, 'If you want to see some material for prudence sake I don't keep in the house....' This said, he awaits my reply. 'You will show me another time,' I tell him. His air of mystery really irritates me. 'This summer I'll be coming back with my family to the sea, to Cecina. I'll come back to see you. Will you take me to the place of discoveries, up there, on Monte Vaso?'

"Coppino tosses the black garbage bag containing the things I acquired into the trunk of my car. He shakes my hand without answering. It then begins to rain and I watch Coppino walk slowly back to his house in the rain and he disappears among the ancient alleys of the old town of Rosignano Marittimo.

"Who knows, if I had presented myself as a journalist, instead of a collector, he would certainly have taken me up on Monte Vaso for the pleasure of the notoriety."

No one has ever seen the dogtags which Coppino claims to possess. He has steadfastly refused to show them to every person who has asked to see them. It is possible that Coppino is lying and that the tags do not exist. Those bodies found on Monte Vaso are unidentified after fifty years. So an air of mystery still surrounds the mountain that was so costly to the 363rd Infantry Regiment.

Fernando Gemignani has never returned to Rosignano Marittimo.

16 . Strootman, Ralph. *History of the 363rd Infantry.* One Regiment of the 91st Division in WWII. Infantry Journal Press. Washington. 1947. Pages 23-24.

17 . Bell, James E. Letter to the author. 28 July 1993. "You may also note some of my comments do not agree with Strootman's history," Bell wrote. "That's understandable as Strootman wasn't there. For sure, Vaso was never correctly recorded. Very little has been written by the survivors. It was not a battle anyone would want to write about. I've often compared the 363rd's assault on Hill 634 with the 34th Division's fight on Hill 609 in North Africa."

18 . *History of the 363rd Infantry.* Page 29. Carberry was later promoted to captain and took over Company E after the wounding of Captain Franks.

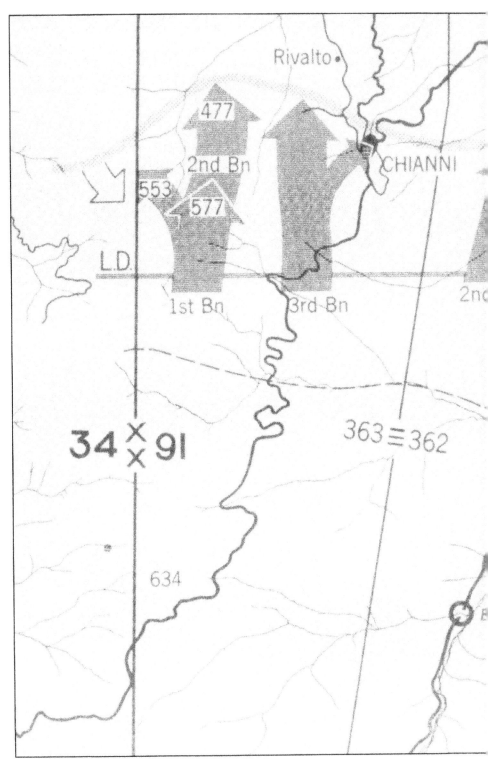

The 362nd enters combat.

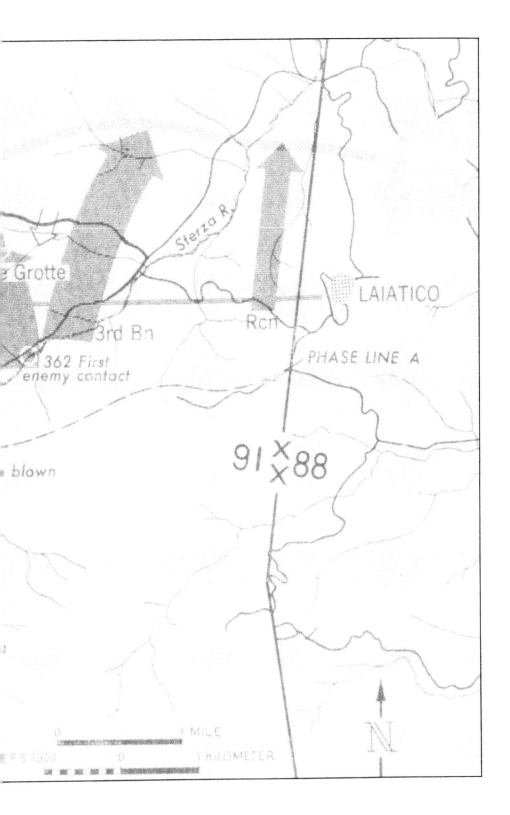

91st Division Artillerymen.

CHAPTER FOUR —
THE 362ND GOES IN

I

At approximately 1400, 5 July 70 officers and 2702 enlisted men of the 362nd Infantry unloaded from a contingent of LCIs in the Roman port of Civitavecchia and boarded trucks for the trip to the front. The move to the port had been uneventful though the roads were congested and the traffic heavy. Many civilians clogged the highways on their way back to their ruined homes and there had been rough seas into Civitavecchia. The regiment spent four days getting into position to go into the line and at 0100 on the morning of the 11th it reached its assembly area. Several hours later Colonel John W. Cotton, regimental commander, gave his staff the estimate of the situation and the order of march. The line of departure was 8 kilometers south of Chianni which was still occupied by the Germans. Colonel Cotton told his men that moderate resistance was expected.[1]

The first troops moved out near midnight and slogged over the mountainous terrain as had the other two regiments before them. The long columns on foot were followed by the regimental organic vehicles but they were almost immediately stopped by two freshly blown bridges. Earlier, reconnaissance had disclosed these bridges to be intact, but this was yet another ruse of the enemy...to blow bridges right under the noses of the advancing Americans. The convoys were stopped but the foot troops continued on. Company B, 316th Engineers made temporary bypasses around the bridges and the regiment moved forward.

At 0415, Company C of the leading 1st Battalion made contact with the Germans two miles southeast of Chianni and the 362nd Infantry was officially "in combat". The forward elements of the company continued to advance until they were stopped by grazing fire that spread out from a number of machine-gun positions. The leading platoon, caught out in the open, was receiving fire from all directions. Seeing the plight of the Platoon Sergeant Roy Harmon pushed his squad forward to a ravine to the right of the beleaguered unit. When the squad got within range, it fired tracer bullets into three haystacks near the enemy guns trying to set them afire. When this didn't work Sergeant Harmon told his men to hold.

"I'll see what I can do about this," he said.

While the German gunners tried to cut him down Harmon crawled within 20 yards of the enemy positions. He tossed a phosphorus grenade and set one of the haystacks afire. When the two enemy gunners tried to run, Harmon killed both of them. He started for the next position but was immediately hit and wounded. Dragging himself to within several yards of the haystack, Harmon tossed another grenade which killed the enemy gunners. He then ran nearly thirty yards straight into the fire of German guns. Again he was hit and almost fell, but regained his footage and kept going, leaving a trail of blood behind him. When he was twenty-five yards from the enemy position Harmon rose to his knees to throw another grenade;

Col. John W. Cotton, CO, 362nd Infantry

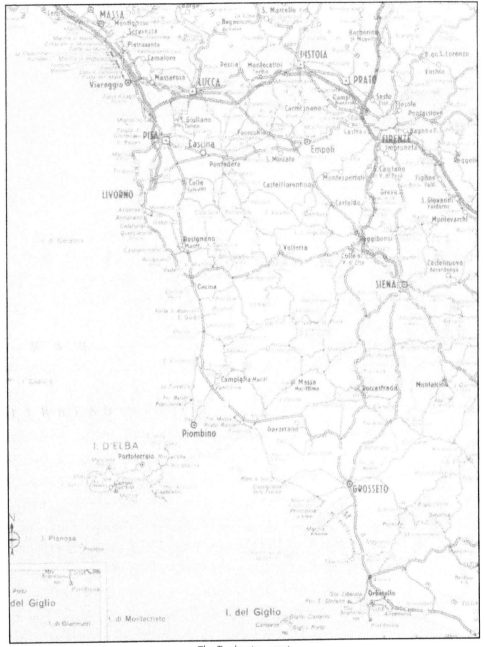

The Tyrrhenian coast.

however, rifle fire cut him down. He got to his feet once again, and with a final heave, tossed his last grenade. For a few second the Germans poured fire into his body. Harmon fell to the ground, dead. The gallant sergeant was later awarded the Congressional Medal of Honor.[2]

The infantryman's first day of combat is undoubtedly the day he remembers above all days: the day he discovers what war is all about.

Wade Hawsey was a member of 2nd Battalion Headquarters:

"Chianni was a small village fifty miles southwest of Florence. There our column of trucks and troops

A platoon of Company F, 362nd. Italy, June 26, 1944.

came to a halt. It was 8 o'clock, the morning of July 12, 1944. They'd been on the march since two a.m. Now we were on a small dirt road in a valley of vineyards, surrounded by a magnificent mountain range. It was calm. The calm before the storm. 'What a beautiful country,' I thought as I sat among a row of grapevines eating my C rations and looking at the mountains which seemed to envelope me in their various shades of yellow, ochre, purple and green. As my fork tore into the can of beans, the first enemy shell thundered into our lead company. With my fork in mid-air, I thought, 'My God, what's next?' I'd left my entrenching tool on the truck. There was no time to run back for it and already shells were bursting all around me. Amid the explosions, I thought of something a combat soldier had told me. 'If you have to, you can dig in with anything.' Anything? All I had was a can of C rations and a fork. I stared at the fork in my hands and yelled, 'I'll try.' The ground in the valley was hard and dry and my first thrust brought me nothing but frustration. The fork bent and doubled up into my fist. The shells kept coming. My hands moved the loose dirt and I dug myself as close into the ground as I could. Some of the shells were now hitting a mere forty feet away.

"As I lay there, flat on my stomach, I could hear a noise above the shelling. It sounded like bees then something hit the ground. It was shrapnel! A piece the size of my hand was only a foot from my head.

"Lee Kilpatrick, our truck driver, was in a ditch about fifty feet away. 'Get the hell over here, Hawsey!' he yelled. I sprinted for his ditch, diving headfirst into the back wall, almost knocking myself out. Finally the shelling let up. We saw a jeep with four guys in it stop on the little bridge that crossed our ditch. They jumped but a shell hit two of them and killed them instantly. The other two guys jumped for our ditch and knocked us down amid a mixture of legs, dust, dirt and rock.

"I left the ditch finally. It seemed hours since I'd left my shovel. Things had been, and were, busy all along the line on our first day of battle. The smoke, the sound of the shelling, the hollering, the smell of cordite, the smell of fear, and always, the stench of death: the sights and sounds all came together that 12 July, 1944."[3]

For Chris Hanson, another 362nder, it was also his first day of war:

"It was a scorching hot day and I was scared. The ground was hard and dry from lack of rain and yet the leaves on the grape vines were lush and green. The mountains surrounded us and we moved out in a column. I watched the foot soldiers and I thought I was lucky to be driving a jeep. It wasn't long before I wondered if I wouldn't be better off in a truck, or on foot. We continued forward all day. As darkness approached, the shelling began. Before I knew what was happening my jeep was out of control. I was to learn later that the battery had been hit dead on. I rammed into a tree and as I wasn't about to stay with my vehicle, I grabbed my rifle, and wishing I could hear for the rear, I took off as fast as I could. All I knew was I had to get the hell out of there. I ran into an open field and dropped down and tried to dig myself in with my body. Would you believe I had forgotten to pick up my shovel? 'So this is what it's all about,' I said to myself. 'If I can make it out of this I can make it the rest of the way.'"[4]

Information obtained by Major Thurber, S-2, from 0400, 12 July to 1800 13 July, indicated the Germans had no apparent front lines but were utilizing small pockets of resistance to the best of their advantage. Snipers were also causing considerable trouble in the regimental zone, in addition to heavy artillery fire from 88s, SPs and 105s. The enemy still held the high ground to the north and was able to set up good OPs. What couldn't be determined was their supply and evacuation routes, nor the extent of their reserves. The German tactics were simple: delay. This they did by extensive mining of the roads and the blowing of bridges.

So the enemy slowly withdrew to the Arno River, falling back yard by yard.

Close to noon on the 13th, the 3rd Battalion was 600 yards beyond the east-west Chianni road meeting only slight resistance. That same afternoon the 2nd Battalion, under friendly fire, advanced slowly and by evening was abreast the 3rd. Casualties for the day had been twenty killed and forty wounded with nine cases of exhaustion reported.

Sgt. James W. King would recall his third day of combat:

"The night before, we were a back-up unit for Company F. Breakfast had been good for we'd found some ripe fruit. We were in reserve so we took a few hours of well-earned rest. By now we were at the top of a hill and we set up our anti-tank gun in the center of a field close to the corner of a vineyard. We moved into position as fast as we could and I told the squad,'Dig in!' Hawsey and I tried to spot the enemy tanks but they beat us to the punch and spotted us first and opened up with their guns. On the third shot our gun was hit. The shelling finally stopped and we assessed our damage. The gun was lost but only one man was hit, Corporal Wilkins was hit with a bullet through the leg. The shelling then started up again. And we hit the dirt again. With our gun gone we were almost helpless. After the shelling eased we found Schneider with a large hole torn in his back. He was bleeding badly. 'Hawsey!' I yelled. 'You're in charge!' and I headed to the rear to try and find a medic for the wounded. As I ran I realized that Company F was shot up badly and that all their medics were working. I finally stumbled across a stretcher and headed back to my squad. The lieutenant ordered me not to go back, but I headed out anyway. I went back to the boys and we carried Schneider and Wilkins back to the aid station, then returned to the vineyard. The shelling eased and I realized this was the first time I had ever waded in blood. The ground was muddied with the blood from the wounded.

We moved in and took our objective that evening. It had been a busy twelve hours and I felt at least 20 years older."[5]

The laconic and indistinctive regimental history, dated 14-16 July, tells us:

"A report was submitted on enemy operations and conditions. The 6th Company, 1059th Regiment of the German 92nd Grenadier Division, is revealed to be facing our forces. They are still using the same tactics of small strong points, that is, changeable 88 SP positions. They had one armored car and two tanks and their artillery was heavier the preceding day. Losses in the 6th Company had been small but morale was not too good. The men have been ordered to advance or be shot and there are some desertions. Yesterday they received their first rations in three days. The company has approximately 60 men in two platoons of three squads each. They have six or seven medium machineguns, one heavy machinegun and two small anti-tank guns. The battalion commander is Captain Kanebol. The company commander is 2nd Lt. Zellerman. The 1st Bn of the 1059th had very heavy losses of 5-10 July and part of the battalion staff was captured during that period. Enemy capabilities tend to a continued delaying action and it is thought the unit is withdrawing to new positions south of the Arno River defense.

Riflemen of the 361st walk through the rubble that was Pontedera.

"For 14 July we reported these casualties: 12 killed in action and 95 wounded.

Another day dawned, the 15th. The weather was clear, visibility was good off the roads but due to the extreme dust, driving the roads was extremely hazardous.

"For the twenty-four hour period 15-16 July, the regimental S-2 report indicated very little enemy change. It did appear that the enemy action had stiffened and that the German withdrawal had slowed down, but the artillery fire was growing heavier and was the cause of most of our casualties with very few coming from small arms. During the two days period twenty-five prisoners were captured. They told how our own

General Livesay (left) and staff. July, 1944.

artillery had caused many deaths to personnel and destruction of equipment. Around 2100, a company of foot and motorized enemy infantry, supported by five tanks, attacked the left flank of the Regiment. At the same time a counter attack was thrown against Company K; however, our troops repelled the attack. The following morning 88s shelled the village of Soiana and a P-47 zoomed over and strafed our own men near the vicinity of San Pietro which is south of Capannoli. The troops promptly shot the plane down to halt the strafing. By mid-afternoon the enemy artillery had decreased but by evening it started up again and threw in some heavy volumes. It seems German morale, in spite of everything, is fairly good. The terrain to our front now consists of a low line of hills running east-west, then flat country to the Arno River. North of the Arno there are high mountains again.

"One interesting S-2 detail came through. It seems a partisan at Casanova, one Marionelli Aladino, stated he found a Lt. Walter Ford, ASN unknown, wandering around the area approximately sixteen kilometers northeast of Casanova. This goes way back to 16 May. Ford's unit is unknown. What he was doing there is still a mystery. Aladino sheltered and fed Ford until 20 June. Ford then left and told Aladino to tell the Americans when they arrived that he was safe. Aladino did not know which way Ford might have gone when he left.

"At the conclusion of the 16th, battle casualty reports were 14 killed in action, 96 wounded and 8 injured but not evacuated."[6]

On the evening of 14 July General Livesay had held a meeting with his staff officers and had told them, "There is no justification for believing the Germans will withdraw any faster or farther than our pressure compels them to, as long as the terrain is reasonably suited for delaying operations which it is to the Arno. We must keep on their heels, on their very backs if necessary, but let them know we have every intention of pursuing them at top speed."

General Livesay's advice was followed to the letter. By nightfall of the 17th the 362nd had made steady progress through the hills and ravines in the countryside north of Chianni, slowed only by mine fields and blown out bridges. There was a feeling throughout the regiment that after nearly six days of hard fighting a breakthrough to the Arno River was imminent and that the Division's mission, the occupation of the south bank of the river, was close at hand.

The 362nd's attack continued the next morning but without opposition. Delayed somewhat by the terrain, minefields and demolitions, the regiment closed on its objective at 1500.

So ended the first week of combat for the 91st Division. Over 2,678 tons of ammunition had been fired by the Artillery, with a peak of 323 in the one 24 hour period of 16-17 July. The Division had suffered 904 casualties: 12 officers and 131 enlisted men killed and 37 and 724 enlisted men wounded or injured.[7]

Meanwhile, at 0900 16 July, General Livesay had telephoned Colonel Broedlow, the 361st commander. "Broedlow" he told the colonel, "You'll swing your regiment west of Cotton's and proceed rapidly toward the Arno through the town of Ponsacco up to Pontedera on the river. Attack with the 1st and 2nd Battalion. The remainder of your regiment should be prepared to advance or resist counterattacks and will establish and maintain very vigorous patrolling north of the river."

A member of the 1st Battalion was in on the drive:

"I remember the Arno River was our first real fight after our rest the first part of July. On the morning of the 17th we ran into some pretty stiff resistance just before we got to the little town of Cevoli. We advanced

Division artillery near Chianni.

on through the town, but once on the other side, we ran into some extremely heavy 88 fire and withdrew back into the town. It was one of the heaviest barrages I was ever in in all my days of combat and I was in some pretty rough ones. When we got back into Cevoli we took refuge in some wine cellars that proved to be excellent shelters from the deadly 88s. As luck would have it, in one of the cellars there were two big casks of wine and of course everyone crowded into that one cellar, filling up their canteens and drinking out of their tin cups. More damn wine than I ever saw in my life. With each shell that went over we drank a toast to a dead Jerry. We even found a piano on the first floor of the house and we really had a party going until it was time for us to move out.

Anyway I can look back now and laugh like hell at the party we had in that cellar, with everyone carrying on with the piano just a-going and the mortars and 88s crashing outside. It was one of the lighter moments of the war.[8]"

In spite of massive artillery fire, the advance of the 361st continued through the night and the following afternoon, two platoons of Company I and another of Company K were inside Poncsacco just three miles from the city of Pontedera on the Arno. The 3rd Battalion rapidly occupied the town and an hour later Colonel Broedlow telephoned the battalion commander, twenty-two year old Major Dick Oshlo, and told him to press the attack. By 0830 of the 18th the 1st Platoon of Company K was within the city limits of Pontedera. Here they encountered a German strong-point in the freight yards consisting of machinegun and sniper fire, with the enemy using the buildings as pillboxes. All buildings within the city were heavily boobytrapped. The Germans were quickly driven out of the city and at exactly 0900 Company K reached the south bank of the Arno River, the first American unit to reach that objective.

Captain Chris P. Hald was the CO of Company I:

"Major Oshlo called a meeting of company commanders in the kitchen of a farmhouse in Cevoli somewhere around 0100 in the AM, 17 July at which time he issued his battle orders. I remember this meeting rather well because I was extremely tired and fell asleep while Osh was giving the orders which pleased him in no way and though we had been close friends for a very long time he laid it on me pretty severely.

"The attack began in the morning at about 0700 as light was breaking. We had a platoon of Company M machineguns with us and were on the left side of the highway which ran north through Ponsacco and Pontedera. Company K was over to out right. The terrain on both sides of highway was flat and generally covered with vineyards. There was a typical number of farmhouses along the road and there were some out-buildings off the road in the fields in both company sectors.

"Company I attacked with two platoons on line and a platoon in reserve. A Company M mortar section was set up to give us some supporting fire. A number of tanks kept close to us and we moved up the highway and were fired on by some snipers hidden in some of the houses, but a volley of fire from our own troops kept them pretty well bottled up as we advanced slowly northward by fire and movement. By noon we could see the rooftops of the village of Ponsacco.

"The firing was so hot and heavy that we ran out of ammo by 0100, the first time that had happened since we were in combat. I called back to Battalion and shortly a weapons carrier with a basic load, drove up the highway and a couple of GIs began to distribute the rounds. From somewhere up the highway an enemy tank opened up on the jeep and made a direct hit. One of the men was hit in the leg, laying it open to the bone. We quickly bandaged it and he was evacuated to the rear.

"The attack continued and as we approached the outbuildings of the town we opened fire on the doors and windows with all weapons in our possession, including the bazookas, which may have missed a few of the tanks, but did a great job knocking down doors. We captured three enemy soldiers and they reported a company of infantry was holding Pontedera.

"It was now about 1630 hours. The terrain was quite flat and the vineyards had given way to more open country. Ponsacco sat astride the highway directly in front of us and there was a low wall on the south side of the town. I met with the commander of four light tanks, a major whose name I can't recall, and discussed the battle plans. I remember he said quite distinctly, 'Thank God for this flat country. This is the first time since I've been in Italy where we can use tanks the way they're supposed to be used.' It was decided we would take his four tanks and continue the move north, encircling Ponsacco, while the infantry companies made a frontal assault against the town.

"We attacked on the left side of the highway and met some small arms fire. The sound of the moving tanks and our firing must have frightened the defenders as the fire slackened considerably as we approached. We were now able to scale the wall on the south side of the city. By this time darkness had fallen and we set up camp for the night, established a guard, rations and ammo were brought forward, and we prepared to jump off for Pontedera the next morning.

"At daylight the attack continued. No resistance was met on the march from Ponsacco to Pontedera, a distance of some two miles or so. Company K entered Pontedera first with Company I close on its heels. As we moved along the highway into town the lieutenant forward observer from the 916th Field Artillery was with me as were his two sergeants and his radio equipment which was in communication with the 916th fire direction center. Captain Sigmen and I were standing in front of a very large building that could have been a bank or hotel. As we were talking the artillery lieutenant said, 'I think I'll go upstairs so I can get better observation and see what's going on on the other side of the river. He stepped into the entryway which had a mosaic design. As he stepped on this design, booby traps blew down the entire front of the building, killing him instantly. After this episode, we sent out orders for everyone to be extremely careful and to make a complete search of all houses. Company I was then directed to move to the left in order to set up a defense and to control the airport that was in that direction.

"There was a highway on the south bank of the Arno River, paralleling it, and a short distance from the river on the south side of the highway were a number of apartment houses between three and five stories high. After the company had assumed its defense of the airfield, company headquarters sought out a building, both as headquarters and one that would give us observation of the river. Such a building was found and we entered it safely through a back door and went up to the third floor. This area was a large apartment and a big picture window faced the Arno and through it we could see across the river to a very large villa a half mile or so beyond. The artillery radios were with me and we also had the 75. mm SPs mounted on the half tracks that were supporting us. From the very back wall of the living room we could observe the Germans without their observing us. We set up the radios and soon established contact with the 916th. We explained our situation and reported the death of the lieutenant. The 916th told us, 'You guys can have our battalion if you want it. We've got some one five-fives and some eight inchers that aren't occupied and you can call in and direct fire to them if you need it.' We also had contact with the mounted 75s and contact with Captain Bob Cuzick's Company M and its 81.mm mortars.

By now it was about 1400 hours. The visibility was clear and it was a beautiful sunny day in Italy. With field glasses one could see the enemy moving around the villa across the Arno. An anti-tank gun was observed digging in, several machineguns were dug in beside it. Two German jeeps drove up to the front of the villa which faced our side of the river. Upon observing this activity, the 916th fire direction was directed by me at the targets around the villa. An 8-inch battalion made a direct hit on the anti-tank gun being dug in and it seemed to disintegrate and explode in mid-air while the men around the gun were blown in all directions like so many rag dolls by the force of the bursting shell. Continued fire nearly destroyed the villa along with the machinegun positions, as were the jeeps sitting on the lawn.

It was now about 1600 and the Germans were still unaware of our OP in the apartment house. About this time a wire-carrying crew came roaring up the road in front of our OP and stopped. The driver got out and shouted, 'Captain Hald! Captain Hald! Are you there?' Upon hearing that I was, the wireman immediately began throwing wire along the front of the apartment and entered the big bay window to wire us into battalion.

This ended our peaceful existence and it was just a few minutes until the roof started coming down around our heads from enemy artillery fire. We withdrew rather reluctantly from the OP and Pontedera was left to Company K and its supported elements."[9]

By 23 July the troops of Fifth Army were poised along the south bank of the Arno on a 35-mile front extending from the sea to the Elsa River 20 miles west of Florence. The 91st Division now directed its main effort to the organization and improvement of a strong defensive line along the river, taking advantage of the high ground south of the Arno.

Endnotes for Chapter 4

1 . Colonel John W. Cotton, chief of the 362nd Infantry, was considered by some to be the best combat leader of the three regimental commanders; however, his record for administrative details, for whatever reason, did not measure up to his skills in the field. The regimental staff of the 362nd kept a wretched record of its actions in Italy. When it came time for the division historian, Colonel Robert A. Robbins, to write the history of the 91st Division in World War II he had to call in Colonel Cotton and other members of the regiment to help fill in the blank spaces. The after-actions reports are very superficial. There is no mention of regimental strategy or tactics, nor are there any personal narratives or personalities. Some of the monthly histories were written weeks after the actions. The Unit Journal is a meager, time dated, list of patrols, telephone calls and artillery reports. There are few, if any, details of combat operations, but there is much about rear echelon activities. The 362nd Regimental History is a historian's nightmare. The author had to dig deep to come up with even a fourth-rate description of the battle record of the regiment. In contrast to the terrible chronicle of the 362nd, the other two regiments kept excellent histories.

2 . The gymnasium at the Presidio near San Francisco is named in honor of Sgt. Harmon.

3 . Hawsey, Wade and Wahlfeldt, Betty. *War Journey* Gregath. Cullman, Alabama. 1986. Pages 41-46.

4 . Ibid. p. 46-47.

5 . Ibid. P. 62-63.

6 . 362nd Regimental History. 11-18 July.

7 . *The 91st Infantry Division in World War II.* Page 75.

8 . Livengood, Roy. *Thunder in the Apennines.* Waukegan, Ill. 1981. Page 73.

9 .Captain Hald's description of the Ponsacc-Pontedera actions comes from a cassette tape made for the author.

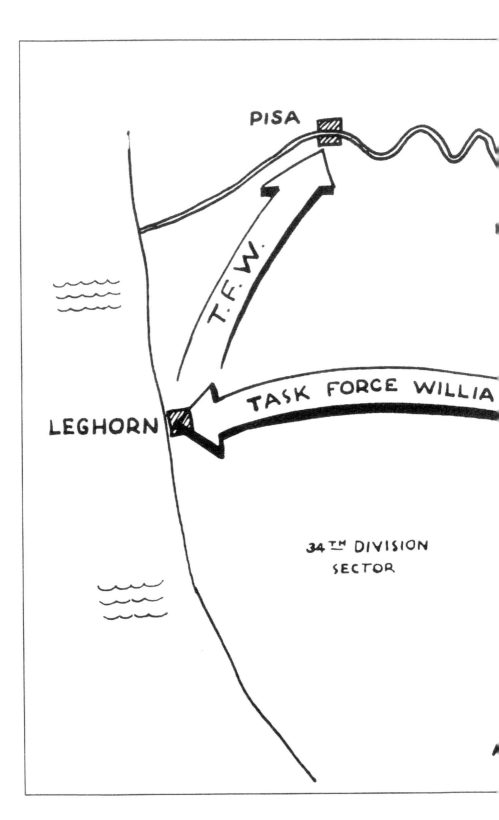

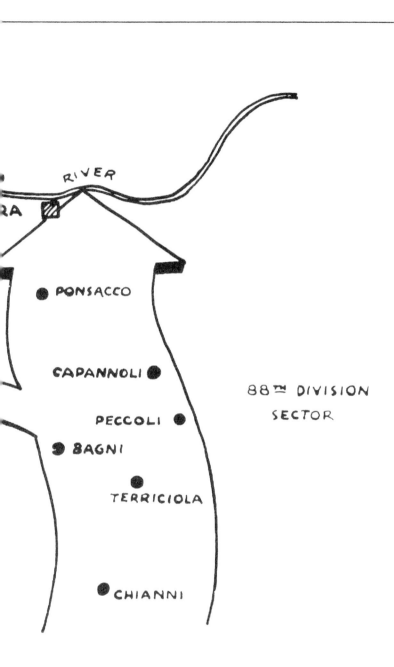

RIVER

RA

PONSACCO

CAPANNOLI

PECCOLI

BAGNI

TERRICIOLA

CHIANNI

88ᵀᴴ DIVISION
SECTOR

"HE FIRST STAR"

OF 91ˢᵀ DIVISION TO THE ARNO RIVER

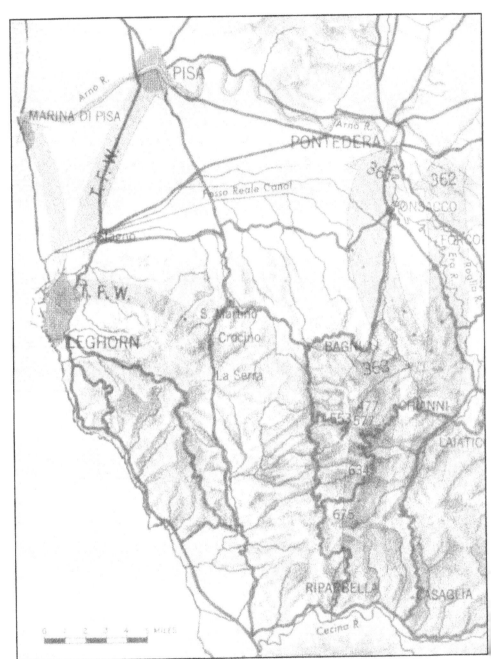

The route of Task Force Williamson.

CHAPTER FIVE —
THE CAPTURE OF LEGHORN AND
PISA: PATROLLING THE ARNO

"You can't know it without being in it and once you're in it, you can't get out of it. Nothing that anyone did made any sense, unless you were there, and then it was the only thing to do."

Vietnam veteran Captain David Loehr.

I

The port of Leghorn lies some 250 miles north of Naples. Since the capture of the southern city on 1 October, 1943, the Allies had used Naples as their primary depot in funneling supplies to Fifth Army troops fighting up the boot of Italy. The seizure of Leghorn, which lay just west of the attacking 34th, 88th and 91st Divisions, would mean that the overland shipping route could be greatly shortened. Although the Germans had not planned to give up the port so quickly, they did manage to destroy the facilities and block the harbor with sunken ships. All quay walls were wrecked and the masonry pushed into the sea. Many ships were scuttled alongside the piers and the harbor planted with mines. Leghorn had suffered the same fate as Naples. However, Army and Navy engineers estimated that at least three weeks would be required to repair the port once it was in the hands of the Americans, when this was completed, ships could again dock and Leghorn could meet all the needs of the Fifth Army north of Rome.[1]

During the afternoon of 17 July, Task Force Williamson was formed. It was this unit that was given the job of liberating Leghorn. Brigadier General R.E.S. Williamson, the Assistant Division commander, was chosen to lead the specialized force which was assigned to the 34th Division but would act as a separate unit. General Williamson had served for many months in the South Pacific before coming to the 91st Division. The Task Force was to consist of the 363rd Infantry; the 2nd Platoon, 91st Recon Troop, Company A, 752nd Tank Battalion, Company C, 804th Tank Destroyer Battalion and Company A, 235th Engineers. Its mission was to make an "end around play" and capture Leghorn by flanking the city from the west while the 34th continued driving north.

At 0210, July 18, twenty-five minutes after the task force elements had closed into the assembly area eight miles east of the port city, General Williamson issued the attack order.

The 3rd Battalion passed through the Japanese-American 100th Battalion and moved across country in a direct line to Leghorn. It met no opposition until Company K took some rifle fire from south of a trail that led to the hamlet of Ceppeto, 2,000 yards from the initial jump-off point. Here, mortars were called for and Company M replied, routing about 50 enemy dug-in a nearby field.

A couple of hours later the 1st Battalion, moving out on foot and in a column of companies, B, A, C, D, slogged up an unimproved road leading north. After a mile and a half, the road forked, with the left fork following a valley straight into the seaport. An hour later the 2nd Battalion hooked up with the rear elements of the 1st and joined the march north.

By noon, Company B was advancing swiftly toward Leghorn, but was stopped for a short while by three German machineguns which killed three men before the guns were silenced.

Throughout the hot afternoon Task Force Williamson continued forward and at 1730 Company A, now in front, reached the high ground about two miles outside the city. Pushing rapidly north the troops moved into one of Leghorn's public squares. Lieutenant Stephen Kish, now the company CO, quickly organized street-fighting platoons and cut all streets leading into the square.

Shortly after 0100, 19 July, Company B outposted Garibaldi Avenue, one of the main streets, for a distance of 750 yards, blocking the retreat for any Germans forces being driven north by the 34th Division. This small band of 1st Battalion troops then spent the entire night alone in the newly captured port.

At 0610 the next morning the 2nd Battalion entered Leghorn and occupied the waterfront area. They outposted and patrolled the docks finding barbed wire, all types of barricades and unburied anti-tank mines.

The 3rd Battalion then moved into the city and took over a sector to the north. Now, the 363rd Infantry had complete control of the valuable port of Leghorn. Later in the morning, the Regimental command post set up in the downtown area and plans were made to continue the northward advance to the Arno River and the city of Pisa ten miles away. Even later in the day, General Mark Clark made a triumphant tour of the port and looked over his new prize.

A member of the 2nd Battalion made the entry into the newly liberated city:

A division jeep patrols the streets of Leghorn.

A poker game occupies the time of the infantrymen of Company E, 363rd at a street barricade in Leghorn. Sam Patranella deals while Dick Garretson (standing) looks on.

"We were ordered to dig in along the ditches that paralleled the coastal road, then move into the town at dawn. First light came slowly and with it the outline of Leghorn up ahead of us. All was quiet as we moved forward, the silence was broken only by the faint clinking of equipment; rifles, mortar plates, tripods and the shuffle of boots on asphalt. We left the roadside and moved into the city, walking closely up against the buildings which were damp with early morning wetness. The streets were shadowy and dark and in the greyness of morning a German cyclist came pedaling toward us, pedaling easily and smoothly. We shot him quickly and he fell from the cycle and rolled over in the gutter. The cycle continued on for several feet then collapsed in the middle of the street. We left the German lying on the pavement. He was our only opposition.

"We continued on into the city proper along walks that were lined with bright red flowers which we

A member of Company C, 316th Engineers takes cover behind a destroyed German vehicle as his comrades detonate mines on a street in Leghorn.

plucked and put into the netting of our helmets. Sort of our 'badge' of liberation. Leghorn had been completely abandoned: not a civilian was in sight. There may have been some around, but they were well hidden. The harbor was in ruins and some of the ships had been blown clear out of the water and up onto the sidewalks. The shutters of the shops were closed and many of them had been wrecked by bombs. A large theatre was without a roof and a big movie screen was white and clean in the early rays of the sun. Up the street was another theatre, intact. The letters were still on the marquee. The movie was 'Sun Valley Serenade' starring John Payne and Sonja Henie. Their smiling faces looked at us from the frames of the glossy prints by the golden entrance door.

We moved on to the city square, took a break and ate our rations. We had been resting for a couple of hours and lazily patrolling the docks when we heard the high scream of a siren and General Mark Clark and his entourage hove into sight. There were at least a dozen jeeps in the column. The general, wearing his usual yellow neckerchief, gave us a half-hearted salute and disappeared around the corner.

Later we set up headquarters in the lobby of a hotel. Lieutenant Knowland took over a two-room suite on the first floor and called a meeting of platoon sergeants. They were informed that no more than four men were to occupy each room. I didn't understand why, but Knowland always had his reasons. Sgt. Wolfe, the Scholar, Birdy and me took a room on the second floor. The Scholar was a tall, lanky kid with a shock of straw-colored hair. He wore thick, steel rimmed glasses. He had the unlikely name of Willis Knight so we had nicknamed him The Car, but when we found out he was such a studious reader who could read through an entire paperback novel in a single evening, we renamed him The Scholar and that was the name that stuck.

"The hotel beds were without sheets and the mattresses had been tied and thrown into a corner. Sgt. Wolfe and Birdy went out to explore the city and the Scholar and I cut the cords around the mattresses and put them on the floor. They were sheer luxury and we stretched and gaped and lay down and fell into a deep sleep.

"I do not know how long I had been asleep but I was awakened rather violently by Birdy yanking me hard at the front of my shirt. I bolted up from the mattress. I thought the Germans were counterattacking.

"'Wake up! Wake up!' yelled Birdy. 'Get the hell out of that sack! Get your helmets and canteens and anything that will hold the stuff! We've run into a brewery down the street!'

"'What the hell is going on?' asked the Scholar who was groggy with sleep.

"'I'm telling you, we've run into a brewery down the street!' said Birdy. 'Let's go! Let's go!'

"'Go?' said the Scholar. 'You can go to hell!' And he lay back quietly and closed his eyes.

"I got up and put on my steel helmet, even though I still didn't know what was going on, put on my web belt with the two canteens and followed Birdy down the stairs and out into the street. As we ran along he explained that someone in Company F had discovered a brewery in the basement of a bombed out building down near the docks. We made our way down a long flight of concrete steps near a sea wall and through a long tunnel to the brewery. There were 25 or 30 men scooping up the beer from a huge vat with helmets, tin cups, canteens, messkits, bottles and other assorted utensils. Sgt. Wolfe was pouring the liquid into a tall, green wine bottle about three feet high. He greeted me with a whoop and continued his pouring. The bottle was half full of foam and half full of beer; an immense head of foam was also on the vat. Some of the men were already feeling the effects of the beer and there was much good cheer and camaraderie. I emptied my canteens of water and filled them with beer, then Birdy and I helped Sgt. Wolfe carry the big bottle out of the tunnel and up the steps. It was heavier than hell.

"We finally got it into the hotel lobby and Birdy began racing through the corridors yelling, 'Free beer! Free beer!'

"In our excitement we had completely forgotten about Lieutenant Knowland. He came stalking out of his suite and exploded.

"'Tenshun!'

"We straightened up the best we could.

"'Exactly what in hell is going on here?' asked Knowland.

"'We found a brewery down the street, sir,' said Sgt. Wolfe.

"'This is the goddamnedest thing I've seen in my life' said Knowland.'Sergeant Wolfe, you know better than to get your men drunk.'

"'None of us is drunk, sir' Sgt. Wolfe said.

"'You damned well better not be,' said Knowland. 'And I mean not,'

"Then, Knowland actually smiled and we were astonished.

"'If I were back in garrison,' he said, 'I'd have every damned one of you punished. And I mean punished However, since we're in a state of combat, I'll overlook this for now. I know some officers who would have your necks for acting like this. Thank your lucky stars I'm not one of them.'

"Knowland was wearing his sidearm which he took from his holster, removed the clip, and walked over and smashed the butt of the forty-five against the glass bottle. The bottle shattered on the tile floor and the beer and foam ran in rivulets across the lobby. Sgt. Wolfe looked sick and Birdy even sicker.

"We moved out of the hotel a couple of hours later and began walking toward the northern outskirts of Leghorn where we were to form for an attack on Pisa. In spite of Sgt. Wolfe's early remark, a few men in the platoon were higher than a Georgia pine and there was much sipping at canteens. How Knowland had ever missed them is beyond me. There were a few attempts at humor among the men of the platoon which Knowland cut short with a stream of earthy commands. He was enraged over the beer incident but he knew there was nothing he could do about it so he simply walked at the head of the column and glared. Birdy kept a low, steady monotone all the way to the assembly area.

"'What a goddamned shame. All that beer. Who do you think will get it now? Well, that ain't hard to figure out. Well, the rear echelon, that's who. The goddam rear echelon. Well it's not fair. It's just not fair. That's the frigging army for you. Nothing for the combat man. Nothing for the guy who lays his life on the line. All for the sons of bitches in the rear echelon. Well, I'll tell you this. I'm about ready to go over hill. I'm serious. I'm not kidding, I'm serious.'

"Finally, the Scholar said, 'Give it a rest, Birdy.'

"Birdy said, 'I can't give it a rest and I'm not going to.'

"Later that night we dug in under the pine trees along Highway 1, the road leading into Pisa, and Birdy kept up his endless harangue about the lost bottle of beer, saving his choicest adjectives and obscenities for Lieutenant Knowland. Of course, there was no way we could have made off with the huge wine bottle of beer and we knew it but it did give us something to bitch about and it fueled our hatred for the lieutenant."[2]

II

Few structures in this world are as well known as the Leaning Tower of Pisa. The 185 foot white, marble bell tower, or campanile, sits north of the Arno River. The building was started in 1174 but the foundations were unstable and it had already begun to lean by the time it was finished in the 14th century. It now tilts more than 17 feet from the perpendicular. The tower has 69 antique columns and some 249 steps corkscrew up to a terrace at the top; from there one can see for miles out over the Pisan plain. So the Germans did the obvious: they used the tower as an observation post. From this vantage point the enemy observers were able to pin-point fire on the troops of Task Force Williamson. General Mark Clark had issued orders to spare the famous landmark if at all possible which meant that the 91st Division's 347th Field Artillery, though the fingers of the cannoneers were itching to pull the lanyards, had to seek other targets. The fact that the tower is north of the Arno and not south probably saved it from destruction during the battle for the city.[3]

On 20 July plans were made to secure crossings over the five canals north of Leghorn and move to the river. The 363rd Regimental history describes the fight to get into the outskirts of Pisa:

"At 0500, 20 July, the 1st Battalion company commanders and staff went forward to reconnoiter the area which they were to outpost, the Fosso Reale, the third of the five canals. North of Leghorn the motor convoy received strong artillery fire from beyond the canals but with the help of the 91st Recon Troop the convoy made its way up to the town of Stagno between the first two canals. After clearing the village they were forced to take cover from machinegun and artillery fire in the vicinity of a church in Stagno. This shelling completely cut off their route of withdrawal in addition to severing the one communication wire to the battalion command post. Lieutenant Fabian Allen went back through the fire and contacted the 1st Battalion commander, Lt. Col. Ralph Woods, then returned with some Cannon Company observers who laid fire on the enemy positions. As 1800 Companies A and B began the fire fight and with splendid mortar and artillery support they drove the Germans back from their positions and across the canals and formed a bridgehead where Company C, 316th Engineers could complete the supply route.

The crossing of the first canal was made via a bypass constructed and mined by the Germans. The 1st Battalion captured the bridge over the second canal near the Stagno church although 700 pounds of explosives were taken from it the next day. The third and fourth canals were crossed on foot-bridges built under fire by the rifle companies and the battalion A and P Platoon from rocks, parts of the blown bridges, planks and engineer sandbags brought up for the purpose. The last crossing was easily made by the infantry because of faulty demolition by the Germans. Instead of being blown to pieces the bridge merely broke in the middle with both ends remaining in position, the center resting on the bottom of the canal in a V shape. With a little planking the battalion walked down one side and up the other without getting its feet wet.

By 2200 Companies A and B were north of the canals and dug in for the night. Contact was made with the 135th Infantry, 34th Division, in the sector to the right.

Meanwhile the 2nd and 3rd Battalion moved up into assembly area close to the five canals although they were not yet committed. While engineers went to work bridging the canals on 21 July, the 1st Battalion continued to attack to the north with the Tombolo Railroad station as its objective. The Stazione Tombolo was 3000 yards north of the five canals and was taken at 1635 by Company B which advanced in its zone to the third phase line, a straight road running across the Task Force sector. Company A and C, however, ran into machinegun fire and were held 1500 yards to the rear of the second phase line, another road. This trouble spot held up the advance of the 2nd Battalion which was moving into a new area north of the railroad station. So the 2nd cut off Highway 1 and swung east of the station, then took another left turn to meet the highway again at the overpass at Sofina which was 5000 yards south of Pisa. By the end of the 21st, the 2nd had moved

Men of the 3rd Platoon, Company E, 363rd Infantry on the lookout in Pisa.

into an assembly area and the 1st Battalion was sending patrols into Pisa. The jump-off for the city was set at 0300 on the 23rd.

On the morning of the 22nd the 1st Battalion resumed its advance. By 1700 in the afternoon Company B was less than a mile from the Arno River and had met little opposition. By 0100 the next day it had reached the river, the first regimental unit to do so.

Two hours later the 2nd Battalion jumped off as scheduled. Company E, preceded by patrols, led the attack. One of nine patrols got as far as the very outskirts of the city on Highway 1 before receiving fire from Cimitero Nuovo, the New Cemetery, and part of the factory district 500 yards to the north. Another Company E patrol reached the airport on the east side of the highway a mile south of the city before it was hit by small arms fire from a railroad overpass halfway from the airport to the outskirts of town.

Lieutenant Carberry, who had taken command of Command E after Captain Franks was wounded near Chianni, planned to move down the highway in a column of platoons past the airport to the vicinity of the overpass, turn left there and deploy at Barra, 500 yards west of the highway. The company was to proceed into the city using the highway as the right boundary and the Navucelli Canal, which flowed parallel, as the left boundary. However, upon moving forward to the point of deployment, the leading patrols discovered a branch canal running across their route which was too deep and too wide to ford. Company E had no bridging material, therefore it swung back on the highway, moved up beyond the canal to redeploy near the cemetery and the group of houses just outside the factor end of Pisa. Here the leading elements were fired on first by a sentry, then thirty seconds later the entire German final protective line, composed of an estimated eighteen machinegun, opened up. Company E pulled back 500 yards and sent patrols out to look for another crossing over the lateral canal. One of these patrols led by Corporal (later Lieutenant) Steven Angle moved around to the left flank and found that instead of one canal, Navucelli, there were two canals with a dike in between.

Leading his squad in the dark down the dike between the two canals Angle emplaced them flanking the enemy machinegun positions and opened fire. Two platoons of Company E then moved forward on signal. The fight lasted for more than six hours. Supported by their own heavies and mortars, the platoons knocked out the German guns and forced their crews to withdraw one by one.

Company F, also with a platoon of Company H machineguns, attacking under light enemy resistance to the right of Company E east of the highway, was now in position in and near the airport buildings. The 2nd Battalion forward command post with Companies H and G moved forward into positions to the rear of Company F. As they crossed the airport from the southeast to the northwest corner they were hit by an enemy gun, but the fire was high and no casualties were suffered as the companies continued across, arriving in position at 0430.

During the hours of darkness, the fire power of the machineguns of Companies F, G and H, in addition to the Company H mortars, supported the Company E fight. With the coming of daylight the battle spread to the airport gradually engaging Company F. Friendly artillery fire was used by the enemy was well hidden and it was difficult to spot his location. German artillery scattered rounds at the airport buildings but inflicted no casualties.

At 1130 Companies E and F assaulted the enemy positions forcing a German withdrawal. The canals were flooded which hampered the advance but did not halt it. Once these positions were overrun the assault companies continued on into the city of Pisa meeting only sporadic sniper fire and no organized resistance. Both E and F proceeded to their prearranged sectors along the Arno River setting up final protective lines and sending patrols down to the river banks. The 2nd Battalion was completely closed into southwestern Pisa by the middle of the afternoon, 23 July."[4]

At 0300 the following morning 24 July, the battalion received an order to withdraw from Pisa and return to the assembly area near the over pass at Fte. Sofina.

The disgruntled members of Lieutenant Knowland's platoon were in on the action:

"The plan was to cross the canals and move straight up the highway in a column of platoons to the river. We got as far as the outskirts of the city before we were fired on from enemy guns located in a cemetery and in part of the factory district to the north. One of our squads reached the airport east of the highway where it met a small force of machine gunners who were on the railroad overpass. In spite of the occasional gunfire it was a quiet night and very dark and over the noise of the bursts we could hear the throaty cries of the Germans as they yelled commands to their men. We kept moving forward.

"Then, a lone sentry near the highway squeezed off a single round; seconds later, the entire enemy final protective line opened fire on us. Our platoon quickly moved into some tall grass near the cemetery to the right of the highway and we began firing with everything we had. We hauled up a couple of air-cooled 30s and put them into action and the weapons platoon mortar squad dug in nearby and began lobbing shells at targets along the river. By dawn we had advanced about 50 yards or so, then were pinned down by the tremendous fire of the Germans. They really let us have it.

"With first light we could see the Arno ahead of us and the curve of the river and the electric lamp posts that followed the curve and the riverside buildings, most still undamaged, though with the increasing artillery barrages, the shells smashed into the sides in quick, sudden puffs of grey and the stones and concrete rolled into the streets, some splashing over the walls and into the water.

"From dawn until nearly noon we lay and listened to the bullets rasp over us. The tall grass bent in the breeze, helped along by the force of the German fire. To stand meant certain death, so we hugged the earth and cursed the war and the exploding shells and tried to work our way out of our ordeal. Even in the early morning the July sun was hot and heat waves hung over the grass and the machine gun fire seemed to rip open the waves and burn its way over us.

"By one o'clock we had made our way almost to the river's edge. A final, ferocious barrage of artillery forced the Germans from the southern bank and we moved up and began digging in along the concrete walls by the water. We were at the far end of the railroad yards. The ground was dry and sandy and our shovels sank easily into the dirt. Lieutenant Knowland came up from the rear. His face was streaked with sweat and grime. He wore his usual scowl, though it was more severe than normal.

"'Dig in deep,' he told us. 'I mean, deep. We'll be here for awhile.

"So I joined forces with Birdy and the Scholar and we took to our task with a will. When we had dug nearly four feet into the grainy soil we spotted a large metal door to our right and we fitted it over the hole and tossed dirt on the top; soon, we had a fine little bunker and we took a break and broke out our rations. As we munched our canned eggs and ham, gunfire still came from across the river but the enemy artillery had slackened.

"After we finished our rations, we set about digging our bunker even deeper, throwing the dirt on top and patting it down with our entrenching tools.

As we worked, Sgt. Wolf came over.

'You can knock it off now,' he said. 'We're moving out. We're being relieved.'

'No shit?' said the Scholar. 'Hooray!'

'What!' shouted Birdy. 'What!'

'We're moving to the rear,' said Sgt. Wolfe.

'We can't be,' shouted Birdy. 'We just finished this hole! Look, sarge! We worked our ass off!'

'You want me to sign a TS slip for you?' asked Wolfe.

'First the beer, then this,' said Birdy. 'It's just too much. It's just too goddamned much!'

"'Knowland said we'd be here for awhile,' said the Scholar.

'No kidding,' said Sgt. Wolfe.

"We moved out of the railroad yards and headed back to the highway, the same route we had taken into the city. The northern sector of Pisa was strangely quiet. There was little artillery or small arms fire. We were being relieved by a group of anti-aircraft artillerymen who had recently been converted to infantry. This was to be their first action.

"As we marched along the route out of Pisa, a 5th Army jeep drove up and stopped and a Signal Corps photographer got out and walked up to us. He was attired in a freshly pressed set of ODs and his paratroop boots were polished to a high gloss. He told us to drop our packs and walk back down the highway for a short distance then march past him as he focused his camera on us. When we had walked about twenty yards, he waved, got back into his jeep, turned around and headed to the rear.

"Later on, the photograph appeared in an edition of the *Stars and Stripes* with the caption, 'American 5th Army troops triumphantly enter Pisa under fire.'

"From Pisa we moved several miles to the east and occupied positions along the Arno River and patrolled the banks night after night.[5]"

III

Once the Fifth Army reached the Arno River General Mark Clark decided to halt the offensive and rest his weary troops. His divisions had been in combat since the 11 May attack against the Gustav Line below Rome and the last 20 miles of the advance to the Arno were peppered with hard fought engagements. The 34th Division was exhausted. The old Red Bull outfit had had few respites since fighting in North Africa in 1943. Both the 85th and 88th had been on line for months on end. The 91st, in its first few weeks of action north of Rome, had fought one difficult battle after the other. The 3rd, 36th and 45th Divisions had been withdrawn from the front and were preparing to leave for the invasion of southern France. In all, nine full infantry divisions and the equivalent of a tenth left Italy in the period 1 June to 1 August. General Clark now had only five divisions—the 1st Armored Division, and the 34th, 85th, 88th and 91st Divisions—and two corps, the II and IV. General Joachim Lemelsen's German Fourteenth Army was in even worse shape. By throwing reserve divisions into the line and rushing reinforcements to battered veteran divisions, Field Marshal Albert Kesselring, the German commander in Italy, had been able to restore a semblance of organization in his order of battle and now he had the jagged peaks of the Northern Apennines behind him, reinforced by a series of a fixed defenses even stronger than the Gustav Line. The war was put on hold. Unless Kesselring decided to withdraw his forces from Italy, Fifth Army was faced with yet another arduous mountain campaign. Our troops, too, were worn out and they had outrun their supply lines. It was now time to rest and regroup.

The Arno River rises in the Apennines to the east of Florence and runs about 140 miles through the central Tuscan plain, emptying into the Ligurian Sea seven miles below the city of Pisa. Though it is navigable for barges as far as Florence, during the summer months it becomes narrow and shallow but with the coming of the autumn rains it can become a rampaging torrent. The largest river in the Fifth Army's Zone of operations, the Arno varied in width from 60 to 600 feet with an average of from 200 to 250 feet. The depth also deviated greatly, ranging from only a few feet in periods of drought to over thirty feet in flood stage.

During the latter part of July the 363rd Infantry had outposts along the Arno on either side of the city of San Miniato. The 362nd Infantry, occupying positions along the river near La Rotta, had the mission of holding its sector against enemy attacks and to learn as much as possible about the enemy's slightest activity, their strength, position and firepower. The regiment's task was also to scout the river, investigating every part of the banks, sounding the depths, locating the sandbars, observing types of foilage, the angle of slopes on both sides and the type of terrain on the German held north bank—all this with the objective of supplying information to Fifth Army in preparation for a possible assault crossing. The men of Colonel Cotton's regiment had their work cut out for them. Company K of the 361st had reached the south bank of the Arno at 0900 on July 16, the first unit of Fifth Army to reach the river. The regiment outposted Pontedera and held the town for the remainder of the month. A member of Company K remembered his first night along the Arno:

"There were no civilians in Pontedera at all. The airport buildings were about all down. The center of town had taken a lot of shelling. The church had two big hits in the top of it and another in the front which left one of the big doors hanging at a crazy angle. The telephone office was in perfect condition while on each side of it, the buildings were flat. The main street which ran east and west was filled with rubble from the buildings the Germans had blown. Along the streets you could see houses that had just one or two walls. One had three sides knocked down while the windows in the other wall weren't even cracked. At night the only noise in town was the screaming of several cats and the occasional sound of a brick falling and the creepy noise the wind made as it blew through the shells of buildings, causing old windows to scrape against the walls."[6]

Pfc. Robert R. Schmieding was at Pontedera with the 2nd Mortar Section, Company H, 361st:

"The scenario for Company H at this time was as follows. We were bivouacked in an olive grove on the forward slope of foothills overlooking the Arno River, a short distance south of Pontedera. Our puptents were lined up neatly beneath the shade-producing limbs of the age old olive trees and each man's slit trench was just a step or two away. The July climate was hot and dry with the exception of an occasional violent summer thunder and lightning storm. On one occasion, a strong gusty wind flattened many of our tents in the middle of the night. The wind was accompanied by a heavy rain shower which soaked our belongings—washing some items down the hillside. During this period of time one Heavy Machinegun Section and one 81mm Mortar Section was on line in Pontedera. Our sections were rotated on a three or four day basis. On the night of 20 July our section of mortars and a section of heavy machineguns moved up into positions at Pontedera to assist in keeping German patrols from crossing the Arno. The machineguns took up positions along the river bank north of the town and our mortars were set up in a courtyard about 500 yards south of the river. We hadn't anymore moved in when a seven-man Jerry patrol tried to infiltrate across the river. The patrol was preceded by a furious artillery barrage which blasted the town, but in spite of this, the machinegunners drove the Germans back across the Arno. The mortar OP was located in a three-story building only 200 yards from an enemy OP on the north bank. Our OP was manned constantly for a period of 72 hours during which time the mortarmen fired over 2,000 rounds and stopped patrol after German patrol. During 24 hours of rapid fire, we burned out two mortar tubes. After every barrage it was necessary to immediately take cover because the Germans would return fire as soon as our mortars lifted. In a seven day period a total of 10,000 rounds of ammo was fired by our mortarmen and time and again German snipers fired into the OP window but our group maintained the position and not once during the entire week did an

Troops of Company E, 363rd Infantry pass a sign on their way into Pisa. This was a posed shot by a Signal Corps photographer. The cameraman had the men shed their packs, walk back down the highway, then walk forward past the PISA sign.

enemy patrol cross the Arno. We were fortunate we had plenty of ammo and we were ordered to fire for effect on anything that moved on the north bank of the river."[7]

Corporal Alfred Vonderscheer was 1st gunner in the 1st Section of the Mortar Platoon of Company H:

"We had an OP in a house on the south bank of the river and during the night, we would sit by the windows and listen for noises on the north bank. Our maps indicated distances and features of the terrain—our potential targets were plotted, thus, when some poor Kraut wanted to move his tank or had to leave his position when nature called, he was greeted by a few rounds of 81mm fire. The Jerries finally had their revenge one day when Sgt. Warren was caught outside as the enemies' mortar rounds came cascading down around him. He dove for the door opening but was a trifle late as he caught a hot piece of shrapnel in his posterior and he had to take a few days off and collect a Purple Heart.

"I was a butcher by trade before the war and I was always on the lookout for knives and steels. I spotted a butcher shop in Pontedera and could see knives and steels hanging in the shop but the windows were protected by iron bars and the door was well secured. I did not have any plastic explosives so I tied a bunch of hand grenades to the door and pulled a pin or two. A foolish thing to do! Results were a terrific explosion but much to my disgust the lock and the door remained intact. During the nights the Germans attempted to terrorize us by using their Nebelwerefers. We referred to the rockets as 'screaming mimis' and some of the fellows thought the noise resembled a large pack of howling dogs. For some time Rhoades, Pignotti, Kruse and I talked about rigging up our own 'screaming mimis' to scare the hell out of the Germans. Finally we decided to give it a try, so we did. We took an empty C-ration can, put holes in the sides of the can and fastened the can to the nose of the mortar round—using wires which were fastened to the fins. We moved over to our gun position and I carefully placed the round in the tube and let it go. POW! The round traveled about 30 feet in the air and then we experienced, first hand, a friendly 'air burst'. Cpl. John Barney, who was bringing in some ammunition, cried out, 'I'm hit!' Pfc. Latham was totally obscured by a cloud of dust as the shrapnel chewed up the ground in front of him, but miraculously he wasn't hurt. We took Barney to the aid station where he was patched up. He got a Purple Heart and I received an Iron Cross for my efforts!

"The action was intense during one 24 hour period as Rhoades, Kruse and I serviced our two mortars throughout the night and were finally relieved by another crew in the morning. We had just stretched our tired bodies out on the floor of the mortuary when three enemy shells hit inside the courtyard. Weaver excitedly burst through the door with the news that two of our men had been hit. We rushed outside and carried the two men inside to safety. One man suffered a bad wound just below the arm pit where a piece of shrapnel had entered one lung. The other man, Pfc. Pignotti held his stomach and groaned, 'I'm dying". But upon closer examination we found that a piece of shrapnel had hit his belt buckle thus knocking the wind out of him and badly bruising his stomach"

Sgt. Gilbert Zigler was also with Company H:

"My first entry into Pontedera was on a rainy night and we set up our mortars in a courtyard of a mortuary. I then proceeded to post some guards just down the street from our position for I suspected there still may be some Jerries left in town. After posting my guards, I began my return journey down the street past the bombed out building with a feeling that at any moment a German sniper might have me in his sights. A few minutes later I saw something move in a second story window and I immediately froze in place as it appeared some one would look out the window for a second duck down, move over a few inches, then look out again. I decided the next time he stuck his head up I'd cut loose with my Thompson. In less than a minute the object appeared again and I let off a short burst as the object disappeared. All was quite once more. I waited for what seemed to be an eternity and then cautiously entered the dark building and sneaked up the stairs. The old stair case creaked and squeaked with every step but I finally reached the head of the stairs and entered the room with my trusty Thompson poised for action. To my surprise, the room was empty with the exception of a bullet riddled body of a poor old black cat. I slowly returned to our mortar position, but I never told the boys what all the commotion down the street was about."

During the daylight hours 31 July preparations were made for the relief of the 361st Infantry from its positions along the Arno River. At darkness, Combat Command B of the 1st Armored Division commenced relieving the regiment, man for man. At 0500 on the morning of 1 August the 361st closed into an assembly area west of the village of Lari and waited for further orders.

The 362nd Infantry had organized defensive positions along the south bank of the Arno and was maintaining strong combat and reconnaissance patrols to the river. The regimental sector covered a front of over eight miles. During the day there was very little activity other than artillery duels; however, at night, German patrols, often forty to fifty men, crossed the Arno to probe the Allied lines. Sometimes, during the daylight hours, the patrols hid in houses on the south bank and made raids by night, but all ordinary patrol methods used by the Germans failed and in a final effort to acquire information, the enemy commanders ordered their patrols to bring back prisoners at any cost. It was reported in some sectors the Germans offered a reward of a two-day furlough, twenty Reichmarks (about four dollars), and an Iron Cross for each Allied soldier brought in unharmed or slightly wounded.

Night patrolling by the 362nd discovered the Germans were using deep foxholes instead of slit trenches and at some of the outposts bird calls were used as signals when the 362nd troops approached. After darkness on the 20th, a three-man German patrol started toward Pontedera to determine whether 91st troops were inside the city. Instead of completing its mission the patrol surrendered to a Company C outpost. The sergeant in command of the patrol told his captors that any German soldier who did not comply with orders was to be automatically shot.[8]

Sixbys of the 363rd inside Pisa. The Leaning Tower is in the center.

On 21 July, a combat patrol from Company C, led by S/Sgt. Fred P. Crane, made the first crossing of the Arno by an American unit. Crane and his men advanced 400 yards into enemy territory and reported on German installations along the river.

And so it went, night after night. The 362nd patrols scoured the banks of the Arno, venturing deep into the German lines. Throughout the period, excellent work was accomplished by the Anti-Tank Mine Platoons and by the attached Company B, 316th Engineers. Most troublesome were the Schu mines, small wooden boxes which were placed in strategic positions along the trails to trap unwary infantrymen. Because the boxes were wooden, the detectors, which picked up only metal objects, were unable to function and had to be patiently, very patiently, probed by the hard working, sweating and nervous crews who crawled on their hands and knees and poked laboriously with their bayonets. Near the town of La Rotta, a number of wooden boxes were found along with six unopened S mines and 200 Teller mines! Quite a haul for the mine crews.

In mid-afternoon of the 25th the regimental staff moved from its comfortable quarters in the village of Forcoli, to an even more comfortable CP in a beautiful villa at Monte Bicchieri (Glass Mountain). The principal part of the villa was taken over by headquarters while the staff personnel found billets in unused rooms. The occupants of the villa, who had little choice, were quite hospitable and friendly toward the staff. The owner was the chief electrical engineer of Naples and as soon as the troops made themselves at home he got on his motorcycle and sped to the southern city which was badly in need of his talents. The regimental staff promised to take care of his villa, said to be more than 700 years old. It even included a small church used by the family and neighboring civilians. Church attendance was excellent for the church was only a few yards from the Headquarters Company chow line! When told of the cushy life of the regimental staff, an officer in Company L remarked, "How interesting! And what are the front line troops doing?"

Meanwhile, up at the Arno River, the two forward battalions of the 362nd had taken over a normal regimental sector and each line company was covering an entire battalion front. The situation further complicated the communication problem. The 362nd had 13 switch boards installed and over 300 miles of wire were laid to front line battalions and to the rear. The artillery and supporting units laid about 100 miles of wire. All this was necessary because the lines were constantly being cut by German patrols and therefore lines had to be strung over alternate routes. The wire section worked day and night to keep communication intact.

The zone of the 1st Battalion included the town of San Miniato on the right front of the 363rd. The town, a sprawling village of some 7,500 people, was located along the ridge of a high hill overlooking the south Arno bank. One of the first things that occupied the attention of the 1st Battalion was the atrocity of the Germans in murdering 27 civilians and wounding 70 others inside the Cathedral di Duomo. The Germans had ordered the entire civilian population who were still in the town to assemble in the cathedral on the morning of 22 June. When 1500 townspeople had gathered shoulder to shoulder, the Germans exploded a time bomb at the church altar. This monstrous act was in reprisal for the uncooperative attitude of the Italians toward the harried Germans.

A departure from the daily routine occurred on 4 August when General Livesay visited the CP to award the Regiment's first battle decorations. Seven men and an honor guard were formed in the courtyard of the

73

villa and as the presentations were made, an eight inch rifle, located in the immediate area, blasted an appropriate ground shaking salute using live rounds. General Livesay told the men, "The 362nd Infantry has come up to every expectation I had for it. Every man and every officer is to be congratulated on doing such a fine job. I wish we might be able to hold a Division review in honor of you men who today are receiving these awards, so that those of you who are getting them and those who should get them could all get together. But we'll have that review when the time is more appropriate."

On the night of the 5th, eight enlisted men from Company K were sent to the river to set up an outpost. It was located in a railroad station on the right front just south of the Arno. By dawn there had been no report

"THE PROPOSITION

from the OP. At noon, still no word, so a patrol was sent to investigate. When they arrived at the OP they discovered an extremely heavy artillery barrage had hit the building. The acrid smell of cordite still hung in the air. The packs and mess gear of the men were found just inside of the front door but there was no sign of a struggle or a fire fight. In the basement was a light machinegun and 500 rounds of ammo. The M-1s belonging to the men were stacked neatly against the wall. There was not a trace of the Company K GIs. After a thorough search the investigating patrol concluded that the OP personnel had been surprised by the Germans after a coordinated barrage and that they were captured before they could make a move in their own defense. Yet, if the men had been captured by the enemy why would their M-1s have been left behind? And why didn't the Germans take the machine gun and ammo? The men from the OP were never seen again.[9]

Two days later, in the 2nd Battalion sector, a heavy machinegunner left his platoon to go forward and relieve a comrade who had spent the night in the river positions helping man the machinegun. As he neared the gun site, he noticed a patrol of about six men moving along the path. They wore ODs and steel helmets and carried M-1 rifles. The relay gunner then noticed that the men quickly veered off the path and in the direction of the enemy lines. He was shocked to see both the machinegun he was to man and the GI he was to relieve were being herded by the patrol. The men of the patrol were not Americans but Germans in OD uniform! The group dropped below the river bank and disappeared before the eyes of the astonished 362nd gunner. So much for the wiliness of the Germans.

On the evening of 15 August the 362nd Infantry was finally relieved of its role at the Arno and moved into Corps reserve in the vicinity of the town of Cusona. Once again, the regimental staff lucked out and located a luxurious villa for its OP. The estate was owned by Count Gicciardini and had been presented to him by none other than King Victor Emanuel. By 0500 on the morning of the 16th the entire Regiment had closed in.

It was at Cusona that the men of the Regiment were awarded their Combat Infantryman Badges. They were also qualified to sport a Bronze Star on the European-African-Middle Eastern Theatre Ribbon.

As of 28 August, 1944 the 362nd Infantry was the most decorated unit in the division. The 1st Battalion was the most decorated battalion in the 91st Division.

For the men of the 3rd Battalion the month of August closed with a bang. On the night of the 28th, a German plane strafed the battalion area southwest of Certaldo setting fire to one British gasoline lorry and starting a fire inside Certaldo; however, the fire was soon under control and the enemy plane buzzed off into the unknown.

While troops of the Fifth Army were vigorously patrolling the Arno River, the 13th Corps of the British Eighth Army, now under the command of Lt. Gen. Sir R.L. McCreery, was battling for the Renaissance city of Florence which was located some 25 miles east of the 91st Division positions at Pontedera.

Striking to the right of the famous Chianti Hills the 13 Corps fought for more than two weeks to reach the high ground five miles southwest of the city. Faced with the near impossible task of supplying, not only his own troops but the entire population of Florence, Generalfedmarschall Albert Kesselring selected a number of paratroopers from I Parachute Corps to cover the withdrawal out of the city. Though the German commanders had declared Florence an open city the fury of the battle threatened to engulf the entire region. British artillery destroyed the power lines, the Germans cut off all water supplies, and shells from the Allied fire, smashed into the quarters south of the Arno. On 31 July as the British closed in on Florence, General Lemelsen, commanding the German Fourteenth Army, ordered the destruction of all bridges within or near the city with the exception of the Ponte Vecchio. By the morning of 3 August the enemy was in full retreat across the entire corps front. The following night the Imperial Light Horse of the 6th South African Armoured Division entered the southern sector of Florence and the next day reached the Arno. Kesselring's paratroopers had strict orders not to make a stand within the city so they retreated to the Mugnone Canal on the northwestern edge of Florence. After first providing the Florentines with a two-day ration of bread, the Germans withdrew the last of their troops on 7 August. As the paratroopers left the city, local partisans quickly occupied the southern sector. For several days it was a no-man's land where the partisans roamed the streets. Finally, on 17 August, Kesselring decided to abandon the entire area. That night British forces moved over the Ponte Vecchio and the nightmare of the Florentines was over.[10]

At the end of August troops of the 91st Division were bivouacked among the sun-drenched vineyards and olive groves of northern Tuscany. Though the job of patrolling the Arno River had been a hectic one, August was to be the most relaxing month until the jump-off into the Po Valley eight months into the future. The days of August were training days: hikes, drilling, night problems, visits to the towered city of San Gimignano and getting acquainted with the Italians whose homes were opened to the friendly GIs of the 91st. Those days would end quickly.

On the 15th General Livesay wrote a letter to all division members to celebrate the second anniversary of reactivation. He told his men:

"The Division is now of age. It is a division that has met the enemy under the most trying circumstances of terrain and has driven him back with heavy casualties. I feel certain that the German High Command has this division registered as one of the first-line fighting divisions. The campaign to the Arno, the taking of Leghorn and the investment of Pisa leave no doubt in my mind that I have the honor to command an organization of top-class fighting men.

With all my pride in you, I am still inclined to sound a note of warning. Let us steel ourselves in all of the things we have learned, so that nothing can stand successfully in the path of the Division."[11]

Endnotes for Chapter 5

1 . Fisher, Ernest F., Jr. *Cassino to the Alps*. Washington, DC 1977. Pages 276-77.

2 . *The Powder River Journal*. June. 1988. "The Capture of Leghorn and Pisa." Pages 46-48.

3 . Regarding the shelling of the famous Tower, Charles E. Brown, C Battery, 346th Field Artillery, later wrote,

"The popularity of church steeples among artillery observers carried through World War II. A classic example was the Tower of Pisa which commanded a good view of the flat plain between Leghorn and Pisa. Highway 1, the main road from Leghorn to Pisa, crossed this plain. It was one of the main routes for the Americans advance on Pisa. I visited the tower shortly after it was captured by our division. Right beside the doorway leading to the stairway up to the tower was a sign in German which read, 'Work of art. Not to be used for military purpose." Right beside the sign were two strands of red German field wire running up to the top level of the tower. Obviously, it had been used by the Germans for an observation post (OP). To the combat soldier the sign and the wires created an understandable contradiction. Such signs were put up by the rear area commanders who with their sophisticated staff members had time to philosophize about the ruinous effects of war and after so doing would, on their own initiative or on orders from still higher authority, post such signs.

"Now the pressure on a front line infantryman and his supporting field artillery forward observers are very literally life and death matters. There isn't time to think a whole lot about the philosophical implications of destroying an enemy observation post, and there is considerable motivation to do every last thing that can be done to save your skin and the lives of your comrades in arms about you. In such circumstances those people have no problem in running their field telephone right up beside the sign forbidding such use. Similarly, under terrific life and death pressures of front line fighting, the infantrymen and artillery forward observer, would, where necessary, fire at the Tower of Pisa, St. Peter's or the Louvre, if any of these structures are being used by the enemy to reign death and destruction down on you and your own people. There is little difference of opinion on this point among those who bear the brunt of the battle.

"Thus it was that one of our own battalions did indeed begin to shell the Tower of Pisa, hitting it at least once in the lowest window facing to the south. (When I visited the Tower in 1975 this damage had been repaired.) The shelling of the Tower was promptly stopped by h higher headquarters more distant from the battle."

Because the famous tower still continues to list, it was closed to the public in 1990 and continues so to this day.

4 . Strootman, Ralph E. *History of the 363rd Infantry in World War II*. Washington. 1947. This book is based on the regimental history written during the 363rd Infantry's actions in Italy. Much of the material is word for word. Though it contains error, as do all records that were kept in combat, the history is one of the better units histories published during the post-war years. The Infantry Journal Press closed its door several years after the end of the war.

5 . *The Powder River Journal*. June. 1988. Pages 49-51.

6 . Livengood, Roy. *Thunder in Apennines*. The story of the 361st Infantry in Italy. Waukegan, Illinois. 1981. Page 77. This narrative appeared in July, 1944 records of the 361st Infantry. The narrator is unknown.

7 . *The Powder River Journal*. June. 1986. "Echoes of the Past." Pages 2-5. The narratives of Alfred Vonderscheer and Gilbert Zigler also appear in this same article.

8 . 362nd Regimental History. 19 July to 31 August, 1944. The regimental history for this month and a half of combat numbers only eight pages!

9 . Ibid. Page 5.

10 . *Cassino to the Alps*. Pages 288-293.

11 . Robbins, Robert A. *The 91st Infantry Division in World War II*. Washington. The Infantry Journal Press. 1947. Page 91.

A meeting of the Brass. General Mark Clark outlines his plan to division commanders. The chap in the hat is Oliver Littleton, the British Minister of Production.

CHAPTER SIX — THE GOTHIC LINE

"And it is awful to die at the end of summer when you are young and have fought a long time and when you remember with all our heart your home and whom you love, and when you know that the war is won anyhow. It is awful and one would have to be a liar or a fool to not see this and not to feel it like a misery, so that these days every man dead is a greater sorrow because the end of all this tragic dying seems so near. The weather is lovely and no one wants to think of those who must still die and those who must still be wounded in the fighting before peace comes."

Martha Gellhorn....The Face of War-The Gothic Line". September, 1944.

I

The brief days of August ended and September, with its approaching autumn, came to the valley of the Elsa River where the division lay sprawled in among the gentle Tuscan hills near the towns of Certaldo, Gambassi and Poggibonsi. Certaldo was the hometown of the great Italian writer Giovanni Boccaccio; unfortunately, this was unknown to the bomber pilots or they were not readers of Renaissance literature for bombs from the 15th Air Force all but destroyed the house of the renowned author. The village of Gambassi is undistinguished but Poggibonsi, which sits atop three beautiful hills, is famous for its Chianti wines.

While the Powder Rivermen worked and trained the American commanders were completing their plans for the Fifth Army's offensive into the Northern Apennines. In spite of all the problems and the near disasters which occurred in the Southern Apennines and the sheer tenacity of the German forces, there was an almost unbelievable optimism among the Allied leaders. The invasion of the French Riviera had been picture-perfect and the U.S. Seventh Army was now north of the city of Lyon 200 miles from the invasion site. Troops of the U.S. First Army had liberated Paris and the jubilant infantrymen of the 28th Division had marched down the Champs Elysees as their comrades continued rapidly eastward toward Germany. Since June 4, the warriors in Italy had driven 150 miles further up the boot and had stopped at the Arno River only to rest and regroup. The morale of the men had never been higher, and to help boost that morale, newspapers and radio, at home and abroad, told of victory after victory. The 14 August edition of the Mediterranean Stars and Stripes declared the German army in Italy was finished! This over-optimism even spread to the general officers who should have known better. On 6 September, Major General Geoffrey Keyes, commander of II Corps, sent out a letter to all his men. "Victory is in the air!" Keyes told his four divisions. "You have set the stage, softened the enemy and have prepared him for the knockout. Tear in and make this the final round!"

It seemed to the men of Fifth Army that the Germans could not hold on much longer. Their casualties had been extremely heavy during the drive out of the Gustav Line and some of the prisoners who had been

Thirsty GIs of 2nd. Bn. Hqs. 363rd.

captured in the hills north of Rome had surrendered without a fight. The majority of them seemed to have little heart for the war. They had been hit so hard and for so long and had suffered so much from the air strikes and the artillery that surely they wouldn't fight to the bitter end in the northern mountains.

At a staff meeting in late August, General Mark Clark, had discussed the coming offensive with his officers. Clark could not remember any operation of the Fifth that had begun with so much uncertainty as the approaching attack. There were strong rumors that the German Army in Italy was about to surrender, but General Clark thought the Germans would probably decide to withdraw from Italy altogether. If the enemy stayed in Italy, Clark told his men, it still wasn't clear whether they would elect to hold their delaying positions in strength or would pull all the way back to the Adige River along the northern edge of the Po Valley and make a stand. There was also the possibility that Chief of Staff General George C. Marshall would ship the Fifth to France and leave Italy to the British Eighth Army. At any rate, Clark said, the important thing was for his army to knife quickly through the 50 miles of mountains and into Bologna. After that, it was all gravy.

At the beginning of the planned Allied offensive the U.S. II Corps was delivered a tremendous stroke of luck: the Germans decided not to make a stand at the Arno River. For weeks the 91st Division had been training for just such an attack and was primed and ready to lead the assault. Since a river crossing is a difficult tactical undertaking even against the slightest opposition, the division would have taken substantial casualties. The high dikes which protected the river's channel meant that the attacking troops would have to go down the banks by ladder, mount assault boats, ferry the stream and use ladders to scale the other side. The American commanders had only to remember the 36th Division's catastrophe at the Rapido to understand what might have happened had the enemy elected to resist a crossing.

Considering the mountainous terrain lying between Florence and the German line 20 miles to the north, one has to wonder why Kesselring did not attempt to seriously contest this outstanding defensive area. Had he chosen to fight a deliberate action as he had all the way from Rome he would have extracted an ample toll upon the Americans moving toward his main positions.

Marshal Kesselring, however, had other ideas. He had pulled his forces back into the rugged mountains where, for nearly a year, the forced labor of the Todt Organization consisting of mostly conscripted Italians, had toiled to complete the defenses. The bulwark of mountains facing the troops of Fifth Army ran from the vicinity of Massa on the Ligurian coast forty miles northwest of Leghorn along the ridge line of the main Apennines chain to foothills near the Foglia River. From there it ran along the crest to Pesaro on the Adriatic, fifty miles northwest of Ancona. It totaled a distance of 180 miles. The name given this line of fortified positions would forever be burned into the memories of the men who had to fight their way through it. To the Germans it was the Goten Stellung; to the Americans, it was the Gothic Line.[1]

The towering peaks facing the men of the division ranged in height from three to six thousand feet, one in front of the other, like the endless links of a chain. Ragged ridges, broken spurs and long, narrow valleys

A couple of members of Cannon Company, 363rd send a round into the Jerry lines.

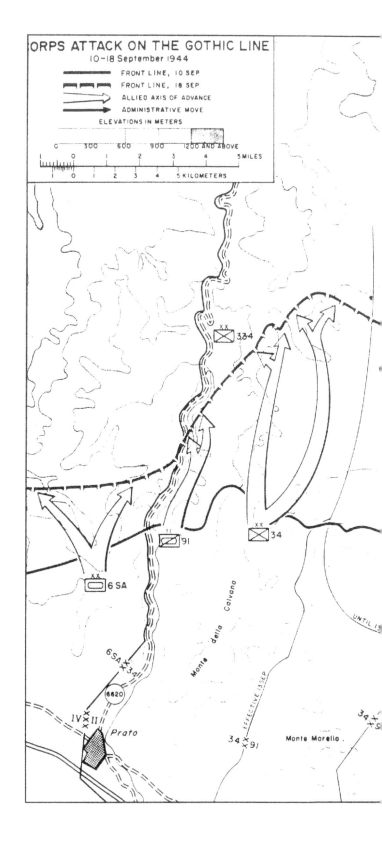

CORPS ATTACK ON THE GOTHIC LINE
10–18 September 1944

FRONT LINE, 10 SEP
FRONT LINE, 18 SEP
ALLIED AXIS OF ADVANCE
ADMINISTRATIVE MOVE
ELEVATIONS IN METERS

0   300   500   900   1200 AND ABOVE

0   1   2   3   4   5 MILES
0   1   2   3   4   5 KILOMETERS

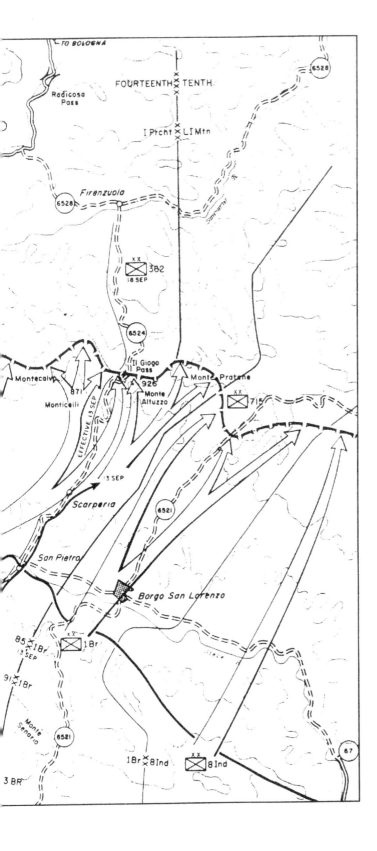

Idyllic view of the Apennines. Pre-war photo.

presented the Germans with ideal defensive locations. In the autumn of 1944 seven roads connected the Arno and Po valleys; the best being Highway 65, a hard-surfaced macadam two-lane, which snaked from Florence to Bologna. Two passes topped the spines along the highway, Futa Pass with an elevation of 2,962, the lowest of the passes, and Radicosa Pass the highest peak along the highway. The other roads, branching off Highway 65, were subordinate roads and all were marked by hair-pin turns, twisting curves and narrow corridors. The winter rains brought frequent landslides blocking many of the roads and once the bridges over most of the mountain streams had been demolished they were impossible to bypass. The mountains were so sharp and steep any movement by trucks or tanks off the roads was out of the question. The only way to supply the front line infantrymen was by two-wheeled carts and mule trains. Along the roads the villages were small and often built right into the mountains. Farm houses dotted the countryside along with poled haystacks. Wheat fields, vineyards and olive groves were cultivated on the jagged slopes. Never had American troops been confronted with such a formidable barrier.

The Germans had built their strongest positions at Futa Pass. Air photos showed an area of minefields laid among low wire entanglements, then another wire obstacle and another one. The principal feature at Futa was the anti-tank ditch which was over 4000 yards long. Behind the ditch were steep slopes converted into tank obstacles. The ditch was covered by machinegun positions and was reinforced with concrete; covering the minefields was a network of infantry emplacements and bunkers that were dug into the sides of the hills; two of the bunkers were topped by Panther tank turrets. Every house in the area was used by the enemy as a billet and most were heavily fortified. This had been the practice of the Germans throughout the Italian campaign. Some of the houses even sheltered tanks.[2]

The original plan of Fifth Army's II Corps was to attack up Highway 65, through Futa Pass and into Bologna, then to advance as far as possible into the Po Valley. However, since reconnaissance, photographs and all other reports revealed the strength at Futa to be awesome, General Clark decided instead to direct the main Fifth Army effort at il Giogo Pass on Highway 6524 southeast of Futa.

The German defense of il Giogo (The Yoke) was based on two 3,000 foot peaks on either side of the highway: Monte Altuzzo on the east and Monticelli on the west. Both mountains had to be taken before there was any hope of capturing the pass. The two mountains, mutually supporting, overlooked the highway and though one should fall, the other still denied the Americans the use of the road through the pass. Even though II Corps had been reconnoitering il Giogo for months very little was known about the actual defenses. The optimistic mood of Fifth Army had seeped down to G-2. On 15 August a report was issued to the top brass:

"The enemy has been developing Il Giogo for some time. He is no doubt aware that his main position at Futa Pass could be outflanked by a thrust up Highway 6524 to Firenzuola. Nevertheless, the Il Giogo position still consists of minor defenses only and in no great number. The road which this position is intended to block is inferior to the main Florence-Bologna road and also more tortuous especially south of the Pass where it runs through very rough, steep, wooded country. Topographically, it is stronger than Futa although defenses are very much less developed. Air photos show only one pillbox and a few machinegun positions. There are two long stretches of wire in the area. The second stretch is about 1000 yards behind the first, but no defenses have appeared to be north of it. Ground sources report strong points consisting of gun positions and trenches. These are sited on Monte Altuzzo. The enemy is expected to continue to develop the defenses: details of alignment between the il Giogo Pass and Borgo San Lorenzo are still not available."[3]

Since Fifth Army was relying primarily on air photographs, these failed to pick up the cleverly concealed pillboxes and emplacements built by the German engineers. Once they got into the mountains the division infantrymen would discover the sour truth. A battalion commander would later write:

"Higher commanders should be very careful of their choice words used in 'Orders and Reports' for often these words have a detrimental effect on morale. The II Corps order for the attack on il Giogo used the phrase, 'II Corps will capture objectives, breach the Gothic Line and debouch into the Po Valley.' Anyone who had studied the map of Italy at all knew that after this attack there still remained 40 miles of the most difficult mountain fighting before reaching the valley of the Po. Another expression used in a G-2 report was 'After the capture of Gothic Line the going will be all down hill'. True enough, that proceeding north, each mountain peak was a little less in height, but also the starting points were also a little less in height which of course left the relative height of climb the same for the infantrymen. If the writer of these statements could have heard the bitter remarks thrown in his direction I'm sure his next order or report would have stuck a little closer to fact."[4]

So the II Corps attack into the Gothic Line began on a highly auspicious note, full of promise, and the Fifth Army staff was writing a happy ending. Meanwhile, in the bunkers of the Line, the German troops talked in low voices and scanned the valleys below for the first trace of advancing infantrymen of the 91st Division. Youngsters in field gray, carrying bolt-action Mausers slung over their shoulders, silently walked the trenches and waited. On 8 September each soldier of the 12th Parachute Regiment, 4th Parachute Division, the unit defending il Giogo Pass, had received orders that...."the position is to be held to the last man and the last bullet even if the enemy breaks through on all sides as well as against strongest artillery or mortar fire. Only on authority of the company commander may the positions be abandoned."[5]

General Keyes planned to attack on a two-division front with the 91st on the right and the 34th, under Major General Charles L. Bolte, on the left. The 91st was to secure a crossing of the Sieve River on a broad front extending from Borgo San Lorenzo to the vicinity of Barberino to the west of Highway 65.

At 0530, 10 September the 91st Division moved forward with the 362nd Infantry on the left and the 363rd on the right. The first objective was the high ground south of the Sieve River. No contact was made with the Germans during the morning, but the troops proceeded cautiously due to extensive demolitions and the ever present threat of mines. During the afternoon they caught their first glimpse of the higher peaks of the Northern Apennines. Five miles to the north loomed a massive wall of mountains shrouded in the azure haze of the early autumn afternoon. The Sieve is a narrow, shallow stream which is easily forded. Before dawn on 11 September both regiments were across the river and moving ahead against slight resistance. The plans for the 362nd was to send its 3rd Battalion along Highway 65 in a frontal attack while the other two battalions were to flank Futa Pass by moving between there and Il Giogo. It was also to capture Mt. Calvi, Linari, Alto and Gazzaro...no small achievement! The 363rd was to advance along Highway 6524, capture Monticelli, Monte Altuzzo, Castel Gerrino and Mt. Verruca. A most ambitious undertaking! Once a breach had been made at Il Giogo Pass the 85th Division was to enlarge it and tail the Germans north

Infantrymen of the 91st Division climb through the foothills of the Apennines towards the mountains of the Gothic Line. 10 September, 1944.

towards Bologna. For the difficult job of supplying its troops through the mountains II Corps had available nine Italian pack-mule companies, each containing 260 mules.

By the afternoon of 11 September both the 362nd and 363rd had crossed the Sieve River Valley and were entering the foothills of the mountains. One of the first things the men of the division learned about the mountain fighting in Italy was...travel light! So most men carried only the bare essentials: a shelter half and blanket. Mess kits were left back at the company kitchens and used only when the troops were off line. Some men carried raincoats, many didn't. Few hauled along more than three boxes of K rations. Combat has a tendency to kill the appetite. The front line soldier usually packed a bandoleer of ammo and a few men carried two and they were crossed over both shoulders in the manner of a Mexican bandit. All during the day of the 11th the 363rd Infantry filed slowly upward. By nightfall it was 2000 yards south of Monticelli and the towering summit of Monte Altuzzo. At 1900, Colonel Fulton Magill briefed his staff. Like many other Fifth Army officers, Magill was brimming with confidence. "We expect to take our objective tomorrow without too much of a struggle," he said. "I don't think the Germans will try too hard to hold on after the beating they've taken. It won't be too many days and we'll be out of the mountains and we can all look forward to that."

In an old stone stable near Scarperia, the men of Company G bedded down for the night. A private in the 1st Platoon remarked: "When we break the Gothic Line tomorrow, I hear the regiment is gonna get a four day pass to Rome. Hot dog!⁶

In the morning, the 363rd's 1st Battalion made good progress toward Monticelli moving northeast nearly one mile from its positions near the village of Sant'Agata, then small-arms fire from the front and from Mount Calvi on the left stopped any further movement one mile short of its objective. To the right of Highway 6524 the 3rd Battalion made a simultaneous effort to reach the summit of Monticelli from the east. Companies K and I led the attack along the axis of the highway, followed by Company L, which was to branch off to the right to capture Monte Altuzzo. The 3rd Battalion companies were moving through the hills along the highway which wound its way up to l'Uomo Morto a small group of buildings that sat directly off the road. The English translation was an ominous one: "The Dead Man". The summit of il Giogo Pass is about 2,000 yards above l'Uomo Morto, then the highway drops steeply down to the town of Firenzuola which sits at the bottom of the Santerno River Valley. Earlier, Colonel Glen Long and his staff had laid out the plans for the battalion attack which called for Company I to move to l'Uomo Morto and directly assault Monticelli with Company L moving to the east for its attack on Monte Altuzzo. With the fall of darkness, Company L was to move to the valley in the vicinity of Parento, then cut left to the

Near Terricola. The Recon Team of the 316th Combat Engineers.

Rocca Draw which ran due north to the west side of Monte Altuzzo. Once the company reached the draw, it would hit the trail leading directly up the mountain. The 347th Field Artillery was to fire white phosphorous shells timed to strike the peak of Altuzzo. This would help Company L sustain its direction in the darkness and guide the men to their objective, using both the distinctive sound and sight of the bursting shells. At least this was Colonel Long's plan. The same method of guidance was to be used by Company I during its movement up Monticelli.[7]

Company L's mission was highly questionable. It had to move over a long stretch of rugged terrain and in doing so would be separated from the other troops of the battalion. To be blunt, Company L was on its own.

As Captain Tom Draney and his men approached the base of Monte Altuzzo, it was impossible for them to see the white phosphorous shells bursting in the crest of the mountain; however, they could judge the movement by the sounds of the exploding shells. Even so, Captain Draney had an extremely difficult time finding a pathway up the slope.

Meanwhile, as Company L was working its way up Altuzzo, Company I was moving to attack positions for its assault on Monticelli. Company K remained in battalion reserve near l'Uomo Morto. Guided by a deep gully to its left, Company I jumped off and by 0430 in the morning, 13 September, had reached the protective wire belts which were covered by the machineguns of the defense. In trying to reach this obstacle, Captain Willie Kriel's company suffered 25 wounded. Company I found itself in interlocking bands of fire from weapons located in well protected bunkers and pill boxes; mortar concentrations and grenades filled in the dead space. The company had advanced to within 500 meters of the crest of Altuzzo only to be forced back down the hill to the only location which would give them any protection: the houses located at l'Uomo Morto...the Dead Man. It was here, at first light, that Captain Kriel also became a casualty when he was shot through the shoulder while trying to supervise the defense of his company's positions.

Company K, to the south of the Dead Man, was now completely exposed to the overlooking Germans who now had both companies under observation.

During the actions at l'Uomo Morto, Captain Raymond Stewart, commander of Company K, was seriously wounded by mortar fire. The 3rd Battalion had lost its second company commander.

Company L kept moving toward the summit of Monte Altuzzo. Somehow, in the darkness, it slipped undetected up the mountain paths. It was so successful that it totally surprised the Germans and reached the crest before daylight. By 0835, it had fought its way to the protective wire and was finally hit by combined mortar, machinegun and rifle fire. The company took up the fight from a slight escarpment which lay along the trail it had been following.

Here, Captain Draney was twice shot through the chest. Being a physically powerful man, he was able to make his own way down the mountain and back to the aid station. At 0920 2nd Lieutenant William Tisdale radioed that he was the only officer left in the company and was assuming command and that casualties were mounting because the enemy could now see where the attackers were located. He requested permission to withdraw to the protection of a small hill at the base of Altuzzo. Battalion granted his request.

The efforts of the 3rd Battalion had come to naught and it had lost three veteran company commanders who had led their companies through training and through the first three months of combat.

It was time to regroup and reorganize and to put the shattered battalion back in order.

Pfc. Robert K. Palassou was with the leading platoon of Company L:

"As we approached the outposts of the Gothic Line, my new 2nd Platoon was designated to lead with two scouts in front, followed by Lt. Robert Queisser III and me. Just a little before dawn, we started to move up a dirt road when the static on my radio became unbelievably loud so I slung my rifle and cupped my hands over the earphone to muffle the sound. You may recall the fear we had of losing contact with a column at night, even though each man had a small strip of white tape on the back of his helmet. I had glanced back several times but this time when I looked back, no one was there! I turned around to tell the lieutenant and he had also disappeared! I tried my best in the early light to determine what had happened then, out of the corner of my eye, I detected some movement at ground level directly ahead of me. I reacted quickly and dove to one side of the road as a German machinegun fired in my direction. I found out later in the day that a German had challenged our scouts but due to the static on my radio I did not hear him. Thus, everyone but me had split and left me on the road.

"Our lead scout, who was armed with a Thompson, returned the fire as we tried to locate the enemy's machinegun in the dark. The situation soon deteriorated for us as our lead scout, Frank Pestana, was killed. Captain Draney, who was at the rear of the platoon, sensed we were in a bad position and hollered, 'Get the hell out of there!' I repeated the order and the men quickly moved back down the road.

"It was now light and we regrouped and tried to size up our situation. We determined we were about a quarter mile east of Monte Altuzzo, so we resumed the advance. The 1st and 3rd Platoons were to lead the attack with the 2nd in reserve.

"As we started to climb the Altuzzo ridge I spotted a lone German outpost man moving swiftly at an angle up the side of the mountain—no doubt on his way to warn his buddies. I raised my rifle confident I could drop him, but my common sense prevailed. I decided to let him go because my shot would instantly alert the enemy in the entire area and much quicker than this solitary soldier could. I was right for we advanced a good 400 yards up the ridge before the Germans started to fire. For the moment we had the momentum as our 1st and 3rd Platoons rolled over the Kraut positions.

"The advance slowed as firefights developed and the going became increasingly hot and heavy. The attacking platoon's forward movement halted as it drew up to a barbed wire apron which helped protect some of the enemy's fortified positions. We then began to receive fire from Monticelli to the left of us and from another ridge to the east or right of our position.

"Now it appeared our attacking platoons were pinned down but Pfc. Jack Buchanan, a good friend of mine from the old days at Camp White, rose to his feet, crouching low with his rifle held near his knees, and started to pick his way across the barbed wire apron. Suddenly, a large German paratrooper moved around the side of the pillbox in front of us, firing his machine piston at Buchanan. Buck didn't have time to raise his rifle but he fired it from knee level. The German spun around as the bullet entered his left jaw. Buchanan continued his fire fight, killing several more paratroopers and wounding five or six more. The attacking platoons, inspired by Buck's performance, crossed the barbed wire barrier and continued their advance as they overran the enemy positions.

"Now, the unexpected happened as our hard-pressed enemy received some help from an unlikely source. Our supporting tanks and tank destroyers, positioned in front of our division artillery, fired two barrages which fell short and into the midst of our attacking platoons, causing so many casualties that our advance was stopped cold."[8]

While the 3rd Battalion was busy with its problems, the 2nd Battalion had made its move into the hills and up the paths leading toward Monticelli. Very early in the morning of 12 September, 1st Lieutenant Thomas B. Keys, the Company E commander, was up at first light and reported to Colonel Ernest Murphy. Keys was a reluctant commander. He had just returned to the Regiment after being wounded in July and Murphy had told him he was to take over Company E. The lieutenant was not too anxious to take command and wanted to remain at his old job of Battalion S-2, but the colonel told him Company E had had no regular commander since the wounding of Captain Ed Carberry and he was his replacement. That was that. At the meeting Colonel Murphy issued his battalion attack order. Company E, as lead unit, was to ford the Sieve and advance on an azimuth roughly north northwest for several miles to the crest of a hill. It was quite dark when the company was guided to the jump off point on the south bank of the river. Colonel Murphy had advised that the Germans were on the north bank and that he expected it to be a bloody river crossing. When Lieutenant Keys led the company across he discovered the water was only knee deep and the north bank was only four feet high. He aided all the men up the bank and the company continued onward.

Not knowing how far the Germans had withdrawn, Keys advanced cautiously over the rough terrain which was covered with thick underbrush. The lead platoon was fanned out to avoid ambush. Soon, both battalion and company radios were jammed by continuous German voices that prevented sending or receiving messages for the remainder of the night. Twice flares were launched above the company, causing the troops to freeze in position until the flares burned out. When Lieutenant Keys reached the area he took to be his objective, he ordered his men to dig in. The Company E command post was located in part of a farmhouse and in an adjacent small field there were several haystacks. By the time the men had completed digging in, the haystacks had vanished, leaving only the center poles. Hay made softer beds than dirt and rocks.

Lieutenant Keys later wrote of the further actions of Company E:

"On the morning of 13 September I reported to battalion and we were ordered to continue our advance. We moved northward across country toward the base of Poggio al Pozzo, a ridge leading up to Monticelli, across which ran the Gothic Line. We heard a distant humming sound and looked up and saw hundreds of Air Corp bombers at high elevation. As the bombs detonated on Monticelli some of the men cheered and a few threw their helmets up into the air. I saw the horizon shake and much dust was raised. Our route led across a field and at the entrance the Germans had placed a sign reading: "Achtung! Minen!". I questioned an Italian who was in the area and he replied that there were absolutely no mines there. I told him that if he lied I would kill him. As I led the company single file across the field I looked back and saw that each soldier was intent on looking downward and placing his feet precisely on my foot prints.

"We slowly moved forward along the western slope of Poggio al Pozzo following Company F. When

Movin' on. Troops of the US II Corps slog along a mountain trail accompanied by artillery and a kitchen.

the column halted I went ahead and met Colonel Murphy and Captain Eugene Crowden the company CO. He told me Company F's leading platoon, under Lieutenant Robert Hatcher, had suffered several casualties in a mine field, but that most of the platoon, including Hatcher, were beyond the field, but out of communication. Aid men had gone to tend the wounded and in turn had also stepped on mines. Colonel Murphy had sent in a section of the A and P Platoon under Sergeant Wilbert Merx to clear a path. However, while Merx knelt to dig up a mine he lost his balance and struck the mine with his other knee. It exploded, severing his leg. Because of the extreme peril, the battalion commander would allow no one else into the area until dawn. Sergeant Merx's ordeal, as he called for help and screamed with pain until he bled to death, was something I wish had not happened and I had not heard. The wounded men who had been rescued beforehand by valiant volunteers, each had a leg blown off. As they were borne back along the column on stretchers, several propped up on their elbows and talked cheerfully about leaving combat while still alive.

"We dug our holes and slept on the slope. An artillery forward observer, consisting of a green lieutenant and three enlisted men, had been attached to us and the next morning, 14 September, I accompanied the team to the highest elevation on the ridge where the team's observation post was established. I had wire strung from there back to our command post. Later I returned to the observation post with 1st Sergeant George Reid. We found the lieutenant and his men busily digging and not observing. Through field glasses I could see a squad of Germans descending southward from the peak of Monticelli about 100 yards below the summit and about 1,000 yards to our front. I designated the target to the artillery officer and told him to bracket the target. Using the radio he gained permission, and rounds were fired and corrected, and quickly the target was bracketed, then the artillery fired for effect. Sergeant Reid borrowed by glasses and said he saw one of the enemy blown upwards. Later the Germans shelled our ridge, cutting my telephone wire in several places but the wire man and I spliced the breaks in a short time.

"In late afternoon I was ordered to reconnoiter a route to Casacce. I took Pfc Perez with me and a couple of sergeants. We proceeded along the cleared path, marked with white tape, on through the mine field, crossed a rugged, steep ravine and reached Casacce 300 yards north. I sent the two sergeant back to guide the company on up. Perez and I waited for a long time, but no company. We attempted to contact our people by radio but got no response. I retraced my steps and found the company column halted on the south side of the ravine. The guides had forgotten the way beyond that point. I then guided the men back to Casacce and deployed the platoons on the steep slope of Monticelli and ordered them to dig in deep. The command was placed in

Mule Train in the Mountains. These pack trains were made up of mules, but horses and donkeys were also used. The trains were also used in Sicily and in the southern Apennines. Without the trains the Italian Campaign would have been very difficult. To supply the basic needs of an infantry regiment in the line two hundred and fifty animals per day were required.

an old abandoned house. Lt. Mann objected to the steepness of the area assigned his platoon. I listened to his harangue without comment.

"We remained in this position for the next two days."[9]

II

The 4th Parachute Division, the enemy unit facing the 91st along the Gothic Line, had extended its regiments from west of Highway 65 to the east of il Giogo Pass where it tied in with the 715th Grenadier Division. The 10th Parachute Regiment was in the Mt. Frassino area, the 11th Regiment opposed the 362nd Infantry on Mt. Calvi and the 12th Regiment was in and around Monticelli and Monte Altuzzo. The 4th had been greatly reduced by heavy losses south of Rome but had received a large number of replacements in

August. In its defense of both passes, the division had committed every possible man to fight as infantry— anti-tank gunners, engineers and even men from a Lithuanian labor battalion.

The troops of the 11th Regiment on Mt. Calvi were located in eight bunkers in the middle of the forward slope. The bunkers were built deep into the mountain and one prisoner of war stated that direct hits did little harm to the men inside, but exploding phosphorous shells were terrifying because of their burning effect. Each bunker had three machineguns and three .8cm mortars. Ammunition was brought in at night and there was a sufficient supply. In order to track the advance of the forward moving 91st Division, the Germans set up a 25 man outpost on the front inclines of Mt. Calvi. The men were to observe the movements of the Americans and were told not to fire. If contact was made they were to retreat to the bunkers on top of the mountain where they could bring their enemy under fire. The plight of the men of the 11th Regiment is captured in its War Diary dated 14 September:

"Weather cloudy. Enemy attacks at dawn. Our positions on Mt. Calvi under heavy artillery fire. Enemy was able to penetrate into our lines and held gained ground. While attacking, our Co. received murderous mortar fire. Larger part of our Co. consisted of young unexperienced soldiers and that was the reason why counterattack failed. In the afternoon enemy was observed taking positions on Mt. Calvi in strength of one company. Later, enemy received reinforcements from the south taking positions on north side of ridge. Since the start of the attack Lt. Ligntzer and his platoon are missing. At 1900 hours enemy attacked in strength of one platoon in the sector of the 5th Co., 11th. Attack was supported by artillery and one machinegun of 6th Co. and two of 8th Co. were deserted by direct hits."[10]

Though the Germans on Mt. Calvi were well supplied with ammunition they were desperately in need of rations. They had had no bread for three days because the division bakery had been destroyed by artillery, and their morale was gradually sinking.

The same day the 11th Regiment made its diary note, Lt. Joseph A. Pena, the S-2 of 3rd Battalion, 363rd, made a reconnaissance to the slope of Monticelli, two miles east of Mt. Calvi. Lieutenant Pena discovered what Fifth Army G-2 had failed to detect:

"We arrived at the base of Monticelli which stood in all its grim bareness. There was nothing on its slope that afforded any cover or concealment all they way to the top which was 2390 feet high. From the Battalion OP I scanned the mountain with my glasses. I could see many pillboxes and dugouts, all so well camouflaged they were invisible to the naked eye. These were all so placed that there was mutual protection for each one. Feeling that even more protection was necessary, Jerry had strung rows of barbed wire a foot high and twenty feet wide at one hundred yard intervals. Still not feeling secure enough, he had sown small mine fields in the two ravines leading to the top and also in between the rows of wire. Inspection of one pillbox revealed it had a roof covered with three feet of logs and dirt, large enough to accommodate five men and with a firing slit six inches high and three feet long. This was typical of all those found on the hill. On the reverse slope of

Monticelli were numerous dugouts used as living quarters. These had been dug straight back into the mountain for a distance of seventy-five feet and were big enough to house twenty men. Over thirty wounded Germans were found in two of these dugouts. On a small hill about three hundred yards north of Monticelli we found a huge dugout which had been blasted out of solid rock. It was in the shape of a "U" and in it we found cooking utensils, sleeping quarters and large amounts of equipment and ammunition. It was probably a Battalion CP."[11]

By midmorning of 14 September, the 1st Battalion, like the two other battalions, was moving into the defenses of the Gothic Line. Company C drove straight ahead from Pgio al Pozzo while Company B swung from the base of Montaccianico to the east towards Monticelli. The objective of Company B, under the command of Captain Lloyd J. Inman, was the tiny hamlet of Borgo on Monticelli's southwestern slope. From there the company was to gain the crest of the western ridge and push on to the summit. Company A was held in reserve. A platoon of heavy machineguns was attached to Company B. Narrow foot trails led to Borgo but beyond the hamlet there were no trails and the steep upper slopes would make supply and evacuation of wounded extremely difficult.

At 1400 Company B, with T/Sgt. Charles J. Murphy's 1st Platoon on the left and 1st Lt. Bruno Rossellini's 2nd Platoon on the right, crossed the line of departure. Off to the right Company C began to move. For the first thirty minutes the two platoons gradually made their way up the narrow mountain paths, then a voice broke into the battalion SCR-300 radio and asked that the 347th cease fire because the artillery was falling on the men of Company C. Captain Inman knew this was false because he could observe the shelling and he pleaded to the artillery commander to keep firing, but he was unable to convince the officer back at battalion. It turned out to be an enemy ruse for no sooner had the barrage stopped then the Germans opened up on the forward platoon of Company B.

It was heavy going for the rest of the day but by nightfall the platoons of Murphy and Rossellini had reached Borgo and had made their way some distance beyond the hamlet. During this period Company C had advanced through small arms fire to Casacce where they were halted by a wall of enemy cross fire.

Company B had sustained severe casualties and its ammunition was running low so Captain Inman ordered his men to dig in for the night. The captain also wanted to locate the guns that had stopped his company. Lieutenant John G. Kearton volunteered to lead a six man patrol to search for the bunker that had caused so much misery. Shielded by darkness, the seven men crawled up the mountainside until they were stopped by barbed wire. Lieutenant Kearton proceeded on alone and was nearly to the embrasure of the pillbox when hand grenades forced him back. Satisfied that he had found the exact location of the guns, Kearton returned to report his find to Captain Inman.

There was little enemy infantry activity during the night, but enemy mortars and artillery remained constantly active.

The following morning, 15 September, the Company B commander called in artillery fire on the German position. When the firing stopped, Lieutenant Rosselini and his men attacked the bunker and captured the five living enemy inside. The company immediately regrouped and moved forward, inching its way through the folds in the ground until it was on top of the hill and a reserve slope defense was set up.

Meanwhile, the troopers of Company C had been meeting with some success and had been working to the right on four machineguns which they finally neutralized; they then started forward only to be pinned down by another gun which was placing flanking fire across the entire company front. Both commanders of the two leading platoons, Lieutenant Walter Wolf and Lieutenant William Hopkins were wounded by the fire. Additional artillery and mortar fire put the gun out of action and the company moved on.

Back in the Company B sector Captain Inman's men had reached their objective: the northwestern end of the Monticelli ridge, but enemy fire had reduced the company to about seventy men and ammunition was again running low. Inman called battalion headquarters and told them to send reinforcements, ammo and a new radio battery. The men were still digging in when around thirty Germans launched a counterattack against Sergeant Murphy's platoon which was on the company's left flank. Battalion was quick to reply to the captain's orders. A 17-man unit of riflemen and a machinegun section under 1st Lieutenant Ross A. Notaro from Company A arrived in the nick of time to disperse the enemy. Shortly afterwards, a large group of Germans launched a second counterattack but Lieutenant Notaro and his men were well dug in to the left of Murphy and gunned down the attackers.

Things were not to let up: early that evening the Germans mounted a third, and by far the heaviest, counterattack. Swarming up the mountainside, the enemy closed in on the foxholes of Inman's men. The captain adjusted the artillery fire so closely that an occasional round fell inside the company's perimeter. The fire took a ghastly toll of the Germans, some of whom were so near that, when hit, they tumbled into the

Company B positions. American grenades and German potato mashers exploded all around and though the infantrymen had fixed bayonets for hand-to-hand fighting, no live German got that far.

Ignoring casualties, and they were suffering a considerable number, the Germans kept coming. Lieutenant Notaro's small band was particularly hard pressed but Sergeant Joseph D. Higdon, Jr., a section leader, picked up his machinegun, cradled it in his arms and charged into the Germans, firing as he went. That courageous and unexpected action sent the Germans reeling back. Higdon was hit by a grenade, then another one and a third time by small-arms fire. When the enemy had fled the sergeant made it all the way back to his foxhole, but when his buddies reached him he was dead.

III

By the end of 14 September it was apparent to both staffs of Fifth Army and II Corps that they were in for a bloody battle. The possibility that the Germans would withdraw from the Gothic Line without fighting was gone and so was the over-exuberance of the Brass. The 363rd Infantry had its hands full with Monticelli so Corps sent the 85th Division's 338th Infantry up the slopes of Monte Altuzzo, the new objective of that regiment. On 12 September the 363rd Infantry had sent a lone company to capture Altuzzo, now forty-eight hours later, an entire regiment, the 338th, had failed to capture the peak. So much for the initial optimism of the officers of the attacking regiments. The enemy was fighting a skillful defensive action, laying in his mortar fire in every draw, gully and creek where the men of the 91st sought cover and raking the open slopes of the mountains with automatic fire. The German defenses were proving far more extensive than previous G-2 reports had indicated. The enemy locations were exposed only as the forward troops came within range of the hidden emplacements or when the bursting shells of the artillery slashed up the earth and tore away the protective camouflage. Under these circumstances the II Corps commander, General Keyes, had no alternative but to feed additional companies and battalions into the attack. Antitank guns, tanks and tank destroyers were brought up to employ direct fire on pillboxes, and the heavy caliber 8-inch guns and 240mm howitzers fired precision adjustments to destroy bunkers too strongly constructed to be destroyed by light or medium artillery. The guns of II Corps and those of the divisions' battalions sent harassing fires on the reverse inclines of the mountains. The experience of the fighting at Cassino was proof that, when well dug in, troops could withstand prolonged periods of shelling without suffering heavy losses. As always, it remained for the infantry to drive the enemy from his positions and to hold the ground.

After the failure of the 363rd Infantry's actions of 13 September it became necessary to concentrate the entire regiment on Monticelli. This left the 362nd Infantry with a front of nearly five miles. To relieve some of the strain on the 362nd General Livesay threw the 361st Infantry back into the line and it entered the battle at 0530. Its mission was to pass through the left elements of the 363rd and swing around Monticelli.

Pfc. Milton Morgan was with the leading Company I:

"We were awakened at 0430. I remember that religious services were held a few minutes before we moved into battle. At about 0530 we moved toward the little town of Casa Lazzari. A heavy barrage of artillery was launched to soften up the German lines. We began to advance up some of the most rugged terrain I have ever seen. We were constantly under mortar and machinegun fire from every side. It was around 1000 in the morning when we were caught in a heavy crossfire. My buddy, Leonard Mistler, and I were lying side by side as concentrations of machinegun fire were whipping off leaves and limbs just above our heads. All around we could hear the cries for help from men who had been hit and some killed. Suddenly, a burst of fire hit me in my left leg, then another in my right hip. Leonard immediately began giving me first aid. After several minutes when the German fire had slackened, Mistler placed me on his back and carried me two or three hundred yards, heading southwest. Several times we spotted Jerry patrols and had to hide from them. We moved out again and as we crossed a small creek we saw another patrol coming towards us. The only cover we had was to slide into the creek by the edge of the bank and go under the water for what seemed like several minutes. When we came up for air the Germans were out of sight.

"We continued on until late evening, then decided to hide in a German dugout. All during the night we heard enemy patrols come right by the dugout but never did they look inside. I was beginning to hurt like hell, but still hoped that by morning we would be able to head back. As dawn came, Leonard packed me on his back again and this time we headed due south. Rest stops were more frequent now due to the fatigue of Leonard. We finally found a road and decided to stay by the roadside until, hopefully, we could see some Americans.

"It was early afternoon of 15 September when we spotted an American tank. We waited until we were sure, then Leonard ran out and told the crew that he had a wounded buddy who needed to be taken to the hospital. The guys quickly responded and brought out a litter, put me on it and placed it on the side of the tank. We rode about a mile and a half until we came to a small farmhouse where an ambulance was waiting. I was taken to an evacuation hospital where surgery was performed on my leg and hip.

"I remember the doctor told Leonard that he should stay and rest, but he said no he'd go back and try and find Company I.

"I didn't see him again until one day in February, 1945 when we met in the 45th General Hospital in Naples."[12]

It was clear from the fighting of 15 September that extensive use of mortars and machineguns would be necessary if any marked advance by the 361st was to be made. Late in the day General Livesay visited the regimental command post and told Colonel Broedlow, "Fire all the ammunition you can haul! Hold every inch of ground you gain. Lose nothing. Stabilize for the night and continue on your mission tomorrow." Colonel Broedlow then passed the word along, "Consolidate your positions for the night. Resist any attempt at counter-attack. At all costs! No change in the attack plan. 1st and 3rd will continue on their mission. Time of attack, 0600!"[13]

In the pre-dawn darkness of early morning a Company D jeep, bringing ammo forward to the 361st, hit a mine and was totally destroyed. The blast killed the driver and ignited the ammunition which exploded with a tremendous roar, causing a great deal of commotion among a platoon of GIs who were dug in close by.

As planned, the 361st jumped off at 0600. In the 3rd Battalion sector, Captain Chet Sigmen and his men of Company K had worked all night to clear the barbed wire entanglements in front of the company. By 0800, with the aid of bangalore torpedoes, they were through the wire and moving forward. Beyond the wire they cleared a pillbox and captured eight Germans. One was badly wounded in the leg and another attempted to escape but was gunned down by the trooper who was leading the prisoners back to the stockade. By noon Company K had reached the vicinity of Lilliano and Company L was outside the village of Vallappero. Five times Company L tried to breach the barbed wire to its front, then finally had to swing around to the rear of the village where it again moved forward. Here, Lieutenant Watkins, the acting CO, was hit in the arm and evacuated. An hour or so later the company was stopped once more by machinegun fire. Lieutenant John Gaultney immediately crawled forward to the front of his platoon and searched the terrain for an avenue of approach which would enable him to neutralize the fire and allow the company to continue. Gaultney observed a shallow draw 30 yards to the front; however, two bands of barbed wire protected it. Ordering his men to cover him, the lieutenant worked his way through the wire and reached the draw. From there he pitched several hand grenades and fired his carbine into the enemy stronghold, enabling three of his men to follow his path to the draw. They then assaulted the machinegun position and killed the Germans who were manning it.

The fighting continued throughout the day. At 1840 hours the 1st Battalion aid stationed received a direct hit from an 88 which killed two men and wounded eleven and completely destroyed the station's equipment. By 2215 the Regimental surgeon reported that for 16 September the 361st had sustained 138 wounded. A count of the number of men killed was impossible but by the middle of the afternoon of that day 17 men had already been listed as KIA.

The commitment of the 91st's reserve regiment served to pin down enemy troops who might otherwise have moved over to Monticelli, but it failed to achieve the outflanking of the troops facing the 363rd.

IV

In the 1st Battalion sector the coming of daylight on 16 September found that Company C had reached a point within 200 yards of Company B, while on the left, the 2nd Battalion's Company G which was attached to the 1st, was in positions to Company B's rear. Such was the situation when shortly after first light a sudden burst of German small arms fire struck and wounded Captain Inman. The command of the company passed to Lieutenant Bruno Rosselini. Lieutenant Notaro's group now totaled nine men. Sergeant Murphy's platoon was down to seventeen.

Throughout the 16th and well into the following day the Germans attacked again and again against Company B. Yet somehow the little band of Americans held. The left flank of the company was now the most vulnerable spot of all and the enemy knew this as evidenced by his repeated attacks against it. A five foot embankment ran along Company B's front and gradually diminished in height until it reached a shallow draw. It was here that the men dug in, where the embankment was about a foot high and dwindled down to nothing. And it was here they braced for the coming counterattacks. Among these men was Pfc. Oscar G. Johnson, who was to be awarded the Medal of Honor for his actions. Sergeant Frank Drazkowski had sent the affable Johnson, who was a mortarman without ammunition, to help defend the hotly contested spot.

The Regimental history describes Johnson's actions:

The Battleground.

"When the enemy resumed his counterattacks at dawn preceded by artillery and mortar preparations they continued pressure against the key left flank. As the platoons returned the fire, Johnson coolly stood in his slit trench to get a better field of fire and emptied his carbine into the advancing Germans, ignoring machinegun fire which killed and wounded men all around him. His carbine now useless for lack of ammunition, Johnson ran to fallen men, grabbed the weapons they dropped, and kept them hot until the attack was repulsed. During the interval he gathered weapons from those men who had been killed or seriously wounded and evacuated, going out into the shelling and small arms-fire with which the enemy kept chipping away at the top of the embankment even though none of his troops were attacking. Altogether Johnson accumulated four M1 rifles, a BAR and a Thompson submachinegun, which he placed within easy reach of his trench. To retrieve the Thompson Johnson crossed 30 years of open terrain in plain view of the enemy emplacements. The severe fire and infiltration tactics kept up all day, the grazing machinegun fire from the crest forcing Company B to remain behind the bank, the snipers picking off men from the rear, and enemy mortar rounds falling throughout the entire area. The company was now down to less than 50 men.

"All during the day of 16 September repeated German counterattacks were repulsed, the enemy several times getting close enough to toss fragmentation grenades. Out on the flank Johnson, his weapons and ammunition arranged around him, was standing up, sweeping the Germans in an 180 degree arc. When the Thompson ran out of ammo, he grabbed the BAR. When the magazine for that were empty he began firing the M1 rifles so fast that they sometimes failed to function properly. When that happened he worked the operating rod by hand. Between attacks he kept more Germans from infiltrating around him by either killing or wounding each one who tried it or making it so hot that none dared try it. He also found time to gather more ammunition and tear down the rifles in an attempt to cannibalize them into one properly functioning weapon. By now Johnson was the only remaining member of the original group which had been put in to guard the left flank. All others had been killed or wounded."[14]

All during the long, ghastly hours on the godforsaken slopes of Monticelli the aid men of the 363rd Regimental Medical Detachment performed their great and laborious services. Among them were T/5 James L. Christopher, Pfc. William J. Enck and Private Joseph Pirog. These men went out into the fire to bandage and give morphine; they crawled through minefields, hauled litters and brought up much needed medical supplies, these angels of the battlefield.

Lmg. Machinegun Squad. Company F, 363rd. L-R. Front row: Robert Sadowsky, Clifford March, Eino Wirta. Back row: Damian Caffrey, Henry Sagmo, Lee Gray and William Weaver.

Early on 17 September two German soldiers carrying a white flag emerged from an emplacement 100 yards in front of the Company B positions. Being a non-combatant, Medic T/5 James Christopher was sent forward by Lieutenant Bruno Rosellini to find out what the flag was all about.

Christopher later described the incident:

"Lieutenant Rosellini asked me to go meet the white flag the Germans were waving. As I approached the area where the flag was being waved a couple of Germans stopped me. An enemy sergeant who spoke English escorted me down the hill to a bunker where I met a German captain. I was taken inside the bunker and saw furniture, a bed, a radio and the general comforts of a permanent quarters-like room. The captain was clean-shaven, neat and dressed in a fresh uniform. I immediately sensed I was dealing with a professional. I smartly saluted the officer, which he returned. I asked the captain if he spoke English. He replied that he did. I then explained we would be glad to evacuate his wounded to our hospital for treatment. I assured him they would be given the same treatment as our wounded and advised him that I had heard most all German prisoners were returned to the USA in short order.

"There were many wounded Germans in the room. One had a serious leg wound that was bleeding badly. I asked the officer if I could treat the man. I was given permission and applied a tourniquet, bandaged the wound and gave the man a shot of morphine and made him comfortable. He thanked me, then broke into tears.

"I then asked the captain if he would meet with my captain and arrange a truce to evacuate the wounded. He replied, 'That's good. That's fine.' I then asked that he place the wounded man I had treated on a stretcher and bring him with us. On the way down I explained he would have to surrender the revolver he wore. He did so without hesitation. We proceeded to return to our lines where I introduced Lieutenant Rosellini as Captain Rosellini. While he and <u>Captain</u> Rosellini were engaged in conversation about 30 other German soldiers came running down the hill and surrendered to Oscar Johnson. It was said they had seen their captain coming down with me and thought he surrendered everyone including them.[15]"

The German officer quickly realized he had been tricked by the fast talking Christopher. He spoke to his men and ordered them in German not to surrender. He told them it had all been a trick. His men refused his order and went quickly down the hill with the wounded man. Seeing his men giving up, the officer too submitted. Although the surrender took some of the pressure off Company B, reduced to a handful of men, heavy fire still prevented Lieutenant Rosellini and his group from clearing and occupying all of the Monticelli ridge in their sector.

That afternoon after making plans with Captain Edward J. Conley, the commander of the attached Company G, for a final assault to sweep the ridge, Lieutenant Rosellini was returning to his command post when he was shot through the heart. Captain Conley absorbed the remnants of Company B into his own command.

V

From the heights of Monticelli to the Sieve River, an airline distance of over five miles, the Germans not only had direct observation of the steep forward slopes, but also of the broad Sieve Valley. This made for an extremely difficult route of supply up to the forward positions of the 363rd.

The regimental supply point was located in the town of Scarperia about three miles from Monticelli. Despite enemy interdictory fire on the road and towns, supplies moved forward at all times. Each battalion had dumps for ammunition, food and water but it was necessary to split the dumps in the event one was knocked out there would still be another from which to re-supply the troops. Initially the 1st Battalion supply dump was located near S. Agata and the 2nd and 3rd Battalions near Ponzalla. At about 1700 16 September the 1st Battalion dump was shelled, causing damage to both ammunition and food stock. By the 17 September it was necessary to start using mules to resupply the front line troops. Battalion S-4s drew the supplies from regiment and transported them by jeeps to the mule park near Scarperia. There, under the supervision of Lieutenant Thompson L. Wood, regimental mule train commander, they were loaded on the mules. The trains were usually made up at about 1800 and left for the front an hour later under the cover of darkness. They moved along the main highway from Scarperia to a point near l'Uomo Morto, branching off to the mule trail at that spot. Mess sergeants, cooks and mail clerks accompanied their own particular train forward to the relay points which were about 500 yards to the rear of the front lines. This trail was so narrow that a rigid traffic control was necessary. First priority was given to evacuation of the wounded, both serious and walking cases, as it was not always possible to get them down the mountains during daylight. This evacuation began immediately after dusk and with the assistance of extra litter bearers placed along the trail, the wounded were soon cleared from the battlefield. By the time the wounded had been evacuated, the mule teams had arrived and were ready to ascend the mountain paths.

When the teams reached the battalion release points, the supplies were transferred to carrying parties from each company and were made up from kitchen personnel, replacements, A&P Platoons and from the Anti Tank Company. When the mule teams were unloaded they were reloaded for the return trip with the wounded who had come in since the arrival of the teams. Although the carrying parties started from about

Infantrymen of the 363rd manhandle rations up the steep trails of the Gothic Line.

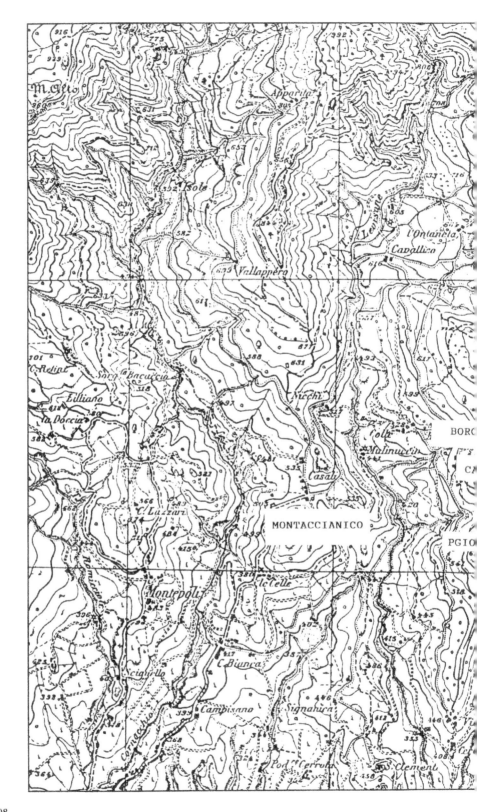

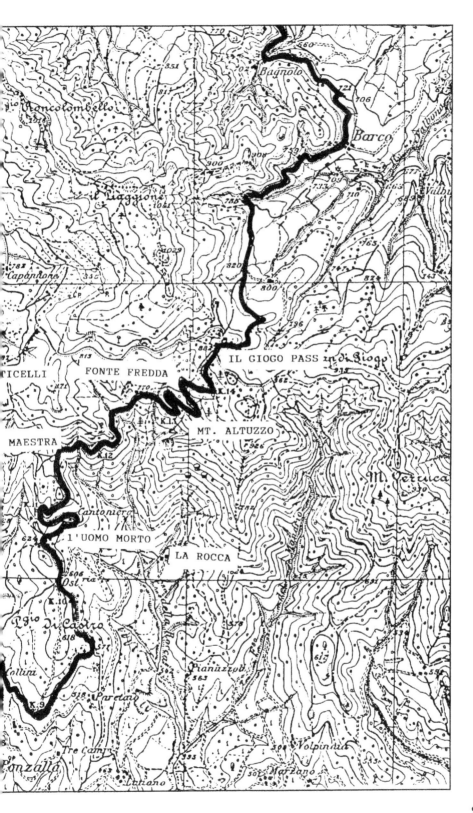

Pfc. Robert K. Palassou. Company L, 363rd. 1945. *Lt. Thomas B. Keys. CO Company E, 363rd.*

500 yards from their company positions, it took them an average of three hours to climb the paths up to their individual units.

As the attacking companies moved forward the regimental S-4, Major Edward L. Beauchamp, established regimental supply points near Fonte Fredda to facilitate the resupply of the 363rd. These were always within two miles of the battalion command posts. Though the road past Ponzalla was under constant shell fire, Captain Jack Lynch, the regimental ammunition officer, kept the forward companies well supplied. The trains made 85 mile trips each day to rear echelon dumps and during the first three days of fighting on Monticelli the regimental train hauled about 100 tons of all types of ammunition.

While the men of the 363rd were fighting desperately to gain and retain Monticelli, the members of the Anti-tank Company were engaged with errands of mercy. The number of lives saved by this group cannot even be estimated. Every night they set aside their weapons and carried litters. It takes a special kind of courage to advance into enemy small arms fire when you too are armed, but an infantryman without a rifle feels nude in the face of the foe and it takes guts to put down an M1 and shoulder a stretcher and walk out into the battlefield to rescue your wounded. These men of the Antitank Company played a major role in supporting the front line troops, laboring not only with the wounded, but also carrying rations on their backs night after night.

The mine platoon also made its contribution working without relief to clear paths through the fields and to open the vital approaches and then eliminate the lanes and paths of Schu-mines which were always a touchy affair.[16]

VI

On the morning of 16 September General Livesay made his way to the 363rd Infantry CP arriving there about 0820. The general was becoming increasingly concerned about the lack of progress by all Corps units. He had witnessed the failed efforts of the 338th Infantry on the right and was most upset with the almost yard-by-yard struggles of his own regiments. The 34th Division, on the left, had slowed to a complete halt before the strong defenses of Torricella Hill. Beyond the hill lay 3,500 foot Mount Coroncina and the even taller Mount Frassino. And after that one there was Mount Citerna. It was a discouraging picture. Battalion commanders in both the 91st and 85th were frustrated at the failure of their companies. The commander of the 1st Battalion, 338th, Lieutenant Colonel Willis Jackson, would later comment:

"On the 16th we hoped that somebody else would do what we were trying to do. Our 2nd Battalion was bogged down, they weren't moving. The units on our right were bogged down, the 91st Division on our division's left was not moving. It was frightening. I said, 'God damn it, won't we ever take these mountains? Won't somebody get through?' I could not believe that everybody was having the same tough time as we were, but apparently they did.[17]"

At 0825 on the 16th a 363rd regimental order was issued to the 3rd Battalion. Three hours later Colonel Magill directed Colonel Glen Long to move out as quickly as possible and to prepare for an attack which was to be made just after dark. Because of the mauling the battalion had taken during the previous two days, Long was faced with replacing all the rifle company commanders. 1st Lieutenant Steve Ehyerbide took over Company L, while 1st Lieutenant Joe Wessendorf was given command of Company I and Captain William B. Fulton, the battalion S-1, was the new Company K CO.

When Captain Fulton reported to the company CP to meet with the 1st Sgt., he found the top kick, who had been a member of the original cadre and the only First Soldier the company had ever had, in the process of declaring himself unfit and in need of hospitalization due to an old football injury he had received while playing with the 1st Cavalry Division during the far away days at Fort Bliss. The one bright spot for Captain Fulton was that all of the original platoon leaders who had been with their units at Camp White Adair were still with their platoons.

The attack plan called for Company L on the left to move up the east side of Pgio al Pozzo and then proceed up the ridgeline which led to La Maestra at the foot of Monticelli. Company K was to move up Highway 6524 after darkness and pass through Company G, 338th Infantry which was still located at l 'Uomo Morto.

Captain Fulton and his men reached the buildings of The Dead Man at 2155, then continued their climb, cutting northwest along the road embankment to a steep ravine that rose northward toward La Maestra. The ravine led to the very crest of Monticelli. As the company worked its way parallel to the highway the Germans detected its approach and began firing flares that lit up the entire mountain slope. The Company K troopers, who had now reached a barbed wire apron, remained motionless until the flashes blazed out, then placed bangalore torpedoes under the wire. At that moment, two enemy machineguns opened fire, one from the right and one from the left. Both were perfectly interlocking and completely covered the crossing point through the wire. It was obvious to Captain Fulton that to attempt a breach of the obstacle would be foolishly suicidal. He decided that an alternative route would have to be found.[18]

At almost this exact moment, Lieutenant Ehyerbide guiding Company L along the western ridge, stepped on a Schu mine which blew off his foot. This was a stinging blow to the lieutenant's men who had now lost yet another company commander and their forward progress was halted by the confusion. When the news reached Colonel Long he radioed Captain Fulton to withdraw back down the mountain to a position just northeast of Collini. During

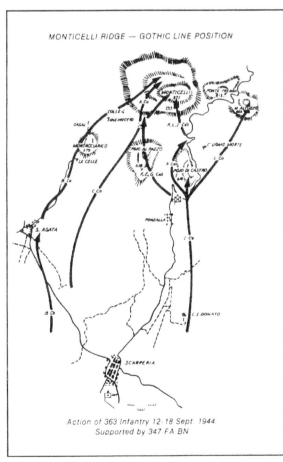

MONTICELLI RIDGE — GOTHIC LINE POSITION

Action of 363 Infantry 12-18 Sept. 1944.
Supported by 347 FA BN

the conversation Long suggested the captain detonate the bangalores for effect. Fulton replied that the automatic fire covered the route of withdrawal and the explosion would undoubtedly bring down all the enemy's defensive fire making it very difficult to get the unit back down the slopes without incurring even more casualties. During its move the company had already suffered three killed and 20 wounded.

By daylight on the morning of 17 September, Company K had found a little defilade in a protected position above Collini and had bedded down on the rocky ground to grab a couple of hours of sleep before taking up the action again.

l'Uomo Morto. September, 1944. From this spot, Company I jumped off for Monticelli. It was open to direct fire from the peak.

The situation on Monticelli was rapidly building up to a climax. Enemy information assembled from observation, prisoner interrogations and intercepted radio messages indicated the Germans losses had been extremely heavy and that reinforcements were being brought into the line from Bologna, Firenzuola and from adjacent sectors to reinforce the 12th Regiment, 4th Paratroop Division. The 12th had been relentlessly attacked by the 363rd's 1st and 2nd Battalions who had been slugging away on the western slopes of Monticelli. The efforts of the battalions had resulted in the decimation of a large portion of the defenders of the 12th who had launched counterattack after counterattack during 14, 15, and 16 September.

In preparations for more counterattacks the enemy had moved the remaining 45 men from the 10th Company, 10th Regiment, from Futa Pass into the 12th's area on Monticelli. The 1st Company, 11th Reconnaissance Battalion, in the vicinity of Bologna, was also sent to reinforce the 12th.

At 1115 hours 17 September, Generals Livesay and Keyes arrived at the 363rd regimental CP and issued the attack orders to take Monticelli. Colonel Magill was informed by both generals that if the objective was not taken by sundown of that afternoon he would be relieved of his command. The two officers then went to the 3rd Battalion CP where General Livesay told Colonel Long, "The 3rd Battalion," he said, 'will follow a rolling barrage up Monticelli at 1400. This will be furnished by the Division Artillery. II Corps will be requested to thicken the barrage by firing on targets in the rear area. Take the ridge at all costs. Go up, and don't stop until you get to the crest."

"I'll get them up there, General," replied Colonel Long, "but I don't expect to have many men left."[19]

VII

Meanwhile, by dawn, 17 September, the 2nd Battalion's Company E had completed its climb to the immediate rear of Company G which had taken 26 prisoners the previous day. First light brought a beautiful day. Monticelli's summit was about 600 yards to the east northeast and Lieutenant Tom Keys' company was on the slope of the major ridge running up the crest. There was no vegetation and the area offered little or no cover. On the right was a gully leading part way up the mountain. Beyond the gully was another ridge and to the southeast, out of sight, were the positions of Company F.

Shortly after his arrival on the ridge Lieutenant Keys received word that Lieutenant Maddox had been wounded at Cassace. This left him only two officers: Burton and Edwards.

Lieutenant Keys described what happened next:

"Colonel Murphy ordered me to send a squad to the gully on my right rear to clear out Germans who had reoccupied several pillboxes and to leave a man or two in each emplacement to guard it. I selected Sergeant Beryl Baker's 2nd Squad. Baker did not have much liking for spit and polish garrison duty but in command he was in his element. He was courageous and he had a natural bent for tactics.

"After the squad left I sat on the edge of my trench and searched the gully with my field glasses. I located an enemy bunker 150 yards to my right rear. Light reflections and German helmets were visible from the position. The emplacement was situated on ground that was raised above the surrounding ground, like a blister, so that it would be difficult for Sergeant Baker and his men to attack. I alerted the platoon around me to fire on the target that I would designate with my fire. I fired about seven rounds on the dugout, kicking up dirt, then the men commenced firing M1's and BAR's. I observed some excitement among the

The Dead Man. A rebuilt l'Uomo Morto. The Gothic Line offensive began here.

Germans who threw out a dozen potato mashers on the south side of the position. They probably thought they were under assault by Sergeant Baker's squad. Within a matter of minutes a white cloth was waved from the mouth of the dugout. I ordered cease fire and counted eleven Germans as they exited, hands over head, and walked southward into the hands of Baker. Lieutenant Burton, sitting on the edge of his foxhole three yards from mine was exhilarated when he saw the prisoners walking to the rear and he jumped to his feet and cheered with his armed raised; at that moment, he was hit in the shoulder by a rifle bullet that knocked him flat. His sophomoric action deprived Company E of a fearless and much needed officer. He walked disgustedly to the rear and I keenly felt the loss of him. Now I had only one officer under my command: Lieutenant Edwards.

"Enemy fire was becoming so intense that it became necessary for the men to remain in their trenches. I then received a call from Colonel Murphy who told me, 'Keys, today you'll get your Oak Leaf Cluster to your Purple Heart.' He said that Division Commander Livesay was at the 2nd Battalion CP and that there was to be a general attack all along the regimental front. Captain Conley and me were to attack straight toward the summit of Monticelli. The 1st Battalion was on our left and the 3rd on our right and they would also attack at the same time: 1400 hours. Corps artillery would commence firing on the enemy immediately to our front and continue for ten minutes. When this artillery fire ceased, we were to assault the crest. When we reached the objective, we were to establish all-around defense, reorganize and prepare for counterattacks.

"Viewing the terrain over which 1st and 2nd Battalions were to attack, it was my opinion that accomplishment of the mission was impossible and that the undertaking was suicidal. It was nothing less than murder to send these men against the fire they would receive from the summit. I then realized the idiocy of war. I assembled the platoon commanders and gave my order. Men were to fix bayonets and all were to leave their holes when the artillery ceased and advance toward the top of Monticelli.

"Corps artillery died away and we got out of our foxholes and started for the summit amidst the heaviest concentration of fire I had ever witnessed. Looking back, I saw one of the platoon sergeants coming up with 12 or 15 men. I called for him to bring up his whole platoon. He cried, 'This is the whole platoon, lieutenant!' I called for Perez, who had stuck right beside me, so that I could contact the rear platoon sergeant by radio and order him forward. Sergeant Sprik, the communications sergeant, yelled, 'Perez is dead and his radio is smashed!'

"As we crawled a few more yards, I looked back and called and gestured for the rear platoons to keep moving. I bumped into one of my dead soldiers and skirted around his body. I saw no troops on our left or right. There was no cover on the bare ridge and we were advancing against a whirlwind of German fire. I saw the cruel casualties the company had suffered and I judged that the men of Company E had already paid too high a price. I terminated the attack and ordered the men to get into any holes they could find."[20]

VIII

After General Livesay left the 3rd Battalion CP, Colonel Long met with Captain Fulton and gave him the attack order. It conformed with the operation of the night before with Company L on the left, Company K on the right with Company L in reserve. Colonel Long told the captain that he was to go with his lead platoon and not stop until he had reached the crest of Monticelli.

Just as Company K moved out, completely exposed on the mountain slope, a concentration of enemy mortar fire landed in the draw to the left. This was to be the only German response until Fulton's men reached the final line of protective wire. By 1350 hours, the company had reached the wire and scouts went out to find a path through the obstacle. The men were exhausted from the brief but rapid climb. It was a hot, bright day and the fear of the unknown, coupled with the heat, had the troops reaching for their canteens. The Time on Target barrage that General Livesay had scheduled was to be fired at 1400 hours, only minutes away.

Suddenly, one of the forward scouts yelled that he had found a path through the wire. It had been used by enemy carrying parties, outpost reliefs and as a route of withdrawal. Finding the path was a stroke of luck for Company K and at that moment the artillery began to fall just above the wire in a line extending from La Maestra across the entire slope. The spirits of the weary infantrymen soared and if there had been any hesitation about moving on, it had completely vanished. Captain Fulton led the charge through the pathway crying, "Follow me!" He had expected a hail of bullets from the covering bunker, but there was none. The German machinegun crew had taken cover from the tremendous barrage being delivered by sixteen artillery battalions ranging from 240mm to 155mm and 105mm guns. The din, dust and dirt from the detonating shells along with the thunderous explosions had driven the Germans deep into their emplacement. Not a single shot was fired as the company charged up the path and deployed on line to commence their movement to the top of the mountain.

General Livesay apparently had directed a standing barrage to assist the crossing of the barrier and this he had done admirably. However, as the charging riflemen continued their advance upward, they were approaching the impact area of the exploding shells. Captain Fulton, accompanied by his radio operator, Sergeant Theodore R. Thompson, radioed a request to battalion to lift the barrage 25 yards and to continue to do so at request. This was done and the artillery was marched in increments almost to the top of Monticelli. At this point Fulton called for a cease fire as a protective measure for troop safety. Immediately, as if by signal, the Germans came out of hiding and began firing at the advancing line of infantrymen. This caused the captain and his group to veer to the right to gain the protection of the mountain's curvature and they continued their climb to the top of the mountain.

Turning upward, Fulton and two of his men reached the top of Monticelli where they found an observation bunker.

It had been cut into solid rock and was tall enough for a man to stand upright. It was reinforced with 24 inch logs and then covered with six feet of earth. Fortunately, it was unoccupied and the men hopped into the bunker and awaited the arrival of their comrades.

Machinegunners of the 363rd Infantry in the Monticelli area, September 16, 1944.

104

Several minutes passed and it soon became obvious that no other company troops were going to join Fulton and his group at the top of the mountain. From the bunker the captain could see the reverse slope of Monticelli which was quite steep and sparsely covered. Just above Fonte Fredda Fulton observed a huge cave on the opposite mountain. As he scanned the slopes with his binoculars, he saw a German also gazing through binoculars and looking directly at him. By now the sun was behind the crest to the south making detection of anything on Monticelli impossible.

Before the command group had moved toward the summit of the mountain Captain Fulton had left a squad along the rim of the ridge about 25 years down from the crest. He made a quick decision to send his runner to the squad and bring them up the hill. They immediately responded to his order and climbed the slope and dropped into the bunker. Fulton then radioed a message to Colonel Long.

"This is Captain Fulton," he told Long. "I'm on top of your goddamned mountain. I've got ten men with me. We're played out. Now, what the hell do you want me to do next?"[21]

The time was 1448, 17 September.

Il Giogo Pass after the breakthrough of the Gothic Line. The pine forests have been leveled by fire. The hairpin turns of Highway 6524 snake to the top.

After the disastrous attack of Companies E and G, Lieutenant Tom Keys moved among his men trying to get them into any foxhole that was available. He moved quickly, slapping each man on the back as they jumped into the holes. When he reached his original trench he called Colonel Murphy and told him he had ended the assault because of the casualties and no possibility of success. The colonel agreed he had done the right thing but he advised the lieutenant it was reported an enemy squad was on his right and he ought to do something about it. Rather than call any of his men, Keys decided to take a look for himself. He grabbed a carbine and walked to his right flank. Kneeling on one knee he looked down at the gully, searching for the Germans. At that moment he was struck by enemy fire and knocked unconscious. When he regained his senses he was lying on his back. His helmet held his head up enough so he could see his torso, but he was unable to move any part of his body. He could barely rock his head half an inch to the right and left. He was later to learn a small caliber missile, probably a rifle bullet, passed through his neck from right to left, causing a compound fracture of the fourth cervical vertebrae. Alternately losing and regaining consciousness, he had a vague memory of someone pulling him into his trench.

Day turned to night and no one came to the aid of the wounded officer. For more than eight hours Keys lay alone on the slope, then he heard a faint voice above him exclaim. "My God, Lieutenant Keys, I thought you had been evacuated!" Before the trip down Monticelli, the medics tied a cardboard plasma box on each side of the lieutenant's head so it would not roll from side to side and further damage his spinal cord. At the aid-station he heard the voice of Captain Paul J. Maloney, the 2nd Battalion surgeon, say, "Tell Murphy Keys is here."

Staff Sergeant Ennis M. Beeson, the Platoon Guide of Company E's 3rd Platoon, was also in on the Monticelli action:

"The day of the week or month didn't mean much in the situation we were in. About all we knew was, 'Yesterday, today and hope for tomorrow.' It was on 14th of September, 1944 when Company E dug in for the night on a low wooded ridge at what seemed to me to be the southwest corner of Monticelli. Our platoon set up a listening post about 50 yards out in front of the company. I remember telling the men to dig deep and tunnel back on each side of their foxholes so they could get away from shrapnel in case we got a tree-burst. It was a bad place to have to dig in because we were just at the edge of the timberline, the rest of the

T/5 James L. Christopher.

Lt. General William B. Fulton whose Company K first reached the peak of Monticelli. General Fulton later commanded the 9th Infantry Division in Vietnam. U.S. Army photo.

way to the peak of the mountain was barren ground. Off to our left we could see other GIs digging in and to our left front an German ammunition dump was burning. Sometime before daylight word was whispered through the company, 'Get them ready! Get them ready! We're moving up! We're moving up!' Company G had already moved. It had moved further up the slope of Monticelli and dug in. We were to follow them into the attack whenever it was ordered.

"All that day there was heavy fighting. We didn't seem to be going anywhere. Units on our right and left were not advancing either and there were heavy casualties. The Jerries were not about to give up without a fight. Around 1400 someone noticed a white flag waving up on the slope and to our right. The men in the forward holes began yelling at the flag. In a few minutes a German medic, holding a Red Cross arm band, came out and slid down toward our position. He said there were about 20 Germans in a bunker who wanted to surrender, but they wanted to be sure we did not fire on them. We told the medic to have them hold their hands over their heads and come out. As they did, their own troops fired on them.

"I remember Paul Dean, a Company G man, a close friend of mine from my hometown, came half walking and half crawling down the mountainside dragging a bloody leg. He had been badly wounded. I crawled out of my foxhole, helped him with a bandage and found a large stick to use as a crutch and sent him on down the mountain.

"By dark all of the rifle companies had taken severe casualties, but Company G, being the assault unit, was hardest hit. There was a deep draw to our right; I think this is where Company F was located. Mortars constantly pounded the area. Between Company E and the main body of Company G there was quite a bit of timber and a dirt bluff about four feet high. Company G had gotten high enough up the mountain to be out of the timberline, but there was a lot of brush around and the ground was very rocky.

"That night we inched our way forward trying to get into position to push through Company G for the coming attack. Most of our company had passed through the timber and over the embankment before daylight. With the coming of dawn we were directly behind Company G and some of our men had even pushed on into the company and shared the same foxholes.

"It was during the night, about 30 feet below the cliff that we found the body of Robert Braun. He had trained with us back in the States, a big awkward boy who had no business in the infantry. So we recommended that he be kept from combat and we had thought he had been transferred to a support unit, but instead he had gone up Monticelli as a stretcher bearer and had been killed the day before.

S/Sgt. Ennis Beeson. 3rd Platoon. Company E 363rd.

"All morning long sniper and machinegun fire poured in on us. Mortar rounds fell with deadly accuracy. We seemed to be open on every side. Little did we know that 24 hours later every officer and every platoon sergeant in the two companies would be dead or wounded.

"About 1000 hours, Sergeant John Rice, a weapons platoon non-com, trying to keep a light machinegun in action 20 yards to our left, took a direct hit from a German mortar. If we had not known what had happened, we would have been unable to recognize his body.

"It wasn't long before orders came down that we were to attack at exactly 1400. Every man would leave his foxhole in an all out assault. Word was passed from hole to hole 'We going to the top at fourteen hundred! 'We're going to the top at fourteen hundred!' Squad leaders moved through the platoons making sure their men knew what to do. We decided to leave everything but our weapons, ammo, belts and canteens. The less we carried the faster we could move. Some of the men fixed bayonets, other took them from their packs and put them in their belts. I was carrying a Thompson submachine gun. I took a trench knife and stuck it in my combat boot. The Germans had us under complete

Troops of Company E, 363rd Infantry move up Highway 6524 after the breakout from Monticelli. L-R. Sgt. Ysbrand J. Sprik, Lieutenant Robert G. Benckart and Sgt. Richard T. Garrestson.

observation and knew exactly what we were going to do and had every mortar and artillery piece zeroed in on our area.

"As soon as we began the attack, they unloaded everything they had. We hadn't gone 10 yards until we were cut to pieces. Company E was hit so hard and lost so many in those few minutes it was impossible to hold the men together. Many never made it through Company G. I jumped off with the 1st Squad, 3rd Platoon. Sergeant Julius Hunley and Private Johnny Burklow were in front of me and I was trying to catch up with them. They were both in a dead run up the mountainside. I could see Hunley bent forward and running, then suddenly I saw him straighten up, drop his rifle and put both hands to his chest and neck. Blood covered his hands. He twisted and fell into a foxhole. Burklow was somewhere in front of us. Then, a mortar shell hit, knocking me crazy for a few seconds. I jumped into the hole on top of Hunley. He was hit bad. He was shot in the shoulder and arm and the upper part of his body, but he was still able to bandage himself. In between the blasts from the mortars I could hear Burklow calling for Hunley. He was in front of us and caught on open ground. He called two or three times before he died, and he died very quickly. Hunley never did hear him.

"The Germans most certainly would have overrun us had it not been for the units on our flanks and especially our Cannon company. I later learned that the Germans rallied for a counter-attack but our Cannon Company laid down such a ring of fire that they literally built a fence around us. In the four days of hell on Monticelli those cannoneers stood behind us like big brothers. It was one of the best outfits in the 5th Army.

The attack was called off, of course, and as darkness fell, some of the firing let up a little and became harassing fire more than anything else. It was intended to keep us down, and it did.

"The mountain was covered with dead and wounded and as soon as it was dark enough we had to get litter teams into the area to haul out the men who were unable to move. Litters were made of anything we could find and men were waiting for darkness to fall so they could carry a buddy down the slope. Replacements were already being brought into Battalion Headquarters. The men were rapidly formed into litter teams and sent up the slope to pick up the wounded. Despite the mortar and machinegun fire many of the men left the safety of their foxholes to go to the aid of their friends.

"I finally got Sergeant Hunley to his feet. He was steady but able to walk and we started down the mountainside. As we moved from hole to hole, I would call the names of the men I thought were there. I wanted them to know it was me and not the Germans going down the mountain. They were men of my platoon. Most of them answered. Some were badly wounded, others had been evacuated. Some we did not find and, of course, many were dead. Everyone helped everyone else, but there were just too many wounded, and some of the men had to be left on the slope until we could find a way to get them down. I half-carried Hunley and picked the easiest route I could. I remember talking to him in a soft manner and being extra nice and easy with him. He said, 'Damn you, Skinny, quit being so goody-goody to me. Cuss the hell out of me like you usually do and I'll feel better.' So I did. In those days the guys called me 'Skinny' after the popular orchestra leader, Skinny Ennis.

"We were a few yards from the aid-station when we met 1st Sergeant George Reid. Though he was wounded and nearly exhausted, he had gathered about 30 or 40 replacements, formed them into litter teams and was leading them up the hill. So I traded places with him. He and Hunley went on to the aid-station and I took the litter teams and started back up Monticelli. I never saw Sergeant Hunley again.

"All night we worked our way up and down the mountain. Most of the men carrying the litters had never seen combat before, but they were formally introduced to it that night. We worked in the Company E and G area and went the same route every time. A boy named Novotny had dug in by the four foot embankment and each time we climbed the small bluff I called to him and when he answered I knew we were in the right place and that the Jerries had not infiltrated down the paths.

"The stretcher bearers kept working. I left them and went back to the edge of the draw and started up the hillside again. As I moved up I knew about where my platoon was supposed to be. I kept calling the names of the men I knew. I found part of the 3rd Squad above the embankment. Some of the men had dropped back thinking they were alone on the hill. Before daylight what was left of the 1st and 3rd Squads had moved into the foxholes in the exact spot we were in before the two o'clock attack. We didn't find any of the 2nd Squad. We assumed they were all dead.

"Shortly after sunup everything became very still. The machineguns up the draw had stopped firing and the harassing sniper and mortar fire had ceased. Complete silence fell over the battlefield. We waited for something to happen. Death was all around us. Bodies were sprawled everywhere. Packs, helmets and all kinds of gear were scattered clear up to the top of Monticelli. Since dawn we had been trying to sort out the men killed during the attack and during the night. Some were newcomers, others were old friends who had left Oregon with us many months before and had trained with us in North Africa. They were men we had learned to love like brothers, but who would be left behind on the slopes of that damned mountain.

"I don't know what really happened. You never do in combat. I do know we got some welcome help from our 3rd Battalion and from the 85th Division on our right.

"Shortly before noon, Sergeant Sprick, our communications sergeant, came over and told me to take what few men I had and follow a telephone wire down through the draw to a bunker. We would find more of the platoon there. As we went along we picked up canteens of water and bandoliers of ammo from our fallen comrades. When we came to the bunker we found what was left of the 2nd Squad! We were absolutely

Il Giogo Pass today with the hotel-inn at the summit.

overjoyed to see each other. We hugged. We cried. We thought the entire 2nd Squad was dead somewhere up on Monticelli.

"We holed up for four or five hours in the bunker until we could get our replacements together and the remainder of the company formed. Each replacement carried either a jerrican of water, ammo or K rations. These men were fresh out of basic training in the States. I stood at the door of the bunker and as each man handed me his rifle so it would be easier for him to get down the bunker steps, he would say, 'Be careful with that thing, it's loaded' They didn't know what they were getting into. When the company was finally formed, replacements assigned to different squads, ammo and rations distributed, we moved out. Up the draw, across the lower slope of Monticelli and east of the highway.

"When we moved over the ridge, Charlie Gainer, one of the men in the 1st Squad, dropped out of the column and started back down the mountain by himself. I tried to stop him, but he said, 'I'll catch up with you. I've just got to go back for a minute.' Charlie had to take one last look at his good buddy, Bob Hagemen, who had been killed beside him.

"With a column on each side of the highway, we headed north again. In a little while Gainer caught up with us and fell in with the 1st Squad.

"Monticelli was behind us! As we rounded a curve in the road, I could feel the first cold winds of winter blowing down from the Alps. It would be a long and difficult autumn and winter and God knows we were lucky we couldn't predict the future."[22]

The men who survived Monticelli, like most veterans of major battles, would forever remember the date of the attack: 17 September. At the time probably few, if any, of those soldiers of the 363rd were aware of another battle that took place on 17 September 82 years before. It occurred at Antietam Creek in the state of Maryland between the forces of General George B. McClellan and General Robert E. Lee. When the fighting ended nearly 6,000 men lay dead or dying and another 17,000 were wounded. It was the bloodiest battle in American history.

The 2nd Battalion's valiant but futile attack on the summit of Monticelli had cost Companies E and G, 32 killed and 59 wounded with almost all the casualties happening within the first few minutes of the assault. Captain Conley was the only officer left in Company G; Company E had no officers and no platoon sergeants. Two section sergeants and five squad leaders were also lost to the company.[23]

After dark while the evacuation of the wounded was still progressing, Company F, 361st Infantry, which had been attacking in the sector to the west and north of the 363rd, was attached to the 1st Battalion to protect the still exposed left flank of Company B where casualties were heavy and the indomitable Pfc. Oscar Johnson was still holding for his third sleepless night.

X

All during the afternoon of the 17th Captain Fulton and his small band of men held their ground atop Monticelli. Shortly after reaching the summit the men could see the Germans assembling for a counter attack on the opposite slope. Fulton quickly called for artillery and indicated the would adjust the fire.[24] Pfc. Jessie Taylor had taken up a position near a communications trench and was firing his BAR at anything that moved, including the Germans who were forming for their counterattack. A sniper located near the crest to the east of Monticelli made life miserable for the little group and kept taking pot-shots at the men in the bunker. Pvt. Clayton Quayle was shot through the left eye and a round tore into the huge log beam supporting the ceiling splintering the wood and drawing blood from Captain Fulton's face.

Three times the Germans tried to rally for an attack but the artillery of the 347th foiled each effort. Even so, a small number of the enemy were able to make their way toward the bunker. Finally, Fulton decided to bring fire directly down on the bunker and he transmitted a fire request to Captain George D. Bunnel, the 347th liaison officer, who followed through with the order.

At 1710 hours Colonel Long and his men were moving rapidly toward the summit of the mountain when an 81mm white phosphorous shell exploded and the smoke moved down the draw obscuring his group. Under cover of the smoke, Long's entire staff rose and charged with him the remaining distance to the crest where they were warmly greeted by the small band of defenders.

By 0830, 18 September, over 300 men of the 3rd Battalion were on Monticelli Ridge with the remainder of the unit on the south slope close to the top. Earlier, the 338th Infantry had secured Monte Altuzzo, the 339th Infantry had taken Monte Verruca and the 337th Infantry had captured Monte Pratone. By mid-morning the last German resistance had ended at Il Giogo Pass and the enemy was in full retreat towards the heights north of Firenzuola. That same day General Keyes, the II Corps commander, again sent a message to his troops:

"You have broken the Gothic Line. I congratulate you upon this significant victory - the first step toward the ultimate destruction of our enemy. You must not pause in your gallant and determined drive, but push the enemy relentlessly, giving him no rest. The final goal is in sight and I have every confidence that the men of II Corps will give the Fifth Army another Speedy Victory."

On 6 September General Keyes had told his men to go in for the knockout. While Fifth Army had not accomplished a knockout it did have the Germans reeling backwards.

Some hours after the breakthrough Sergeant J. Denton Scott, a staff correspondent for Yank magazine, went up front to take a look at the troops. He wrote:

"WITH THE FIFTH ARMY ON THE GOTHIC LINE—This section of the Gothic Line is loaded with dead bodies, a nauseating stench and grim men who have scarcely eaten, slept or shaved for days.

"You got there by waiting until the doughfeet of this Fifth Army regiment cracked the line in the predawn hours of 18 September. Slow moving, endless streams of Italians leading their heavily laden black mules up the passes with supplies and medical equipment makes rapid progress almost impossible. Even jeeps can't climb some of these hills. They are rocky, sheer, narrow and in some places completely untraveled. The GIs came this way carrying their weapons and ammo and nothing else. They moved fast into the Gothic Line and are moving faster on to the other side.

"The battle of the Gothic Line has a tragic tinge that is evident in the conversion of everyone. News reached the men of the Fifth, while they were beating their heads against the Line, that the war was all over but the shouting, that the Allies were in Germany and maybe it wouldn't be too long before they would all be home. That news was still in the heads of these men when they lost an entire company. For five days and nights they watched their dead being brought in and they mulled over this news of a near peace. To most, the Gothic Line was the toughest of them all. The Germans had every possible angle planned. The only approach was frontal.

"A short time ago we were walking up one of these mountains trying to contact a regimental CP. We stopped to inspect one pillbox of thick concrete and with a dug-out so close and so well fortified our artillery couldn't knock it out. We moved up in slow single file ten yards apart, every man looking for snipers. We were deep in German territory or at least what had been their territory and we knew it was a favorite Jerry trick to detail clusters of snipers to delay advance.

"We ran into a trail with another long line of mules moving down it. They were moving slowly and they had cumbersome bundles on their backs. Great streams of flies flowed down the mountain after them. Italians leading them were silent and perspiration streamed from their bearded faces. We by-passed the funeral procession of mules and Italians and hit the regimental CP which was just being set up in the one section of a stone farmhouse left intact.

"An officer sat on a box munching a piece of cube sugar and talking to his men. The infantry companies were moving out again in about fifteen minutes. I walked around to the other side of the farmhouse and found some GIs sprawled on the ground, most of them silent, resting.

"One GI looked up at me and said, 'What's a correspondent doing here? Don't you know the war's over? Don't you read the papers?'

"It was beginning to get dark and cold. I noticed that the men around me weren't carrying any blankets. Just ammunition and weapons and a few boxes of K-rations.

"One of them looked up and grinned. 'We'll be in Firenzoula by dawn,' he said. 'I hope the Tedeschi haven't stolen all the good vino out of that town like they have most of them. I'll probably need a shot by then.'

"Five feet from me two large lumpy squares of canvas were gathering shadows and I walked closer and saw two pairs of motionless GI boots sticking out from under the canvas. A doughfoot sitting close waved at me as I walked past.

"'Tell the boys we're doing fine,' he said.[25]"

Endnotes for Chapter Six

1 . Chapter One of the Fifth Army's Volume Seven, The Gothic Line, gives an excellent description of the fortifications of this major German defense line in the Northern Apennines. To date, there has been only one definitive history written exclusively about the actions that broke the Gothic barrier. Titled, The Gothic Line, and published in 1967; Its author, British historian, Douglas Orgill, served with the Eighth Army in Italy. No comparable history, on this phase of the war in Italy, exists by an American historian. In the years following the war, articles began to appear in newspapers around the United States that the 10th Mountain Division, which arrived in Italy in January, 1945, had broken the Gothic Line in February of that year. This myth was helped along by stories written by veterans of the division. Some of these men, for whatever reason, truly believed the 10th had broken the line. In 1972 a book, The Ski Troops, authored by a chap named Hal Burton, was published by Simon and Schuster and caused a firestorm of protest by veterans of II Corps whose divisions had actually broken the Gothic Line. In his attempt to glorify the 10th Mountain

Division, Burton plays fast and loose with the truth. The book contains distortions, inaccuracies and downright lies. The first half of the book is a good account of ski troops down through the years, but once Burton arrives in Italy, he loses total control of his material and shows an appalling ignorance of the history of the campaign and of the other divisions of Fifth Army. Unfortunately, veterans of the 10th accepted Burton's book as gospel and this resulted in some bitter exchanges between the veterans of Fifth Army and of the 10th Mountain Division; even fifty years later, many of these feelings of rancor and bitterness still exist though many Fifth Army men have been greatly amused at the wild distortions and gross exaggerations of the 10th Mountain. Ironically, though the 10th was one of the last U.S. Army combat divisions to be sent overseas and had one of the shortest period of combat, it has received more publicity than any other World War II unit. Over the years, the exploits of the division have been inflated almost to the point of absurdity.

2 . Fifth Army History. Part 7.

3 . II Corps G-2 Report marked CONFIDENTIAL. 15 August, 1944.

4 . Cole, Robert H. Lt. Col. The Battle at Il Giogo Pass. The 2nd Battalion, 338th Infantry. Undated. Monograph, The Infantry School. Ft. Benning.

5 . Captured orders to soldiers of the 12th Pcht Regt (4th Pcht Div) 8 September. 338th Infantry S-2 files.

6 .This rumor spread throughout the regiment the day prior to the Monticelli attack.

7 . These actions and the subsequent battles of the 3rd Battalion at Monticelli are taken from an excellent narrative written by General William B. Fulton for The Powder River Journal. It appears in the June, 1992 edition.

8 . The Powder River Journal June, 1992. Pages 37-39.

9 . Lieutenant Keys' Monticelli story was originally written for publication in the 91st Division Association Journal. The author served under the lieutenant during the battle for the mountain.

10 . 361st Infantry POW Report #13. 24 September, 1944.

11 . Kennedy, Captain Henry A. The Initial Breakthrough of the Gothic Line by the 5th Army. Captain Kennedy was a 363rd regimental historian and wrote this outstanding 30 page history of Monticelli during the early winter of 1944. Though Lieutenant Pena's reconnaissance to Monticelli was supposedly made on the 14th it almost had to be made later, perhaps even after the battle.

12 . Livengood, Roy. Thunder in the Apennines.Waukegan, Ill. 1981. Page 112.

13 . Ibid. Page 113.

14 . 363rd Regimental History. Pages 76-77.

15 . The narrative of James L. Christopher was written for the author September, 1993.

16 . Kennedy Narrative.

17 . Morris, Eric. Circles of Hell. The War in Italy 1943-45. Hutchinson. London. Page 384.

18 . Fulton Narrative.

19 . This conversation between General Livesay and Colonel Long appears in both the division history and the 363rd Regimental History.

20 . Keys Narrative.

21 . There are several versions of exactly what Captain Fulton told Colonel Long when he radioed from the summit of Monticelli. The words in Fulton's narrative are probably correct. According to the 363rd Journal the captain supposedly said, "I, Captain William B. Fulton, am on top of Monticelli. I've got ten men with me, we're played out and I'll be goddamned if I know what to do next!" Whatever the words were, Captain Fulton certainly got his message across.

22 . The Powder River Journal. June, 1980.

23 . The battle casualties of the 363rd Infantry from 11-19 September, 1944 totaled 85 killed in action, 349 wounded and 195 non-battle casualties. The battle casualties for the three attacking divisions, the 34th, 85th and 91st for the period 13-18 September were: 34th, 611; 85th, 873; 91st, 1,247. From the beginning of the attack against the Gothic Line on 10 September to the fall of Futa Pass on the 22nd the three divisions suffered 3,903 casualties of whom 688 were killed. Heaviest casualties were sustained by the 91st Division.

24 . During the Monticelli battle the Division's 347th Field Artillery and the Regimental Cannon Company supported the 363rd. The following are the number of rounds fired each day:

Date	347th F.A.	Cannon Co
12 Sept.	1757	985
13 Sept.	2216	967
14 Sept.	3711	1706
15 Sept.	4217	1101
16 Sept.	1814	1698
17 Sept.	4055	1328
18 Sept.	1666	306
Total Rounds	19436	8091

When Captain Inman of Company B was observing one of the many counterattacks forming against his position, Cannon Company, commanded by Captain Ernie Land, fired 750 rounds in the period of one hour with such effect that the German attack was never able to effectively materialize.

Monticelli could never have been taken without the help of the 347th. The artillerymen of Lt. Col. Woodrow W. Lynn's battalion. Beginning with the assault on the summit the 347th fired all day and all night, three rounds per minute. This was later cut to two rounds per minute, then one round every three minutes. The 155 rifles of Corps augmented this fire at the rate of battery one round every five minutes. The effects of this fire can well be imagined. Many of the POWs were dazed and shaken when they surrendered.

25 . Yank. MTO Edition. September, 1944

91st members receive Holy Communion before going into battle.

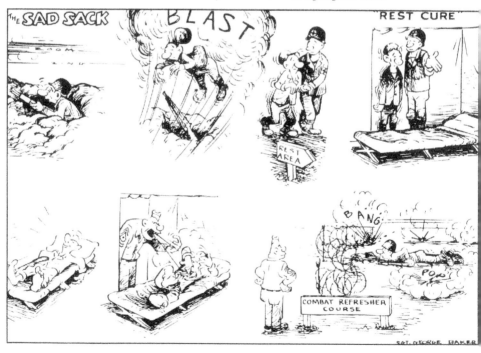

Captain Smith. Company commander, Headquarters Co. 316th Engineers.

CHAPTER SEVEN — FUTA PASS

"Futa Pass, with an elevation of 2,962 feet, is one of the lowest of the passes and the terrain here is less precipitous than in other portions of the range, and Highway 65, connecting Florence and Bologna, is the best and most direct road through the mountains. Since Highway 65 was the logical route for an attacking force to follow, the Germans made Futa Pass the strongest point in the Gothic Line defenses."

Fifth Army History. Volume Seven. Page 8.

I

For centuries Futa Pass has been north-central Italy's most famous region. Early maps drawn as far back as 1500 show the area encompassing nearly all of the district between Fiesole and Bologna and the towns and mountains paralleling Highway 65 which is known as the "Futa Pass Road", or to most Italians simply, "la Futa". During the Middle Ages and the days of the Renaissance the highway followed the exact route it does today coiling around the slopes of the Apennines and through the little villages. A postal schedule charted in the 1700's indicated stops were made at Pianoro, Loiano, Feligare, Covigliajo below Pietramala, Fontebuona and Florence. In 1789 Louis Dutens, a Frenchman, wrote him fourteen hours to travel by horse-drawn carriage from Bologna to Florence. Many of Europe's most distinguished authors have written about the Futa: Goethe, Casanova, Montaigne, Stendhal, Shelley, Byron and Huxley and some in the most poetic terms. An Englishwoman, Lady Morgan, wrote in 1820:

'"The stars were still burning brightly in the clear dark blue heavens as we ascended the pass on the following morning, but they soon, though gradually, 'paled their ineffectual fires'. A sort of sapphire light fell like a shower on the eastern summits of the mountains and ushered in the rising sun, which ascended most gloriously, most awfully, above those mighty elevations where the sublimest spectacle of nature is most sublime. Many a salient point of bleached rock sparkled with refracted rays, and hung above the rolling vapors of the valleys beneath like beacon lights on the ocean's verge; and many a changeful meteoric illusion cheated and charmed the eye until the first burst of day dispelled every atmospheric mist and cloud, and left distinctly traced and brightly gilt the forests, turrets and meandering rivers of the vast and varied scenery which beautifies the descent into the Valley of the Arno."[1]

A division infantryman looks over a destroyed Panther tank turret at Futa Pass.

In the 17th Century the most beautiful villa in the Futa was <u>La Delizia di Cafaggiolo</u> located near S. Piero a Sieve and owned by the Grand Duke of Tuscany. Its magnificent towers could be seen for miles and the parklike grounds stretched on and on and on, vineyard after vineyard, fence after fence; it seemed as big as a village. Today it sits along the highway, abandoned and empty; the rooms dim, dark and dreary. Like the war, it has passed into history.

Beginning at Barberino del Mugello and running over the mountains just west of Highway 65, over Passo della Futa, over Monte Bastione, over Monte Venere, Monzuno and Monte Adone and disappearing into the valley of the Po, is the old Roman road <u>Flaminia Militare.</u> It is actually an extension of the Via Flaminia in Rome and runs from there across the spine of the Northern Apennines. It is an astonishing feat of engineering dating back to 187 B.C. The old Roman route is several yards wide and in constructing it, the workers first put down a layer of sand, then a layer of pebbles, a layer of rocks, a layer of larger stones, many two feet in diameter, then flat pieces of rock were fitted vertically between the stones. The logistics of the operation must have been tremendous and just hauling the material up the mountain passes had to require a monumental effort. During the battle for Monte Bastione some of the men from the 34th Division removed the large stones from the road and placed them in a circle around their slit-trenches, probably praying that the added protection would save them from the red-hot shrapnel of the exploding German artillery. Since most infantrymen are not students of Roman history it's highly unlikely the 34th soldiers realized the significance of those huge rocks. Every kilometer of the road was marked by a small, upright pillar in the same way our highways tell us the distance by signs.[2]

The antitank ditch near Futa Pass.

A few miles northeast of Radicosa Pass, in this land of the Futa, stands one of the strangest geological features in all of the Northern Apennines: Sasso di San Zanobi. This surrealistic serpentine bulk of cinder-looking rock rises from the fields of the Idice River Valley. For centuries a church stood in its shadows but it was destroyed during the war and never rebuilt. In the distance is the towering peak of Monte Canda. Zanobi seems to be geared with wings and ready for flight. So sinister looking is the site that for centuries it was reported to be occupied by Satan.

II

By the morning of 18 September the 85th and 91st Divisions had clawed their way through il Giogo and had seized a sector seven miles in width on either side of the pass. The badly battered 4th Parachute Division, assisted by horse drawn carts, heavily laden infantrymen and any vehicle that would run and carry equipment, was in full retreat towards the mountains north of Firenzuola. Troops of the 91st were pouring through the pass in an ever-increasing rushing as the roads were repaired by the men of the 316th Engineers.

The race for the Po Valley had begun.

When the expanding intensity of the German resistance at Monticelli forced General Livesay to commit the 361st Infantry the 362nd Infantry was left with the responsibility for a zone four miles wide extending from the west of Highway 65 to Mount Calvi, a vast amount of territory for one regiment to control. Captain Fred W. Booth was the company commander of Company L. He would later write:

"I don't doubt that our zone was four miles wide. I often felt very lonesome out there with my company. From the time we started the advance along Sixty-five, somewhere south of S. Lucia, we were on the left flank of the division. All the way to Futa Pass and beyond I never knew who was on our left, west of us that is. I never saw anybody there and our orders never mentioned anybody over there. Hell, most of the time I didn't know where Company K was except that it was somewhere east of us. Company I was usually attached to another battalion. If the regiment was spread out that far, over four miles, that would explain why I never saw any other companies."[3]

To the right of the 362nd sector and running northwest of Mount Calvi is a ragged, broken-toothed chain of hills which forms the left wing of the amphitheater into which the 361st and 363rd Infantry attacked and which joins the main divide at Mount Gazzaro, the highest peak in the line of mountains overlooking the Futa Pass defenses at S. Lucia. To the left of Mount Calvi are two wide north-south ridges with open, rolling farmland. Colonel Cotton planned to focus his main force in the mountains to the east in an effort to accomplish, on a regimental front, the same flanking movement that II Corps was carrying out at the Il Giogo Pass.

The 362nd's 2nd Battalion was given the chore of capturing Mount Calvi while the 1st Battalion was held in reserve and the 3rd drove north along Highway 65. The forward slopes of Calvi were long, gradual

91st Division Artillery kitchen along Highway 65. General Keyes, CO, II Corps, has a word with General Hospital the artillery commander who was never seen in boots. He preferred the old style leggings.

and rocky and, except for a few sparse trees and brush, almost devoid of any kind of cover. The 2,454 foot mountain was well fortified with concrete pillboxes, mines and wire.

The 2nd Battalion attacked at 0400 14 September. S/Sgt. George M. Morris was with Company G: "That morning we jumped off on the push for Mount Calvi. It turned out to be bitter, bloody and one hell of a battle. It was about four in the morning and we were laying there waiting to move out when word came whispering down the line, 'Man with the tommygun up front.' I started to pass the word on when one guy said, 'Hell, Morris, you got the tommygun. They're talking about you.' So I crawled up and reported to the captain and he said, 'We've got a couple of engineers here with two rolls of tape. They know their way through the mine field so go with them and act as a guard. They'll mark the field and we'll go on through it.' The field was an open meadow of about five or six acres and was uphill all the way to some trees. The engineers knew what they were doing and where they were going and all went well until we got right in the middle of the meadow and the Krauts started shelling the hell out of us, but it stopped about as quickly as it had begun. At any rate, we got the tape up through the meadow and the engineers took off and I reported back to the captain who led the company up through the field. We climbed a short distance then ran into another meadow. The fog was right down on the ground which gave you an eerie kind of feeling. It was an extremely cloudy day and had rained a little. As we passed through the meadow the fog was waist high and you couldn't see the ground. I'd never seen conditions like that. We began to run into unseen objects with our feet that were hidden by the fog. Most of us had our raincoats and we started using them as fans to wave off the fog which revealed the bodies of several Germans as many Americans.

"As we got up on Mount Calvi our fighting with the Germans was kind of a rear guard action on their part. It took us a couple of days to take the mountain but by the time we took the peak there were only 28 men left in the company. Many of them had stepped on mines but most got caught by the enemy artillery fire. By the time we reached the top we were exhausted and thirsty. We had no water. Our canteens were dry.

"So we captured Calvi and our next objective was Hill 840 which was just as damned tough."[4]

The 2nd Battalion moved rapidly up the long smooth slopes and by dark of the first day Companies E and G were within one half mile of the summit. At 0612, 14 September Company G reported it was fifty yards from the top of Mount Calvi and twenty minutes later Battalion sent back the word that the company had passed over the crest of the mountain, had run into a sharp firefight but that all was quiet now and Calvi was secure.

The battle of the 2nd Battalion for Mount Calvi was later written up by Correspondent Jack Bell and appeared in the MTO edition of The Stars and Stripes.

WITH THE FIFTH ARMY IN NORTHERN ITALY. Lt. Col. Keith Thomson, a young man from that famous old town of Cheyenne, Wyoming, will never forget the mountain known as Calvi. It was there that he led a battalion of the 362nd Infantry through one of the bloodiest battles of the campaign.

The Allies drive was northward. And many an American lad is dead today because all through this part of Italy the Apennines are filled with great hills, the south side of which are almost vertical rock. On top are Germans who can see every move we make, and shoot from well-concealed positions on the northern slopes of the mountains. Plus which they cover each flank with every known type of fire.

Mount Calvi was such a hill, a cliff rising some 300 feet. Colonel Thomson's job was to get it. Westerners know about mountains, but this Wyoming officer didn't know the Germans had fortified a saddle just south of the Calvi cliff. He did know he had to go over that saddle to flank the cliff. Americans and Germans tangled that night on the saddle, a wild, confused battle that lasted until dawn, leaving hundreds of men on the battlefield.

The colonel got his outfit organized and moved to the southeast because they had found their left flank unprotected. All that day and on into the night the Americans fought up the west slope, veered right, and when daylight came next morning the remnants of what had been a well-equipped battalion stood on Mount Calvi. Men had been killed, wounded, lost German and American dead lay everywhere. Thomson's men were jittery, hungry, exhausted ... but they had the hill! Thus, through hundreds of miles of mountains Americans fought, taking hills and machinegun strongholds. Everywhere you turn is evidence of their war, a hill by hill struggle against an enemy which them Jerries could see our tonsils as we fought up to 'em."

The communiques say, "The Americans captured three hills north of Florence" and reading it, say, "Is that all? They must not be trying."

Near the top of the cliff some trees and bushes grew. Below that it was rock ... straight down. Just below the crest the Jerries had two machinegun nests, caves in the mountain side. Their guns were set back so they couldn't be seen even with glasses, yet they commanded every foot of the valley below. The gunners sat not far apart. Each had a chair behind his gun, so he could shoot at ease. Beside each gun was a shelf on which were books, cigarettes, shaving kit. Beside each was a pulley and rope. When the gunner needed more ammunition he merely grabbed the rope and pulled a case up from below. And below? Down there the gunners lived. It was a big cave, back in the rock far enough that the artillery couldn't dent it. A ladder ran down from each gun. If the enemy did shell their nests they merely ran down the ladders. They had stoves, beds, lights.

But the crowning achievement of this ingenious crew of Germans was in front of their cave openings. They had rigged up doors, painted the exact color of the cliff, which they could drop—and even the best scout couldn't see where they were hidden.

The nests were discovered by American soldiers after the hill had been captured. They chanced on a little path that wound down among the trees and bushes, and there it was![5]

A wet day for Fifth Army artillerymen.

The capture of Mount Calvi was the first breach by any element of the Fifth Army of any portion of the Gothic Line. It took some very superior observation away from the enemy and relieved the pressure off the 361st and 363rd Infantry Regiments.

At the time of the bitter fighting on Mount Calvi, the 362nd Anti-tank Company was sent around the flank to capture the town of Gagliano because the wide gap between the 2nd and 3rd Battalions made it difficult to prevent enemy infiltration. The small village was well behind the forward lines.

The two battalions continued the attack at 0600 15 September. The 3rd Battalion pushed one mile up Highway 65 just short of the village of Montecarelli where it dug in for the night.

At 1230 the 1st Battalion was committed with the task of making a flanking attack from the west through the village of Morcoiano which was about four miles from Futa Pass; however, only slight gains were made before dark. Sgt. J. Denton Scott, of Y<u>ank</u> magazine followed Company B through its actions in and around Mount Calvi. His story appeared in the November 14 issued titled "Gothic Tales":

Pfc. John Czinki of Detroit, Michigan, a mild, quiet-spoken, undersized company messenger was advancing with his company against a Jerry strong point located on the left flank of a ridge near Futa Pass. Another company was supposed to be moving up on the right of the same ridge. Czinski was sent to check up on possible enemy positions near the right of the ridge. "I looked down," he said, "and saw two pillboxes with a guy sticking his head out of one. You can hardly tell the difference between our helmets and the Jerries at that distance, so I called over and asked the lieutenant near me if we had any men down there. He said, 'Hell no!' I fired 20 rounds at the guy down there and started down, but before I started I asked the man beside me to give me some hand grenades. I never carry those things because I'm a messenger and just carry a rifle and ammo. Finally he got them out and gave them to me and I went down.

"I threw one at the nearest pillbox. Nothing happened. I turned around and looked up toward the hill. Right under it were three more pillboxes bigger than the two I was standing near. I went up to the first one while Lieutenant Haley came down and covered me. There was a Jerry standing halfway inside of it. I pulled the pin of the grenade and made like I was going to throw it in. The Jerry hesitated for a minute then he came out toward me while the lieutenant covered me. I went over to the second pillbox and stuck my head in and hollered for them to come out. Out came fifteen. I went to the other three pillboxes and did the same thing. Altogether fifty-two Jerries came out of those boxes. The lieutenant and I got them lined up and by this time the company started down the hill and took over the prisoners.

The American Military Cemetery at Pietramala. During the post war years all bodies were disinterred and taken to the permanent burial ground at Greve, near Florence.

"The next day I started to feel nervous and jittery as hell and kept telling myself what a damn fool I'd been. I could've been killed!"[6]

T/5 Errol Graham of Vallejo, California, a medic, got himself some prisoners in a different way. "I had lost my shovel," said Graham, "when all this artillery started pouring in and around us and I wanted to dig in. I thought I had left it back in an open field. One of the guys told me it was safe to go back and get it because there wasn't any Jerries around because they wouldn't be throwing all that stuff at us. So I went back and found it in the middle of a big open field. As I straightened up, my shovel in my hand, I saw six Germans right in front of me. There were two sergeants, a corporal and three privates. One of them had a gun on me, so I put my hands in the air and walked over to them. I said, "Sprechen sie Deutsch?" They said, "Ya." And that's as far as we got. I don't speak German. They searched me and put me in front of them and we started marching. I led them right up the hill between C and D Companies and started pointing and said, 'American here, American here, American here, American here and there.' We talked to each other in sign language and I made it plain that if they went with me and gave themselves up they wouldn't get killed, but if they didn't that they'd get knocked off sure as hell. So they started coming over and giving me their guns. They had three machineguns, a burp gun, two sniper rifles, two P-38s, one 38 automatic and assorted ammunition. I started walking them in. I stuffed my shirt with all the weapons and swung my shovel in my right hand. I got them back to the company OK."

S/Sgt. Chester M. Hollis, Dallas, Texas, was ordered to take a squad out to Hill 1021. "The first squad up on that hill had been gone four hours already and we hadn't heard from them," he said. "It looked like they ran into trouble. As we started out two men from the 1st Squad came back bringing two prisoners with them. The GIs said they had left two wounded and that the rest of their squad was dead. It was about eight in the morning when we started out. As we started our company decided to flank the hill. They did, then started to dig in. We went as far as we could and dug in too. It wasn't long before Pvt. Horace Biggs and I began to hear voices. We went out to investigate but still couldn't tell if they belonged to our men or Jerry. Finally we met three Jerries coming up the hill. We hit the ground and they walked within three feet of us. We didn't try to knock them off because we were in there amongst them and it would have been foolish. We spent the next fifteen minutes or more trying to find out how many Germans were up in there. Then we crawled back to our own platoon. We started blasting them. We took nine prisoners and killed three that I know of. Then they counter-attacked. They gave us bazooka and mortar fire all night and we lost plenty of men."

Pfc. Steve J. Smolarek of Hamtramck, Michigan, carries a heavy machinegun over the mountains. The

The site of the cemetery today. Mt. Oggioli in the background. Nothing remains now but a large field of bright yellow flowers.

Entrenched in the foliage of the Apennine forest, two machinegunners of the 362nd Infantry wait for a target.

gun weights about fifty-one pounds and he carries all his regular equipment besides. One morning, the morning his outfit took Mount Calvi, Steve lost both heels off his shoes, lost his machinegun and fell down the mountain eight times before he could get his heels back on.

Pfc. Bernard R. Barker of Chicago fought right next to Smolarek during the night and following morning of the battle for Calvi. "Soon as it got daylight," said Barker, "the Jerries let us through, and we found out soon enough it was just so they could encircle us and then blast the hell out of us. Our platoon and the platoon below us was pinned down. A short way ahead of us were two small farm houses. We kept blasting at the farm houses until we wised up that they were re-enforced from the inside and nothing but real heavy stuff could do them any harm. Suddenly we see a Jerry coming out of one of the houses waving a white flag. We stopped firing. Some of us even stood up. Then they opened up on us with their machineguns. They got a louie and a sergeant on my left. They shot they sergeant's lip off and got the lieutenant in the stomach. A gunner right beside me got in in the temple, the neck and the arm. All around me men were blowing up. They were stepping on mines. The place was lousy with them. We lost a lot of men that day by mines. All of a sudden someone shouted that tanks were coming. Thank God they were ours. The tanks and our artillery began to open up on the two farm houses. The Jerries had dugouts and ditches all around the houses. When the artillery and tanks started blasting the houses, the Krauts ran into the dugouts and ditches. When we quieted down they'd run back into the houses. That's when we had our picnic. We chopped them down by the dozens. It got so bad we were fighting over the machineguns to see who would knock them off. A lot of the guys were about crazy. They had lost good pals a few minutes before and wanted to kill as many Germans as they could. Pfc. Omar Smith was pushed away from his machinegun but he didn't fight for it. He picked up an M1 and killed six Jerries in about ten minutes. He got killed a little later on. They brought the dead off Mount Calvi for days after and I think they're still bringing them down. There were hundreds of dead Germans around those houses. When we came by the next day they were already beginning to stink. It'll be a long time before I forget what happened that day."

Sgt. Jesus Armendara, San Bernardino, California, is being congratulated for refusing to obey an order. "It was like this," said Jesus. "Me and my pal, John Flores, were in this foxhole and the lieutenant behind us to our right rear gave the order to cease firing. He didn't see the platoon of Jerries going up the hill toward us. John and me did. I had this machinegun and I cut loose and John M-oned the bastards. The Jerries kept on going for a few seconds before they realized what was hitting them. They started to scatter, but it was too late. The lieutenant was swearing at the top of his voice at us. But we just kept firing. I think we got that whole platoon. At least no more of them went up the hill. You see, the lieutenant just couldn't spot them up the hill. I was right in disobeying that order, don't you think?"[7]

At 0430, 16 September, all three battalions of the 362nd Infantry attacked. The 3rd Battalion moved quickly north until it reached the huge antitank ditch that cut across Highway 65. Here the battalion stopped and sent patrols into Santa Lucia.

The 2nd Battalion moved out toward Hill 840 but descending the sheer northern slope of Mount Calvi made for slow going and called for the qualities of a mountain goat and Superman, as the division history put it. Moving from Calvi to Hill 821 and Hill 840 involved some of the most difficult fighting the regiment had yet encountered.

S/Sgt. George M. Morris was still among the survivors of Company G:

"It was raining and we were pinned down on top of Hill 821, I think it was. Fred Geison came up to me and said, 'I want to borrow your tommygun. I'm going with Sergeant Owens and I want you to watch my platoon. We're going to try and get some help and get out of this hopeless situation.' We were right on top of the hill when all of a sudden, through the rain, we saw the Krauts jumping up from their positions where they had been shooting at us and they started running back away from us. Here I had this platoon I didn't want and I said, 'Come on, we're going to follow them!' Everyone hollered that I was crazy. But I said, 'No for God's sake, they're going to shell the hell out of us. We don't have much time!' They quit arguing with me and we all ran after the Krauts and sure enough we had no more than cleared the area when the 88s came pouring in. They were getting their people out so they wouldn't hit them while they were shelling us. They didn't get us because we were right behind them. We started going down the face of the mountain which would have been the north side of 821. It was steep as hell. The backside of the mountain had a lot of small trees on it. We dropped in elevation about one hundred or one hundred and fifty feet and then it started to get hot. It had stopped raining and was really muggy. We found a little clearing in among the trees which were two to two and one half inches in diameter. When we were settled in the clearing it turned out that we only had about twenty men, in both outfits. We were that far down in strength. It was so hot and so sultry and the barometric pressure so low that everyone almost immediately went to sleep. I posted guards then I went to sleep and when I woke up I noticed everybody was asleep! I went around kicking guys and said, 'We've got to stay awake! We've got to stay awake!' Pretty soon all the men were aroused and I told them, 'Punch the other guy. Keep each other awake or we'll all get killed in this damn mess!' I was standing close to Sergeant Noce who was one of our squad leaders and I could hear someone coming toward the clearing that we were in, just one step at a time. It sounded like a German scout. Here I had Fred's carbine and I couldn't for the life of me remember when the damned carbine was on safety or when it was on ready. I was switching the safety back and forth and we were in such a position that we didn't want to move or make any noise whatsoever. There was absolute silence. Everybody could hear the steps. I whispered in Noce's ear, 'If that guy comes in and I don't kill him, you be sure you kill the son of a bitch.' 'OK', said Noce. We waited and waited and finally a big bull stuck his head into the clearing! Well, the tension was relieved for a little while.'"[8]

The regimental plan for the capture of Futa Pass called for a pinchers movement. The 1st Battalion would attack and take Mount Gazzaro, then move northwest along the ridge to come in from the east. The 3rd Battalion would assault from the southwest. The jump off was to take place at 0430 but supplying the 1st Battalion proved extremely difficult. The 3rd Battalion was slowed by mortar and long range machinegun fire. At 0830 Companies K and L were west of Santa Lucia. Division and Corps artillery had shelled the village so effectively that the forward German troops were all but cut off from supplies. A number of enemy gun positions were also destroyed including a Panther turret which commanded the valley approach.

During the day, Company K captured Santa Lucia while Company L moved along the pine-covered slopes west of Highway 65. By dusk it had outposts in the pass itself. Futa Pass had been entered but not until the afternoon of 22 September when Hill 952, west of the highway, was taken was the 3rd Battalion assured of the complete control of the terrain.

To the 362nd Infantry had fallen the honor of liberating Futa Pass which more

Pietramala. Division encampment in the palace yard.

than any other was a symbol of the Gothic Line. However, some of the credit was also given to the 346th Field Artillery Battalion which so ably assisted the infantry. Captain Charles E. Brown who commanded C Battery describes some of the work done by the Battalion in and around the pass:

"During the drive for Futa the fighting became so intense that the 346th fired approximately 5,000 rounds a day in support of the 362nd Infantry. After days of heavy fighting the initial zone of antitank ditches, reinforced concrete pillboxes and blockhouses was penetrated, leaving the Division facing the natural fortifications of the steep, rocky, forested mountainsides. Here the Germans were dug into caves and bunkers to withstand our artillery and mortar fire. When the artillery was lifted so the infantry could advance, the Germans popped out of their holes to man their various weapons. To counteract this, Captain Robert Scott, our Liaison Officer to the 1st Battalion, 362nd, proposed a World War I type of 'rolling barrage'. In such barrages our infantry follows close to the lower edge of the bursts of the artillery concentrations which are moved forward on schedule with the infantry moving close behind the artillery bursts so as to be on top of the defenders before they can leave their caves and bunkers to man their weapons. This technique was employed and was highly successful.

"By 24 September, the leading elements of the Division had captured Futa Pass and were moving towards Monghidoro. The batteries of the 346th were firing at approximately 6,000 yards. Although with Charge 7 the 105 can reach out 12,500 yards, a little over six miles, it is most effective at ranges between 3,000 and 6,000 yards and we did our best to stay within those ranges. At this point we had a real problem. The terrain was so rugged between our positions and Futa Pass that it was not possible to find suitable artillery positions for that zone. The nearest available ones were just through the pass in the southern approaches to the town. Unfortunately, these 'nearest' positions were within 600 to 800 yards of the German front lines and they had perfect observation on any movement in the area from a prominent peak which rose sharply to the left of the pass. Nevertheless, in order to give our infantry the best possible support, it was determined to make the move. Colonel Barry assigned position areas to the Batteries and the Battery Commanders selected specific positions. They moved from the old to the new position was made that afternoon. A fact that did not escape the attention of the German forward observers. Battery C had just pulled off the road and Lt. Aickin was directing the howitzer sections into position when the Germans started raining 120mm mortar shells down on us. There was a wild scramble for ditches, holes or any slight depression in the earth. Corporal Bob Kaempf, the Firing Battery Recorder, was close by Lt. Aickin. Simultaneously, they both spotted a heaven-sent haven of safety - a German slit trench, or at least what appeared to be one. They tumbled in in great haste only to discover their slit trench had been a German field latrine. They took instant note of this but gave no thought to leaving their shelter until the shelling had subsided. Looking up they could see the give away as to the nature of the trench. A low log rail positioned two feet above the ground on two upright logs was right at the edge of the trench. In contemplating their decision in calmer times, they concluded that even had they seen the rail, they would have sought the shelter. No one who was there at the time has ever argued with that conclusion."[9]

On 24 September the 362nd Regimental CP moved into Passo della Futa while the 316th Engineers struggled to rebuild Highway 65 and the secondary roads to be used as supply routes. Later in the day word came down that the Regiment was to be relieved by the 363rd Infantry. The great Futa had been conquered along with Mount Calvi, Mount Alto and Hill 840 though many men had fallen in the draws, valleys and on the mountainsides.[10] On 25 September Colonel Cotten sent word to all his men:

"You are now in Futa Pass which you have captured. You did much more than your assigned mission; you decisively defeated the 4th Parachute Division and in doing so, captured the most important

Radiscosa Pass. The summit of the Northern Apennines. Late September, 1944. The building to the right is the old chalet.

feature of the GOTHIC LINE, the key to the PO VALLEY. When we reach that valley you can all know that YOU, the 362nd Infantry, unlocked the gate. Each member of the Regiment can take great pride in the job done and in the years to come all will be able to look back upon one of the most remarkable efforts of the American Army, in that on so broad a front you defeated such an enemy and took such dominating ground so cleverly defended."[11]

Early in the morning of 24 September the 363rd Infantry left its rest area near Villanova and trucked up the highway to the vicinity of the pass. Enemy shells were still dropping on the turnaround point on the highway, so the troops unloaded from the convoy and marched through the cold rain and fog arriving at the area at 1800. By the time the men began to form for the march to the lines, every man was soaked to the skin. And to add to the misery the Germans sent over a harrassing artillery barrage forcing the march column to hit the ground. After the shelling died away the men arose cold, muddy, wet, miserable and wretched, and swearing.

Along with first light came the horrendous weather for which Futa Pass was noted. A violent wind blew down from Radicosa and sheets of rain pelted the troops as they struggled toward Traversa. The wind reached such a velocity that many of the trees that had been weakened by shellfire toppled over blocking the highway and causing casualties. After reaching Traversa the 1st Battalion cut west of the road at Sasso di Castro, an enormous mountain of rock, and continued through the mud towards Mount Freddi, the first Regimental objective.

Sitting along the highway like sentinels in file were three huge mountains: Sasso di Castro, Mount Freddi and Mount Oggioli, the latter just northwest of the town of Pietramala. Across the highway a mile south of Pietramala was Mount Beni another formidable obstacle which was in the zone of the 361st Infantry fighting to the right of the 363rd. From the heights of these four mountains the Germans could prevent any forward movement of 91st Division troops up Highway 65.

At 1600, after a fifteen minute barrage laid down by Cannon Company, the 363rd jumped off. Companies A and B pursued the enemy over the rugged slopes and by 0630 the next morning, after a bitter night attack in the rain, both companies were on Mount Freddi having killed or captured eighty Germans. The 3rd Battalion then struck out for Mount Oggioli. By early afternoon on the 28th Company L and elements of the 361st Infantry had taken and outposted Oggioli. At 1620 that same day Company G, 361st had two platoons on top of Mount Beni. The 1st Battalion then moved forward and all units spent a quiet but cold and wet night on the mountain.

The capture of Mount Beni had been a miserable affair as remembered by a Company G trooper:

"The only route of approach was to go up a slight draw between two smaller hills then climb hand over hand up a loose rock wall some 20 feet high. Every time we took two steps we would slip back one. On this hill we had several trees for cover and we went around on the side on Beni before we were ever stopped. Once on Beni itself all we had for cover was rock—we would move from one to the other and all the while the machineguns were cracking around us. Beni is little more than just a big rock itself. On one side there is a

The rebuilt chalet at the peak of Radicosa.

rock wall 800 feet high. The only trees on the mountain were on the reverse slope and Jerry had that. At a spot about a hundred yards from the top the 3rd Platoon was separated into two groups—one to go around one way and the other to go around the other and meet them. Each section was about half way around when machineguns opened up at point blank range. The squad spread out and in a few minutes had killed or captured the 16 Jerries that were on top of the mountain—to the loss of one American. It was a hot fight while it lasted with the two groups so close that they had to hold grenades in their hands for a couple of seconds for fear the Germans would have time to throw them back. The Jerries had three light machineguns dug in for the protection of this hilltop and all we had were rifles and tommyguns. On top of Mount Beni there is a table like surface

The summit of Futa Pass today with its hotel and restaurant.

some 20 years square and on this was a pole some three feet high...somebody had the idea it was an artillery marker so we had to move on up and tear that down. At this point, Lieutenant Hagen, in charge of the Bn OP group, moved up to set up an OP on top of Beni to direct fire into Pietramala and into Germans positions on Mount Freddi. Late in the afternoon the mist began to clear and with the sun at our backs we could see some large buildings in the distance, an on looking closer with the glasses and as more of the mist blew away, Lieutenant Hagen found he was looking at the city of Bologna and part of the Po Valley."[12]

Pietramala is the last mountain town before Radiocosa Pass which has the highest elevation in the Futa range. An ancient town, Pietramala was an important stop along Highway 65 because it had its own customs station and travelers, over the centuries, were sometimes forced to spend their nights at the local inn which one Englishwoman described as "that single, solitary and wretched inn which tops one of the loftiest acclivities—the dreary hotel of Pietramala. The inn is the only habitation in this lonely spot and it is almost as striking within as the scenery is without. Its dark stone stairs and passages; its cells to sleep and common hall to eat in; its rude kitchen with a little forest blazing and hissing on the vast concave hearth; the gaunt figures and marked countenances of the attendants—all were pictures, and compensated in some degree for the want of more civilized accommodations which were missing."[13]

Though the Englishwoman may have considered her surroundings as miserable, the troopers of Company F, 361st who passed through Pietramala, would have given much for the comfort of the blazing hearth. One member recalled the capture of the town:

"Just after daylight and through a steady rain we moved up Highway 65 into Pietramala. The road leading into the town runs around and along the bottom of two hills and on the left of the road was a small wall. Above this wall leading up to the hills was a little wood. Most of the trees had either their tops blown off, cut into or chopped off at the ground from the artillery barrage of the day and night before. Sitting on the last curve before town was a Jerry SP gun that had taken a direct hit—the ammo was scattered all over the road. On the edge of town the first two buildings were completely torn down from shell fire. A small bridge had been blown and the road was full of shell holes with a few large bomb craters. We moved on into town and reorganized our company, in a large walled court yard. In this courtyard there was a huge building that Jerry had used to store supplies and house troops. On the first floor there were big piles of lumber and boxes of nails, a complete field kitchen and lots of communication equipment. On the second floor the rooms had double beds. These rooms were filled with parts of the roof that had poured in these holes leaving about two inches of water in the rooms. Several houses in the town were badly shot up—some torn down. At the north end of the town one house was being used as an ammo dump. One room was full of mortar ammo, and two rooms full of small arms and grenades. The Krauts had pulled out in a hurry. On the road leading out of town were two German trucks standing in the middle of the road—both unhurt in any way. One truck had several boxes of silk hose in it. All along the road you could see the Jerries personal equipment such as packs, belts, extra clothing and ammo that he was trying to get away from our artillery."[14]

A Company G man described the 361st advance out of Pietramala:

"About noon we moved out of Pietramala and up the road that leads into Radicosa Pass. The fog now was so thick we couldn't see more than a hundred yards and the wind was blowing the rain so hard we had trouble hearing what the man in front said. Along the road up to the pass we could see more signs of how fast the Germans had pulled out. Near the entrance to the pass was a Jerry ambulance that had taken a direct hit. It was laying on its side and couple of dead Germans were laying nearby. As we came down around the curve that leads into the pass we could see more of the damage done by our artillery—the trees were all torn down—several telephone poles were laying across the road. A big sign that read 'Passo di Raticosa' had been shot up. There were dead horses with carts still hitched to them. Dead Germans were laying on the road and in foxholes at the side of the road. One was standing up leaning against a side of the trench. He must have stood up just as a shell hit near him. While we were walking through the pass we were looking for Jerry to open up at any moment. We knew that all the Germans didn't have time to get out and that they must be somewhere up on the side of the hill in that fog. The fog worked both ways—we couldn't see them and they couldn't see us. We only found one German in the pass and he was ready to give up after a couple of shots. We moved on over Radicosa Pass into the village of La Posta where we got orders to hold for the night. We also learned we were to be relieved. We moved into some houses there and built fires because the fog was so thick the Jerries couldn't see the smoke. It was the first time we had had a chance to dry our clothes in days. After cold rations the eggs and chickens we found tasted pretty good. The only problem was wood. We solved that by burning the furniture and sitting on the floor."[15]

In the early hours of 29 September, the 362nd Infantry moved through the positions of the 361st and the latter regiment was quartered in assembly areas near Mount Beni where rehabilitation could be carried out. That same morning the 1st and 3rd Battalions of the 363rd continued the attack to the left of the 362nd. The 363rd plunged northward through a heavy fog. The weather continued wet, cold and wretched. The next objective of the 363rd was the huge 911 meter Montepiano or "Flat Mountain", a name that was terribly misleading. The mountain stood directly north of the town of Monghidoro. It commanded the entire area and was admirably suited for defense.

The actions of the 91st Division during the month of September were the most bitter yet for the Powder River men. The battles of October would be even worse.

Endnotes for Chapter Seven

1. Written by Lady Morgan in 1820 and published in Italy. Publication date unknown.
2. For a description of the old Roman Road on Monte Bastione see "Monte Bastione, the Roman Road, Futa Pass and Other Places" written by the author and published in the December, 1992 issue of *The Powder River Journal.*
3. Letter to the author, November 27, 1993.
4. Morris, George Martin. *The Replacement.* Independence, Mo. 1991. Pages 108-09.
5. Jack Bell was a war correspondent for the The Miami Herald and filed some excellent stories on the actions in Italy during the autumn of 1944. Some of these stories were later reprinted in *The Powder River Journal.* During World War I Bell served with the 363rd Infantry and lost an arm during the fighting in the Argonne Forest. Bell's stories are used with the permission of the Miami Herald.
6. Two days after being interviewed by Sgt. Scott. Czinki was killed in the action.
7. Reprinted in the *Powder River Journal.* December. 1987. Pages 44-45.
8. Morris. *The Replacement.* Pages 117-118.
9. Brown, Charles E. "Futa Pass. Pages 3-4
10. During the 17 day period from 10 September to 27 September, 1944 the 362nd Infantry suffered 656 battle casualties with 123 killed in action.
11. 362nd Infantry Regimental History. 25 September, 1944.
12. Livengood. *Thunder in the Apennines.* Page 118.
13. Lady Morgan.
14. *Thunder in the Apennines.* Page 119.
15. Ibid. Page 120.

Hqs. Staff, 316th Engineers. Sgt. Moran, Corporal Mayo, Sgt. Festerman and Major Wolfe.

CHAPTER EIGHT —
HEADED NORTH ON SIXTY-FIVE

"Against the mountains the shells burst and exploded and the reverberations, swelling, rising, ringing, gradually diminishing, then growing again, tying in with the sounds of the newer shells, then dying away, rolled night and day.

"It was a heartbreaking sound, a distressing sound, a fear-filled sound, and yet, sometimes a beautiful sound, piling up, surging, then fading away. The guns worked from the roadsides, in the valleys, in the mountains, on the hills, from saddles and crevices, from bridge abutments and dooryards and river beds. They splashed shells everywhere tracking the enemy. They disrupted communications and destroyed buildings and wounded men and killed men and caused other men to go out of their minds with terror. Their shells and ours, in turn.

"The guns accompanied all our efforts, day after day, we who were hemmed in by our own weariness and ignorance, taking each hill or house or road or town as it came, and, always, carrying out our wounded. Down the innumerable mountain paths, across the many streams, along bare paths, along mined paths, along wooded and ever-descending paths, beneath hot skies and in the falling rain, waiting and waiting, and finding in our exhaustion, now and then, that we had come either too slowly or too late."

—John A. Lynch. "In Emilia, at Melpomene".

I

Radicosa Pass is a rocky, gloomy, bleak and desolate place. Even during the clear days of summer, which are a rarity, the winds blow loud and cold down through the valleys. Beginning with the autumn rains, the peak becomes shrouded with fog and remains so throughout the long months of winter and into early spring. On those rare summer days one can stand along Highway 65 and look towards Monghidoro and out over the northern range of the Apennine mountains which stretch to the horizon, then one can turn around and view the same scene of the southern range, looking down on Pietramala: mile after mile of canyons, ridges, precipices, slopes, gullies, tributary streams, bluffs and hills, with the ever present winds howling and gusting, sweeping the grass and blowing through the branches of the pines and firs, and the highway, looping and curling, winding and bending.

This was to be the terrain for the next thirty miles to the very outskirts of the city of Bologna.

The troops of the 91st Division were now over the 968 meter pass and moving slowly north. They had captured four huge mountains that had barred their advance up the highway: Sasso di Castro, Mount Freddi, Mount Beni and Mount Oggioli, but many more lay ahead and the difficulty of securing these increased with the coming of October rain, mist and haze.

After the fall of Radicosa Pass the Germans fell back four miles to a line of defense that crossed the highway at the town of Monghidoro. This little village was to be the objective of the 362nd. During the night of 29 September the regiment crossed the line of departure and jumped off at 0730 the next morning. A thick fog lay over the mountains which made a rapid advance virtually impossible but the men slogged their way over the hills, taking the little winter resort town of La Posta, then working their way onward to Monghidoro to take a heavily fortified hill called 852.

Although the Division artillery fired 10,587 rounds to support the attack on Monghidoro only minimum gains were made on 1 October. The next morning the 3rd Battalion cut Highway 65 to the north of the village while the 2nd Battalion captured the high ground overlooking the Idice River Valley to the east. Meanwhile, Company C, supported by nine tanks of the 755th Tank Battalion and two platoons of tank destroyers, fought its way into Monghidoro and cleared the streets house by house. The S-3 Journal of the 755th recorded the actions of those desperate days:

"Sunday, 1 October. Pietramala, Italy.

"Company C moved two platoons of tanks from Selva to assist the 916th Field Artillery. The position was very difficult to get into and two tanks threw their tracks and were unable to get out. By 0400 we had eight tanks in position. Everybody was in a big rush to have every available gun firing for the 91st Division attack today. The weather was very bad. The tanks fired missions throughout the day. Because of the rains the road to our Company C guns is impassable. Company B is supporting the 362nd Infantry which is driving straight up Highway 65.

It was quite an exciting time to keep so many people happy during this god-awful weather and the lovely terrain."

"Monday, 2 October. Pietramala, Italy.

"Rainy weather. Visibility nil. Company B sent one platoon of tanks into Monghidoro which is an enemy strong point. The fog was so thick the gunners could not see their sights. The tank commanders directed fire from the turrets and great work was done which saved a few of the lives of the infantry. When we entered the town we caught the Germans off guard and the 362nd captured two enemy tanks along with a couple of SP guns, including the crews. The weather could not have been worse. At 1700 we got into the town and set up two road blocks and A and C fired indirect fire. Our supply problem is serious due to the bad roads and I don't know if we will ever get any damned supplies. Major Fowler received word that he will be sent back to the General Staff School at Fort Leavenworth, Kansas in the one and only good U.S.A. What a break! Company B had one man seriously wounded by artillery fire in Monghidoro. The CO of the 362nd wants all tanks available to go into the town. Some people do not understand common sense! One platoon is ample."[1]

A platoon from the 91st Reconnaissance Troop, entering the village from the north, knocked out a machinegun position and captured 29 Germans who had hidden in a house. By late afternoon 2 October, Monghidoro belonged to the 362nd.

It was a difficult struggle for the 364th Field Artillery to get into firing position to back up the 362nd because the roads were a quagmire. After much winching and cursing the battalion moved through the mud to just southwest of Monghidoro. The position, in an open field, was still strewn with the results of the fighting. Many dead Germans and a few Americans were sprawled grotesquely about the still green meadow. The town itself was a shambles. The battalion CP was set up in a barn near an old stone house that sheltered a group of Italians who, that very day, had witnessed a family tragedy. Several of its young men had refused to work for the Germans. As a result, the men and six others were found in a house in Monghidoro with their heads bashed in by rifle butts.

Monghidoro was discovered to be the straw hat center of Italy and many pieces of assorted headgear were in evidence after men of the 362nd had been in the town for a few hours.

After the village was clear a few troopers of the 755th Tank Battalion got their belongings together and bedded down in one of the houses on the main street. As inspection of the house revealed several bodies had been left by the enemy in an adjoining room, so the tankers took another room and laid down to rest. When morning came it was discovered that the "dead" bodies were a dozen Jerries very much alive but fast asleep.

Radicosa Pass. Looking out across the valley towards Monte Oggioli.

On the 363rd Infantry front, the regiment was preparing to assault Montepiano. The plan for the downfall of the mountain called for two battalions on line and one in reserve. The 2nd Battalion was to make the main effort while the 1st assisted in the attack.

To defend Montepiano, the Germans had set up a number of outposts in several small villages and farmhouses surrounding the mountain which looked out across the wide valley of the Savena River. This broad expanse of ground was sliced into large sections made by the tributaries of the river. Swollen by the recent heavy rains, these streams tumbled and roared through channels whose banks were often 50 feet high. Only at certain places could the men of the 363rd cross. Everyone of these approaches was zeroed in by the enemy.

The 2nd Battalion, now under the command of Lt. Col. John W. Angell, jumped off at 0600, 1 October. The leading companies, E and G, quickly attained their objectives. Company F was then called up from its reserve position and joined the fight at Villa de Mezzo. The 2nd Platoon received orders to move out and clear the ground for the advance of the company up a slope that had been the scene of bitter fighting two days before. This slope climbed toward Monghdoro and was wooded with a heavy growth of evergreen trees. After an unopposed advance of some 400 yards the platoon leader, suspecting a trap, halted his men.

The regimental history narrates the actions:

Monghidoro under fire.

"Heavy casualties had occurred in Company F during the previous week and many men were recent replacements who were seeing only their third or fourth day of combat. As the 2nd Platoon moved forward its leading elements were hit by a burst of machinegun fire which killed the squad leader who was only one of two men with more than a few day's battle experience. Realizing the squad leader was dead, the platoon leader asked the shaken men if anyone wanted to take over. After a short silence, Pvt. Howard E. Weaver, who had been with the company for three days, answered back, 'I'll take over, sergeant. I know what to do.' Weaver quickly moved to the front. Entering a clump of bushes, he

Monghidoro. The town was captured by the 362nd Infantry on 2 October along with 103 prisoners.

Monghidoro today. The road sign at the right is approximately the spot where the 362nd soldier dug his foxhole.

located a well-concealed enemy machinegun emplacement, crawled to within 35 feet of it, pulled the pin out of a grenade and let fly. The grenade rolled into the position and exploded, killing one German and wounding another. The squad continued up the hill. Near the crest, Weaver and his men came to a road which looked like good cover for his men. Here he spotted a sniper in one of the trees and killed the German with his M1. Continuing onward, the squad came to a house at the top of the ridge, the company objective. Weaver entered the house and found two more snipers whom he captured, making a total of two killed and five prisoners taken by the private in the short time he assumed command of the squad. Weaver was awarded the Distinguished Service Cross for his actions and was later given a battlefield commission.

The 1st Platoon, under the command of S/Sgt. Ernest L. Johnson, had gone forward with the 2nd in its fight up the slope and, after taking a little group of houses to the east of the hill, the men went inside to investigate. In the kitchen they found wood burning in the stone fireplace. In a metal pot, hanging over the fire, was water coming to a boil. On the table was a chicken all cleaned and ready for the pot. To the ever hungry GIs, who had been existing on a diet of K rations, this was manna from heaven. Shortly after the meal was finished, a German runner who was obviously unaware of the presence of the Americans, came into the house with a message. He was promptly captured. While the men of Company F were resting and savoring their chicken, the guards outside the house spotted a loaded enemy pack train of three mules moving down the road.

"This was a sight.' Sergeant Johnson said. 'We knocked down one mule and saw a second take off. Two Krauts were trying to get the third mule across an open field to some cover. One man was dragging on the reins for all he was worth, while the other was pushing the mule just as hard from the rear. They couldn't budge him. We soon put a stop to that. After we had eliminated the Jerries the mule made its way down the slope to our position—so we took it prisoner, too.'

"When inventory was taken the mule had donated 56 cans of salmon and sardines, 30 loaves of bread, 3 gallons of butter and several cans of beef—all to the Allied cause. They were divided up between the squads and the mule was given water for its service. The German runner was offered some of the captured rations, but he refused saying he'd been eating enough of that stuff. He chose a K ration."[2]

As the attack continued on north, Company F ran into a German outpost barricaded in a group of buildings midway between it and Montepiano and a fierce firefight began that lasted all the rest of that day and far into the night until the enemy pulled back the next morning.

The company then pushed forward with Company E and by the middle of the afternoon 2 October, the battalion was slowly forming a ring around the mountain. As darkness closed in so did Company G from the south, Company F from the southwest and Company E from the east, behind a curtain of artillery fired by the 347th. At 2100, Company G radioed it was atop that mountain and had made contact with the other two companies. Montepiano was then secured against counterattack.

Resistance was light along Highway 65 on 3 October as the Germans withdrew to their next line of defense. Both the 362nd and 363rd Infantry drove forward to within one mile of Loiano before dark, an advance of nearly three miles. Italian civilians had been put to work constructing a strong natural line of

defense through the village. Four miles further on was a third such line that ran through the town of Livergnano; another four miles up the highway was yet another line that passed through Pianoro which was on the outskirts of Bologna. As soon as one of these lines was penetrated, the enemy would fall back to the next and the 91st Division would be forced to regroup for another attack.[3]

II

The first phase of the II Corps' October drive for Bologna closed on 4 October. During those four days the Corps front was pushed northward four miles or one mile per day. A total of 858 prisoners were taken and enemy killed and wounded were thought to be very high. The Corps casualties were 1,734 in the four line divisions: the 34th, 85th, 88th, and 91st.[4] On the basis of these figures and the character of the October battles the Fifth Army brass anticipated that II Corps would reach the Po Valley before the October rains turned to snow. As they had been since the invasion of Salerno a year before, the officers of Fifth Army were, once again, overly optimistic.

By 4 October the 91st Division was poised to renew the attack though the fighting had never ceased.

Highway 65 runs directly through Loiano which clings to the side of a mountain called Bastia. Upon entering the town, the highway becomes the main street, Via Roma, then exits at the north end and

The main street of Monghidoro today with the church in the background. In rebuilding the town, the people constructed a very wide street and so it differs from the other villages with their narrow, crowded medieval streets.

continues on toward Livergnano. The west side of Loiano is open and so was under observation from enemy occupied peaks to the north. From the top of Bastia one can see out over the Zena River Valley and, far in the distance, the famous observatory tower of the University of Bologna which is dedicated to the Italian astronomer, Gian Domenco Cassini, who died in 1712. This tower was to become yet another landmark for all veterans of the Division.

General Livesay's scheme to capture Loiano was to keep both the 362nd and 363rd Infantry on line and also bring in the 361st, thus all three regiments would be in combat. Once the town was secured the 362nd would swing west and pinch out the 363rd which would go into division reserve, then together the two other regiments would drive on Livergnano.

Prisoner of War Reports indicated the 4th Parachute Division was dug in on the slopes of Mount Bastia and along the high ground stretching eastward to the zone of the 85th Division. One POW reported there were fifty Germans and six machineguns inside Loiano. During the night of 3 October the 362nd Infantry had estimated at least one hundred enemy were in the town. On the morning of that same day, SS troops in Loiano had rounded up all the male citizens they could find and had taken them to Bologna. Twenty trucks were parked near Pianni but no one knew exactly why.[5]

The 4th Parachute was becoming an old foe to the men of the 362nd. They had met in a furious battle on Mount Calvi. Now, they would meet again at Loiano. A captured German soldier of the 2nd Company, 12th Parachute Regiment told his captors that Field Marshal Kesselring had said, "I shall hold in Italy even if I have to go back to Berlin with a box car full of dog tags."[6]

The weather report for the next three days of October was, "Scattered showers over high ground.

Visibility good. Winds moderate southerly becoming westerly. Some fair periods but occasional showers and periods of rain."[7]

Beginning at 0548, 5 October, the Division Artillery began a concentration of 1,000 rounds in twelve minutes on the enemy defenses across the 91st Division front. At 0600, the three regiments attacked.

Captain Fred W. Booth was the commander of Company L, 362nd. He had been ordered to go in and take Loiano.

"Of course we relish beautiful, sunny days in combat. It is more comfortable to fight and die in the sunshine. Even in the first light of day 5 October, 1944, we could see it would be a beautiful day. Warm. No wind. The sky to the east, all clear. As we moved out I could hear the thunder of a monstrous artillery barrage somewhere east of us and it roared on for several minutes. American artillery. I could tell by the massive sound of it. Our guys on the right must have run into trouble early.

"Our objective this day was Mount Bastia maybe two miles north along Highway 65. Bastia was strongly defended, according to our battalion headquarters. My company was to attack it from the southwest, K Company from the southeast. Orders always make things sound so simple.

"Because we had fought along Highway 65 for several weeks, Company L had considerable experience fighting through small towns and we had found that hand grenades were the most effective weapon. The night before, when I saw Loiano looming large on my map, I called battalion and ordered up all the grenades they had in stock.

"We moved out that morning with hand grenades hanging all over every man. We moved out from high ground overlooking the highway, ground we had taken from some very stubborn Germans the day before. We moved fast past several dead bodies and a badly wounded enemy soldier who looked at us helplessly and hopelessly. Had we known he was there we would have picked him up the night before. One of our medics attended to him now. Not much life left in him, I thought. After all the casualties Company L had suffered in Futa Pass and the days following, we couldn't work up much sympathy for a wounded enemy soldier.

"We continued slowly northward along the west side of the highway in a column of platoons with two scouts about a hundred yards ahead. This company had been in brutal combat for seven or eight days in a row. We were tired. We were not in a hurry to get anyplace. And we expected small arms fire and artillery any second. When not in contact with the enemy I preferred to move in a column of platoons. I had better control and I could quickly move one or both of the rear platoons right or left into action when we hit an enemy stronghold. This morning we hit one almost immediately. Our rear platoon had just barely started moving

Roland Smith, Hqs. 316th Engineers, gazes at several German crosses that mark the graves of enemy dead.

in the column when the scouts and lead platoon came under small arms fire from high ground directly ahead, maybe two hundred yards. Then came the artillery, a storm of shells for a couple of minutes. No damaged except for our blood pressure. That shot up a notch.

"The platoon leader moved up the scouts, through the artillery barrage. While hugging the ground, we examined the enemy position very carefully and decided it was an isolated stronghold with few Germans. Probably one of the hit and run units we ran into so often along Highway 65. They used vehicles which they hid along the side of the road. They occupied high ground with good fields of fire. They opened fire as we approached, hit us with artillery and, as soon as we deployed to attack, they would head for their vehicles and disappear. This was a very effective delaying tactic and it cost us casualties almost every time. My standard solution was to circle a platoon around their flank. When they saw the platoon coming in on their rear, they took off, usually with an outburst of small arms fire.

"That's what happened this day, but it took an hour or more to deploy the company, move a platoon around the flank, and then slowly attack up the hill using text book fire and movement tactics. As usual, the German were gone. Our guys reported a German vehicle heading up the road toward Loiano. Luckily, we had no casualties this time. All we lost was about an hour and a half. Good thing for America it wasn't paying us by the hour.

"It took another half hour to reorganize the company and move out. This time, with my runner and radio man, I stayed up with the scouts. I was anxious to get a look at Loiano. I expected big trouble there. The scouts always got a big kick out of it when I moved along with them ahead of the company.

"Hey captain, better be careful. It's dangerous up here in the front lines."

"Somebody has to keep you guys from losing the way."

"Gosh, if we knew how to lose the way, we sure would."

"I was always amazed how loose our guys were most of the time. We were all combat weary. We had just come through a testy artillery barrage and some frightening small arms fire. We knew we faced a big battle ahead. We expected a huge artillery barrage any moment. But these guys still kept wise-cracking along. When you know that the next second may be your last second on this earth, maybe the only way to handle it is with a wise crack. Wise cracks can cover up a lot of fear. Once under fire, however, our guys were all business.

Loiano fell to the 362nd Infantry 5 October. After that date it served as a focal point for troops moving into the Winter Line. Although the town was nearly destroyed by our artillery, the Germans continued to plaster it until the spring offensive.

"Suddenly we were looking at Loiano, a typical Italian town with stone buildings and narrow streets, but very beautiful and graceful the way it was built into a mountain on the east. We moved very slowly. Less than a half mile away now. Still no artillery. I stopped and knelt behind a small rise in the ground. Studying the town through glasses, I was surprised at all the action, especially where the highway ran through the town. The road was alive with German soldiers moving in and out of buildings, crossing the street, moving up and down the road. They acted as if we were not around, but they must have known where we were. I couldn't figure out what all the action was about.

"My radio man poked me. 'Major Coleman on the radio, sir.'

"Major Coleman was battalion S-3. 'Yes, sir, Major.'

"'Division headquarters intelligence just called to warn you of a huge concentration of Germans in Loiano.'

"We're looking at them,' I said. And I'm thinking, the only time in this war that I get intelligence information from higher headquarters, I already know it.

"'Well,' Major Coleman said, 'division advises that we proceed cautiously.'

Loiano. A photographer catches the exact moment of a shell burst.

The Loiano church, San Jacobe e Marguerita, in pre-war days before it was destroyed.

The restored church and plaza, a meeting place for townspeople.

And I thought, how the hell do you know that? But being very young and very cocky, I said, 'Major, call the Germans and warn them that we're going in.'

"And he said, 'That's about what I thought you'd say.

"I called up the platoon leaders and we lay there for several minutes looking at Loiano and all those soldiers hustling about. Strange. How should we attack this place? Maybe there's more of them than there is of us. I knew we had massive amounts of artillery on call and it was zeroed in all over town. I had direct radio contact with an artillery lieutenant who was itching to pull the trigger. I also knew that I did not want to get trapped in those buildings. This was something we had drilled into our men since last July when a patrol from another battalion had been trapped in a building and captured. Don't get trapped in buildings. That was gospel. You can't fight out of buildings. You can't run, you can't retreat, you can't maneuver, you can't see. So I wanted a base of firepower that could move outside the village and be able to fire into it while the rest of our guys inside the village moved from building to building, throwing hand grenades and shooting anything that moved. Loiano set up perfectly for that tactic.

Highway 65 seemed to be the main street and it ran along the west edge of

A division chaplain holds services in the rubbled Loiano church. October, 1944.

town. Buildings hugged the east side of the highway. Going east, each street paralleling the highway was higher and higher up the hill so the buildings up there all looked down on the buildings below. Those buildings seemed to be built right into the hill and a row of buildings lined the top of the ridge overlooking everything. I worried about those houses because from there the enemy had a perfect view of everything we did until we got up against the wall of the first building. My worries proved to be deadly right.

"On the west side of the highway there were no houses as far as I could see through the town. A platoon could move along the west side of Loiano completely free of buildings and be able to cover the highway with small arms fire. It could also cover the doors and windows of buildings facing the highway as well as windows of buildings on up the hill. So I ordered the third platoon and weapons platoon to move to the west outside of Loiano and to follow along as the rest of us moved through the buildings. Those two platoons must also be ready to cover tanks coming down the highway with small arms fire to keep them buttoned up. We had found early in combat that enemy tankers became very nervous when they had to run buttoned up. They had very limited vision and, from their actions, we decided they feared what might be going on that they couldn't see.

"While those two platoon moved into position, the rest of us crept closer to the first building in town until we reached a low bank that gave us some protection to the front. It was then I noticed the streets were empty. No enemy in sight. Suddenly a ghost town. Where had all the Germans gone? Our two western platoons were now in position. I was about to call for artillery and rush two squads across open ground to the protection of the walls of the first building. This was a run of about a hundred yards. I didn't fear fire from the front because the buildings had no windows facing us and we could keep the Germans off the streets with small arms fire.

"Suddenly a man appeared on the highway maybe a hundred yards into town. Through my glasses I could see that he was a civilian, an old man. Rifle shots sounded, probably from the western platoons, and he went down. I was momentarily sorry but also pleased to know that these platoons had control of the highway. We later found that the man was a civilian and very old, probably confused. He was the only civilian we saw that day.

"Now I called for artillery. I always had respect for our artillery, but this was something special. Unbelievable! Awesome! Hell delivered by air express! Suddenly that town blew up under what must have been hundreds of shells. Buildings shattered. Buildings falling. Smoke, dust, debris rising over the town. All of this happening immediately in front of us with an agonizing thunder that numbed the eardrums. Two squads of the first platoon sprinted to the first building on main street. One man went down and didn't move. Another doubled over, went down, struggled forward and fell. Two of our men came back and helped him to the wall, all the time under fire. That small arms fire had to be coming from buildings up on the ridge. I

139

The 91st Infantry Division Monument in Loiano. It sits in a small park along the Via Marconi.

called the artillery lieutenant. 'Can you cover those buildings on the ridge?' He could and he did. Under that barrage we turned two squads of the second platoon loose up the hill into the eastern part of the village. They covered the open ground without trouble. Shortly after that we sent in the rest of the first platoon to take the first street paralleling main street.

"I stayed behind with one squad from the second platoon watching the action ahead, ready to cover our company from the rear in case the Germans tried to slip in behind us. I still worried about all those Germans we had seen in town. The first platoon was now maybe five buildings up main street, throwing hand grenades through doors and windows where buildings were still standing. Four of our men lay flat on the highway looking forward, rifles ready. They had the drop on any enemy soldier who tried to step out of a doorway or out from a corner of a building to fire on us. Two of our guys came out of a doorway herding four prisoners. They forced them down on the side of the road. Another of our guys came around a corner with two more prisoners. He stayed to guard the six prisoners.

"All we had to do was keep on going, hand grenade after hand grenade, building after building. But not so simple. What we all dreaded now showed up, a tank. Truly a frightening sight. No matter where you are that big gun seems to be looking right at you. German soldiers moved behind the tank. An enemy head looked around from the top of the tank. But that head ducked down quickly so I assumed our western platoons were pouring fire on the tank. And the soldiers behind it suddenly dispersed, some running back up the highway. I was very happy that we had sent those platoons out on the eastern flank. The tank fired two quick shots, mostly in fear, I think. It obviously was not aiming at anything. The shells screamed over our heads, a frightening sound, but we were too busy to be frightened. The tank kept inching forward, buttoned up. Suddenly, a head appeared out of the turret, looking for targets. I think one of our guys got him because the head slumped down and they disappeared. Immediately the tank backed up out of sight after sending a couple of more shells screaming down the street and out into someplace. I'll bet we could have jumped up and touched those shells, they sounded that close to our heads.

'Now the Germans came after our western platoons with artillery. I could see the shells exploding out there. A call came in on the platoon radio. Usually those radios did not work very well. This call came through clear from the third platoon leader. And he reported, "We can see a lot of German troops pulling out of town heading north on Highway 65."

"How about the tank?'

"We got the son-of-bitch looking out. It's gone!'

"Are you getting hit?'

"Not yet. Shells are falling behind us and west of us. We're going to move up now to the north end of Loiano.'

"Okay.'

"The ground is very rough. We should be able to find good positions to defend against counter attacks.'

"How cool he sounded. Thank God for experienced platoon leaders. With the remaining squad I now moved into the village. We seemed to be in complete control. The first platoon had left two men to guard fourteen prisoners lying face down on the road. We found a dead Company L man in a doorway and another Company L man lying dead around a corner of a building. Farther up the street our medics were treating half a dozen wounded Company L men. Those wonderful medics!

"I saw a lot of dead Germans lying around inside buildings and around the corners of buildings I caught up with the platoon leader where the highway headed out of town. We could still hear hand grenades exploding as the second platoon swept through eastern Loiano and up the hill. We figured the battle was over. But it wasn't. Somebody yelled, 'Tank!' Down the road toward us it came, several hundred yards away, running buttoned up. It was flanked on each side by what looked like a hundred German soldiers running and shooting. The tank launched a couple of those big shells over our heads. They exploded in buildings behind us. Frightening, yes, but we knew they were firing wildly. Those Germans never had a chance. Our western platoons opened with a tremendous barrage of small arms fire and the enemy melted away. Some hit the ground. Some were hit. Many of them turned and ran. And the tank backed up until it was out of sight.

"Loiano belonged to us. How long did it take? About three hours from the time we sent our platoons around the west flank. I'm sure glad we did that. And I'm sure glad the Germans chose to stay in the village rather than fight us from the wide open ground to the west.

"Now we could no longer see the retreating enemy. No tank, either. But that tank crew decided to go out with a bang. It fired a bunch of shells into the north side of town and we all hugged mother earth lovingly when they came in. Not much damage. Just a few more shattered buildings in what had once been a lovely, quiet, peaceful Italian town. Our men were stretched out along the highway heading north. Some were lying down, some sitting, some eating K rations, some smoking, some trying to heat coffee by burning ration boxes.

Personnel of the 346th's fire direction center line up outside a shell scarred CP.

I walked among them thanking them for a great job. They hardly looked up. They were tired, too tired to care about much of anything. I saw young faces with sweat running through the dirt, young eyes full of sadness. No wise cracking now. They had done a lot of killing and a lot of wounding. Some of their buddies had been killed and wounded. We lost four killed and seven wounded, all from one platoon.

"Two first platoon men came up to me. One of them said, 'Maybe it was our fault that Hanson got it.' "How come?'

'The three of us went into that room after throwing hand grenades. We thought it was all clear. Two Germans came from nowhere. One of them shot Hanson point blank. Then they dropped their rifles and put up their hands. We weren't taking prisoners then. We blasted their heads off.'

"You did great,' I said. Maybe talking about it made them feel better.

"I thought we had already done a pretty good day's work but we hadn't reached our objective, Mount Bastia. It was mid-afternoon, still a beautiful day. No more time to rest. Before dark we would meet that tank plus one more. Some of us would get badly shot up. More shattered bodies, them and us.

"By sundown we had fought our way almost to the top of Mount Bastia. Company K, after running into plenty of trouble of its own, came along on our right to help out. Shortly after dark we secured the top and set up a defensive position. We counted our dead and wounded and sent the count back to battalion headquarters. After a while rations came up. Ammunition came up. Orders from battalion came up for the next day's attack.

'There's another mountain up there named Casterllari. There's another village up ahead called Anconella. There are more Nazi soldiers up ahead. There are more tanks up ahead. Think about that and try to sleep on top of a very hard mountain.'"[8]

142

Pvt. Earl Schoelles of Company I followed Captain Booth's men into Loiano:

"Late in the afternoon of the 5th we began moving into the town. I remember, as we came into town, the rubble was piled high. We kept working our way up the main street. I was out front of the column crawling over the rocks and rubble, headed for the north side of the town. The Germans opened up on us and we finally had to pull back to the edge of town. It was beginning to get dark, fast. The sergeant picked me and three other guys and led us down the main street over all that rubble to the far side of town where we went inside a house. We were left there as an outpost. We took turns on guard as the rest of us tried to sleep. About midnight it was my turn at guard and shortly after I took over I heard German voices coming from somewhere. I was hoping all the time that the rest of the guys wouldn't wake up and make any noise to give us away. I prayed the Germans would get the heck out of there. They finally did.

"The next morning 6 October, our sergeant came up to our house and told us we were moving to the church on the other side of the town. From there we moved up the mountain and up to the very top of the ridge and started moving north. The Germans began shelling us and it continued as we walked up Highway 65. We stopped a short way up the road and I went into a house with a medic and a few guys from my squad. It was about 1100 hours. We could see out the windows in the back of the house and could see the men of Company L down in the valley. They were pinned down by artillery fire and the Germans were making it sheer hell for them. Finally we were ready to move again. I put on my pack, slung my rifle, went out the door and started up the highway. We had gone only about 50 yards when the shelling began again. I dropped to the ground. A few moments later I heard one of our guys yelling in the field opposite the road. I raised up on one knee to get a better look because a good buddy of mine was out in the field. At that instant, just as I went to drop back on the ground, a mortar shell exploded to my right. A piece of shrapnel entered the right side of my neck, traveled all the way across to the left side and went into my neck a couple of inches. Another piece tore through the calf of my left leg just below the knee joint. I screamed for a medic. It seemed it took him forever to get to me. I was bleeding badly. The stress at what was happening to me was almost unbearable. I was finally put into a jeep. I can't remember what happened before that. Maybe they carried me on a stretcher. I was taken back to the battalion aid station. I was hit around 1200 hours and by 1800 hours they had me on an operating table. Luckily we were along the highway. I owe my life to that medic. I wish I could recall his name. I recovered from my wounds in the 24th General Hospital in Leghorn."[9]

At 0959 6 October, the 363rd was ordered into Division reserve and the unpleasant task of moving on northward was left to the 361st and 362nd.

By 2100 both Company K and Company L were dug in on the slopes of Mount Bastia. At the end of the day, 6 October the 3rd Battalion was prepared to continue the offensive. In little more than twenty-four hours the Loiano line of defense had fallen.

Captain Charles E. Brown commanded Battery C of the 346th Field Artillery:

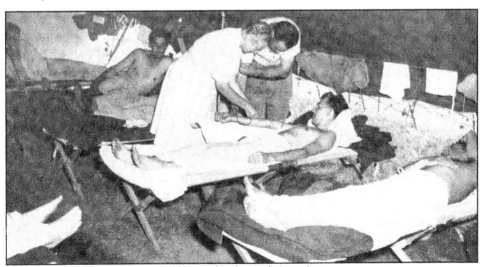

Field hospital in the North Apennines.

"Charlie Battery's next firing position was on the southerly outskirts of Loiano. The area assigned to the battery was on the right side of Highway 65 and was exposed to observation. Within our sector there was a spur ridge going in an easterly direction, almost at right angles to Highway 65. Placing the guns as near as possible to the base of the cross ridge offered as much screening from enemy observation as it was possible to get. Keeping in mind that it was always desirable to have as low a minimum elevation as possible, the guns could not be placed right at the base of this ridge. Minimum elevation is the lowest the gun tubes can be lowered without hitting the mask (trees, hills, buildings, etc.) ahead of the guns. Having a low minimum elevation provides maximum coverage out in the target area.

"By noon we had the howitzers in the Loiano position and had most of the other equipment out of the mud at Monghidoro. The Morning Report for the day reads, 'Position very muddy,' which indeed it was. But not as bad as Monghidoro. There did seem to be a bottom to it, mostly because there was a better drainage.

"The next day one of the Regimental Cannon Companies moved into position not more than fifty to seventy-five yards to our left flank and a little bit ahead. Their four cannons were sawed off 105's, with a lighter carriage and lighter trails. As twilight settled in some of the people in the cannon company built a rather large fire, much to the horror of Bill Aickin, Charlie Battery Executive Officer, and myself. I hastily made my way through the mud toward the bonfire to 'counsel' with the cannon company people. Surprisingly enough, the Company Commander was in the group around the fire. There was some question as to what sort of a reception I would get. When you're soaking wet and cold from rain and mud a fire feels mighty good. But the fire could not be tolerated. I got right to the point, explaining to the Cannon Company commander that the fire was like a neon sign and we could expect to be serenaded with country battery fire since the Germans had undoubtedly already seen the bonfire. The captain seemed unaware that the Germans were still on the peaks off our right flank. Having the information I had just conveyed to him, the Cannon Company commander ordered the fire put out.

"Unfortunately my prediction turned out to be more accurate that I really wanted it to be. The following day from 2345 to 0200 the general area was shelled off and on, most of the shells landing within our area, at least it seemed that way to us. Fortunately, we suffered only one casualty—one of the men in the ack-ack section. The low number of casualties was the direct result of our people being well dug in. Men of the Battery did suffer considerable loss in the way of shredded pup tents, clothing and gear. A farmer's straw stack behind the guns was mostly scattered to the winds.

Division sixbys in the mud near Sabbioni. October, 1944.

144

Men of Battery C, 347th Field Artillery. L-R. Capt. Mel Cotton, S/Sgt. Van Tassel, Cpl. Schelp, Muschatt, Owens, Urban, Powers, Lt. Root. Kneeling — Pfc. Takkinen, Pfc. Rohloff and Pfc. Tech.

"The Cannon Company moved out the next day, leaving us to sweat out the counter battery fire for three more days. If anyone had any question about whether we would receive any more counter battery fire, that question was answered by the Krauts that evening. They began to shell us about 2200.

"The shelling was not stretched out for as long a period as the night before, but the shell fire was more concentrated on our position area. In order to get as much personal protection as possible from the ridge ahead of us, I had dug in an army folding cot on the slope of the the ridge ahead of the line of guns, but roughly between the line of fire of the second and third howitzers. Nonetheless, it was a pretty noisy bivouac. Over this excavation I pitched my pup tent. That night the shells came right down the slope of the ridge close enough to snap the canvas of my tent like shaking a blanket. After the first time of that I rolled off my cot, sleeping bag and all, so as to get on the very bottom of the excavation and up against the uphill wall.

"When we were satisfied the shelling had ceased, I went down through the position to assess the damage. J.L. Coffey, one of the cannoneers in the Fourth Section, had been hit in the upper back and was evacuated. The damage other than that was more shredded clothing, pup tents and equipment.

"The rain continued and more and more we were fighting the mud. It was at this position that we received our issue of Shoepacs. This piece of foot gear was an exact replica of L.L. Bean's Maine hunting boot. The lower part was rubber and the upper part was leather. Three sets of felt insert pads and three sets of heavy wool ski-type stockings came with each set of boots. If you wanted to use one pair of heavy stockings, you would leave in all three pads. With two pair of stockings, you would leave in two pair of pads and with three pair of stockings, one pad. Those boots were heaven's answer to the water and mud. The combat boots we were wearing were the old army shoe with about a 5" leather cuff sewed to the top. The cuff was closed by two leather straps and two buckles. With those, your feet were wet most of the time in the water and mud we were encountering."[10]

The morning of 7 October dawned clear and bright and a radiant sun rose over the northern mountain range burning off the heavy fog that had rolled through the valleys the previous day. The first blue sky in more than ten days was a welcome sight to the men in the rain-soaked foxholes. The melancholy S-3 of the 755th Tank Battalion recorded the events of the day:

Saturday, 7 October—Del Boschi, Italy.
Company C tanks moving north to support the 361st Infantry. Clear sun shining today! A very unusual sight! Allied planes overhead, however they bombed and strafed our own infantry! It's a damned peculiar situation when our own planes cannot fly into enemy territory and drop their bombs. Our own troops fear our planes more than they do the Jerries because there are more of them. The infantry could not advance

because of the heavy resistance and because of the terrain. Traffic is moving up the highway continuously. 240mm guns moved into Loiano today. They can shoot into Bologna so the tempo is rising. We are now on high ground, however the terrain is rough and bottle-necked. The CO of the 804th TD Battalion came to the CP today more than a little miffed. There seems to be a misunderstanding in the use of armor between the regiment and the front line officers. There will be times when tanks and TDs can fire, but they say, 'No!' Well, "Cest la Guerre."[11]

At the end of the night attack of 6-7 October, the 362nd's 1st Battalion had succeeded in taking Hill 705 just to the south of Mount Castellari and the 3rd Battalion had pushed on to the village of Anconella. At 0800 the next morning both battalions jumped off, attacking without artillery support in an attempt to surprise the enemy on Castellari. All attacks failed due to the intense small arms, artillery and mortar fire.

Very early the next morning, at 0430, Colonel Cotton brought up the 2nd Battalion. The troops jumped off into the darkness and into the rain which had returned during the night.

Pvt. John Roice of Company G had recently joined the company as a replacement, just in time for the attack on Mount Castellari:

"Replacements were almost always used for scouts in an attack. This meant that the first scout was forty or fifty yards ahead of the rest of the platoon. The second scout was about ten yards behind the first scout. We were to the left of the highway attacking toward the mountain. As this was my first attack I was assigned as second scout. After moving forward a short distance we were pinned down in the middle of a brushy flat. Being pinned down away out in front of the rest of the platoon is a pretty lonesome feeling. Every time there was a movement, the Germans opened up with machinegun fire. Finally, we were able to move to the left and into a ravine. After a short while we could see smoke a mile or so down the ravine. The lieutenant said, 'Let's go see where that smoke is coming from.' So he took five of us and we moved down into the ravine to discover that the smoke was coming from a group of Italians who had moved off the road and set up camp in the trees to avoid the combat area. They told us that there was a machinegun nest on top of the hill in front of us and that the Germans came down every day for eggs or whatever else they could get. The lieutenant said, 'Well, let's go get 'em.' And we started up the hill through the timber. We had been moving very slowly all afternoon and it was now near sundown. The lieutenant asked me to go back to the platoon and move them down about a half mile from a small cluster of houses we had pass through. I said, 'Me? Alone?' He said, 'Yes.' I asked if I could just go around the hill and he told me, no, because he didn't want me to get lost. As soon as I was out of sight I cut around the hill. When I splashed water crossing a small creek one of our guards halted me. I had come out exactly where I wanted to! We moved down to where the lieutenant told us to dig in but it was so rocky that was impossible. I then went back to the group of houses to wait for the lieutenant and his patrol to return. I waited and waited but no one showed so I returned to my platoon and tried to get some sleep. The sergeant told me, 'Since you're the one whose had to run around all day, you won't have to pull guard tonight.'

"I woke several times during the night and shook the water out of my eyes and went back to sleep. The rain had never stopped. All we had to keep us warm was our jackets. At daybreak the sergeant woke me and said, 'We're getting' out of here.'

"We hit the road early, walking in the rain. Some of the guys said there was so much water in the air they were afraid of drowning. That night the kitchen brought up hot chow but everyone was so tired very few of the men ate anything."[12]

Rain and fog slowed the 362nd's push up Mount Castellari and enemy fire from the mountain swept the entire area. After fighting all morning the forward elements of the 1st Battalion were within seventy-five yards of the crest, but the going was slow. Company C lost all but one of its officers during a mortar barrage. Company B was stopped by heavy fire from some concrete machinegun emplacements and the thick haze that hung over the battlefield made it difficult to coordinate the movements of the troops; however, three hours later the attack continued. The battalion beat off a counterattack, then Company B worked forward under the cover of the fog and cleared the mountain. Patrols, using rope ladders, then scaled the rocky crest. At 0215, 9 October, the mission was accomplished. That day Company L occupied La Guarda, Company I moved into Farne and Company F to La Balzi where it captured fifty prisoners.

During the first week of October the 362nd Infantry had broken the defenses at Monghidoro, had taken Mount Bastia overlooking Loiano and the Idice River Valley and had conquered the peak of Castellari, but the price paid for this high ground was extremely costly and the advance up Highway 65 was minimal: some three miles.

To achieve this meager gain the Division had sustained 383 battle casualties.

The rainy and foggy weather worked entirely to the benefit of the Germans. Artillery planes were grounded. Air missions were cancelled. Attacking companies were unable to coordinate. As the troops moved over each rain-soaked mile, the problems of supply increased.

The high hopes of the 5th Army staff for a quick thrust into the Valley of the Po were now fading with each long, dreary October day.

Endnotes for Chapter Eight

1. The Journal of the 755th Tank Battalion is one of the most interesting of all the S-3 Journals that were written during combat operations in Italy. The author never fails to express his own opinions and his criticisms of some of the 5th Army actions.
2. 363rd Regimental History. October, 1944. Pages 1-8. The author used the monthly regimental histories that were kept in the field. The 363rd history published in 1947 is based on these documents.
3. Fifth Army History. Volume 7. Privately printed. 1946. Reprinted in the "The Powder River Journal". June, 1987. Pages 21-31.
4. Ibid.
5. 91st Division Headquarters. G-2 Periodic Report No. 61. 4 October, 1944.
6. Ibid.
7. Ibid
8. Captain Booth wrote this account of his actions in Loiano in July, 1993.
9. "The Powder River Journal". June, 1985. Page 10.
10. Brown, Charles E. "Loiano". 1993. Pages 1-4.
11. 755th Tank Battalion S-3 Journal. 7 October, 1944.
12. Roice, John. "World War II Memories" Unpublished manuscript. Undated. Pages 10-12.

General Mark Clark visits Battery C, 916th F.A.

CHAPTER NINE —
THE LIVERGNANO ESCARPMENT

Stay with me, God. The night is dark,
The night is cold: my little spark
Of courage dies. The night is long;
Be with me God, and make me strong.
This poem was written on scrap of paper and found in a slit trench in Tunisia during the battle of El Agheila.

I

As the weary-worn troops of the Division prepared to resume the attack up Highway 65 in the fog, mist and cold rain, ahead of them lay the most formidable natural line of defense north of the Gothic Line: the Livergnano Escarpment. A precipitous, sheer rock wall nearly 1800 feet high and three miles long, this huge barricade ran from the village of Livergnano eastward to the hamlet of Bigallo. The escarpment was an almost impossible objective. From their vantage point along the rock rim of the wall, the Germans commanded every approach from the south. Any movement by the advancing infantrymen could be observed by the enemy gunners atop the escarpment and on the hills behind it. The entire 91st Division zone was completely covered for a depth of over five miles. Each approach was blocked by interlocking bands of fire, sealed tight by prepared mortar barrages. There were only two breaks in the wall: Highway 65 which ran through the village and a foot path one and one half miles east of Bigallo. If the Division was to pass through the escarpment it would have to be at one of these breaks.[1]

Just east of the village of La Guarda, the highway curved through a cluster of buildings called Predosa and ran on north past an ancient house, La Fortuna, which sat to the left of the road, then continued to the base of Hill 603 which rose like a colossal sphinx guarding Livergnano. The highway wound around 603 and into the village. The hill was honey-combed with caves that had been hollowed out by the natives and taken over by the Germans for defensive positions and living quarters. The highway made a U-turn into Livergnano meeting another hill, number 554, on the north side of the main street. It was to become known to the attacking troops as "Livergnano Rock". The nose of 554 jutted out almost into the center of the village. A secondary road branched off the highway and ran very steeply alongside the hill and up to the village church. At the top of the hill were more houses and the local cemetery. In the old Italian custom, several houses were built back into the escarpment and were called the "cliff" houses.

To the east of Highway 65 across a narrow gorge formed by Zena Creek, in the zone of the 85th Division, lay Monte della Formiche a 2,092 foot high mountain topped by a fortress-like church, Santa Maria di Zena. The west side of the mountain is a near vertical precipice and half way down is a huge cavern that was said to be the cave of the hermit Barberio. The church was used by the Germans as an observation post. To the west, the enemy defenses were tied in with the Monterumici hill mass in the 34th Division zone.

So the stage was set for what the troops yearned for: the final drive into the valley of the Po. Once over the escarpment, the Apennines begin a gradual slope downward and if the momentum of the drive could be sustained there was still hope that the offensive could succeed.

On 4 October the German 65th Infantry Division began relieving elements of the 4th Parachute and taking over positions along Highway 65. It was this enemy division that was to face the 91st all along the rugged escarpment front. The 65th had been badly mauled at Anzio but was reconstituted during the summer of 1944 and had suffered comparatively few casualties during the autumn fighting. The division shoulder patch was a potato masher grenade and so was known as "The Handgrenade Division."

The 361st Infantry had gone back into the line on 5 October. At 0130 on the morning of the 8th, the 3rd Battalion jumped off for the escarpment. Captain Chris P. Hald commanded Company I:

"I know that many of us lived the battle of Livergnano and, to all of us who were there, it was certainly a phase of our life that none of us will ever forget. I doubt sincerely that the human emotions of fear and courage were ever jointly more tested than they were in the several days that this battle took place. Success in this battle depended on, as have all battles, trust and confidence that each of us placed in his superiors and subordinates, recognizing that rank alone does not import God-like attributes in judgements or prognostications. Each one of us, from the division commander to the front line rifleman, lived and saw the battle through our own eyes and so provided descriptions of it that, surely in large measure, should be similar but has the right to be totally different from that described by other participants."[2]

Captain Hald's company had spent the night of 7 October at Casoni some two and a quarter miles south of Livergnano. At around 2000 he received a call from Colonel Broedlow. The call was a surprise to the captain since he usually received his orders from the 3rd Battalion commander, Major Dick Oshlo. The colonel told Hald he was to swing to the right of the highway and attack through the villages of Trebbo and Barbarolo then continue on northward and cut Highway 65 where he could and hold the road till the rest of the battalion pushed up to meet Company I. Cutting the highway, the colonel said, would block the escape route of any Germans south of that point. "Tonight," Colonel Broedlow told Hald, "we will make I Company famous."

The captain immediately sent two patrols forward in the direction of Trebbo which was a small group of houses about 500 yards southeast of Barbarolo. One of the patrols was led by 1st Lieutenant Mel Krieger and the other by the company 1st Sergeant, Frank Meyer, who was of German descent and could speak the language fluently. Captain Hald and Lieutenant Krieger were the only officers left in Company I.

It was raining heavily as the two patrols headed for Trebbo. The only knowledge Krieger had of the terrain was an aerial map that Hald has shown him. Upon reaching the tiny village a scout reported back to the lieutenant that he had spoken to a soldier of the 1st Battalion. When asked who was out ahead of him, the 1st Battalion soldier responded, "Only the Jerries." This information puzzled Krieger since he had not been told the 1st Battalion was also in the area.

The lieutenant radioed this information to battalion and was told to take both Trebbo and Barbarolo and to keep moving. The little group moved on through Trebbo, reorganized, then struck out for Barbarolo.

At 0730 Captain Hald and the remainder of his men moved out from Casoni to follow the forward elements of his company. The rain continued and daylight brought a typical early morning of rain squalls and low cloud banks with a heavy fog masking the mountains.

Sergeant Meyer's platoon reached Barbarolo at 0810 and seized the village along with three German prisoners whom he questioned and learned the main enemy force had pulled out during the night. Sending the PWs back to the rear, Meyer gathered his men together and, shielded by the fog, pushed on to Vaiarano, to the east of Highway 65, and captured it after overpowering an outpost. It was exactly noon of 8 October. The stouthearted sergeant then led his men onward towards Prato di Magnano and arrived there an hour later only to receive orders to thrust west and cut the highway.

In the meantime, Lieutenant Krieger and his small band of troopers, followed on the heels of Meyer up a narrow cart trail between the highway and a creek to the left. The rain now fell in torrents and the fog limited visibility to only a few yards. Movement was extremely difficult and some men had to grip the ammo belt of the man in front. As the two platoons reached the high ground just east of La Fortuna they could hear vehicles, tanks and German voices but were unable to see what was going on because of the fog. Krieger radioed back to battalion and suggested heavy weapons and antitank weapons be sent up to help them out. He was told in no uncertain terms that there wasn't time for reinforcements and to proceed with his mission.

As Krieger and his platoon plodded on west they met an Italian farmer coming towards them along the cart trail. The lieutenant asked one of his men who spoke the language to ask the farmer about the location of La Fortuna. He told Krieger there were two houses at La Fortuna and another one to the east of the highway. After Krieger's platoons had moved forward a short distance, they could see the highway and the outline of the buildings through the fog. At that moment they were spotted by the Germans who opened fire; however, the Powder Rivermen quickly subdued the few enemy soldiers and seized La Fortuna and the adjacent section of Highway 65. The lieutenant then radioed back that the highway had been cut. It was now 1800 hours.

Sergeant Meyer and his men moved into a house about one hundred yards down the highway and to the left of La Fortuna. Each window was manned by a GI with a BAR or M1 who quickly settled down for a long night's wait.

Darkness was falling fast when the last of Company I moved up the draw and into La Fortuna. Captain Hald ordered Krieger to take some of his men and put them in a small house behind Meyer's position. He then instructed the 2nd Platoon to occupy a small knoll-like strip of ground just to north of La Fortuna and to the left of the highway; here, the road curved into the village. From the knoll the platoon would be able to bring fire on any German troops coming down the highway. The platoon spread out and began digging in. Captain Hald's headquarters took up positions under an outside stairway on the north wall of the La Fortuna house and other members went up the stairway where there was a window that looked out toward Highway 65. The house itself sat just a few yards off the road. In the wine cellar below were two windows facing the highway and one could look up the road toward Livergnano.

Meanwhile, a section of Company M machineguns from 1st Lieutenant Bill Boeker's 1st Platoon moved up the highway and occupied a house near the bend in the road. After the section had set up their guns Boeker told them to erect some type of roadblock. This would maneuver the enemy off the highway and into

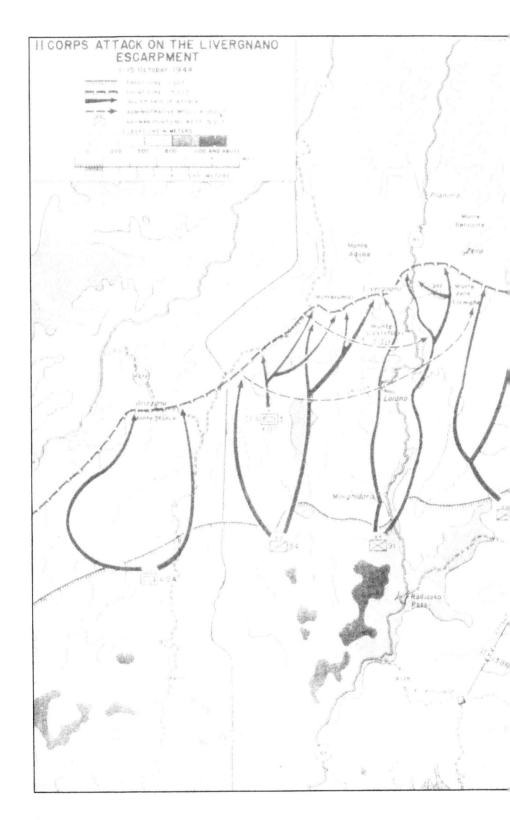

II CORPS ATTACK ON THE LIVERGNANO
ESCARPMENT
1-15 October 1944

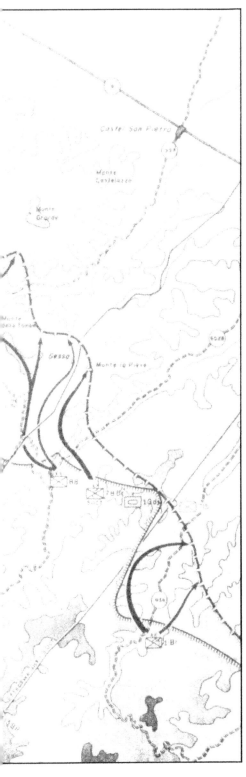

the machinegun fire of Company M. The roadblock was a makeshift affair of anything the men could find; two large pieces of farm machinery and a couple of big logs that were lying in the farmyard and other loose ends that were in and around the building.[3]

Shortly after dark, a German truck bringing supplies for the enemy troops in the area, drove slowly down the highway south and directly into the guns of Lieutenant Boeker's section. One man had a bazooka which he loaded and quickly fired. The first round hit the back end of the truck. It skidded for several yards then stopped at the edge of the road. The driver jumped out and ran off into the darkness. The machinegunners then pushed the truck into the middle of the road beside the farm machinery.

By 2200 most units had dug in for the night. Out on the northern knoll, the mission of the 2nd Platoon was an intolerable one. It was hopeless trying to dig foxholes in the steady rain and the water-soaked ground, so the men simply lay in their shallow mudholes and watched the highway. There were no guards posted because sleep was impossible. The rain fell endlessly and though the sounds of battle had slackened there was still sporadic fighting around the village of Cant where Company L was fighting off a counterattack.

At Predosa, eight hundred yards south of Captain Hald's command post, two enemy troop carriers, shielded by the mountain mist and darkness, sat in the yard waiting to move north to Livergnano. These Germans of the 145th Grenadier Regiment of the 65th Infantry Division were completely unaware they were surrounded by a handful of American infantrymen. Beside the carriers were two long nosed assault guns also waiting to move.

Promptly at 2230 the troop carriers fired up their engines and with a good deal of clanking and creaking, headed up Highway 65. At his outpost in the house down from La Fortuna, Sergeant Meyer heard the sound of the carrier motors and peered out of window to have a look. He was shocked to see so many of the enemy coming up from the <u>south</u>! Meyer was a veteran of many battles and knew it would be self-murder to order his men to fire, so he told them just to sit tight and he watched, fascinated, as the carriers, loaded with loudly talking Germans, lumbered on up the highway towards Lieutenant Boeker and his gunners. Like Meyer, Boeker realized his little group wouldn't stand a chance against the overpowering fire of the two truckloads of infantry. They watched closely as the Germans stopped, dismounted, moved the stalled truck to the side of the road, proceeded to board the carriers again, then swing out around the roadblock and up towards Livergnano.

Unknown to these men of the 3rd Battalion, the 361st Infantry was the very tip of the Fifth Army arrow thrust into the enemy's escarpment defenses. Having penetrated deep behind the lines, they were caught in

a vise: German infantry and tanks were coming up from the south and down from the north. Squads of enemy soldiers roamed the hills and ravines and patrols drifted in and out of the fog and darkness.

At 2300 the Germans began the first counterattack to drive the 91st Division troops from their positions along Highway 65. About a company of infantry, following three Mark IV tanks, moved cautiously out of Livergnano and toward La Fortuna. One of the tanks halted just short of Boeker's machinegunners and shot up a flare. In the brilliant glare of the brightness the Germans moved quickly to remove the obstacles of the roadblock. The 1st Platoon instantly opened fire on the Jerries. The lead tank, still sitting in the middle of the highway, fired a round into the farmhouse yard. A second round tore into the farmhouse knocking down a corner of the wall. The gunners sent forth a murderous fire that sent the Germans retreating back up the highway into Livergnano.

Once the tanks and infantry had retreated Captain Hald moved some of the machinegunners to the opposite side of the road and the bazookas were placed in more convenient positions. The captain then sent his non-coms around to each man with a word of encouragement to hang on.

At 0100 the Germans hit again.

The three Mark IV's came down the highway with their guns booming and attacked the 2nd Platoon dug in on the open knoll. They drove over the mudholes, swirling their treads and scattering the men in all directions. The bazooka men stood firm and exhausted their ammunition but they did little damage to the sturdy Mark IV's which kept coming. One of the tanks shot up a flare, then all three began to fire armor piercing shells into the north wall of the La Fortuna house. A round ripped into the outer stairway and with a thunderous crash it dropped down on the headquarters group crushing six men.

The wounded were hauled into the house and placed in the wine cellar below the two small windows that looked out upon the highway. Captain Hald, who was to become a surgeon after the war, walked among the moaning men trying to put in a word of cheer. One man had a serious sucking wound in the right upper chest. Hald stuffed the wound with several first-aid packs and tied a number of others around the man's shoulder. Though he was severely wounded the man was not in shock. He asked Hald, "Captain, what do you think is going to happen to us?" "If we're hit again, " the captain said, "the odds are we won't make it. We're out of bazooka shells, we're nearly out of ammo and we don't have very many grenades." Hald told the wounded man it was six of one or half a dozen of the other as to what he did. "You can stay in the wine cellar and run the risk of being killed or captured," the captain told him. "Or you can take your chances and try and get back to battalion by going back along the telephone wire with other wounded."[4]

The wounded man chose to try and make it back to the rear. Hald later learned the man did make it and lived to fight another day.

At around 0300 the Germans launched another counterattack. This time the tanks, accompanied by a fresh platoon of infantry, again moved down from Livergnano and pulled up one hundred yards from La Fortuna and again began spraying the house with machinegun fire and armor piercing shells. By this time Captain Hald had gotten everyone out of the upper stories and down into the wine cellar. Even though the shells knocked down portions of the walls the men inside the cellar were safe.

Very quickly the enemy infantry circled the house and fired into the wide door that led to the cellar. In this ferocious uproar it was impossible to tell Americans from Germans. Grenades flew in and out of windows. One sailed through the small cellar window and exploded among the wounded killing Pfc. King Clark who had just arrived at the house to offer his assistance.

Captain Hald had to make a decision whether to stay inside the house and risk having his company killed or captured or to make a wild break for the outside where the men could get some concealment in the darkness. He chose the latter.

The men grabbed as many grenades as they could, pulled the pins and tossed them out into the farmyard, then rushed outside with their weapons blazing. This tremendous volley of fire forced the Germans to withdraw back up the highway and again regroup.

After the firing had ceased the captain took inventory of the Company I situation and discovered his ammunition was nearly gone, as were the bazooka shells. The machineguns that had been placed out on the knoll had been smashed by the Mark IV's, so Hald sent a few men out to retrieve the ammo boxes and the belts. The rounds were pulled from the belts and distributed among those still able to function. Each man ended up with about six cartridges, but the grenades were gone.

Down the highway, the Germans attacked the farmhouse where Sergeant Meyer and his beleaguered men were hiding.

Two enemy infantrymen knocked down the front door and made a dash for the stairs but Sergeant Meyer cut them down. Another German was killed while climbing through the front window. Amidst the shrieks and raucous cries of the men, the smoke and fire, and the bitter smell of cordite, potato mashers and fragmentation grenades bounced off the outside walls and the old stone building jarred with the explosions.

After what seemed like an eternity to Meyer and his men, the enemy attack was beaten off. Later, the bodies of nine Germans were found outside the door of the farmhouse.

By 0700, a chilly, ashen dawn was breaking over the Highway 65 battlefield and the 361st troopers began to assess the damage wrought on them during the night. There were only thirteen men left in Company I. The others had not all been killed or wounded for some were still widely scattered over the countryside in foxholes and houses. Since Hald's supply of ammunition was nearly consumed he asked 1st Lieutenant John Windle to form a patrol to go back down the road and attempt to find friendly forces that might be able to bolster his supply. Windle was a Company K officer whose platoon had been sent to La Fortuna the previous afternoon to help out Captain Hald and

A reserve company of division infantry moves into the line.

155

company. Several men volunteered to go with Windle. They crept out the wine cellar and started south down the highway.

The patrol had gone only a few yards when Lieutenant Windle noticed, in the dismal first light of morning, what appeared to be a battalion of Germans moving toward him from Predosa. He could make out some tanks, a few motorcycles, a half track, a recon car, and behind these, an infantry company on foot. It seemed to the lieutenant that the entire countryside was moving. Where in the hell, he asked himself, are all these damned Germans coming from? He motioned his men off the road and down under a culvert. Here they remained motionless until one of the men, unable to stand the stress of waiting silently, panicked and ran out into a vineyard. The marching Germans took no notice of the terrified American.

Lieutenant Windle and his patrol remained under the highway as the enemy column passed over them. "Had we had troop strength," Windle later recalled, "we could have wiped them out. I'm sure we later fought most of them in Livergnano."[5]

Up at La Fortuna, Captain Hald could hear the sound of the approaching Germans. Company I had no ammunition that could possibly stop the tanks. They had no communication that would allow them to call in artillery fire, so the captain promptly sent a runner up to Lieutenant Krieger's house to tell his elements to stay the hell hidden and not try to contest the advancing column. He then gathered together all his wounded and the rest of the men and again

Captain Chris P. Hald (left) and 1st Lieutenant John Gaultney.

took refuge in the wine cellar. Hald felt the cellar was his only hope. The open field to the back of La Fortuna was much too wide for the company to cross. The tanks would have had them under fire immediately. Years later Hald could still remember sitting before the tiny cellar window and watching the hob-nailed boots go by. Fortunately, the Germans did not bother to investigate either La Fortuna or the house of Lieutenant Krieger.

Shortly after the passage of the enemy column, Company I, or what was left of it, once again established radio contact with battalion. Hald talked first with Major Oshlo, then to Colonel Broedlow who gave him a severe tonguelashing for failing to engage the Germans. The captain did his best to explain his situation and the colonel finally accepted it. In any event, Hald let the Germans through and his men survived and this indicated, at least to the captain, that they were experienced infantrymen who knew their capabilities and limitations.

As the last of the column moved into Livergnano an enormous blast thundered through the mountains and a geyser of earth gushed up into the air just north of La Fortuna. The enemy had set off demolition charges in the middle of the highway. Now, Sixty-five was closed to any 91st Division traffic.

At Lieutenant Krieger's farmhouse his platoon was also taking stock of the situation. They were out of ammunition and all but a few were wounded. All were exhausted. Krieger conferred with Sergeant Meyer and told him he felt the walking wounded should be given a chance to either stay and fight or try to make it back to the rear. Meyer questioned each man and all asked, "What are you and the lieutenant going to do?" The sergeant answered the two of them were going to stay and fight. "Well," each man said, "I'll do the same."

When the rest of the battalion moved up to join Company I, most of the survivors, including the lieutenant, were evacuated with battle wounds. Krieger ran into Major Oshlo at the battalion CP who said to him, "There's the hero of La Fortuna."

"No sir," replied Krieger, 'The heroes are no longer with us.'"[6]

Meanwhile, far, far back down the Italian boot on the Naples waterfront, the troops of the Peninsula Base Sector, the most hated rear echelon unit in the Italian Campaign, were clustered around a sound truck listening to the end of the World Series which was being picked up via short wave radio. Some of the men were drinking beer, others were exchanging currency from bets won or lost on the game. The St. Louis Cardinals had beaten the St. Louis Browns four games to two.

II

Along the escarpment front the supply problems were now at a critical point. The forward elements of the Division were drastically short of medical supplies, radios, small arms and mortar ammunition, rations and water. The only available road up to the 91st front was Highway 65 and it was extremely dangerous for any vehicle to venture too close to the fighting, all other routes were rugged secondary roads, trails and paths. So getting provisions to the infantry was a chore left to the individual soldier.

Ralph Rustad was a member of Antitank Company, 361st:

"On the night of October 8th we received word that Companies I and K had cut Highway 65 behind the enemy lines. Regiment was asking for volunteers to take a mule train to these two companies because they were out of supplies and ammunition. Our 3rd Platoon volunteered for the trip. I don't remember the exact strength of the platoon at the time but it must have been about twenty or twenty-five.

"We did not leave with the pack train until sometime after midnight, the idea being to get as many Germans bedded down as possible. A pack train usually consisted of twenty-five mules, each accompanied by an Italian soldier, so I assume that was what this one was. We went up Highway 65 until we made contact with the forward elements. As we traveled up the road we had to pass through a fairly long cut in the hillside. The rain had stopped temporarily and the clouds had become broken with the moon shining through on occasion. As we traversed this cut the moon moved out from behind the clouds almost turning night into day. There were about a dozen German soldiers standing up on the rim of the cut watching us as we passed through. To this day I've never been able to figure why they never opened fire on us. As far as we were concerned this wasn't the time or the place to start a firefight so we just kept on walking and they kept on watching and seemed content to just let us go by. They really had us boxed in if they had decided to make a fight of it.

Officers of Battery C, 348th Field Artillery. L-R: Lt. William T. Lonz, Captain Julian Hogan, Btry CO, 2nd Lt. Steve Stevens and 1st Lt. James M. Jenks.

"As we went on up the road we could hear small arms fire up ahead but by the time we got to our destination and removed the supplies from the backs of the mule the fighting was all over.

"For the return trip we loaded the wounded on the mules and were accompanied by the walking wounded. We were concerned that the Germans would be ready for us this time and would have an ambush ready. But as it turned out one of the Italian soldiers who must have been a native to the region knew an alternative route, a foot trail through the hills. This was above the highway on the west side, so we followed the path. We didn't pass any buildings or meet any Germans. We came out of the hills and into the back street of a tiny village that sat near the road. The sky was just beginning to lighten up in the east.

"The next night we had to take a pack train up to the 2nd Battalion sector under the escarpment, up near Sassi. We were given Medic arm bands, helmets and stretchers. We were ordered to make our way to Companies E and G who were isolated up on the escarpment. Just before we left, a major showed up with a jeep full of ammo. He told us to carry as much of the ammo as we could so we took off our shirts, placed two bandoliers across each shoulder, then put our shirts back on. We stuffed four grenades in our pockets and headed on up the trail. I don't believe this was in exact accord with the Geneva Convention but then all's fair in love and war.

"Our trip on the way up was uneventful. Just to the south of the escarpment, down in the bottom of a draw, were some buildings and a group of Germans were just leaving the place. There must have been forty or fifty of them and they marched out of there in a column of threes just as pretty as you please. It sure would have been a nice spot for an artillery observer. Believe it or not, the morning was bright and sunny and these guys all had their pants legs stuffed into the top of their boots. The sun reflected from their boot tops almost like mirrors and I remember thinking, those bastards must have spent all night shining their boots. As we were going up a bush covered draw, just before reaching the base of the escarpment, a German opened up on us. Surely, he could see our Medic helmets and arm band but he fired on us anyway. Luckily, he was a lousy shot. Only one of our guys was hit and that was in the leg.

This much reprinted photo of Hill 554, or Livergnano Rock, has been claimed by about every American unit that fought along Highway 65. The shot was taken a day or two after the capture of the village by the 91st. The tank at the left belongs to the 755th Tank Battalion. And one must assume that the men who surround it also belong to that same battalion.

A rustic photograph of Livergnano taken in the 1930s. Every house in the village was totally destroyed by the fighting between the German 65th Infantry Division and the 91st.

"We finally made it up to the point where we were to unload. What a relief that was because we had the feeling that things might have gotten nasty if the Germans had stopped and searched us.

"I can't remember how many stretchers we carried back but there was a long line of us. And we had the usual number of walking wounded. I don't know how we managed to get back down off the cliff, but we did, and without causing any more injuries to the poor guys on the stretchers. The terrain was rugged as hell. The path went down the top of a long hog-back ridge, which we got across just as it was getting dusk. It had taken us all damned day to get to the point where we were. The Germans had set up a defensive position on the reverse slope of the ridge. I believe they had set this up as a temporary position just for the night. Before we cleared the ridge the trail took us past three different Jerry machinegun nests. That was eerie as hell and sent shivers up our spines, walking right there among the enemy. One machinegun was fairly close to the top of the ridge and there was a big heavy-set German on the gun, a really mean looking son of a bitch.

"It was dark before we got back with the wounded, and I mean dark. I would like to say that the soldier that I helped carry was perhaps one of the bravest men I've ever known. He had been shot in the gut, probably the day before, as it was an old bandage. Drainage came out through the bullet holes and turned the bandage into a dirty green color. The man was fully conscious the entire trip down and we were careful not to tip the stretcher along the rough trail, but he never complained, not one time. Whenever we stopped for a short break we lit a cigarette for him and he'd try to carry on a conversation. He never mentioned his wound and was only worried about his buddies up on the escarpment. I sure hope he made it home all right.

"After the ambulances left we went to get our rifles and helmets that we had left in an old stone house, but they were gone. Someone had taken them back to the company. Maybe they didn't expect us back. They didn't leave us any rations either. We were really put out about our weapons being gone, as a matter of fact, we were highly pissed off.

"After the war I ran into Lieutenant Jack Taylor of Company G. He remembered quite clearly our trip up to the escarpment. We had a real good laugh about that. Of course, that was years later."[7]

Early in the morning of 9 October, General Livesay visited the 361st Regimental CP and discussed the coming escarpment actions with Colonel Broedlow.

"We've made a big bulge in the Fifth Army lines," the general said. "We've got to expand that bulge which means we have to take Livergnano, get through the escarpment and on up the highway. The II Corps drive won't mean a damned thing until we do. So, I'm telling you Broedlow, Livergnano is your objective and you take it!"

After the general left, a determined Broedlow contacted Captain Hald and ordered him to send a platoon into Livergnano and find out exactly what was going on inside the village. The captain replied he would send his men forward but his supply of ammunition was so low that if they got into a fire fight they would be unable to respond. The colonel then changed his mind and decided to rely on a platoon from Company K.

The 2nd Battalion, dug in near Barbarolo, had been directed to attack at 0650 and march northeast toward Bigallo, the other break in the enormous mountain wall.

The 1st Squad, 3rd Platoon of Company K was chosen to lead the way into Livergnano. Second Lieutenant Donald Murray, who had come up to the company the night before as an officer replacement, was assigned to the squad. The morning was quiet and the day clear as Murray and his men moved quickly up Highway 65. The cloudless sky offered the Germans, hidden in the caves on Hill 603, unlimited observation. II Corps G-2 reports showed the enemy evacuating Livergnano, but Colonel Broedlow, pondering over the battle at his headquarters, gave little credence to G-2 reports, S-2 reports and most other reports. He remembered the rosy forecasts that had come from Corps prior to the Gothic Line offensive. There was only one way to find out what was up ahead of his regiment and that was to send in his infantry and find out for himself.

Before the 361st struck out for the escarpment the 1st and 3rd Battalion had been shuffled up a bit. The 1st was using Companies K, C and B which were operating along Highway 65. The companies of the 3rd Battalion, A, I and L, were, more or less, on independent missions. The 2nd Battalion had its own companies, E, F, and G.

It didn't take the Germans long to react to the advancing squad of Company K. Just as Murray and his men passed a large four story house sitting along the hair-pin turn into the village, the enemy infantry on Hill 603 opened fire. The Americans hit the ground and almost immediately mortars began dropping among the men. Lieutenant Murray yelled to the squad to get out of the street and into the protection of the four story house. Back down the highway, Private Billy Steele, leading the 3rd Squad into the village, screamed for his men to double time into the house along with Murray's squad. The 1st and 2nd Platoons, also attempting to move up the highway, were stopped by the heavy fire and forced back to their original positions.

At the Company K command post Captain Chet Sigmen watched his men trying to get into the village. He then put in a call to Major Oshlo who told him to hold his platoons until darkness.

As the night settled down over the beleaguered men of the 361st, Captain Sigmen ordered Lieutenant John Windle to lead a small patrol into Livergnano before the rest of the company moved forward. Three men volunteered to go with the lieutenant. Pvt. Harvey Boynton was to go along as the radio man. After receiving final instructions, Windle and his four comrades set out for the village.

The lieutenant's patrol was to become a personal ordeal:

Infantrymen of the 362nd accompany tanks up a hillside near Livergnano. Note the felled tree in the foreground. This was a typical German tactic to stall traffic.

"On 9th October, we moved up into some houses at the foot of the mountain where the highway starts up into Livergnano. Captain Sigmen had sent a platoon into the town but had lost radio contact. Later in the night he received orders to move the company up, but before the company was to move, he sent me with a four man patrol to locate our lost platoon. We didn't know what had happened, if they had been wiped out, captured or just how far they had gone.

"I set out with the radio man, who was from Company I, and three other men. We moved up through a corn field to the east of Highway 65. We could hear some Germans talking and moving toward us, so we laid flat on the ground and let them pass, only about eight or ten feet

More mountains! Another river! Damn this scenery anyway!

from us. As we moved along, the Germans would fire flares over our heads, but did not fire rifles at us. When we would hear the click of the flare launcher up on the mountain we'd lay down on the side of the highway. Most of the way up there was a rock wall on the right of the highway that afforded us some pretty good protection.

"I was out in front of the patrol and fell off into a deep crater that the enemy had blown in the highway. This was the first of four times I was to fall into that damned crater.

"We moved on into the town, and as we reached a house, a man of the lost platoon hollered at us. We ran into the building and found the platoon sergeant with a few of his men. The platoon leader, Lieutenant Murray, had been killed....shot through the back. He had been carrying the 300 radio and the shot had shattered the radio. I remembered he had joined us the day before about four p.m. Most of the platoon in the big room of the house were badly wounded or dead. The sergeant had lost a thumb and he warned us not to go in front of the windows or doors because the Germans were firing at every movement. I told the patrol to stay with the sergeant and I'd go back and bring up the company. I asked them to put out a guide along the highway for me. I figured I could make it quicker alone, so I set out on a dead run straight down the highway. It was dark except for an occasional flare, but again I ran into that crater at full speed. It didn't take

Livergnano. October, 1944. The ruins of the church of St. John the Baptist sits atop the Rock.

me long to reach Captain Sigmen and he moved the company out immediately. This must have been around midnight or later.

"I led the company single file. I warned the men behind me to look out for the crater, but as we came up the road I fell into it again! We moved along the rock wall on up to where I expected to find my guide. I saw a movement in a doorway and walked over toward it. I asked, 'Are you my guide?' At that instant, I was looking down the barrel of a German rifle. I thought if I can just dive into the door next to the one the German was standing in I could get away, but just as I turned he fired, striking me in the right chest. The bullet went through my lung and shattered my right shoulder blade. Upon hearing the shot, the company ran forward and into the house where our men were. I'm sure they thought I was dead.

"I lay in the street for some time. I don't know how long, but I managed to get to my feet. My right arm was paralyzed. I remember staggering down the highway and falling into the crater again. I had to really struggle to get out this time. I reached a house along the side of the road and got inside the door. The Germans came into the house sometime during the night and took my maps, my identification bracelet and other things. I was only partially conscious at this point because I had lost so much blood.

"The next day I heard English speaking voices along the highway and managed to get their attention. It was Captain Anderson and men of Company B. They were headed up to make contact with Company K. Anderson gave me water and sent his radio man back for help. This saved my life. Litter bearers came up and got me and took me first to the house where Captain Hald was. He had his medic patch me up and give me first aid. I remember the house had a terrible odor from the dead and that were buried in the rubble. The sergeant who had lost a thumb and several other wounded were moving back with me and the medics who had me on a stretcher. As we started down the highway, the Germans opened up on us with a mortar barrage. The litter bearers sat me down in the middle of the highway and all ran for cover! The shrapnel flew all over, but didn't hit me. They pretty well shelled the area but I didn't get a scratch.

"I've re-visited Livergnano several times since the war. The old house where the German shot me is still standing. The doors were just as I remembered and there was a step down from the street into the house. It didn't dawn on me until years later why I had such a vivid picture of the house and the German in the doorway and it finally came to me that a flare must have been fired about the same time I was wounded. The evidence of the crater I fell into is clearly visible today in the rock wall along Highway 65."[8]

At 0500 10 October, Major Oshlo reported to Colonel Broedlow that the remainder of Company K had joined the reinforced platoon in Livergnano and were occupying several houses in the southern outskirts. The fighting was still continuing, with the enemy, on top of Hills 554 and 603, firing into the village houses.

III

In the Italian language the grouped consonants gn resemble the English ni as in oNIon, thus Livergnano is pronounced, "Liver-yawn-o", and it didn't take the GIs of the Division very long to twist the word into "Liver and Onions" - fergato e cipolle - and so the village fortress would always be known by the name of an American dish. In among the records of the 361st Infantry is a poem supposedly written by a dejected and exhausted 361ster during the battle. To date, the poet has never been found.

"We're the battlin' bastards of Liver and Onions,
Dog-tired and dirty, we've got blisters and bunions,
But we got no replacements and no ammunition,
No bazookas, no tanks and an impossible mission.
General Clark said, 'Don't worry, the Jerries are beat.
Tomorrow we'll walk up Bologna's main street.'
But a week has gone by, and we ain't got there yet,
The rain is still fallin' and gettin' us wet,
The burp guns are rippin' and the 88s blast,
Darkness is comin' and night's fallin' fast,
And the mortars keep chunkin' and the howitzers slam,
And nobody gives goddam!'"

The continued mission of the 361st on 10 October was to press the attack against enemy positions on the escarpment generally east and west in the vicinity of Livergnano. The regimental zone consisted of the territory astride Highway 65. The west boundary ran north-south to the west of Predosa. The east boundary ran north-south passing the vicinity of Pescara and Fornacetta as far as the east-west escarpment near Bigallo. The 363rd Infantry was in position on the east flank and the 362nd on the west. The 1st Battalion, 361st held the forward positions of the Regiment in close contact with the Germans immediately south of Livergnano. The main route of supply was still Highway 65; however, the troops dug in foxholes a considerable distance from the highway, had to haul their own supplies or have mule trains pack the loads in over narrow, pot-holed trails.

While Company K was holding off the attacks inside Livergnano, the 2nd Battalion had already pushed off for the escarpment nearly three thousand yards east of the highway. Here the perpendicular wall was 592 meters high with the south side being extremely steep. In places it was sheer rock, straight up and down. The route used by the battalion was the only possible point where the troops could ascend and even using this route it was necessary for the riflemen to sling their M1s and use both hands to clamber up the wall. The machinegunners disassembled their guns and each man carried parts in his pockets so he could have his arms free to climb. Men could not carry heavy loads and supply-carrying parties could haul only a minimum essential burden of ammunition, rations and water. Supplies were carried to Sassi by mule pack and from Sassi by small rations details. In order to evacuate the wounded it was necessary for litter bearers to carry the stretchers down the escarpment and remove the men under fire. It was an exhausting task and though the litter teams did a superb job, it was possible only to evacuate at night. Sometimes twenty-four

Trebbo. Mid-October, 1944. Sgt. Ed McElhaney and Phil Scaglia. 361st Infantry 2nd Battalion Aid Station. Right-Note empty K ration case, along with packs of the wounded and dried mud on shoepacs.

Division troops look over the ruins of the cliff houses.

hours passed before the wounded could be given medical attention. It required twelve hours to get a wounded man down from the escarpment to the battalion aid station.

Lieutenant Jack Taylor of Company G took his platoon up the vertical wall to Casola:

"It was only due to the heavy fog and misty conditions that we reached the base of the escarpment. The Germans couldn't see our approach. We were shelled with 88 and heavier fire during this time, but it was completely undirected and ineffective. It would have been impossible to have reached the base during daylight without the fog. From the top the Germans could see any movement for miles.

"We arrived at the base, it seems in the afternoon, in the vicinity of Sassi. After a short huddle of the brass, my platoon, the 2nd of Company G, and a rifle platoon from Company E, led by Lieutenant Vanderburg, were called forward and given the mission to work our way through the cut and take Casola. Frankly, this seemed crazy as hell to send a platoon out of two different companies, but a lot of crazy things happened in combat.

"Anyway, away we went, as always in Italy, single file through the cut. We drew fire several times, but by staying in the timber we made it through without any casualties. There were ridges running back from the escarpment and we moved to the ridge overlooking Casola. After moving about one hundred yards away from the ridge I could hear steps coming through the mud. My carbine was pretty muddy from the climb, so on the spur of the moment I decided to try and capture whoever it was that was coming. I stepped behind a tree and two Germans were within ten feet of me. I stepped out and put my carbine on them and hollered, 'Hands up!' They stopped and the trailing man reached for a rat gun. I fired three or four rounds and they guy screamed as I hit him. I then ran to a ditch only a short distance away, and without looking, tossed two grenades. After they exploded I looked out and both men were gone. A machine pistol lay on the ground and I picked it up and ran back to the ridge.

"So the enemy now knew we were there and we started drawing fire. Vanderburg and I decided one of us must go back and report that we are dug in behind the German MLR. As soon as it was good and dark Van took men and went back the same route we had taken. It was a terribly lonesome feeling to have two platoons behind the lines and unable to get fire support or any kind of help. Van made it back OK and the next morning he led the rest of our men up, accompanied by Lieutenant Coz. They were cut up pretty bad with the weapons platoon getting the worst of it. Our radios, because of the terrain I guess, would not function. Van had brought up the 300 which did give us communication with battalion.

"Now it was just Van, Coz and myself. From this time on the situation got pretty serious. The Germans pulled up some tanks and fired point blank into our positions. Machineguns were firing from all sides and mortars rained down on us. Van and his men were down the ridge and somewhat below me. After a very heavy mortar barrage I could see his position was hit much worse than mine, so I ran down to help him out but when

Captain Chet Sigmen and his men of Company K, 361st. This photograph was taken enroute to North Africa. Company K was lost at Livergnano.

I got there he was lying in a small ditch, a shell had hit him right above his head and the top of his head was gone. He didn't know what hit him. After helping what I could I ran back to my foxhole. At that time my runner was a guy named Keegan. On reaching the hole I found Keegan hunched down and I thought that maybe he was frozen with fear, but he was dead. After a long search trying to find out where he had been hit, I found a very small hole under his chin in the soft part of his throat. He had had his head down between his knees and a small piece of mortar shrapnel had gone straight to his brain.

"The Germans would shell and shell and shell and then attack. We had dead Krauts within twenty steps of our positions. Sometimes they would come out with the Red Cross flags and move forward gathering up their dead and wounded. We always honored the flags but we couldn't trust them to do the same. Many of our men died because we couldn't get them out until night. With so many dead and wounded around us and a seemingly hopeless situation, it says something for man just to be able to keep from going insane."[9]

Staff Sergeant William "Jack" Sansom, also of Company G, climbed the escarpment with his men:

"Ten days or so after we had gone through Rome, we lost our platoon leader and as a platoon guide I took over command, and strange as it seems, I was to become the leader for most of the campaign. We got an officer named Davis during the summer. He was all man but he had recurrent bouts with malaria and after one particularly bad attack I had a couple of the boys take him to the rear and I took command again. During the long months that were to follow, the 1st Platoon was a 'leaderless' platoon, meaning that we did not have an officer commanding.

"By the time we got to Sassi we were leaderless again. Nevertheless, when we reached the Casola escarpment our company commander, Captain Dougan, sent my platoon to the left flank. We held about seventy-five or one hundred yards of the escarpment. Our extreme flank was a perpendicular drop off, so we had no protection from the rear or side.

Also, directly in front of us, was a hillside with trees and underbrush, where there were at least six German machineguns scattered around through the woods. Two of these guns made us keep our heads down at all times! We also got plastered by SP88s from the right, and across the draw we had come up, were a couple of aggravating machineguns that the Germans kept firing into us. We figured they were too far away to do much damage, just pesky and harassing but not very dangerous.

"Captain Dougan had told me that my platoon would have to go in and knock out the machineguns because the terrain between the company's position and the houses of Casola was all open space. To make this attack we had to cross a dirt road in order to take advantage of the shrubs and trees. Jim Quinn went first-running. He was OK and signaled me. I went next with the platoon following me. We found the machineguns, but no gunners. I sent a runner back to the captain and then the platoon went on through the trees toward the

The church at Livergnano. 1940.   The church at Livergnano. 1946.

houses. We found other machineguns, but still no gunners. Quinn and I figured the Germans had pulled out and were not going to make a stand because they had abandoned their equipment.

"We were within rock throwing distance of the main house when an enemy soldier came out waving a white flag. We circled the door as the Krauts came out with their hands up. We backed them up against the wall and then another fellow and myself went into the building to check it out. There were no more soldiers, but we did get a sack full of pistols. I already had a P38 and a Luger from Mount Beni, so most of the boys wound up with a lot of souvenirs."[10]

Early in the morning of 10 October before a new II Corps attack was launched General Livesay had visited the 2nd Battalion headquarters and ordered its advance halted until the 363rd Infantry, which had been sent to the east to help out, had pushed further forward and covered the exposed left flank. The stiff resistance met by the 2nd Battalion, 361st, indicated that all the strength of the 363rd would be needed. The enemy was fighting from excellent defensive terrain and his order of battle was better integrated than in the 85th Division fighting to east. The 3rd Battalion, 10th Parachute Regiment, and the 2nd Battalion, 145th Grenadier Regiment, held the area west of Livergnano; the 1st Battalion, 146th Grenadier Regiment was astride Highway 65; and the 2nd Battalion, 146th Grenadier Regiment, together with the 142nd Fusilier Battalion, held the eastern portion of the escarpment.

When the II Corp attack began Company B, 361st, dug in near Hill 495, was ordered to swing west and move up Highway 65 into Livergnano to help relieve the critical situation of Company K.

After returning from a meeting at 1st Battalion headquarters, Captain Ralph Anderson, Company B commander, alerted his men and prepared to move out. The captain had recently been assigned to the company and, as a former liaison officer, had had very few days of actual combat command.

The men of Company B moved westward to catch the highway which was reached at 0645 hours. Anderson stopped briefly at La Fortuna to converse with Captain Hald. The two officers discussed the situation then Anderson, with a wave of his arm, signaled for his men to follow him. Hald stood in the ruins of the badly battered house and watched the actions of Company B thinking he was damned glad it wasn't him going into Livergnano.[11]

A short distance up the highway Anderson stopped and told his executive officer that he was taking several men with him and going forward on a "reconnaissance" and to hold the company where it was. This was a puzzling maneuver since, obviously, the only way into the village was straight up Sixty-five. To accompany him, Anderson selected four riflemen and two radiomen, one with a SCR 300 and another with a SCR 536. Pfc. Fred Berg was to go along as a runner and once Company K was contacted he was to return to bring up the rest of the company.

The morning was quiet with very little artillery activity. The bodies of both Germans and Americans were scattered along the road all the way from La Fortuna to the entrance of Livergnano. As the men passed a nearly demolished house, they could hear moaning coming from just inside the door. Upon investigation

361sters display abandoned German equipment near Livergnano. L-R: Pvt. Charles R. Williams, Pvt. C.E. Mote, Pfc. William Roche, Pfc. Lee J. Sparkman and Pfc. Walter J. Oblazny.

Years later at a 361st Infantry Reunion. From left- Captain Ralph Anderson, 1st Lieutenant John Windle, Captain Chet Sigmen and Pfc. Fred Berg.

This sketch of embattled Livergnano was drawn under fire by Combat Artist Captain Ed Reep of the 5th Army Historical Section.

they found an American officer face down on the floor. It was Lieutenant John Windle. He was unable to give the captain any information and Anderson let one rifleman remain with Windle and sent Pfc. Berg back to Company I for a stretcher and medic. The party then continued on to the village.

The highway curved to the left and to the right was a sheer rock wall and there was a deep canyon to the left. Beyond the blown crater the road made a sharp 'U' bend into Livergnano. Anderson kept telling his radiomen to stay some distance behind him but they kept closing up, then closing up again. As he walked slowly up the street he could see no signs of life nor were there any shots fired. As the captain rounded the bend he stopped in his tracks. Several yards ahead of him stood a German assault tank! The driver immediately started the engine and fired a round that burst just above Anderson's head. Shrapnel from this shell killed the two radiomen instantly and destroyed the radios. The captain yelled for the two riflemen to go back but they came running forward and another shell burst in the same place killing both of them.

Now, small arms and machinegun fire blazed from every direction in the village. A squad of Germans began firing at the captain. The men of Company K then opened fire on the enemy which allowed Anderson time to take cover in the slushy, refuge of a stable which also sheltered Sergeant Dave Covington and a handful of men. Covington said Captain Sigman was uninjured and was with the remnants of his company in the building next to the stable. Anderson made a dash out into the street and into the four story house.

The shelling had increased in intensity. The Germans were firing into the village from both hills; mortar, tank and heavy artillery rounds burst in the street, and onto the houses and exploded against the wall of Hill 603.

Though Company K was under the control of the 1st Battalion, Major Oshlo had been in radio contact with the company commander all during the early hours of the morning. The battle was desperate Sigmen told Oshlo and the captain kept repeating, "Where in the hell is Company B?" The battalion commander could only assure Sigmen that Anderson's company was on the way into the village to give him a hand.

Back down the highway, Company B was caught in a heavy barrage and took shelter behind a small knoll to the right of the road. Pinned down by the fire, they were unable to move.

When the two company commanders met inside Livergnano it was exactly 0730 hours. As they talked, both realized that the situation of the Company K men was hopeless. Without the support of Anderson's platoons, there was little doubt they would be overwhelmed. Their ammunition was all but exhausted. Many of the wounded, lying on litters, had been killed by falling rocks and debris.

The troops inside Livergnano were able to withstand the enemy's attacks for three hours. Both Sigmen and Anderson agreed there was no alternative but to surrender the men. Any further attempts to hold the house would eventually cost the life of every man in Company K. At 1000 the officers ordered all letters, maps, platoon radios and other items of use to the Germans to be destroyed. Weapons were damaged beyond repair. At around 1015 the final decision to surrender were made. Captain Sigmen volunteered to go out first, but before walking out into the street, he called Major Oshlo and told him he was surrendering. At the other end of the line, the major listened soberly as Sigmen's conversation was cut off in the middle of a sentence.[12]

Captain Anderson made a final search of the house and went up to the third floor window to take a final look outside. The surrendering men were being hurriedly rushed through the village street to the back of the town. Anderson then walked down the stairs and was met by two "well-fed" Germans. He took one look at his watch before his captors removed it from his wrist. The time was precisely 1030 hours.[13]

Pfc. John Shier was one of the Company K prisoners:

"We really didn't stand a chance because without help we were doomed. Germans tanks shot at us from point blank range. Enemy infantrymen were all over the place—even on the roofs. We had no medics and there were many wounded and dead. As we were being herded away I observed a large group of Germans and a number of tanks. There were anti-antiaircraft guns no more than one hundred yards from where we were captured. An RAF fighter plane tried to help us escape by strafing around us, but he couldn't get close enough and we had many guards."[14]

Early in the evening, as darkness was falling, Company I sent a patrol into Livergnano to determine the number and location of the casualties and to assist to escape of any men remaining in the town. Sergeant Ernest Avery's squad succeeded in evacuating twelve wounded men:

"We had the gruesome task of removing our dead buddies from the vacated home. Bodies were strewn from the top floor on down the stairway to the bottom floor. Some of the men's heads were literally blown off. One man in particular I had known personally since the early days at Camp White, Oregon. It was one of the worst moments of my life. The stench of death was everywhere. Hell couldn't have been any worse.[15]

Only ten men escaped the carnage at Livergnano. Shortly before midnight, Lieutenant James H. Scudder, Sergeant Dave Covington and eight men, all of whom had hidden in the stable next to the ill-fated four story house, made their way into battalion headquarters to relate the story of the capture of Company K.

Shortly after dawn 11 October, Captain William C. Goenne, 3rd Battalion surgeon, drove by jeep up to La Fortuna to survey the casualties of Company I. Captain Chris Hald confronted Goenne and asked for a smoke because he was out of cigarettes. No such niceties had been delivered to Company I since before Casoni. Goenne gave Hald a cigarette. Hald attempted to hold the cigarette in his hand but was shaking so badly he dropped it, nor could he light it with a match.

"Chris," asked Dr. Goenne, "when did you sleep last?"

"About four nights ago," said Hald. "I've forgotten."

"Well," said Dr. Goenne, tying a tag around Hald's neck, "Get the hell out of here and go get some rest!"

Captain Hald was taken back to the 91st Division clearing station where he slept for two days, getting up now and then only for a bite to eat. He was then sent back to Florence for a four day pass which he spent drinking too much and having terrible nightmares. During this time Company I was commanded by Lieutenant Mel Krieger. On 14 October, Krieger was wounded. Four days later, Captain Hald, sufficiently recovered, again assumed command of his old company.[16]

IV

The efforts of Company K had ended in disaster; however, the 361s's 3rd Battalion had put a big bulge in the Fifth Army lines and the Germans had reacted violently to this forward push of the 91st Division. Both General Livesay and Colonel Broedlow tried desperately to exploit this success. Company K was fed in on top of Company I. Company B was fed in on top of Company K. Unfortunately, there weren't any more troops available to fully take advantage of this rupture in the German lines. If there had been a regiment, or even a battalion, available to feed into the hole, it may have developed into a major breakout. On the right of the II Corps the 88th Division had driven to within seven miles of Highway 9 in the Monte Grande area, eight miles northwest of Livergnano though the 88th, like the 91st, was near exhaustion.

Hill 603. Exhausted troops of Company B, 361st. Note the fatigue on the face of the infantryman at the right. The soldier still wears the old style field jacket. The man beside him has dug himself a nice foxhole. On the

ledge sits an empty tin from a ten-in-one ration. The heavily bearded GI takes a smoke and stares blankly at the ground, lost in thought. The helmetless soldier at the left seems to be saying, "What next?"

A prewar photograph of Livergnano probably taken during the early part of the 1900s. The ancient houses in the foreground were razed after the war. A filling station now sits at the site of the house at lower right.

Did the failure of Company B to get into Livergnano and help Company K doom the 91st's struggle to expand the bulge? After the war a number of Division officers pondered this question. Colonel Dick Oshlo had a few comments:

"Even if we had gotten Company B up to Livergnano prior to daylight, probably the end result would have been the same. However, would it have been? I don't know how the Germans would have reacted if suddenly another one hundred - fifty soldiers, or however many men there were in Company B, had bounded into that town. I assume they <u>all</u> wouldn't have ended up in the buildings with Company K. If spread around, they might have brought very effective fire on the Krauts. Together, the two companies would have been a tremendous amount of fire-power in that small place. Further, the Germans wouldn't have known whether it was a company, battalion, or what. I'm sure they'd have been very scary and jumpy about the whole thing, too. They may have reacted in our favor. I'm aware there was <u>supposed</u> to have been a battalion of Germans there, but I doubt if they were all inside the village. There just wasn't room for everyone! The enemy battalion was probably in that very immediate sector. I don't know how it would figure out mathematically, if one could do such a thing, but the eighty men captured <u>may</u> have been a relatively light price to pay for the real estate gained at that critical stage of the game. Our casualties had been very, very heavy for several weeks ahead of this action."[17]

At 0230, 12 October, Company C, 361st moved out in a flanking attack to the left of Livergnano. Its objective was Hill 554 and the flat high ground at the top of the hill. The road past the cliff houses which led to the Saint John the Baptist Church was excessively steep and to climb it even at a slow walk was a trying ordeal. The houses built into the hill's wall were completely destroyed and rubble was piled high in the middle of the road making the climb even more of a struggle. By 0745 the company had a platoon and a half on Hill 554.

From the plateau atop the hill the Powder Rivermen could look out over the Savena River Valley and the German lines. The church stood at the rear of the hill and was rapidly being destroyed by shellfire. Originally, it was a clean-lined building with a square campanile. The Germans had used the bell tower as an observation post and were able to spot the movements of Division troops clear across the valleys, north and south. The church dated back hundreds of years and its parish priests were recorded back to 1787.

At the eastern end of the plateau was the village cemetery with its mausoleums, tombstones and graves, all of which had been devastated and ravaged by artillery fire. Many of the graves had been blown out by the violence of the explosions. It was a gruesome and horrifying place. Just beyond the cemetery was the protruding nose of Livergnano Rock.

Colonel Broedlow had ordered Company C to make an extremely determined effort to secure the hill. Company B was to advance against the enemy's east flank positions on Hill 603. When these two hills were in control of the 361st there would be no way the Germans could continue to hold on to the village. Once through the escarpment the Division would be able to drive on up Highway 65 toward the II Corps objective, the city of Bologna and the valley of the Po which was becoming known as the "promised land".

Pfc. Kenneth Tutwiler was with Company C up on Hill 554:

"Incardona and Lutts were the 1st and 2nd scouts and I was next. We climbed up the road next to the cliff houses at daybreak. It was still half-dark and we surprised a Hollywood-looking German. He was cold and alone. He had on his great coat and was swinging his arms back and forth to keep warm. He was a big man, about six-four. When we were about twenty feet from him Incardona hollered, "Hands up!" I'll never forget the guy's expression as his countenance fell. Lieutenant Gloor came up and we marched the German in front of us. Half way up to the church the lieutenant told me to go back down and tell the 2nd Platoon to come on up. I got down to where the road levelled off and I'll be damned if I didn't meet a Mark VI Tiger tank coming right at me. It started up the hill machinegunning back and forth, killing five or six men. A small group of us jumped into the first house and the tank blasted the wall with two rounds of HE and two of AP. One blew me through a doorway. After I got back up we all went down into the wine cellar. I looked out of a little window at the level of the road and saw some GI prisoners being herded back. Some of them were bandaged up and bloody. The tank stopped about ten yards from our house and the Germans set up mortars in the middle of the road just outside our door. We could hear them talking and giving orders, then a squad came over to each house and yelled, 'Come out! Come out! Are you English?' Well, we got our grenades ready and Saunderson from San Francisco got his BAR ready and said the first bastard who comes through the door is a dead one, but we lucked out because they skipped our house and went on to the next one.

"Meanwhile, there was a lot going on up at the church, or so I found out later. The Germans got close to the church and yelled out something in German. They had set up a machinegun nearby. Lieutenant Gloor used his carbine to shoot it out with the Kraut machinegunner and killed him. He then charged the church with his platoon and captured after fifteen Jerries. One of the German officers spoke perfect English and told Gloor that he had lived for awhile in Texas before the war. That was interesting to Gloor because he was also from Texas. The Jerries had a tunnel in the rear of the church and came inside the wine cellar this way. They were throwing up potato mashers and Gloor and his men were throwing down grenades. Everything went fine in the church until a Mark IV arrived and started firing point blank into the church. There was nothing these guys could do if they wanted to stay alive but to get the hell out of the church. Some of them took a chance and jumped down the side of the cliff. Lieutenant Clyde Littlejohn, who related the story to me, hurt his legs, but not seriously. A few of the GIs had broken legs. I don't think anyone was killed from the jump. Incardona, Lutts and Sergeant Modderman were captured there. There were about eight American dead inside the church. All those who jumped down from the cliff got back down the hill to the house where we jumped off that morning.

"Now back to those of us who were in the house. We couldn't get out. The Germans were all over the place. Around 1500 our artillery started coming in and about four rounds hit our house. We bedded down for the night, and it was a long one. About 0400 the shells started to come in again. I said, 'Let's get the hell out of here!' I felt I had rather fight my way out then to be killed by our own artillery. A guy named Frampton agreed with me, but none of the others wanted to go with us. Since day was breaking I knew we had to move out fast. Frampton and I found our way out of the cellar and up to the first floor. It was getting daylight as we walked right out of the house and up the road and, out of the corner of my eye, I noticed two Germans standing

Battery C, 347th F.A. L-R: Captain Mel Cotton, 1st Sgt. Hutchinson and 2nd Lieutenant Stan Young.

by the damned tank . . . no more than twenty feet from us. That big old barrel pointed right at me. We simply kept on walking. I guess they thought we were Germans too. After we had walked about ten minutes we saw some people in the distance. We unslung our M1s and got ready. I was about as scared as any one man can get, then I heard some coughing. I knew that they were Americans. Nobody smoked as much as our GIs!

"I took Lieutenant Lee Hutchins and showed him where our men were. I told him to try and stop the shelling of those houses. He said he would, but he never did. The next night our men got up enough courage to get out of the houses. They were mad as hell at Frampton and me because we didn't stop the shelling, but we did everything we could.

"When Company K was captured we were right across the mountain on the next hill. Harry Hewitt and I were talking and looking out that way when all of a sudden the first house in town, to the right, just exploded in a cloud of smoke."[18]

To the east, Company B began moving up Hill 603. Its mission was not an enviable one. With an elevation of 1800 feet the huge hump of land stood at the entrance to Livergnano like a sentinel ready to defend the village against all comers. The lower slopes were brush covered and half way up the nearly vertical wall the brush became rock. Its many caves had been blasted out of the bluff and some, in addition to living quarters, contained anti-tank guns. The higher the attacking Americans got, the easier it was for the Germans to defend their positions. They could hurl boulders and grenades from the very peak and there was little concealment for the men clambering up the escarpment.

The attack began at 0600 and lasted all morning. By 1145 the company had reached the crest of the hill. Some elements were beyond 603 and were digging in.

Pfc. Fred Berg was with the attackers:

"My platoon, or most of it, was holed up in a house by the side of Sixty-five within viewing distance of the village and the church on the hill to our left. Hill 603 and the escarpment was above us and to our right. While we were staying in the house two captured Germans were brought in. One was a medic attending the other, who was a sergeant, and after some discussion found to be a member of the German Olympic swim team of 1936.

"We watched intently as some of our dive bombers strafed and bombed an enemy self-propelled vehicle on the road just below the church. We could actually see the bomb on the way to the target from our vantage point. Later we pulled back to regroup and by later afternoon we had taken the caves which laced the base of the escarpment bordering the highway. Setting up Company Headquarters in one of the caves, the 1st Platoon was entrenched in foxholes on the edge of a narrow dirt road leading from the town to the caves. That same night, and I can only guess it was midnight or after, a German counterattack was begun against our positions. I would have to say it was a company strength force preceded by a flamethrowing and grenade attack from the top of Hill 603. I remember our First Sergeant was making out his morning report when the first of the flames came across the mouth of the cave. The grenades burst mainly near the holes of our exterior guard, the 1st Platoon. Following this came the enemy infantry moving up the dirt road from town. We stopped their advance until we had time to pull back to our morning positions. The wounded had to be carried in blankets off the dirt road and down to the highway in the dark, no mean trick, since the road was at the top of a fairly steep slope which was studded with short shrubs and bushes. I remember this most vividly because I had a corner of one of the blankets and kept stumbling.

"Early the next morning, Company B, led by the 2nd Platoon, advanced to the east side of the escarpment, or to the side opposite the caves. Fortunately, the German sentries who had had a rough night of it, were asleep in their holes and we routed them out one by one, so that by mid-morning we had control of Hill 603.

"We then continued the same day for about 1200 yards beyond the town where we and some members of an engineer outfit who were clearing the area of mines, held up in some caves to the right of the highway. In this cave that night was accomplished some of the best medical work, at platoon level, that I had ever seen. Doc Mays had to give first aid to two engineers who had feet and legs blown off by mines. His expert aid undoubtedly kept these GIs alive for further medical help. There were other mine casualties that day, mostly from booby traps, the first we had encountered since the early days of June near Grossetto."[19]

By the end of 12 October, the German 65th Infantry Division was still in possession of most of Livergnano; however, eight companies of the 361st and 363rd had climbed the escarpment, and the village was nearly outflanked from the west. After 10 October, clear weather continued almost uninterrupted for the next four days which made possible the first extended period of observed artillery fire since the actions in the Gothic line. Rover Joe, a system of airground support set up at the beginning of the Gothic Line drive

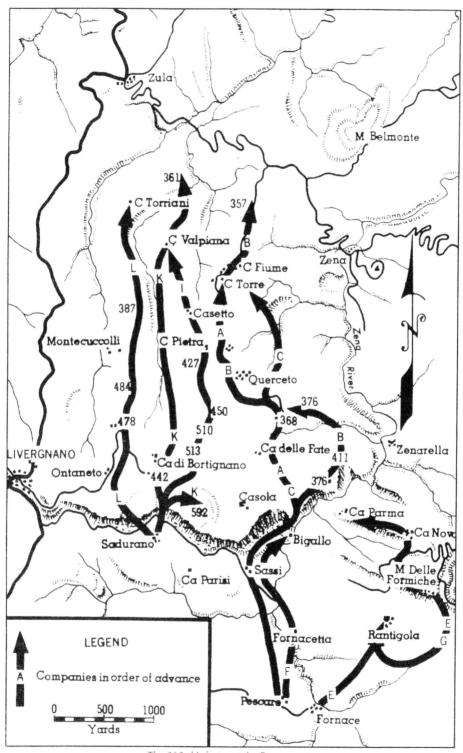

The 363rd Infantry at the Escarpment.

to deal with targets needing immediate neutralization, was again permitted to operate. Forward observation posts (Rover Joe) were set up with front-line divisions and were manned by experienced air and ground troops who directed the P-47s and Spitfires to their targets by radio. These air attacks could be made well within the bomb safety line and often within twenty minutes of the call for support by the infantry.[20]

On 11 October the 363rd Infantry moved up to the base of the escarpment. The regiment had been committed in an effort to relieve the perilous situation of the 361st's 2nd Battalion whose two companies had suffered thirty-one killed and one hundred and forty-one wounded, or more than half the men who had gone up. The regiment was to be on the high ground before morning. This was a direct order from General Mark Clark.

After dark, the 363rd launched a night attack and Companies A and C reached the top of the escarpment to the east of the 2nd Battalion, 361st. These troops consolidated during 12 October while Companies L and B came up to join them. In a coordinated move the next morning Company A struck out for Ca della Fate and Company B attacked from Hill 411 for Hill 376 and the house at 368 (See 363rd Escarpment Map). That afternoon a Company A patrol, coordinating with Company B, moved out, took Ca delle Fate and captured twenty-two prisoners in addition to overrunning the enemy mortar positions which contained ten mortars and a large quantity of ammunition. These were promptly turned around and used on their former owners. Two platoons from Company B went down the draw to the right of Hill 411, swung around in front of the hill, and cleared the house on the reverse slope of 376. While all this was going on, thirty-five Germans, driven out of Ca della Fate by Company A's attack, walked into the trap and were placed in the house under guard. Company B then sent a security patrol to Hill 368 while the remainder of the company moved forward by the same route and established positions for the night in and around the house on 368.

The fire from Captain Ernie Land's Cannon Company located below the escarpment near Sadurano proved highly effective. Strewn about the yard at 368 were a knocked out anti-tank gun, the remains of a blown up ammunition dump, a burning 88 with its prime mover and a blazing German tank.

Beginning on 13 October the German resistance on the Livergnano escarpment commenced to slacken. Up above Bigallo, the 2nd Battalion 361st, after being virtually immobilized for three days, jumped off at 1735 using rocket launchers against the strong enemy positions. At 2000 Company G had taken Casola along with one German officer and 46 prisoners. Colonel Broedlow ordered the battalion to reorganize and then drive west across the plateau. At the end of 14 October it had reached positions where it could dominate Highway 65 to the north of the village.

Back in Livergnano, the 1st Battalion, 361st was still unable to drive the Germans from Hill 554. The battalion commander, Lieutenant Colonel Howard Reynolds, ordered Company A to continue the attack and at dusk another attempt was made to grab the hill but it, too, failed.

On the division right flank the 1st and 3rd Battalions, 363rd had cleared the eastern plateau and during an early morning fight the 1st Battalion captured the village of Querceta more than one mile beyond the escarpment. (See 363rd Infantry Escarpment Map). The seizure of this critical objective meant that Germans inside Livergnano were rapidly being outflanked from the east. To the division left, the 362nd Infantry, after days on line, continued the work of driving the enemy back from the area lying between Highway 65 and the Savena River Valley until the forward units were relieved by the 34th Division. The regiment then passed to reserve.

At 0600 14 October, the 2nd Battalion, 361st jumped off and three hours later Companies E, F and G were moving slowly toward the west through very rugged terrain. By the middle of the afternoon the advance elements were on Hill 481 less than 1000 yards to the east of Hill 603 which Company B had taken some hours before. The commander of that company reported that, at 1445, he had personally pushed to the cliff overlooking Livergnano and could see no sign of the enemy. When the village appeared to be evacuated, Major Oshlo sent a Company K patrol into the town to investigate the situation. At 1740 the patrol returned and reported the Germans had withdrawn from the now famous Liver and Onions.

By midnight of the 14th the tiny mountain town, which had cost so many lives to capture, belonged to the 361st Infantry. The 3rd Battalion records show sixty-six men from that unit alone died in the vicinity of Livergnano and seventy-six were captured. A loss of 142 men to the battalion![21]

On October 19, the 361st Infantry Information and Education Section filed the following report:

"After eight days of fighting, the town of Livergnano is now cleared of all Germans. This obscure little town, hardly more than a quarter of a mile in length, was the scene of some of the most concentrated battles yet fought in the current campaign in the Apennines. The Germans did not spare any men or equipment in their defense of this strong position, which was approximately 2,000 yards wide. More concentrated forces, with abundant ammunition and weather hindered and delayed our efforts. Food and ammunition could not be transported by foot or mule; rather it had to be sent up to the troops attacking

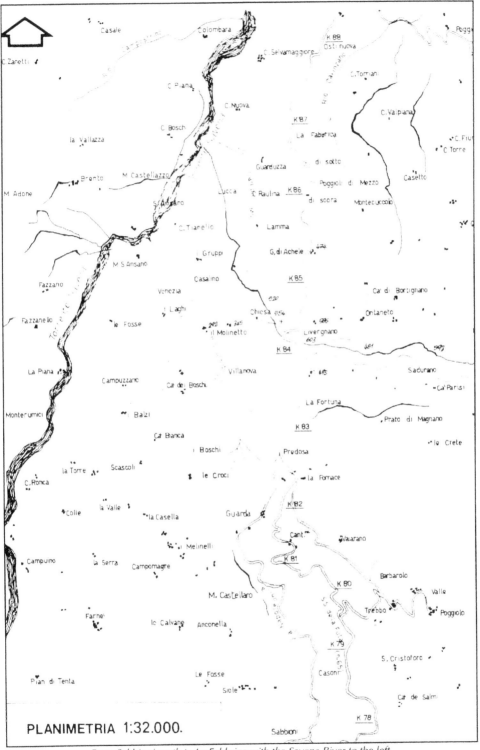

PLANIMETRIA 1:32.000.

From Sabbioni north to La Fabbrica with the Savena River to the left.

177

the ridges by means of hand carry. The weather was cloudy and misty and foggy and rainy, making observation of enemy positions very poor. In addition, German artillery and mortars constantly cut our lines of communications.

The same hard formula was renewed and used daily. It was necessary for the infantry to demolish each gun position, mortar position, cave and dugout through the use of hand grenades and close fighting. All types of artillery fire and tanks and tank destroyers, together with tactical air bombing assisted the infantry in their efforts; but the final annihilation of the well dug-in Germans became the task of the infantry.

The town itself had been reduced to rubble. There is not a building standing. Casualties on both sides have been very heavy. The Germans were given orders to hold at any cost, and their fanatical, determined resistance still continues. North of Livergnano, the Germans have brought up Mark IV tanks and with the use of direct fire and self-propelled guns have inflicted casualties against our advance patrols. Having full knowledge of the terrain and concealed positions, they have placed their tanks in firing positions advantageously. However, given clear observation of enemy positions, artillery fire and bombing missions are quickly placed on these targets.

Progress the past week has been slow, not because of any lack of effort or initiative on part of the infantry. Quite the contrary. Their ability to destroy the formidable German positions has been made much worse by the adverse elements of natural barriers and unfavorable weather."

V

The suffering that resulted from the fighting along the escarpment was not confined to the GIs of the 91st or the soldiers of the German 65th Infantry Division. Like the inhabitants of all those little mountain towns that were destroyed from Florence to Bologna, the victims of the war saw their village smashed, their lives ruined and their families shattered in the wake of the battle that raged up Highway 65. Four men from the village were killed in action in the Italian Army in Greece and Germany. Five were listed "Missing in Action" and never seen again. Though the majority of the townspeople were evacuated from Livergnano during the fighting a few stayed to tough it out and fifteen lost their lives. Five men of the village were rounded up by the Germans and never seen again.[22]

Father Felice Contavalli, the present parish priest of Livergnano, was a young man of twenty caught up in the terrible events of those days:

"I was twenty. I saw the front swiftly pass by. I did not live the tragedy of the combat line. I was taken prisoner and was about to be executed by shooting. These were the days of the Marzabotto massacre. I lived in a drying room for chestnuts in the middle of the wood and underground for a week. The cannon shots would arrive violently. I can still hear the curt and atrocious commands of the SS troops, which in that September and in that part of the front, made the civilians move away, and my eyes can still see the long lines of unfortunate people, with animals, the wagons, and the drags with no wheels on which were the sick, wrapped up in rags. Once more I see the people with bundles of humble things. I listen once again to the cry of the children tightly held in their mothers' arms.

"In Livergnano it was different. It seems that there was no real German organization regarding the civilians and people found themselves on the line of a terrible and lengthy front, caught in the vise of two determined armies. People wandered from one cave to another. Shelters and caves were the homes of men that shared lives in their suffering. Our people lived here from October to November during the first violent battles. They saw the destruction of their homes and their dear ones die. I have frightening testimonies that are part of stories of men, no longer men.

"We were in the shelter among the rosemarys, below Castello and we had finished our food. We went inside the house to fry some 'cresenti'. The Americans arrived. We would go get water at the fountain of the village and the Americans who were well hidden, would give us their canteens to fill. When we returned they would repay us with cans of food. Someone told me that at Maddalena's there was a warehouse of food. One night I slowly went over there and stole a case and when I got home I found it full of TNT. What a fright!

"I still remember the impression that was left on me by a German officer who was killed by a shot in the forehead while looking out a window at Guarduzza. And another who began crying while looking at me. And another that told me of his desire to see his daughters and his wife and then was killed shortly after.

"We were evacuated to Villanova and were present at the destruction of Livergnano. The situation was tragic when the Americans conquered Molinetto. One night the Germans were able to enter the house through a ditch that brought water to the mill. They ended up being massacred. When we were in the Mintfield cave, a German officer who had always been kind to us, told us how a patrol that had been with us shortly before, had been completely annihilated. Everyone caput. Father Giovanni said that while he was going to Predosa to celebrate mass he saw two rows of dead Americans at the side of the road. The priest moved from one place to another in order to say mass in the air-raid shelters. He went to Guarda and offered to go all the way to Tianello, but the Americans wouldn't allow it. 'Because,' they said, 'there is need for you here.' A great tragedy took place in Tianello. The poor people there all disappeared. Nothing about them was ever found out. They simply disappeared.

"Above Bortignano many dead Americans were gathered. Many were brought out wrapped in white cloths. Those people who lived the battle at Garduzza remained in the cellar under the ruins for forty days. That month left enduring traces and wounds on the flesh and life of the people, destroyed from hunger, suffering from fear. It seemed that life did not exist. What one became aware of while talking to these people is the great sense of solidarity and their conscience of being human. The dead are not forgotten. My mother and grandmother died in the first bombardment in the Grotta. In Ca di Luca, my sister was killed by an exploding shell. She was holding her daughter who was thrown away and was safe. The wounded were assisted and the desperate were comforted. I was wounded while rescuing a wounded lady and was treated and taken to the hospital. My home no longer existed. It was completely demolished. When we returned home we found many packs, equipment and munitions.

"We were going to Predosa. We encountered some Italian soldiers with mules. 'Paisa, where is the front? they asked. 'Livergnano', we told them, then fled away.

"When we returned home we slept under what was left of the stable on bedsprings with no mattress and there were many rats. We covered ourselves the best way we could. Some fought their war against the rats, going to bed with a rifle and shooting at every intrusion of the rats on the beams of the ceiling. We returned home on foot. The people proved their attachment to the land. They immediately reconstructed their homes and tilled the fields. So the life of our community resumed with tears and with hope. Hope for a different and better future.

"Life had changed."[23]

VI

The six day period 10-15 October was characterized by the heaviest fighting since the beach of the Gothic Line at il Giogo Pass. Not only was this true for the 91st Division but for the three other attacking divisions of II Corps. During the six days of fighting the 5th Army attack suffered a total of 2,491 battle casualties with 769 in the 91st. In the first nine days of October the four divisions had lost 3,208 men to make a total of 5,699 for the first fifteen days of the month and 12,210 casualties since the beginning of the II Corps offensive on 10 September. It didn't take a mathematical wizard to figure out that if these losses continued the 5th Army would be reduced to an ineffective fighting force within a matter of days, or even hours. A serious shortage of replacements was developing in the Italian theatre and since Italy had taken a back seat to both the Pacific theatre and the war in the ETO it was third in priorities in both replacements and supplies. It was obvious the offensive for the Po Valley was slowing down and each day saw fewer gains by the attacking troops, though the fighting continued savage and bloody. Also Marshal Kesselring was shifting more and more strength to the II Corps front and was showing an amazing resourcefulness in putting together odds and ends to maintain a front. In addition to the 65th and 98th Grenadier Divisions, which were sent into the line before 10 October, one regiment of the 94th Grenadier Division was identified in the 85th Division zone and one regiment of the 29th Panzers turned up north of Livergnano in the 91st sector. At this rate it wouldn't be long before the Germans would have as many troops at the front as II Corps.[24]

On 15 October the still weary men of the 362nd Infantry were sent back into line. Under cover of darkness the regiment moved up Highway 65 to attack a place called Lucca northwest of Livergnano. This enemy defensive position was situated so that the only approach to the houses, which composed the strong point, was over previously cultivated ground completely barren of cover. Maneuvering was virtually impossible as sheer cliffs afforded protection on both sides and the houses were built up against the face of the escarpment. The nature of the terrain made it impossible to deploy more than one platoon at a time.

The Miami Herald's Jack Bell covered the attack:

WITH THE FIFTH ARMY IN NORTHERN ITALY—Lucca isn't a very big city. In fact, Lucca, up on Route 65 in northern Italy, consists of two houses and five haystacks. But they were strategic houses and important haystacks, a key position commanding a lot of war movement up the main highway. They asked Company I of the 362nd Infantry to take Lucca and that's how Sgt. Herman F. Buie, Akron, Ohio, got into the scramble. For he was the oldest man, in point of service, on the company roster, since 10 July 1942. Men had been killed, became ill and dropped out. Replacements came in again and again. But Sgt. Buie stood firm.

He was a fine soldier and because he had proved his ability many times under fire he had been recommended for a commission, a combat appointment. In short, he had earned his bars the hard way. So, when Captain Clifton Peters, Amarillo, Texas, got orders to take Lucca he selected his two best non-coms to lead a unit of some two dozen men on what they knew would be a desperate scrap. One was Sgt. Virgil Moore, a farm boy from Beech Grove, Arkansas, who many times had stood cool under fire and had won a Silver Star. The other was Sgt. Buie. Several more sergeants were chosen because the captain's company had been shot up so badly he dared not sent too crack non-coms out with twenty-two green replacements.

They advanced at dawn, soon as it was light enough to see a few feet but not enough for the Krauts to spot them—so they thought! The Jerries expected the attack, had outposts, and after letting the Americans advance into a draw, they opened up with withering fire. There was nothing to do but drop behind whatever they could find and fire as best they could. German 88's fired point blank. Machineguns kept them hugging the dirt. Snipers took their time and aimed true. No men were ever in more of a hell. First to be wounded was Sgt. Roberts, a veteran from Dearborn, Michigan. Sgt. Drew, St. Louis, was next. Sgt. McChesny got five Jerries before a sniper wounded him. A bullet killed Sgt. Pierce instantly. Another wounded Sgt. Missey, a veteran from St. Louis. Enlisted men were getting it less because the squad leaders put them in more protected spots.

When darkness ended the hellfire, eleven Americans managed to crawl back unhurt. First-aid men went for the wounded and Sgts. Buie and Moore met with Captain Peters to discuss the plan for the next day. They were given more men and arms. Next morning they took off again, and obviously the Jerries hadn't expected them this time. At the first pillbox they surprised and captured three Jerries without firing a shot. This enabled them to surprise and take six more half an hour later. But the Jerry power on the hill was aroused and once more the Americans went through terrific fire. It was during this exchange of bullets that Sgt. Buie was hit in the chest, a deep and painful wound. He refused to pull out, declaring he was going to remain and go into the Jerry stronghold with the rest. But after an hour he became so weak he could no longer hold his rifle and Sgt. Moore took charge and ordered a medic to take him back.

Sgt. Buie and the medic turned toward a hill a few yards away. Buie looked back, the bullets whizzing around him as he moved away, and said, prayerfully, "God damn, how I hate to leave you guys!"

"And he meant it," Sgt. Moore said proudly, "and we went on and took the objective. When Sgt. Buie got hit that made seven non-coms knocked out, leaving me the only survivor. I thought I had it once. A burst of three bullets hit my helmet. I was lucky they didn't come straight, but the glancing bullets only knocked me out. At first when I came around I thought I was dead. Then I remembered feeling my head. My helmet was gone. I figured if I could feel my head and knew my helmet was gone I wasn't dead. And pretty soon I came around all right, found the helmet and got back in there pitchin'. We killed eight more Krauts and captured nineteen before we were through. That night they made a counterattack, but we're better shots with small arms and beat them off. Anytime it's them against us, they're licked."

"And it might be well to remember," observed Captain Peters, "that Lucca, the biggest little town on the road to Bologna—was the only victory later ——by the United Nations on that particular day."

"And that it got me the issue of a new helmet," added Sgt. Moore. "Just as heavy and ornery as the old one."

"When that Buie gets back from the hospital," Captain Peters said. "I'm going to work his tail off. I'll make him wish he hadn't won a commission."[25]

The attack continued all during the morning of 17 October and at 1400 Company I broke into Lucca. Company G then sent a platoon forward to help occupy the tiny hamlet. During the night the 362nd Infantry took over command of the sector of the 1st and 2nd Battalions, 361st and prepared to continue the attack at 0530 the next morning. The regimental objective was the enemy positions at Canovetta.

This small group of houses sat along Highway 65 about 3000 yards north of Livergnano. After three days of a bitter back and forth battle a 2nd Battalion patrol entered Canovetta. It was as far forward as any Division troops would advance in the Savena River sector or up the highway leading to Bologna. At 1650, General Livesay directed the 362nd to consolidate its positions and organize for defense.

In the four day period 16-19 October the 91st Division gained only one additional mile along Sixty-five. In addition to a notable increase in the use of tanks and SP guns the volume of fire laid down by the enemy artillery had more than doubled from that experienced in September. The Germans concentrated their heaviest fire on Livergnano in an attempt to block the passage of supplies up the highway. Elements of the crack 16th SS Division had also moved into positions along the left flank of the Division. Faced with the danger of a possible counterattack by the 16th SS and the 29th Panzers the Division had gradually shifted from the offensive to what was in effect an aggressive defense.[26] Adding to this bad news was a change in the weather. At 1800, 18 October the 91st G-2 Periodic Report gave the following forecast: "Mainly cloudy with rain. Scattered showers in the mountains during the afternoon. Visibility moderate to poor. High SW winds, strong in exposed places." By the morning of the 19th dense rains were falling all along the Division front and fog rolled through the Savena and Idice River valleys.

Despite the miserable weather conditions all efforts were made by the Division units to get anti-tank weapons forward and into positions to meet any armored threat by the Germans. While the 316th Engineers shoveled and blasted and carved roads to get tanks forward, Captain William P. Gooldy, commander of the 363rd Antitank Company, was using everything available to get his guns up front and into action. Mules and oxen, jeeps and bulldozers, trucks and winches and infantrymen and engineers worked together to haul the guns through knee deep mud. One platoon, soaked to the skin from the continuing rain, worked all night with four oxen and eight mules but failed in an attempt to pull a 57mm gun up out of the ooze. The engineers brought up a bulldozer, but even that broke down. Another bulldozer came up but could only manage 200 yards before it slid and tumbled down a ravine. When everything else failed one platoon tore a 57mm gun down into parts and loaded a oxcart, throwing camouflage nets over the white oxen so they wouldn't be recognized if the weather cleared, but an artillery barrage routed the Italian drivers and as one infantryman remarked, "The oxen wouldn't via for me." Finally, five guns were moved forward and into position.[27]

On the morning of 24 October the 362nd Infantry received Field Order Number 25. It was to be relieved by the 361st Infantry and closed in the area around Anconella for three days of badly needed rest. However, the unlucky GIs would not get their rest. Around noon of that same day orders came down for an advance party to go to the headquarters of the 88th Division. That division had just captured Mount Grande and was only 8,000 yards from Highway 9 which runs in a straight line into Bologna. For the 88th to hold on to Grande and also continue the drive, it needed another combat team and the 362nd was the only one available. It was ironic that just to travel the five impassable miles between the old regimental area and the new one, it was necessary to travel back to Radiocosa Pass to get to the 88th Division zone, a total distance of thirty-five miles! At this time the weather was becoming increasingly foggy and rainy. On 25 October, the 346th Field Artillery began the long trip over to back up the 362nd with its guns. The road to San Clemente in the Sillaro River Valley, where the 88th Division was fighting, was clogged with traffic. Atop Radicosa Pass a full gale was blowing and all the little valleys and streams were choked with water.

Captain Robert F. Dunning, S-2 of the 346th, made the trip with his fellow officers:

"On the evening of 24 October, the 362nd was ordered to reconnoiter positions in the Sillaro Valley to reinforce the 88th Division. Colonel Barry, Major Geyer, myself, the battery commanders and Lieutenant Desperate Dan Desper, the survey officer, fell in behind the doughboy column on Highway 65. The Sillaro Valley was laterally only about seven miles to the right of our positions near Route 65, but to get there, we had to go all the way back to Radicosa Pass and take Route 6529 a total of thirty-five miles to get into the valley by the back door. This last named route was a gravel road, but "gravel" is too grandiose a name: it was a "dirt" road.

"It was raining cats and dogs when we left and did so all day. The convoy made good time back over Route 65, but on the dirt road, conditions became bad with a vengeance. There was a good foot of mud which would be plowed off to the side by bulldozers only to be washed back onto the road by the rain a few minutes later. We would move a half mile and then wait half an hour. The peeps being light and low had to be frequently winched out of mud holes.

"Our first stop was at 88th Division headquarters. In the heavy rain we had kept the tops of our peeps up and the side curtains on like civilized sensible people. During the inevitable wait an 88th MP came down the line of peeps rapping on each windshield. "In 88th Division country, all vehicles keep their tops and windshields down," he announced, and we complied. On a bright or even a cloudy day, this makes sense to prevent reflections in the sun, but on this particular day, the Krauts couldn't see fifty feet. We later learned that such quirks were normal under General "Bull" Kendall, the 88th CG who ran his outfit like George Patton and Charlie Gerhardt style. For the rest of the trip, we rode with the driving rain in our faces, once again cursing our helmets which sometimes seemed to channel the water down the backs of our necks under our collars.

"We finally made it down into the Sillaro Valley and our destination just south of the village of San Clemente. The river winds through the valley which is flat as a pancake but only a few hundred yards wide. On each side barren, treeless hills and mountains rise steeply, and there are no sheltering tree clumps and canyons to afford protection. All the decent positions and buildings were occupied by 88th Division people and supporting troops, and we finally had to settle for positions on the valley floor next to the swollen river about a half mile up stream from San Clemente. We were able to find a room for our FDC in the only building in the area called Casa Calanco. The whole Sillaro Valley looked dirt poor. It was sparsely settled, the soil

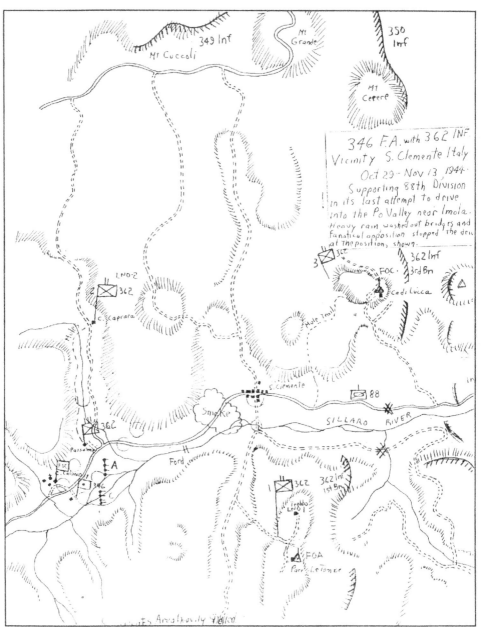

The 362nd Infantry and 346th Field Artillery in the Sillaro River Valley. Drawn by Bob Dunning, 346th F.A.

was too tight for decent farming and what grew was often washed out by the river. The houses were built accordingly. Most Italian "casas" have substantial walls, often masonry more than twelve inches thick and the roof was flimsy, supported by sagging wooden rafters. There already were a number of shell holes in the walls and roof, covered by tarps.

"At the beginning, our FDC would share this palace with Hqs of the 338th Field Artillery, Hqs of the 804 Tank Destroyer Battalion, a company of the 316th Medical Battalion and the supply echelon of the 362nd Infantry. Later, the 338th would be replaced by the Hqs of the 19th Regiment, Royal Artillery. There was no room for our CP, so we planned to install it in a dug-in tent across the road in the valley bottom. With our new positions all arranged for, we returned to our old ones at Valle off Highway 65, slugging and slogging all the way. The rain had let up a little, but it was still long after dark when we got home.

"On the morning of 26 October, at about 8 a.m., still dark under the double daylight saving time that prevailed, the entire 346th Field Artillery prepared to leave Valle for Casa Calanco. Though the rain had slackened a cold dense fog had moved in. I was assigned to lead the column in a command car with a half dozen men to leave off as road markers. Unfortunately, the Headquarters Battery vehicles followed directly behind my car without giving me time to drop off my traffic policemen. I did manage to leave he first marker at Highway 65 to insure that nobody turned north and ended up in the Po Valley in a POW camp. But at the Monghidoro bypass, where we stopped to drop off the second man, the column behind us didn't see us in the fog and the big FDC truck and a couple of wire trucks whizzed by before we could get started again. Now we had a problem. We had to catch up and pass the three errant trucks before they reached Radicosa Pass, missed the left turn at Route 6529 and ended up in Florence, and all of this in a thick fog. We overtook the two wire trucks but the driver of the FDC truck kept speeding up, evidently looking for my command car. All the time we were behind him trying to catch up. As I look back we played a very foolish game for a few minutes at speeds far greater than were safe. But at the time, it was very important to catch that damned truck. And we just did, just before the critical turnoff.

"There, at Route 6529, on top of Radicosa Pass, the fog had lifted, but a cold, wet gale was blowing, making it difficult to stand without bracing yourself. I had to leave a route marker at this miserable place. I sort of closed my eyes and did a mental 'eeny, meeny, miny mo' ending up with Private Henry Tom, a young Chinese-American boy from New York City, the officers' mess orderly. I felt awful leaving him there all alone, shivering and dejected in the wind and rain and wondered if it would be safe for me to eat my powdered eggs the next morning. Later vehicles in the column reported that, as they came down Highway 65 approaching Radicosa Pass, all they could see was a long skinny arm reaching out of a foxhole beside the road and waving them down Route 6529.

"Once on muddy 6529, the bulldozers began in earnest. A bulldozer would plow the knee deep mud on either side of the road, leaving a rocky but passable road bed, then as you watched, the mud would flow back onto the road like molasses and pretty quick somebody was stuck, particularly the peeps. Our entire column quickly caught up with us. It was just before noon when we reached a placed called Villanova, just north of the cutoff road leading over the mountains to the Santerno Valley to the east. We were actually in the zone of 13 British Corp, at this time assigned to the 5th Army and there was a Limey officer in the middle of the road. We stopped the column and I got out to see what was the matter. He pointed to a deep gully on either side of the road just ahead. There had been a bridge there once but it had been blown by the Krauts. Instead of building a new bridge, our engineers had installed a pipe culvert to carry the stream and then filled in the gully with dirt to road grade. The gully was maybe sixty feet wide and thirty feet deep. The pipe was not big enough to handle all the rain; on the upstream side the water had risen to about road level creating a large pond and the road was now acting like a dam. The Limey advised us not to cross. I looked a little closer and could see the filled-in road surface quivering like a bowl of Jello. No way was anyone from our outfit going to cross, so I sent the command car back along the column to report the situation to the Colonel. The question of whether to cross or not quickly became academic. I had barely opened my mouth to give the order when the whole mass of road-fill in the gully gave way with a mighty roar and water and dirt took off like a freight train down into the Sillaro Valley.

"We stood there for about two minutes with our mouths wide open, just about as long as it took to empty the pond. Then I sweated and thanked God none of us were in on that part of the road at that time. I should have also thanked the Limey officer. We later learned that the flood was disastrous to the 362nd Infantry which was already down in the valley. Motor pools washed away, dozens of vehicles were wrecked and several doughboys drowned. Later when we were in position at Casa Calanco, Lieutenant Dave Howie of Headquarters Battery discovered a peep in the river mud. He and his motor crew fished it out and made it run. All such extra vehicles, even captured ones, were supposed to be turned in, but in practice this was seldom done.

"Well, the Limey officer took off to find a Bailey Bridge and we discovered that three other bridges were out more or less marooning the 346th on about a mile of Route 6529. We were even separated from A Battery by one washout and would be cut off from the rest of the army for at least twenty-four hours. The Colonel ordered all batteries off the road and under such cover as was available.

Headquarters Battery was able to get off the road near the wash-out but cover was scarce. The only building for half a mile that could be used as an OP was a rickety old masonry barn in which two white oxen were tethered to a central feed trough. At about this time, the enemy started to shell the road and we were reminded that there were Krauts just over the ridge from us in the Santerno Valley with no friendly doughboys in between. They undoubtedly had observers on the ridge and we were thankful that the light rain and fog made observation difficult. That was the good news; the bad news was everyone was cold and wet as a result of the windshield edict. More good news was that we had our kitchens with us and everyone got a hot meal.

"The Krauts shelling continued all afternoon and evening with a "crack" about every couple of minutes. Everyone not in the CP were in foxholes under puptents and nobody was hurt although nerves were ragged. When it became time to bed down, the Colonel invited Captain Earl Lawitzke and me to sleep in the barn with him and the CP personnel. Earl had not yet joined his infantry battalion as had Captains Chargin and Scott, the other liaison officers. We grabbed our bedrolls and went inside. As cold as it was outside, within it was hot and steamy with the atmosphere permeated by the odor of cowshit and urine. Every nook and cranny was occupied by a bedroll. The floor was wet and filthy, the roof leaked, and in the middle of the room, those two great breasts jostled about, every now and then letting out a plaintive bellow. Then one of them relieved its bladder, the mate swished its tail through the heavy stream a few times and the air was suddenly saturated with droplets that did not come from the leaky roof. "No thanks," said Earl, in his usual calm, polite manner, "I think I'll take my chances outside." I agreed, and we found a small wall tent, pitched it over a pair of foxholes and slept like babies despite the steady "cracking" of shell bursts throughout the area.

"The next morning it was still cloudy with poor visibility but the rain and the shelling has stopped. The Limey engineers arrived early with the bridge equipment on huge flatbed trucks. Now, an Englishmen had invented the Bailey bridge which goes together like an erector set. If decent piers or banks are available it should take no more than a few hours to put a sixty to seventy span in place. In our case, the banks required more work making the job a little more difficult. However, all the regular engineer troops were busy elsewhere, so they sent the Limey a platoon of infantry to do the work. Things didn't go well at all. It was sort of like the construction of the "Bridge Over the River Kwai" before Alec Guiness took charge. The bridge wasn't completed until late the next day, the 28th, by which time the Limey engineer had, I believe, been evacuated in a straight jacket.

"We were the first unit to cross over the new bridge and completed our journey to Casa Calanco without further adventures. By dark, the battalion was in position, the FDC was operational and we helped the 88th Division artillery repel a counterattack. On the 30th, the 362nd Infantry relieved the 351st Infantry of the 88th on either side of the valley just north of San Clemente, all in preparation for a planned attack by II Corps toward the Po Valley and Castel San Pietro on Highway 9. Our liaison officers and observers were all with their respective battalions ready to go. The next day, however, all was called off and everyone went on the defensive. Perhaps, when the brass finally realized that the "relievers" were just as short handed and worn out as the 'relievees' they had to admit that all was 'kaput' as far as reaching the Po Valley at this time. Bad weather, ammo shortage, lack of replacements and battered supply routes may have helped in their decision. Once again, if that fresh division had been available, but enough of that nauseating 'if.'"[28]

All attempts by the 88th Division to reach Highway 9 failed. The fog, mud and torrential rains added to the misery of the infantrymen who were already approaching the limits of their endurance. Several foot bridges were put across the swollen river, but all transport was tied up south of the Sillaro. On the afternoon of 26 October General Keys ordered his troops to pull back and dig in.

By the end of October the Fifth Army offensive that was to take it to the valley of the Po and the plains of Lombardy had bogged down completely. From the start of the offensive on 10 September through 26 October the 34th, 85th, 88th and 91st Divisions sustained 15,716 battle casualties—forty-seven days of continuous combat, or 334 casualties per day.[29]

All along the Division front from the Savena River Valley west of Highway 65 to the Idice River Valley to the east the Powder Rivermen were digging in and digging in deep in preparation for a long and miserable winter.

The atrocious weather did not let up but only worsened. The rain continued to fall. Day after day it washed the faces of the dead who lay along the beaten paths and in the foxholes hacked into the rocky soil north of Livergnano. It drenched the men in the line companies and soaked them with a perpetual clamminess that would not dry. It fell on the reserve troops as they lay shivering in their shallow slit trenches, wrapped in their flimsy shelter-halves. It fell on the plodding rations mules whose hooves sucked rhythmically in the mud as the fog moved silently over the towering hills around Monte Adone and the wind cut a little deeper into the eroding crags. The rain fell on the brown clad corpses as they came down out of the mountains lashed to the pack saddles of the faithful mules who, nose to tail, brought supplies up the slippery slopes and returned with the dead. Sometimes even the mules could not make it and the bodies were transferred to litters and rode the rest of the way down on the bruised shoulders of sweating medics of the 316th Medical Battalion.

The rain fell on the stack of crosses that lay in a waiting pile by the open graves of the Pietramala cemetery. It fell on the pitiful cadavers stretched out in the mud and onto the cold hands of the Graves Registration men as they moved jerkily among the bodies removing the one dogtag and tacking it to the one cross; and it soaked Old Glory, the cemetery flag, so that it could no longer wave in the bitter mountain wind, but only quivered and snapped atop the metal pole.

A 363rd infantryman remembered November as pretty much like October.

"I think it was the first day of November. It had been raining for days. Each day became colder as autumn moved into winter. This particular night we had stopped at the foot of a huge cliff and were preparing to dig in but the soil was so rocky we decided to simply pitch pup tents and try and get some rest. To hell with the artillery. It was so foggy it would have been impossible for the Jerries to zero in on any targets. The lead company had moved on ahead of us and was somewhere in front. A barrage had hit the company as it moved forward and the bodies of half a dozen men lay strewn about twenty feet from the base of the cliff. As we struggled with our tents, the rain fell endlessly, helped along by gusts from the mountain winds. A replacement had come into the company the day before, an elderly looking guy who seemed bewildered as hell. He asked me if I'd pitch in with him. I felt a little sorry for him and told him, yeah I would. After we got the tents buttoned together and the pegs in the ground we decided to strip and wring out our clothes. I know this sound absurd, but that's what we did. I told my mother about this after the war, but I know she didn't believe me. We even wrung out our long johns...our shirts, pants and we even tried to wring out our field jackets, then we put them all on again. It was absolutely goddamn miserable. We were no more then settled under the shelterhalves when a four inch stream of water came trickling down from the cliff and began running through our tent. There was no way we could sleep or even rest so we tore down the tents and put them back in our packs and stood huddled against the cliff for the remainder of the night. Around one in the morning the rain changed to sleet and the temperatures dropped way down. Ice began to form on our helmets, then a thin crust formed on our jacket sleeves. We endured an almost endless night. Finally the day dawned cold, grey, dirty and wet. Early in the morning the platoon sergeant came over and told me I was being sent to Florence for a three day pass. He said I was the last one in the platoon. Everybody else had already had one. I'd gone into the line on 10 September and it was now the first of November so that meant I had been in combat for over fifty days. There was a guy in the 2nd Platoon who was going with me. I guess he was the last one in that platoon too.

"We started back down the mountain to find the Antitank Company where we were to leave our packs and rifles. We then walked over to a sixby and crawled up into the back and were driven to the Fifth Army rest center in Florence. We showered, got clean uniforms and had our first hot meal in days. I went back to the hotel and laid down on my cot and fell asleep. I awoke, racked by stomach cramps, and so began three days of dysentery with periodic races to the latrine. The hotel we were staying in had the old style bathrooms. They didn't have stools but two small pedestals shaped like shoe soles and an round hole in the terrazzo floor. All day long I swayed back and forth on those damned shoe soles and listened to the drunken conversations of men in the stanchions next to me. I checked in with the medics who poured paragoric down me. They told me nearly all the men who came off the line came down with the GIs after eating hot food. They laughed and thought it was funny as hell. Yeah, a real riot!

"After the end of my three days I wasn't feeling much better, but I didn't see any point in continuing my treatment with the medics. Second Platoon joined me on the truck ride back to the Antitank Company. I felt pretty good when we left the rest center but by the time we got to the front I was deathly sick. We no sooner reached the Antitank Company then the Germans threw in one hell of an artillery barrage. Most of the antitank guys were billeted in an old stone barn whose entrances were sandbagged. There was also a high wall of sandbags at the rear of the barn so 2nd Platoon and I crawled behind these during the barrage. About a dozen rounds lit in the farmyard, tearing up a sixby and a couple of jeeps. I didn't even attempt to pick up my pack and rifle. I told 2nd Platoon that I was going back to the aid station and to tell my sergeant. I managed to walk back down the mountain to the 3rd Battalion aid station. It was crowded and there were several bodies on stretchers by the door with their faces covered with blankets. The battalion surgeon saw I had a high fever. He asked me if I was passing blood. I said, yes. He scribbled something on my tag and I was loaded into an ambulance with two guys who had been wounded and were in bad shape. One of the medics asked me, 'What in the hell is wrong with you?' I just pointed to my tag.

"We finally arrived at an evacuation hospital near Monghidoro, I think it was. It was a miserable place, a sea of mud. There were long duckboards down the middle of the tents to keep the patients from walking through the mire. And it was cold. God, it was cold. There was a stove in the middle of the tent but it wasn't very hot. A nurse came over to talk to me. I remember she had a cheery smile and grey flecks in her hair. I had a sudden cramp while I was talking to her so she told me where the latrine was and gave me a cardboard box with a lid on it and told me to bring back a 'specimen'. I sloshed through the muck to the latrine and sat down on the cold boards. It was one hell of a depressing situation. After I returned I laid on my cot and tried to get some sleep. The nurse had given me a glass of chalky powdered stuff to drink. The man on the cot next to me had stepped on a Schu mine and they had amputated his leg just below the knee. He was just coming out of the anesthetic and was moaning and groaning and vomiting loudly into a curved pan held by a wardboy. On the other side of me was a guy from the 34th who had taken some machinegun slugs in the back. He was in a cast from his neck to his waist. The cast was red with blood. After awhile I fell asleep and when I awoke the 34th man was gone. He had died while I was asleep and they had carted him away. Just like that.

"A couple of days later I climbed once again into the back of a sixby which took me all the way south to Leghorn to a hospital by the sea that was absolute paradise. There were sheets on the bed and we were given crisp, clean, new red robes and the hospital had marble floors. One of the Red Cross workers gave me a copy of Hemingway's For Whom the Bell Tolls. I read as far as El Sordo's fight for the hilltop and had to give it up. The writing was far too graphic for me. I broke out into a sweat and had to put it down.

"I was at that hospital ten days before I was ruled well enough to be returned to my company. I eventually headed north again and found my old platoon holding a small beachhead on the other side of the Savena River. It was hell to be up front, but good to see familiar faces again.[30]

Endnotes for Chapter Nine

1. The 361st Regimental History. October, 1944.
2. Captain Hald wrote a sixteen page description of the actions of Company I at La Fortuna for the author during the time he was researching Thunder in the Apennines.
3. Letter to the author.
4. Hald Narrative.
5. Letter to the author.
6. Letter to the author.
7. The Powder River Journal. December, 1987.
8. Lieutenant Windle's narrative originally appeared in Thunder in the Apennines in an edited form.
9. Letter to the author.
10. Letter to the author.
11. Hald narrative.
12. In 1949 Captain Anderson wrote an interesting monograph while attending the Advanced Officer's Training Course at Fort Benning. This study covers his actions at Livergnano. The author sent the monograph to the former 3rd Battalion, 361st commander, Richard C. Oshlo for his comments. Colonel Oshlo's critique is very informative and adds much to the confused actions that took place during the battle for the village.
13. Anderson monograph.
14. Letter to the author.
15. Letter to the author.
16. Hald narrative.
17. Oshlo critique.
18. Conversation with the author.
19. Letter to the author.
20. Fifth Army History, Chapter VII. "The Gothic Line" Reprinted in The Powder River Journal. June, 1987. Page 29.
21. The Livergnano casualty figures are from the records of the 3rd Battalion sent to the author by Colonel Oshlo.
22. Sfondrini, Don Giovanni Battista. "Il mio diario de guerra". Livergnano. 22 September, 1965.
23. Contavalli, Don Felice. "The Impressed Memory." La Resa. Livergnano. 1992.
24. Fifth Army History. Page 31.
25. The Powder River Journal. June, 1988. Pages 27-28.
26. Fifth Army History. Chapter VII. Reprinted in The Powder River Journal. December, 1987. Page 80.
27. 363rd Infantry Regimental History. October, 1944. Page 36.
28. Dunning, Captain Robert. "Hot Time in the Sillaro Valley." The Powder River Journal. June, 1991. Pages 10-12.
29. Fifth Army History. Page 81.
30. This narrative was sent to the author by a veteran of the 363rd Infantry who preferred to remain anonymous.

CHAPTER TEN —
SHORT OF THE PROMISED LAND
AND INTO THE WINTER LINE

"The scenes on this field would have cured anyone of war."
—General William T. Sherman, describing the Shiloh battlefield, in a letter to his wife.

I

The last laborious drive of Fifth Army to break out into the Promised Land of the Po plains had ended in an agonizing collapse, like a miler who tumbles to the track in exhaustion just inches from the tape. The failure was an especially bitter one for the troops of the Division. Those who had survived remembered the early, sunny days of September when it appeared the end of the Italian Campaign was only weeks away. Helped along by the overly optimistic reports that poured fourth from Corps and Army and the overall cheery rumors that filtered down from the U.S. command in France, the final, terrible offensive in late October seemed even more odious to the men in the forward foxholes and an acrimonious attitude seemed to seep into the character of the GIs; their speech; their manner and their language. They were now, truly, combat veterans and had attained the cynicism of the battle-seasoned soldier. It was now a matter of surviving; everything else was secondary. This meant men in the rifle squads had to look out for each other. The platoon sergeant had to ride herd on his platoon. The company commander needed a tight rein on his company. The same applied to the battalion commanders, the battery commanders, right up to General Livesay who had once told his men that an infantry division was like a family and that they all had to look out for one another.

For the next five and one half months the Division would encounter an infinity of artillery and mortar barrages, patrols, attacks and counter attacks, ceaseless days of bitter mountain winds, rain, sleet, snow and digging in, always digging in, on the raw, ragged slopes of the Northern Apennines.

So the Fifth Army, for a second year, would be forced to face another dreaded German line of defense. In the Division zone the line stretched from the escarpment at La Tomba, near Montermici, along the Savena River, past Monte Adone, S. Ansano, across Highway 65 at La Fahbrica, to Zena Creek and into the valley of the Idice. This region was a desolate land of ruined houses, acres and acres of taped mine fields and blood-soaked terrain, pock-marked with thousands and thousands of shell holes.

The first snowfall of late autumn fell on the higher mountains on Armistice Day, 11 November; four days later two inches of snow and rain drenched the Apennines. The Italian winter had begun.[1]

Though the Division was digging in for the long haul, it had not gone into hibernation. The dogfaces in the mudcoated positions were constantly on the alert against any German action. Activity on the MLR and to the rear was sharply reduced. Orders from II Corps stated that "1. No offensive action of more than company strength be made without prior authority from Corps Headquarters; and 2. No troop movement was to be made except during the hours of darkness." No one, the order continued, regardless of rank, or importance of mission was permitted to visit any of the front-line units from dawn to dusk. Night travel was held to a very minimum. The defense of the Second Winter Line had also begun.[2]

With the arrival of November, Captain Robert F. Dunning and the men of the 346th Field Artillery were still in the Sillaro River Valley with the 88th Division.

"So we went over to the defensive, but nobody told the Krauts. They evidently still felt the situation to be dangerous to them and continued to feel the doughboys out with counterattacks. For the first time in our experience, there was more incoming mail than outgoing. Infantry action gradually petered out to active patrolling, but Kraut artillery fire continued at a high rate. Because of a general lack of cover, the 346th had been forced to situate itself in a "hot spot". The Germans had direct observation of our positions from a mountain down the valley directly ahead of us. The rain and later smoke screens across the valley at San Clemente interfered with the observation, but by that time, the Krauts had everyone and everything zeroed in. They could shoot blindfolded and hit someone or at least scare the hell out of him. For once Jerry seemed to have plenty of ammunition.

"The FCD was in the only available cover, and that was skimpy as previously noted. The Battalion CP and everybody else had to dig in as deep as possible, gun positions, battery's CP's, kitchens and each individual soldier—when he had a chance to sleep. The ground was soft and easy to dig but the water table was so high you could only dig so far, maybe eighteen to twenty-four inches at the most if you didn't want

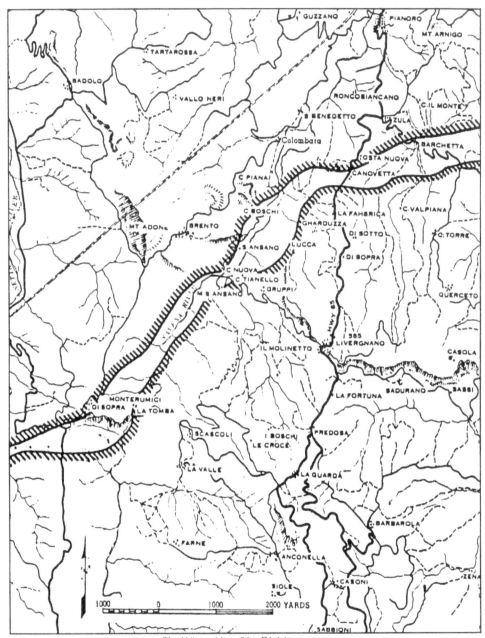

The Winter Line. 91st Division sector.

to sleep in a waterbed without the bed. The howitzer positions were dug in and well sandbagged. The Battalion CP was dug in on a knoll about four feet, sandbagged a couple of more feet, provided with a wooden floor, covered with a pyramidal tent and camouflaged. My foxhole was about twenty-four inches deep and covered by a puptent as was everyone else's.

"Surprisingly, the 346th had few casualties. We had protected ourselves as well as possible and had been well trained and conditioned not to take unnecessary chances and to expose ourselves only when we had to. We all got pretty good at "hitting the dirt" at the sound of the distant pop or the deadly whine. Still, it was nerve wracking, particularly as the weather turned fair for a couple of days and we had to depend entirely on the smoke pots at San Clemente for cover. We also suspected there were Kraut observers in civilian clothes up on the mountain ridge to our right. This was possible since the ridge was on the edge of the salient and a sort of no-mans land. The Jerries were still in force in the Santerno Valley beyond. We could never interest anybody in sending a patrol up over those rugged peaks.

"All areas in the battalion sector were shelled. After a few days, all the tents were peppered with tears and holes and many vehicles damaged from shell fragments. As if the shelling wasn't enough, we had to keep a twenty-four hour alert on the river level. Whenever it rained it didn't take long to overflow its banks and once we had a trailer wash away.

"Casa Calanco took its share of punishment. Shells overventilated the roof and showered debris on the rooms below. In the courtyard, where a dozen vehicles were hidden, a number were damaged. One shell

Soldiers of the
"Avanti"-Division![(*)]

How do you like your new Divisional insignia?

Surely, all of you will recognize the cow in the picture: the good animal has long become your intimate companion and indispensable helper. What would the 715th Division do without its cattle?

Yes, there was a time — up to 6 January — when you were a proud motorized unit! Then the beautiful motor-trucks were exchanged for horses, oxen, and cows. Later there was suddenly some talk about your becoming motorized again; but that was just one of those latrine rumors. No, the MOT has definitely transformed into a HOT and a MUH. (**)

When you will have to «make Avanti» once again, you may not be able to move quite so quickly as in the good old motorized days. Let's hope that your cows are not afraid of water—or else they will hardly manage to get across the Po River, which seems to be a pretty deep and broad stream.

But your leaders have now other worries than the transportation of the «Avanti» Division. The big-shots don't care whether you go to the devil in LKWs (lorries) or in oxen-carts . . .

Well, let's hope that you'll find some other solution — more satisfactory for every one concerned.

Best regards from your comrades in captivity. They are all right!

(*) Nickname of the 715 Div — the expression, «to make Avanti,» meaning in the German soldier's slang, «to retreat»
(**) MOT, German military slang expression for «motorized,» HOT, for horses; MUH, for cows.

The German 715th Grenadier Division was originally a motorized division, but was so badly shot up by Allied artillery and aircraft that by 1945 many of its vehicles were being pulled by horses and oxen. This American propaganda leaflet chides the men of the 715th for their loss of trucks.

landed on the tailgate of a British van where a couple of Limeys had just set up for 'tea' and gone inside for a minute. When they came out 'teatime" was definitely over.

"On 8 November, the 88th Division and the 362nd Infantry began to be relieved by the British 1st Division. The 346th was to remain in place to cover the relief and to support the British as they took over the front lines in the Sillaro Valley. The First had been at Dunkirk and in Tunisia, although like all old outfits, few people were left from those battles. They had just been brought up to strength and moved over from the Eighth Army. We stood outside the FDC watching some of the rifle companies move to the front and we couldn't get over how very young they looked. In the English Army, by this time in the war, everyone seemed to be either greybeard veterans or pink checked kids.

"For four days we were under the control of the British. We got along fine with the Limeys. By the time we left, we even had begun to get the hang of English humor. But when we finally got orders to return to the 91st Division, nobody was unhappy. We had had enough of the barren, shell shocked, muddy, wet and cold Sillaro Valley. On 12 November, at 2230, we left that godforsaken place and returned to our previous positions alongside Route 65 in the little hamlet of Valle near Barbarolo. By morning, except for an occasional bad memory, it was as though we had never left it."[3]

Pfc. John Roice also spent some time in the dismal valley:

"When Company G arrived in the Sillaro we got a location away from the river. God, did it rain! All the bridges were washed out and all the buildings in the area were occupied by other troops. Our squad had three or four shelter halves and we put them together somehow to shelter seven of us. One side of the shelter was open but it let us get out of the rain. A couple of guys thought it was too crowded, which it was, but they went down to a house that another company occupied and went up into the loft and scrounged a place to lay down. After awhile one of them had to go so he just used his helmet and dumped it out the window right on top of some soldiers who were sleeping under the eaves. They came storming up to find out who had poured 'water' on them, but didn't have any luck.

"In a day or two we received much needed supplies and they had built a bridge across the river so we were sent to relieve a British outfit close to the summit of Mount Grande. Shortly after we got there one of the guys got pretty sick and I was sent to escort him back to the aid station. I stayed at battalion all night and the next day accompanied the ration mule team back up. Before that, we saw they were serving hot chow at the battalion so, naturally, we asked for mess kits. All they had was the top half of the kit. You never saw anything that was piled as high as the mess gear! Chicken, potatoes and gravy and everything. We took ourselves out to a stump and started eating and about that time somebody hollered that the mule train was ready to go, so we gulped down the chow and started forward with the mules. About half way up the mountain, one of the mules got down in the mud and we couldn't get him up. We then cut off his pack and left a case of ammunition. The mail bag and a five gallon can of gas was on the other side of the pack and we took that with us. When we got to the company CP I was so mad I told the lieutenant that I never wanted anything to do with mules ever again.

"On the line with us was some Gurkha Indian troops. These guys were supposed to be the most feared soldiers at the front. They sat around all day polishing their rifles and sharpening their swords. The swords were about two and a half feet long and about four inches wide on the outer end.

"The morning we were relieved we were camped in about the same place we were before we went up to Mount Grande. The order came down that everyone was to shave because we were supposed to be going into town for a rest. One lieutenant who had an inch and a half beard refused to shave. And he didn't until the company commander stood by him and made him!

"That night we loaded on trucks and started out of that miserable valley. About ten miles down the road we could hear each truck ahead of us holler when they reached a certain location and we couldn't figure out why. When we reached this spot, which was the crest of the hill, everyone in our truck hollered, too. We had reached the Light Line which was ten miles from the front and the headlights of the trucks were turned on

Highway 65 winds toward the Promised Land. Sketch by Captain Edward Reep.

and we could see the lights all the way to the front of the column. The reason for the hollering was that some of us had not seen an outside light for eight or nine weeks. We reached Pistoia about five in the morning and we bivouacked in Italian barracks.

"Late the following afternoon we marched downtown to a shower unit. It had been seven weeks since any of us had had a bath. Shower companies were moved from place to place. They were capable of cleaning, heating and purifying water. They consisted of three pyramidal tents set close together. In the first tent you undressed and put your clothes in a duffle bag. Jacket, shoes and helmet were put in first. Each bag had a number and the corresponding number was placed around your neck on a chain. Next, you got in the shower, which had six units on each side. If there were a lot of soldiers waiting you were allowed five minutes to shower, then you were pushed out the other end into the third tent where you found the duffle bag with your number. Five minutes didn't seem very long to get cleaned up. I hurriedly soaped and rinsed down twice and felt cleaner than I had in a long time. You handed them a shirt and told them your size and received another shirt as close to your size as they had. The same was true with pants, underwear and socks.

"Whenever you went on pass a shower was the first thing you wanted."[4]

During the first few weeks after the end of the autumn offensive the combat actions of the Division were limited to patrols and artillery duels. Occasionally the enemy mounted small attacks against the forward positions of the companies on line in an attempt to gain a little ground or to recapture a mountain that gave them good observation or just to frighten some of the new replacements, and there were many of them.

Pvt. Frederick de la Ronde submitted his first verse to the **Stars and Stripes**. *At that time he wrote, "These are the first of such verses that the war has brought out of me for better or worse. It is my hope to have a hundred or so of them published in the States under the title of "Fours in Olive Drab," as they are quatrains, that is, four lines to a verse, and the title derives from that and the fact that they are quite plainly the verses of a man while carrying out his part of the war in olive drab. Shortly after writing this letter, de la Ronde was killed in action.*

FOURS IN OLIVE DRAB

Asleep in Africa
Gnarled wires hung in cross-wise spread
Cruide boards for posts and frame, all bare
Such trash my love and once a bed.
I know because I missed you there.

War Cry
Of all the things I yet miss
Most keen your lovely evening kiss;
And all the war that I yet face
Weighs less than loss of your embrace.

Breakers at Anzio
Breakers on Anzio beach come home,
Languishing, hungering, ever and more
Toward the cool sands they will bathe in foam
Amorous, even like me for my shore

Infantry
There seldom are the glory and the fame
Or marches, clamor, bugles, drums and flags;
Instead a silent man's remote acclaim
An outpost, and a wind that nags and nags.

Millennium
Ah, some way there must be to end all this!
Ah, some way there must be to end all war!
Yes, there must be a way-and tiger jaws
Alike shall feel no need to feed more.

Souvenirs in the Meadow
Break not the crocus underneath
The soldier's boot of mire and clay.
The crocus is Love's souvenir
Of what was mine but yesterday.

Suppers Across the Sea
All the good things to eat that are far away
From the great dream of all my morale obtains;
What a tiger I'd be at the beef and the pork
Could I fight out this war with my knife and fork!

O'Donnell
"It's easy staying 'live-just use your head-"
Light words that young O'Donnell dryly said.
He knew, too, the grim and sorry rest
Of war, and died-just used his breast.

Dim by the Ditch
Through Monday's dark when we moved in to occupy our lines
The way led on past muddy sinks of bursted shell and mines
The ghastly mist there almost hid me from his boyish face
Half down the ditch, his head at drink, his dead arms still and slack.

— **Pvt. Frederick de la Ronde**

One of the unique aspects of the Italian Campaign was the use of artificial moonlight. The Fifth Army history describes the practice:

Artificial moonlight became standard procedure during the period of the stabilized front. Sixty-inch searchlights were so placed behind the forward lines that the light from their low-angled beams cast a dim glow over most of the mountains. The light assisted patrol activities and was also an aid to drivers as they inched their black-out vehicles along narrow, twisting trails. Poor weather in some respects improved this system since the lights reflected well off the low-hanging clouds. This type of weather, however, was no aid to the troops in the foxholes and to artillery observers. Six days of November were listed good, ten were fair, ten poor, and four had zero visibility as low fogs hung over the mountains. On only nine days of the month were reconnaissance planes able to take pictures. Many of our forward areas which were under close enemy observation were provided with smoke screens on clear days. This practice was continued during the entire stabilized period.[5]

Each regiment had a policy for the rotation of its companies. The 361st Infantry, dug in along the Highway 65 zone, rotated its battalions six days in the line and then three out, with one company occupying Livergnano for patrols. On 1 November the 363rd Infantry had relieved the 135th Infantry, 34th Division in the Savena River Valley in the shadow of Monte Adone. Its battalions were rotated each ten days. To the right of the regimental sector, the battalions were in line eight days and rested four. On the left, because of the exposed flank, all companies stayed on line for the full ten days.

The relief of the 135th by the 363rd went smoothly and without casualties. The 2nd Battalion, now commanded by Major George Kotchik, was the unlucky unit picked to occupy positions across the Savena River. Because of the heavy rains during the latter days of October, and the continuing steady rains, the river was swollen to twice its depth and width and to ford the stream the leading Company E had to ford the chest-deep torrent holding onto an overhead rope. It took three days for the entire company to cross the raging river since men could only be sent up during the hours of darkness. Supplies had to be portered up the same way by engineers of Company B, 316th. Each day the depth and width of the Savena was different because of the amount of rain that fell and would range from a rushing rapids of fifty to seventy feet wide to a current with protruding rocks. The engineers stretched a cable across and fastened it to trees on each bank and a pulley attached to a rubber boat pulled supplies from bank to bank. The men of the 316th made sixteen trips across the Savena ferrying ammunition, water, rations, barbed wire, tools, mines, shovels and picks with which Company E built up its defenses.[6]

The infantrymen of Company E, dug in near the village of La Piana, which was in their hands, held their little beachhead until 5 November.

Correspondent Jack Bell followed the actions of Company E:

WITH THE FIFTH ARMY IN NORTHERN ITALY — The mountain sides are steep and between them is a narrow valley. Great spaces of bare gray rock show here and there, too forbidding even for the small hardy trees now turned rich brown in autumn. An occasional village clings to a ledge, a few houses crumbled and full of shell holes. 'Way up atop the highest peak of the north ridge the ruins of a town stand boldy against the far-off skyline. 'Way to the bottom of the valley is the stream winding among the rocks, rushing swiftly because of the recent rains. In the north ridge and on ledges down the slope are the Germans. On the south ridge are the Americans. And deep in the valley, on the north bank of the rushing river is a village — La Piana.

One hundred and eighteen Americans — Company E, 363rd Infantry — went into La Piana one night. Heavy American shell fire and a daring rifle company raid had rid the town of Germans — before the rains caused the river to rise. Company E crossed the river in pouring rain, by means of a rope drawn taut between trees on opposite banks. Each man clung to the rope and went hand over hand, through water up to his neck. Two were carried away by the roaring current. Streams continued to rush down the mountainsides into the river. It continued to rise. Company E was in La Piana, on the German side of the river, cut off from the remainder of the American Army...118 soldiers with rifles, machineguns and grenades; 118 men ordered to hold the town against everything the Germans sent at them.

"Now I know what they mean when they say 'at all costs'," observed Lt. Chester R Eckard, skipper of Company E, the 10th company commander the outfit has had since it went into this bitter Italian Campaign.

"Yes," the C.O. continued to his prize first sergeant, George Reid, Flint, Michigan, "it means we keep the Krauts out of town, or else. If they come in force we've not a chance in the world to get back across the river, or to get help from there."

They formed a perimeter defense completely around the village, so that no patrols could sneak in at

WINTER WEATHER AHEAD

The days are shortening and you are still here. "Beautiful Italy" has changed! The bit of sun during the day cannot warm you any more after you have been living for days and days in your foxholes and perhaps knee deep in water.

True enough, Jerry is giving up a bit of ground here and there. Perhaps he will give up a few miles again some day, but only after he has exacted the highest toll of blood from your infantrymen.

WHAT WOULD YOU BE FACING THEN?

The mighty swift-flowing Po river with its deep ice-cold water and a merciless fire sweeping across from the other side.

WHAT WOULD YOU SEE after you had perhaps managed to build a bridge over the river on the bodies of your comrades? Just new fortifications, a maze of barbed wire entanglements, thousands of pillboxes, earthworks, concrete and steel for miles! All the long weary way to the Alps, the highest and most difficult mountain barrier in all of Europe with ridges of ten thousand feet and an eternal winter.

EACH LINE MUST BE STORMED AND THOUSANDS OF AMERICANS WILL HAVE TO GIVE THEIR LIVES!

AND AT HOME?

They know very little about your sufferings out here in Italy. The ignorance on the subject has never been greater than now. The home front warriors, especially the Hebrews, are rolling in cash and praying that this war may go on forever. They are launching "reconnaissance parties" too, but into the bedrooms of lonely women. Their ammunition is a fat roll of bills and their war-cry is: MORE DOLLARS AND GIRLS. They get them!

HAS IT EVER OCCURED TO YOU HOW SENSELESS all this is and that nobody will give you any thanks afterwards?

You can do nothing about it? Oh, yes you can.

You can think of your nearest and dearest at home. You know in your hearts that, whatever their sentiments about dead heroes may be, the very best news any of them can receive is that you are waiting for the end of the war safe and sound in a decent camp.

GEORGIA series comprising 6 pictures. Do you have the others?

A pamphlet in the Georgia series. This one was fired into the Division lines in November, 1944 warning the Powder Riverman about the coming weather.

night. They placed a squad in the village church some 75 yards from the rest of the houses. They put lookouts at each house. Every man stayed awake all night. They were soaked, cold and dared not build fires. Nor did the men of Company E dare move outside in daytime. The Jerries had the town under constant mortar fire and even had machineguns zeroed to keep bullets zipping down the streets. The men were isolated even from each other during the day. They could see, but usually fired not a shot. No point in telling Jerry how strong they were — unless he attacked. La Piana seemed dead by day; actually it was deadly!

The Jerries came that first night, a patrol that slipped down through the rain — and was sent back under a rain of automatic fire. But it was fire that told the Jerries the town wasn't to be given up, no matter how high the river became. That meant mortar fire — and it came. There was no relaxation from then on. The Jerries tried to sneak in along the edge of the river. They tried to draw the fire to one spot, then rush from the other. They tried to slip in close under their own mortar fire, then rush the outposts. They even tried to throw grenades through the small windows of the church.

"This", said Lt. R.C. Benckart, Bloomington, Ind., "is going to be rough."

"If it gets tougher," replied Lt. Dick Sykes, Atlantic City, "Let me know and I'll send for aid. That is, if the radio worked, which it won't, and if the damn Jerry mortars hadn't broken our telephone lines."

'Twas true! Company E couldn't talk to the other Americans. The first three nights it rained almost constantly. When the Jerries came — and they never missed — the men fired low and fast, and their comrades came to their aid. These death struggles in the black night, desperate while they lasted, usually ended soon with the Jerries running fast; and then the Americans dived frantically for cover because they knew the mortars would come.

Late at night their comrades came down to the opposite side of the river and used pulleys and buckets to send food and dry sox across. They had a hospital technician along, with a supply of plasma and splints. They used tiny gasoline stoves to heat coffee, the only hot food they dared prepare.

There is a soldier in Company E — Pfc. Alfred Akers, Joplin, Missouri — who'll be a sergeant when you read this. And what a soldier; what proof of the old legend that you don't know what's in a man until the chips are down. Pfc. Akers has no next of kin. He lost his parents when he was five. He has no brothers, sisters — nobody. He has been a truck driver, a farmer, a carnival man, auto mechanic, just another lad who never had a chance. He came into the infantry just another bit of cannon fodder. But Pfc Akers has what it takes. When the guns started roaring he stood up, a great soldier, a born leader. That's why, despite the fact that he's a private, he's a squad leader. He can handle any gun, and men too. He's the big reason the Jerries repeated efforts to take that church, 75 yards from the town, failed. He just wouldn't let 'em get it.[7]

Company E knew at noon of the fifth day that they were to be relieved at midnight. Two clear days had lowered the river and they could cross, and fresh troops were to take over.

"But I figured we'd not make it, at that," Pfc. Akers told me. "Them Jerries seemed to want us. They come before the moon was up. We had eight men and one BAR gun. We heard 'em all around the church and I kept men shooting at the windows. I heard 'em under my window and tossed a grenade out. Some Jerry threw his grenade in at the same time. I kicked it before it went off, into a corner. It blinded us but no one got hit. Then I sure poured lead at 'em with the BAR gun. They kept coming back till the moon come up. I think we got several, an' wish we could 'a counted 'em. But the boys had to be talked to. They was beginnin' to talk to themselves."

They came out at midnight, after five days and five nights, carrying their wounded and happy they hadn't had a man killed. They were haggard, dirty, unshaven, wet after wading the river. They had been down among the Jerries, down in hell on the banks of the Styx.

"But they started kiddin' as we got up the mountain and out of mortar range," Lt. Eckard said proudly. "I take my hat off to 'em. They've got it!"

I went into the mess line with Company E — corned beef, beans, bread, jam and coffee. "Hot food," they yelled, "just like the Waldorf."

"Where do you go next?" I asked.

"Oh, we're going back in tomorrow night," they said, "but we're gonna get showers and clean clothes first.[8]

Men on Company H, 361st take a coffee break somewhere in the Winter Line.

Company H, 362nd. Montecatini. 10 February, 1945.

Years later, a veteran of Company E wrote about the Savena River positions:
"We were across the river for about a week. The Germans tried every way in hell to drive us back across the Savena, but we held. I thought at the time that there really wasn't any reason to be across the river, that we should have been on the opposite bank. We could have seen damned near as much back across the river, but the brass didn't think that way and maybe they were right. I remember there was an old mill in the river and near the mill wheel lay the body of a German soldier we had killed on the first night. He had lain there for several days. Every night a scrawny, dirty, half-starved cat would come out and sit on the German's chest and preen himself and stare into the darkness. We had one guy who, every night, would grab his M1 and flick off the safety, point the barrel at the cat, then he'd slowly lower it. He simply could not bring himself to kill the poor defenseless creature. We could kill a German, a fellow human being, without a second thought, but a pitiful, hungry cat — well, that was something else. That's a good example of the stupidity of war. The Germans were our enemy but the cat — well, he hadn't done anything to us, so why not let him live.'"[9]

The situation in the artillery battalions was somewhat better than the front line conditions. On 8 November, Service Battery, 348th Field Artillery moved from its area near Filigare to the small village of Poggiolo, a town of about ten houses, barns and stables which had only been slightly damaged as the war passed over it. The constant vibration from the howitzers had jarred the outer walls of the houses until many of the inner walls gradually broke down. This was aggravated by the continual rain which soaked everything. Each day was a little colder than the previous one though the weather during the early part of November was not cold enough to freeze the vast sea of mud and the unstable condition of the ground. A light snow fell on the morning of 10 November, but this only added to the miseries of the artillerymen because the snow melted during the afternoon and made the ground even more sloppy.

It was difficult to tell if the houses of Piggiolo, like all the ancient villages of the Apennines, were houses, barns or stables. The cattle of the peasants normally occupied the ground floor. The people inhabited the floor above the cattle and rabbits, chickens and ducks shared the floor with the oxen, however, so many Germans and Americans had "borrowed" the oxen some of the stables were empty. The men of the 348th bedded down in these. There was a complete absence of hogs since the Germans had slaughtered them for food.

The age of the houses could be estimated by the amount of wear in the stone steps; in some, the stone had been worn away as much as three inches. The Division Redlegs made a determined effort to improve their living quarters. Manure piles were moved away from doors, floors were scraped and scrubbed, walls were cleaned, walks were built and drainage ditches dug. On 7 November the battalion started a project of improving the road leading into Livergnano.

Camp White, Red Flag Quarrantine. L-R Front: Lathrop, Wypysinski Rear: Korte, Krogstad, Erickson.

Italy, Oct 44, Drivers and Radio. L-R Front: Clark, Ostrum. Rear: Chapman, McGee, Hinson.

Camp White, POW Demonstration Squad. L-R: Redjinski, Krogstad, Olin, Korte.

Italy, Radio Section. L-R: S/Sgt. Drowley, Kuehl, Davidson.

Survey Section near Livergnano, 11-44. L-R Front: Krogstad, Hunt, Samuelson. Rear: Trim, Craine, Lathrop.

Italy. L-R: Neumann, FDC, Driessen, OPNS.

347th Artillerymen

Battery C, 347th firing the 100,000th 105mm round.

During the month of November 5,053 rounds were fired by the 348th — a drastic reduction from the month of October.[10]

As winter tightened its grip over the Division front, and all along the Fifth Army lines, Italy rapidly became a secondary campaign. The war news was in France, Belgium and Germany. Few stories on the actions in the mountains before Bologna appeared in the newspapers back in the States. If a story did turn up in one of the national papers it was usually very short and appeared on the back page and almost always contained the brief sentence — *Patrols were active*. And they were active! Night after night the Powder Rivermen probed deep into No-Man's Land trying to capture prisoners and obtain new information other than what appeared in the intelligence reports, though there were precious little we didn't already know about the strength and location of the enemy. Each night at least six or more patrols went into the tiny shattered towns along the front: La Tomba, Canovetta, Boschi, Mt. S. Ansano —names that would be forever etched into the memories of those men who entered the blackness of the unknown and who came out alive.

By late November, the rain was changing to sleet in the valleys of the Savena and Idice, then the sleet changed into snow. The first flakes were big and warm and covered the ground with a gentle layer of white, then the winds came up and the snow blew across the hills and down through the ravines and the wind swirled the flakes in great spirals of white and snow clouds filled the air and it was difficult to tell the sky from the earth. The snow muffled the sound of the guns and softened the crash of the exploding artillery shells, then finally it covered the burned out tanks, the broken houses, the twisted metal wreckage along Highway 65 and back roads and the barbarities of war disappeared under a cover of grizzled whiteness. The Division troops dug like badgers into the frozen soil, then finally abandoned the digging altogether and moved into the windowless farmhouses leaving the snow-blown forward foxholes to the unlucky men on line and taking their turns manning the outposts and pits of the battlefields and running patrols night after night.

Many infantrymen made their share of those nightly ventures into Death's dark country:

"I never did understand why we ran so many patrols. Most of the time our orders were to take a prisoner or two and bring them back for interrogation, but we never did. Those of us who had been in combat for some time weren't taking any chances. And we sure as hell weren't looking for trouble! The Germans could go their way and we'd go ours. Sometimes if a gung-ho sergeant was in charge of the patrol, we'd do some foolish things, but we didn't have very few of those types left. Three or four months on line was enough for a guy to lose his "gungho-ness". There was a patrol known as a "recon patrol" where we tried to get information. There was another called a 'listening patrol'. It was exactly that. We would go out, stop within a few yards of the Jerry positions, and just listen. We had merely to remember the first General Order to 'observe everything within sight or hearing.' One time I went out with the 2nd Squad. The sergeant had just been promoted to squad leader and he was really nervous. It was his first patrol. We were some distance from the German lines when the squad leader told us to stop. This is as far as we go, he told us. No further. That was all right with the rest of us. Just sitting there in Jerry territory and listening was a stressful ordeal.

"One time near the Savena River we were holed up in an old wine cellar. There were huge wine barrels in the cellar and the stale smell of rot and mildew. We used candles in the cellar and were forbidden to go outside during the daylight hours. We spent the time playing cards and dreaded the coming of night. Several yards from the mouth of the entrance to our house was an old hand-dug well and most of the men used it for a latrine because it saved digging a slit trench or going out in the open. Every night we ran patrols. One night we were walking nonchalantly down a steep mountain trail when we ran headlong into a Jerry patrol coming directly toward us. I guess we were two patrols with but a single thought because when they saw us the Germans quickly turned tail and headed back to their own house. And that's exactly what we did!

"Another time we occupied a group of houses in the heart of the Idice positions. During the day we kept a nervous watch inside the big stone houses and at night we ran more patrols. This time it was bitter cold. The snow was butt-deep and we ran the same patrol every night. Some fifty yards or so from the door of our farmhouse was the body of a dead SS trooper. No one had volunteered to haul him away, certainly none of the men in my platoon. He was perfectly preserved with the cold and still wore his steel helmet with its eagle on the side and the bolts of lightning within the small black square. He had a potato masher grenade still in his belt but none of us tried to yank it free. He wore a leather belt with the words <u>Gott mit uns</u> on the buckle and his frozen boots still had a shine. We had a guy in the platoon we called 'Poke' who was from Arkansas. He said, 'You know, Joe Louis said we'd win this war because God was on our side. How can He be on both sides?'

"Anyway, night after night we passed this SS German as we left the house. There was his jacket stiff with the cold and his arms encased in ice. He was our first familiar landmark. We could go down this small hill and into a ravine, then up another hill and along a dry river bed filled with snow and up another hill into

Livergnano Rock. December, 1944. Sketch by Savo Radulovich.

198

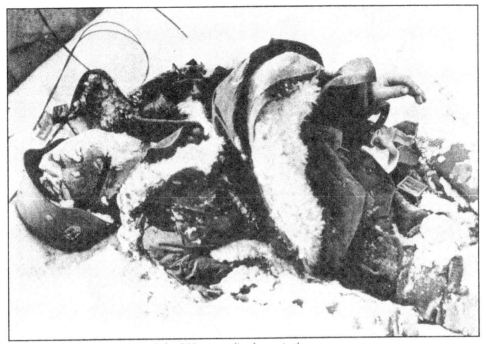

A dead SS trooper lies frozen in the snow.

the farmyard of a demolished house; here we paused and set up a listening post. We were there for about an hour, hearing nothing and seeing nothing. During the nights we were there we never heard or saw an enemy soldier. It was a bone-aching cold and the snow scudded across the frozen ground and we shivered miserably in our white parkas and our feet were numb in our shoe pacs. An old horse drawn rake sat in the yard, its steel wheels covered with frost. Far in the distance, on top of a hill, stood a church with a campanile. Some nights we could hear the Germans shooting rockets or 'screaming meemies'. I don't think I've ever been as cold since then as I was those nights.

"At the end of the appointed time we shouldered our rifles and walked back up the icy path. As we topped the final hill, we saw the body of the SS trooper. Someone in the column would always say, 'Well, there's old Hans.' He was our friend beckoning us to the warmth and safety of the farmhouse."[11]

The division history tells us that Thanksgiving Day was "particularly memorable for its food and good fellowship". The 362nd history notes that "church services were held and a delicious dinner was served to all troops in the park at Villanova". The 363rd history is more detailed: "Highlight of the rest period in Montecatini was the Thanksgiving Day celebration held two days late on Saturday, 25 November, so that cooks would have time to prepare. Mess sergeants and their helpers labored all day Friday and all Friday night in cleaning and roasting 4,375 pounds of turkey in the hotel ovens. Menus included, besides the turkey, sage dressing, cranberry sauce, mashed potatoes, giblet gravy, creamed asparagus, fresh peas and creamed corn." Of course, what the regimental histories don't tell us is that all these goodies were piled on top of each other in the soldiers' mess kit. The 361st Infantry, also in Montecatini, celebrated the holiday by being issued 5,650 pounds of turkey, one hundred pounds of cranberry sauce, eight hundred and eight pounds of candy and 65,000 cigarettes. The Company C mess sergeant, Emmet Hance, said, "I didn't have enough dishes and ranges to cook all the turkey and the rest of the dinner. So we had turkey again the next day. And we had seconds both times."[12]

However, all good things come to an end and on 2 December the 362nd relieved the 133rd Infantry, 34th Division in the Predosa-LaGuarda area. The 363rd moved to Villanova and the 361st went to Pretaglia.

On the night of 9 December the skies cleared and it turned bitter cold. There had been a heavy frost that morning but it melted in the early sun. By noon the sky had clouded over and the entire Division front was blanketed with a dense fog. The following day snow began falling, but turned to a steady and miserable rain in late afternoon and continued for several days. In the 362nd sector the nights were dark and foggy but

Division artillerymen Don Schoof and Lieutenant John Timmons with a Red Cross hostess named Ruth.

patrolling continued. Bit by bit, information was gleaned on the location of minefields, routes of approach, enemy emplacements and fordable river crossings. A combat patrol from Company B was sent up to the village of Tianello to check out a house which was suspected of housing a strong force of Jerries. When the patrol reached the house the men discovered the second story was held by ten enemy soldiers. A fierce fire fight broke out between the Germans on the second floor and the combat patrol on the first floor. The Jerries countered by tossing down potato masher grenades which slightly wounded five members of the patrol. Blood began seeping through the second floor so some of the fire of the 362nders had done its work. The Germans, sensing defeat, finally fled through an upstairs window.

In the 361st sector south of the Savena River the continuous rain, sleet and snow limited the actions of the regiment to extensive patrolling. For the men in their caved-in, water-filled and icy foxholes it was a time of tough, physical hardship. In order to give the men a chance to get some short, well-needed rest and an opportunity to get dry and enjoy some hot food, Colonel Broedlow set up a "rest area" just behind the front lines. Five 12x20 foot storage tents with wooden floors, sidewalks and a kitchen were set up. In just eight hours Company A, 316th Engineers had delivered the lumber, had a dozer clear the mud and level the ground. The troops were then in business.

Pfc. Robert R. Schmieding described some of his time on the Winter Line:

"The 2nd Battalion pulled back to Anconella for a few days of R and R and I recall that we did sleep inside a building on a soft bed of hay for at least *one* night. Then, it was up front again and my mind was jolted back to the reality of war. I checked out my combat pack, my canteen, placed a package of unneeded stationary and a bottle of ink in our squad's jeep for safe keeping. Once again I felt a knot forming in my stomach as I viewed my immediate future. I had survived this exercise several times but the move was always difficult to accept. The same questions ran through my mind once again: I wonder where we are going? Will this be the quiet sector? How much longer will it last? How much longer will it before I'm hit?

"A few hours later we moved out of Livergnano and proceeded up Highway 65 to a point about a mile north of the village. We hiked down an incline to the right and proceeded to dig in. North of this location was a natural cave whose entry was sandbagged, extended and covered. Another mortar was set up just to the north and a sandbagged bunker constructed next to it. On the first night of our arrival our CP was set up in the cave. The 1st and 2nd gunners dug in near the mortars. The rest of us dug in just above the cave. The soil was loose and cultivated which made for easy digging — for a change. The early mornings were foggy which gave us more freedom of movement but restricted our mortar fire. Throughout the first day we remained close to our foxholes as Highway 65, a few yards above us, was being heavily pounded by the enemy who were determined to deny us the use of the highway at all costs. It was the most intense shelling I had ever experienced.

"At night, as the Germans would continue their sporadic and harassing fire, our jeeps would drive up Sixty-five to our positions and we'd unload the rations. Usually a detail of six men would scamper up the slope to the highway and quickly empty the jeeps. We balanced our load on our shoulders as we negotiated the fourteen foot ladder that someone had borrowed from a farmer and leaned up against the mountain. The supplies were then distributed to the various mortar positions and to the CP at the cave. After the first few days we didn't bother to carry the ammo on our shoulders and down the ladder, we just dropped it over the side of the embankment and let it bounce to the earth below to improve our slit trenches and foxholes which simply meant digging them deeper.

"Then the weather turned worse. The skies darkened and a strong wind from the NW started to blow with increasing intensity all day long. We improved our positions by stretching shelter halves over the top of the holes and ditched around them. Early that next morning I noticed several small trickles of water running down into my trench. The rain came down even harder as I tried to deepen the ditch, then the worst thing happened as the edges of my trench started to give way and my shelter half dropped to the bottom of the trench along with mud and water. My blanket and all that I possessed was soaked and filthy.

"We subsisted on the bland C rations. Tom Moore, our squad's 1st gunner and a father of ten who was in the upper pay bracket, receiving over $300 per month, had a solution for correcting the tasteless rations. He always carried a small bottle of sauce, a mixture of vinegar and spices which he liberally applied to each can of rations he consumed, transforming the bland meat and vegetable stew and corned beef hash into something almost edible.

"Guard duty was a very important activity on the Winter Line. Due to the lengthy nights it was necessary for each one of us to be on duty for two periods of two hours each. We were positioned in one spot and remained still throughout our watch. After the snow covered the ground the nights were so bright one could read a book by the moonlight. This condition forced us to stand in the shadows and remain almost perfectly still. At times one would be brought to full alert as a rabbit could be seen as he scampered across the snow.

T/5 Richard Root waits for the 363rd Service Company Kitchen to come and unload his truck. 19 November 1944.

Each squad leader had been issued a G.I. wrist watch which would be passed on from man to man as he was relieved during the night. For a period of nearly one week our squad's watch had gained over an hour per night. Someone had obviously been sitting the watch ahead while on duty. Finally after five or six days the culprit was caught red-handed and severely reprimanded.

"La Fabbrica was the last OP I served at. This almost demolished house was located on the edge of no-man's-land all during the winter. The wine cellar was still intact and was a heavily used piece of real estate. It was a jump off place for our combat patrols. Most of the patrols were based in Livergnano. Every night a patrol, clad in white, would silently pass by us and then in a few hours they reappeared. One would hear them joking and talking as they headed back home. Our only light and heat was produced by several gas filled vino bottles with discarded socks stuffed into the neck of the bottle to serve as wicks. Talk about pollution! I spit up black soot for three months after my stay in the cellar. Our observer and I tried to sleep during the day as we had to direct fire missions at night. One of our prime targets was Canovetta, a small village located in the forward battleground. Our patrols and the German patrols were very active in this area. We had this tiny town zeroed in but one night I was asked to observe our firing mission. I crawled out of the cellar and was greeted by the bright moon and stars. The fresh snow glistened on the rolling hills and fields to the north of me. Under normal circumstances a person would consider this a beautiful night."[13]

During December snow continued to fall and by the waning days of the month the Division front lay under a heavy blanket of white that dazzled the eyes with its brightness. The barren, ice-coated peaks of the Northern Apennines stretched endlessly north, though there were only a few remaining miles into the city of Bologna. Because the city of Monticatini had not been damaged during the autumn offensive, it had been selected by Fifth Army as the major rest center for all combat troops and hundreds of men were rotated back to the City of the Mineral Baths.

The 361st Regimental History for November, 1944 describes life in the rest center:

Troops jammed the Viale Roma, the main thoroughfare of Montecatini, and soldiers of all Allied commands poured into the photo shops, cafes, bars and canteens. Each night there was a dance in one or more of the companies and most 361sters, who had not danced since they left the States, swung to the best of local bands and whirled signorinas around the dance floor. Regular bars were installed in most company areas where the men could buy American beer, Italian wine and even cocktails made from fruit juices and heady local spirits. There were five regular theaters showing movies or stage shows three or four times daily, some starting as early as 10 A.M. There were Red Cross Clubs with spacious lounges with radios and phonographs, big writing rooms and coffee bars and snack bars that were open till curfew. But it was not all fun. During the day one could see groups of soldiers marching at right shoulder arms through the wide streets, while others did close order drill, manual of arms and P.T. In the afternoons, classes were held indoors. Soldiers emerged from medical aid stations rubbing their arms and receiving booster shots. And occasionally there would be long lines of men wearing nothing but raincoats marching down the streets on their way for physical exams. There were dental inspections, medical inspections and rifle inspections. It was garrison all over again. But

Division 105s dug in above Loiano. Sketch by Savo Radulovich.

it was one hell of a lot better than the foxholes north of Livergnano or the shattered houses in the Savena River Valley.[14]

On 16 December, General Mark Clark was given command of the 15th Army Group, the group headquarters command which had been set up under General Sir Harold R.L.G. Alexander to coordinate the operation of Fifth and Eighth Armies. Alexander took over as theater commander and Lieutenant General Lucian K Truscott, who had earlier led the 3rd Division, was brought over from France to take control of Fifth Army. Shortly before his promotion General Clark had worked out a new attack order named the "PIANORO PLAN". It was set for the day after Christmas. According to the plan the 91st Division would attack north across the Savena River, over Monte Adone, Mt. Dei Frati and the high ground overlooking the Po Valley. The Division was to be assisted by the 34th and 85th Divisions. One can only speculate why Clark would put forth such a plan at such a time. The area was the most heavily fortified along the Fifth Army front and the Germans facing the Division were in equal strength. The terrain was buried under several feet of snow. The ammunition reserve for December showed there was only enough to back up fifteen days of fighting and there was no more available until the end of January. What it would have been like for the Powder Rivermen struggling forward over the snow clogged hills and ravines with only a limited amount of ammunition hardly bears thinking about. Later events in April showed how difficult it was to capture this terrain even in the best of weather. General Truscott was violently opposed to PIANORO and thought it to be an appalling undertaking and that there was no chance of the attack being successful under the terrible conditions of the battlefield. Clark was adamant in his defense of his plan and fully intended to go ahead with the attack; however, on 16 December the Germans struck in France and the Battle of the Bulge began. The German Army in Italy also launched a limited-objective assault against the 92nd Division in the Serchio River Valley which guarded the approach to Lucca and Leghorn. The 92nd was driven back six miles before the enemy was stopped. This action, along with the fierce battles going on in France, was enough for General Clark to reluctantly agree to a postponement of Pianoro. There's little doubt that the cancellation of the proposed attack saved the lives of many men of the Division.[15]

On Christmas Day, Sergeant Jack Fosie of *Yank* magazine made a trip up front to the positions around Mounte Belmonte:

You can see so much more on a night like this. The freezing cold keeps you sharply awake. The entire range of mountains is revealed in the snow-reflected moonlight. The blue tinted planet of Venus hangs low enough to be a signal light. The bigness at the front makes you feel more insignificant than you normally think you are. The sound of a single plane can be heard plainly in the still crisp air. It comes down in a whine and strafes a straight stretch on Highway 65, aiming at the headlights. He is gone after one machinegun rattling pass...the first night fighter in many a week. No damage.

You travel now with blackout lights. The road looks so black in comparison to the glistening white fields on either side. The traffic thins out. Soon you're along with just the clink of the chains and the undertone of their snatching on the ice-coated roads. At one point you technically come under direct enemy observation. You jeep on. The bottom scrapes on the crusted center. It's low-low all the time, going up the mountain. You're within mortar range. Everybody there lives in dugouts. The night is no longer quiet; there is the intermittent chatter of machinegun fire, some far away, some not so far, and the occasional crunch of artillery fire.

You can still ride a ways but it's better to walk. And you wear a white parka. Not that you can't be picked up against the snow, but it helps. You reach this summit of Monte Belmonte, but if you're wise you won't stand there. The crest can be swept by German heavy machinegun fire. You reach the forward slopes and you're just about as close to Bologna as any American soldier can be today - seven miles. A recon patrol is just coming in. They wear white parkas, white leggins, white helmets and with weapons painted white. They call themselves a "ghost patrol". The idea was thought up by Lt. John Bannan, a company commander.

You find Captain William Harris belatedly opening up a couple of Christmas presents given him by the unit which he formerly commanded. The presents are an orange marmalade sandwich and a can of bouillon cubes, both wrapped in toilet paper. Harris laughs heartily.

Somewhere off in the distance a machinegun gives out will "shave and a hair cut, six bits." That brings a tired laugh to everyone.

You leave and come back off Monte Belmonte.[16]

The 361st Infantry was the only regiment to spend Christmas Day on line. It was a cold and very white holiday. On Christmas Eve it began snowing heavily all along the regimental front and by morning nearly eight inches had fallen. The sky then cleared and it turned bitter cold, a raw penetrating cold. The previous night a strong German patrol had tried to storm the positions of Company I and for an hour or so a furious hand grenade duel was fought in the falling snow before the enemy was driven off.

The men of the regiment ate their Christmas dinners sitting in the dark, icy caves or battered buildings just yards from the Jerry outposts with a rifle nearby just in case of trouble. They ate in shifts, starting a day before Christmas and ending a day after the holiday.

II

The atrocious weather along the Division front did not diminish with the coming of the New Year and the snow continued to fall all during January. Throughout the entire month the ground was cloaked with a layer of snow to a depth of six to eight inches and in some places had drifted to a depth of eight to ten feet. Bad weather was the watchword and every type was experienced from howling blizzards to a rare, freak thunderstorm.

As 1945 rolled around the men dug in deeper and tried to make themselves as comfortable as possible. No one knew what January would bring, a German counter offensive, a Division attack or another long static winter in the mountains like the one a year before at Cassino; except this year the weather was colder and the mountains higher.

During the first thirty minutes of New Year's Day the sky over both fronts, ours and the enemy, was filled with tracers, flares, rockets and artillery as the Yanks and the Jerries celebrated the coming of another year. Old traditions die hard and not even war can push them aside.

And the troops kept digging to improve their emplacements. Additional mine fields were laid, more barbed wire strung; houses, foxholes and slit trenches were sandbagged and duck boards placed on the bottoms of the latter to keep the GIs from standing and lying in the snow and icy water. White parkas were worn at all times, vehicles were painted white and some units used skis and snowshoes to deliver rations to the forward outposts. One division unit constructed a home-made toboggan and used it.

For the first time the artillery battalions were introduced to the VT (Variable Time) fuse. This highly secret and effective fuse proved especially useful for long range night harassing. It was necessary to fire much high angle fire in the normal barrages which were close in front of the infantry and in deep gullies. The terrible weather made the adjustment of fire impossible to keep because of the changing K's (corrections due to weather changes). The battalions were often unable to adjust fire because of the poor visibility. Another difficulty was finding the burst in the snow. On one occasion, on firing a previously adjusted mission, an observer of the 346th was unable to see the HE, smoke WP or air burst. Finally, in desperation, he ordered a stray round of purple base ejection smoke fired and was able to pick it up immediately.[17]

Rotation of the troops continued.

At Montecatini, officers at the Army sponsored liquor warehouse, which sold spirits at lower rates than in the open market, reported they had grossed $300,000.00 during the month of December. So, the men of Fifth Army were drinking well.

While the city of Montecatini was popular the front line favorite was the Eternal City of Rome and the combat men of all divisions looked forward to a visit to that great place with all it had to offer. Some infantry platoons of the Division were rewarded with eight day passes for jobs well done. A platoon of Company E, 363rd was sent back to Rome for capturing a German bunker near La Collina in the Idice River Valley, but as one member remarked, "That's a hell of a way to get a pass."

But things in Rome were a far cry from what they had been shortly after the city was liberated some seven months before. The Naples rear echelon had moved in, the boys who wore the hated PBS shoulder patch, and a lot had changed. MPs roamed the back alleys searching for drunken infantrymen and high ranking officers had taken over the best night clubs. The citizens of Rome were becoming a bit fed up with the troops of at least a dozen nationalities and the black market flourished. Lucky Strikes were $1.50 a pack, Pall Malls sold for $1.75 and Chelseas and Raleighs were a bargain a $1.15. Sugar was $3.00 a pound, eggs 28 cents a piece, bread $1.40 a loaf and chicken cost $2.00 a pound.[18] Those kisses that were given away free on June 4, 1944, now cost at least $10.00 a night. The girls on the Via Tritone, who made $10.00 a week as typist were making $15.00 a night on the streets; the prettier girls, who waited outside the officer's bars were making $20.00. On Sunday mornings old women marched in penitential processions from St. John's Latern all the way to the church of Santa Maria Maggiore to atone for the sins of the girls.[19] Yet, in spite of everything, all in all, Rome was a wonderful place for the weary combat men of the Division.

With the 361st and 363rd on line, the 362nd, in reserve, was given the mission of preparing an "Intermediate Defense Line" and "Switch Line" which was to be constructed from Loiano north along Highway 65 to Sabbioni. It was to be an elaborate system of secondary defenses with individual foxholes and gun emplacements, sandbagged and revetted to prevent caving in. Tactical wire and mine fields protecting the perimeter were

A Fifth Army patrol north of Pracahia. 7 December, 1944.

A Fifth Army convoy winds its way over the mountains. Highway 65 sector.

strategically placed throughout the network of positions. The extreme cold hampered the digging, but the snow did aid in camouflaging the construction.

By 15 January seventy-five to one hundred per cent of the defensive work was completed.

The early days of February saw a marked change in the weather. The mountain air warmed and the snow began to melt. By the middle of the month it was gone from the lower elevations of the Apennines. The numbing chill was disappearing with the snow and during the days cool, almost warm, winds blew down through the valleys of the Savena and Idice valleys and every morning the men on line noticed there was less snow than the day before. The sides of the mountains resembled huge, dirty-white sheets with ragged holes where the blackened ground shown through and the new warmness brought a wet, foggy haze that hung over the ravines of no man's land. And with the melting snow came the mud.

Pfc. John Roice was still serving with Company G:

"In February we were off the line for several days, then went back up. When we unloaded off the trucks the soupy mud was almost boot top deep. We started up the mountain and I don't know how the mud stayed in place it was so thin and deep. At the first break everyone looked for a rock to sit on because we had been to a shower unit and had clean clothes and hated the thought of getting dirty again. At the second break, we were so tired from the steep climbing that we just flopped anywhere we could. After about two hour climb we reached the top of the mountain and started along a ridge on a cart trail. We met an outfit coming out and also a mule train slogging its way back.

"We stayed overnight in a house at the foot of a big hill and the next night I guided a ration detail down to the platoon at the forward CP. Snow was melting and the trail was muddy so every time I slipped I took an extra step. The lieutenant was with me and he told me part of the path was too skylined and we ought to change our route, so the next night we went down we took a new way but weren't challenged by the guard, but a little later he came in scared as he could be. He said he almost shot us. He thought we were a German patrol because we weren't on the regular trail!

"Another time in this same position the cooks had fried some steaks and put them in heat containers and sent them up on the mule train. One of  the mules carrying a container of meat was killed by a mortar shell. When we got to the forward CP that night the lieutenant said, 'My mouth has been watering all day for that steak'. When I told him I was sorry but the mule with his steak had been blown up, you should have seen the look on his face. I then explained that we had gone through all of the cans of meat and divided the biggest pieces and had brought him his steak after all!

"The mules were never able to get closer than a couple of miles to our positions so every night a detail had to be sent to the spot where the mules were halted. Once when we got back, a bag of socks and two boxes of rations were not with the delivery. Two of us were sent back to search for the missing items but we couldn't find them. The sergeant said I could pick one man and neither of us would have to stand guard that night but would leave before daylight next morning to search again for the socks and rations. We still couldn't locate anything. We made one final effort and were told just to go out a little way and come back later and report that nothing was found. Well, we later discovered that the cooks had traded the boxes for a bottle of vino and that

Snowbound. T/4 Erich Korte. 347th.

A burned out farmhouse sits atop a hill in the snow covered mountains near Mount Dei Frati. Photo taken 18 January, 1945, by the 3131st Signal Service Co.

the missing bag of socks had a gas lantern in it for the officers to play poker by, but it had been sent to another platoon."[20]

III

From 14 February to 23 March the 363rd Infantry occupied positions in the valley of the Idice River running constant patrols and now and then assaulting a bunker. The Idice was a small, twisting creek that flowed past the east side of Monte della Formiche. To get to the regimental sector the supply trucks had to drive to Filigare then turned right on "Easy Street" which the 363rd Journal called a "rough, winding, climbing, descending, corduroyed, gravel and mud road". The 316th Engineers had worked miracles putting the road in shape to use. Every round of ammunition, every pound of rations that "Easy Street" supplied to the forward infantrymen were hauled up front by this route. The 363rd Infantry Regimental history for February describes the Idice Valley:

The Idice Valley in which the 363rd Infantry found itself after traveling the five roller-coaster miles of Easy Street was known familiarly as Death Valley. It was a drab, weary, war-torn, muddy, colorless, desolate stream bed through which the road sometimes led, at other times climbing the slate-grey cliffs which bordered the stream and crossing over more Baileys that bridged gaps blown by the Germans in the road shelf. Although the Idice was now shallow and narrow it had recently overflown its banks and upon receding had left a foot of thick, gooey mud over everything in the valley. In this mud scattered throughout the area was the debris of war — cardboard shell containers, German Rieger, Teller and Schu mines, which had been placed in the bed against the Allies using it as a route of tank approach, and which were now stuck in the mud at odd angles, parts of planes that had crashed, an occasional German body or part of one just uncovered, dead branches and small tree trunks washed along, then left high when the water receded. And always the mud.

As the days passed into spring the patrolling continued night after night after night. Each time the troops were sent out into no-man's-land they came back a little more jittery. It was well known that a major offensive was being planned and would be put into effect once the ground was dry and none of the patrols wanted to be bushwhacked and killed on a useless mission, as most of the patrols were. The 3rd Battalion Journal, 361st recorded each night's actions:

13 March 1945
"L" Company has one patrol tonight consisting of one officer and twelve EM with the mission of capturing prisoners by ambush. Patrol departed at 1930 led by Lieutenant Hinson. Established ambush at

209

Livergnano aid-station. Christmas 1944. Note Christmas bell hanging on wall. Sketch by Captain Edward Reep.

8980-3305. They received machinegun fire from the church, so pulled back. After they pulled back the Jerries shot up flares and mortared the position. The patrol went back after things quieted. At approximately 0415 two groups of Germans could be seen approaching the "L" Company position but for some reason they stopped and withdrew. "K" Company also had a patrol tonight consisting of one NCO and fifteen EM. Its mission was also to set up an ambush. They departed, established positions then began receiving heavy mortar and artillery fire, all throughout the night. No contact with the enemy. "I" Company relieved "C" Company tonight at 1900. All patrols returned safely. Weather, cool and clear. Mule trains are still being used to supply the front line troops.

14 March 1945

Weather, cool and clear. No patrols operating tonight as there is to be a friendly propaganda broadcast in the sector;[21] however there will be listening posts set up to intercept any German personnel who wanted to surrender. At "L" Company's outpost a Jerry managed to infiltrate past the post and approached it from the rear. When the men in the hole heard him coming they

"I'm dreaming of a white Christmas."

challenged him to halt. The German quickly opened fire with a rat gun, killing one man and wounding another. The wounded man fired back but because of his wounds did not fire very accurately.

15 March 1945

"I" Company has one patrol operating tonight with the usual mission of an ambush, led by Lieutenant Roberts. No contact was made with the enemy. A "K" Company patrol, led by Lieutenant Cross, went out with twelve men but made no contact with the enemy and returned at 0500. Weather, clear and cool.

During the middle of March the 362nd and 363rd Infantry were relieved by Italians of the Legnano Group. This was a unit composed of veteran troops who had been fighting fascism since the downfall of Mussolini. The 361st Infantry was not relieved until 2-4 April when the 34th Division took over its forward positions. The 91st Division Artillery was relieved for the first time in six months and had supported not only the 91st but the 34th and 88th. On the night of 20 March the 346th Field Artillery moved to Gagliano having completed 197 consecutive days on the line.

The duty in late March and early April was the best since the division outposted the Arno River seven months before. There was sunshine. The ground was dry. The training was strenuous but there was time for softball, volleyball and relaxation. This was the life. No patrols, ambush or otherwise. No mole-like existence of the Winter Line. Plenty of chow and plenty of rest.

Now spring had arrived and they days were warm again. Mountains of rations were piled in dumps. At Radiscosa Pass there were acre upon acre of gasoline-filled jerricans. Stacks of ammunition stood along the roads. The tanks of Fifth Army had moved well forward. So had the engineers, complete with bridges.

D-day was but hours away.

Endnotes for Chapter Ten

1. Fifth Army History. "The Winter Stalemate." Reprinted in the *Powder River Journal.* June, 1989.
2. Division History. p, 198.
3. Dunning, Robert F. "Hot Time in the Sillaro Valley". *The Powder River Journal,* June, 1991, pp. 10-12.
4. Roice, John. "World War II Army Memories". pp. 18-21.
5. Fifth Army History. p. 13.
6. 363rd Regimental History. November, 1944, p. 44
7. Sergeant Alfred Akers was killed in action 21 February, 1945. By that time he had been awarded a Silver Star, Bronze Star and a Purple Heart with Oak Leaf Cluster.
8. "Fighting Men Jest After Brave Stand at River". *Miami Herald.* December 16, 1944

9. "Christ Has Only One Arm". *The Powder River Journal*.

10. 348th Field Artillery Battalion History. 4 December, 1944. Henry Bahringer sent the author a copy of the battalion history. He signed his letter, "#1 man who pulled the lanyard on #2 gun."

11. "Patrols, Passes and the Winter Line. *The Powder River Journal*. December, 1980, p. 8.

12. *Thunder in the Apennines*, p. 248.

13. Schmieding, Robert R. "Remembering". *The Powder River Journal*. December, 1984, pp. 23-27.

14. 361st Regimental History. November, 1944.

15. That General Clark would purpose such a plane as PIANORO must seem absolutely astonishing to any veteran of the 91st Division who fought through the Gothic Line battles and who spent some time in the second Winter Line. During the month of December the divisions of II Corps were still in the process of being rebuilt and were not only short of supplies and ammunition but of replacements. Anyone familiar with the situation of Fifth Army at the end of 1944 would certainly have viewed an attack on Monte Adone and the surrounding area in December as sheer folly, as General Truscott did. In his book, *Command Missions*, General Truscott tells of his dismay at Clark's stubbornness in refusing to abandon his plan. PIANORO can only corroborate the thinking of Clark's post-war critics who considered him a bad field commander who drove his divisions ruthlessly with little regard for his casualties.

16. "Yank About Italy". *The Powder River Journal*, December, 1987, pp. 7-8.

17. 346th Field Artillery Battalion History. Chapter XIV. "The New Year", pp. 33. The VTF fuse was effective and vicious. It burst from a height of four yards. The 175th F.A., 34th Division fired on a German bridge building crew and the enemy was still picking up the dead the afternoon of the next day.

18. Fifty years later these prices don't seem all that exorbitant.

19. Sion, Sergeant Henry. "Liberated Rome". *Yank* 2 March 1945. MTO edition.

20. "World War II Memories". pp, 23-26.

21. During the period of the Winter Line both Americans and Germans brought up loud speakers and placed them near the front line positions in an effort to persuade men to surrender.

Nothing Merry about this Christmas!

Millions of men are locked in battle in the most cruel and bloody war of mankind. They no longer know the great Commandment "Thou shalt not kill" and they have probably forgotten the lovely Christmas spirit which silently embraced all of us on Christmas Eve in the good old days.

Just imagine that magic door should open and you caught a glimpse of what Christmas tide meant to you in peace time.

There's a church in the valley by
the wildwood,
No lovelier spot in the dale,
No spot is so dear to my childhood
As the little brown church in the vale.

Don't you actually see them walking to the parish church? Men and women, prayer book in hand, girls in hooded capes and galoshes and last — but not least — the noisy pack of scuffling choir-boys in bubbling spirits storming the church door — then suddenly quiet inside.

A minute later they will begin to sing, loudly and a bit out of tune at times, the grand old Christmas carols — and the parish will listen.

This year millions of hearts cannot gladden on Christmas Eve because someone dear is out at the front and Death may close the door at any moment. They dread the future and their hearts cannot warm up even for Christmas. A father, a mother or wife, they fret and sorrow in anguishing pain. They are longing for their loved ones and their spirits sag.

Boys like to fight even if they emerge from the scuffle with a black eye, an injured finger or a plastered face. Choir-boys are no exception. Yet after a while they get tired of fighting and before long they all sing together again in the choir, loudly and a bit out of tune at times, but after all in unison.

Can't we men learn a lesson from these boys?

German propaganda leaflet. Christmas 1944.

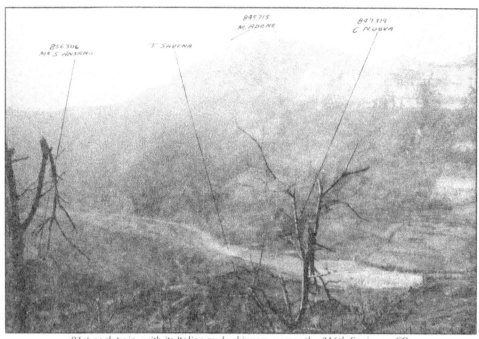

91st pack train, with its Italian mule skinners, passes the 316th Engineers CP.

Monte Adone. The Savena River flows at the base of the mountain. 25 February 1945.

Sandbagged. T/4 Robert D. Lathrop. 347th.

Battle-hardened veterans of Company L, 363rd Infantry in the Idice River Valley. A few of these men have seen months of bitter combat, dating back to the July days of Mount Vaso. There's a war weariness on their faces that

Spring comes to the Apennines. March 1945.

even the smiles can't hide. Note the trooper (opposite photo, right, back row) with the unbuttoned shirt. The GI in the cap and holding the Tommygun (above photo, bottom row second from left) is simply unable to smile.

CHAPTER ELEVEN —
OUT OF THE MOUNTAINS AND
INTO THE VALLEY

"Twenty-five years later some thirty-eight of us with our wives stood on the road near Livergnano and looked across the rolling terrain of the impressive bulk of Monte Adone and its vertical escarpment. My wife, who had seen me shakily standing on a chair to change a light bulb, said, 'I know you climbed that cliff and took that mountain. But I don't see how.' I looked up at that big mass looming up like something in my nightmares and said, shaking my head, 'I don't see how either.'"

Captain Milt Mater, CO, Company F, 361st Infantry.

I

On 25 March, 1945 Lieutenant Colonel E.O. Foster, the Division G-2, sent a memorandum to General Livesay titled, "Terrain Study of Division Sector," which described the defenses facing the 91st and also gave an assessment of the situation along the Division front prior to the coming offensive:

In the division sector the enemy has maintained a high degree of sensitivity to our patrolling and reacts immediately to any penetration by patrols. His mortar and artillery fires are well sighted and adequately cover the available routes of approach. Because of the limited routes along the highway, the Germans have made economical use of their troops and by holding key approaches with a very few men, they have been able to rotate and rest front line units. The winter lull has enabled them to conserve and build up supplies, particularly ammunition and gasoline. POWs have reported strict orders for the conservation of ammo and fuel and maximum use has been made of animal drawn transport.

There has been a reshuffling of troops along the entire Italian front and the 65th Infantry Division is directly opposite the 91st with the 8th Mountain Division to our right. The 8th has recently been renumbered and was previously known as the 157th Mountain Division. Before coming to Italy it saw action in the south of France. The personnel of the division consists mainly of Austrians and Bavarians. Morale seems to be high, so far, and the desertion rate is practically nil. These are first rate mountain-wise men and it is a unit not to be taken lightly.

The terrain under discussion drains generally east and west into the Savena and Setta Rivers. The southern portion of the area is dominated by Monte Adone and on both sides of this huge mountain gullies run down to the rivers mentioned. None of these streams or gullies appear to carry much water but from the depths of which they have cut the mountain it would appear that in time of rain or thaw the water in them might constitute a considerable obstacle. The area has a highly developed ridge system. Monte Adone, the highest and most massive peak in the group, is a key point and dominates the southern portion of the area. The slopes of the ridges are very steep, especially above Setta River. The ridge running north of Adone connects with M. Frati. The greater part of the ridges have very steep sides which are formidable barriers.

From his present positions the enemy is able to observe the entire Savena River Valley. Key Points for enemy observers along this front are Monte Adone, M. Castellazzo, C. Boschi, and S. Benedetto. It must not be forgotten that operations directed against the area in question can also be observed from enemy positions east to the Savena. A ridge running northeast of Canovetta thru Zula to Monte Arnigo also offers excellent opportunities for this. Once Adone and the first ridge on the west side of the Savena has been taken, the enemy will still have observation of our advance from the second ridge and from M. Frati. Once we have gained this second ridge the advantage of observation should be with us, as the enemy will have been forced back on lower ground where his line of sight will be interfered with by the cut-up nature of the ridges. There will be many places, of course, where he will have local advantage of observation but generally speaking M. Frati would appear to be the key terrain after we capture Monte Adone.

The advantage of good fields of fire should always be with the defender in terrain like this. From prepared positions above the Savena River he can fire down on the bare slopes running northeast of Monte Adone. His excellent observation and the length of time he has been in position should render his artillery fire extremely accurate. Even after the initial ridge of Adone has been taken he will be able to employ mortar fire from reverse slopes in the massif with little danger from our artillery due to the steepness of the hills. Only sparse natural cover from vegetation is available but the terrain with its deep ravines, gullies and escarpments should offer excellent cover and concealment except from air observers.

The area under discussion is interlaced with mule trails and foot paths. Some of these may be suitable for one-fourth ton vehicles without engineer improvement. There are a few roads that can be used to supply troops and move motorized equipment. Unfortunately the location and direction of these appears to favor our enemy. As far south as Sasso Bolognese he has Highway 64 at his disposal and to supply troops on Adone he has the road paralleling the Setta River with a secondary road running along the ridge line almost up to M. Frati. Another secondary road runs east and west connecting Highway 64 and 65 and several roads run south from this lateral road to lose themselves in the mountains west of Frati.

So it can be seen that the advantage of terrain in all its aspects goes to the enemy. We will be forced to attack an area of successive cross corridors, up steep slopes of which the enemy holds the dominant features. There is every reason to believe that the Germans will defend their present positions stubbornly and retire only when forced out. The enemy is determined to hold Bologna as long as possible in order to exploit the resources of the Po Valley and ease the growing burden on the Fatherland.

By the end of March it was obvious that the Division troops had their work cut out for them. Unlike the rosy reports that were issued shortly before the Gothic Line attacks, G-2 by now had a far more realistic picture of what faced the infantrymen in the coming offensive to break out into the valley of the Po. Throughout the winter the Division had rested, trained, and rebuilt its shattered regiments. Replacements had been assigned to fill in the platoons and squads and most companies were back up to strength. While all this was going on there was no let up for the men in the line. They had sweated out the winter in the shadows of Monte Adone, Monte della Panna, Monte dei Frati, Monte Rosigliano and Monte Arnigo; now it was time to climb those peaks they had stared at for nearly six months they had now become symbols.

There had been little change in the II Corps front since the previous November; however, in late February, over in the IV Corps sector, the 10th Mountain Division and the 1st Brazilian Division, in a limited offensive, had seized the dominating ground west of Highway 64 which brought the IV Corps abreast of the II Corps in front of Bologna. The capture of the terrain greatly improved the jump-off positions for the major spring offensive.

On 24 March, 15th Army Group had issued Operations Instruction No. 4 which was a detailed plan setting 12 April as D-Day. Fifth Army would make the main attack. The British Eighth Army was to clear the plain east of Bologna. Both armies were to make wide enveloping movements in an effort to cut off the bulk of the German forces south of the Po River. The Eighth would operate to the east, the Fifth to the west. Their spearheads were to meet somewhere on the south bank of the Po. The plan was to be in three phases. In Phase I the British would break through the Santerno River defense. The Fifth Army would leapfrog the mountains into the valley, capturing Bologna. Phase II was to encircle the enemy forces south of the Po and Phase III called for the actual crossing of the river and the capture of Verona which was the gateway to the Brenner Pass.

Along Highway 65 the II Corps was a mere twelve miles from Bologna. On Highway 64 the IV Corps was twenty miles away. The question was: Would the main line of attack be up Highway 65 or Highway 64? The road net along Sixty-five was the best in the Army area, but the Germans had built their strongest defenses on the approach to the city. Every foot of ground of the mountainous terrain was strewn with mines, many artillery emplacements rose up to challenge the attackers and all the other deadly devices designed to stop an army lay in the path of the II Corps divisions. All winter the enemy had been working on this defensive system and the drive up the highway would be a costly one. IV Corps' Highway 64 front, while longer, was far less heavily fortified and the road, which followed the Reno River, was defiladed from the west over much of the distance and was the more protected of the two. It was decided to begin the attack in this sector. The 92nd Division, which had deactivated two of its all-black regiments, and was now made up of the 473rd Infantry, the 442nd Infantry and the all black 370th, was to protect the left flank on the Ligurian coast near Massa and follow up on any German withdrawals.

The 10th Mountain and the 1st Armored would make the main effort for IV Corps. II Corps was to attack with all its divisions in the line and it had a tough nut to crack. The 6th South African Division was to take Monte Sole in the Reno River Valley. The 88th Division would capture Monterumici, the 91st was to drive directly up Highway 65 and take Monte Adone, Monte Arnigo and the town of Pianoro. The 34th would be east of the highway with the Italian Legnago Group maintaining contact with the Eighth Army. The 85th Division was in reserve.

On 9 April the British Eighth Army attacked. The jump-off was preceded by one of the heaviest air-artillery bombardments ever fired in the Italian Campaign. Wave after wave of heavy bombers dropped their payloads and hundreds of howitzers thundered all along the army front. April 12, three days after the British began its drive, the Fifth Army was to attack; however, the upper air was so unstable General Truscott

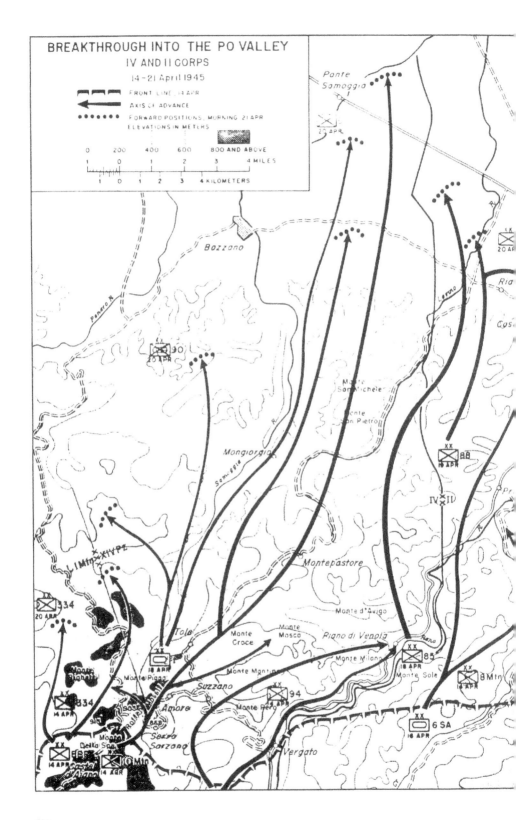

BREAKTHROUGH INTO THE PO VALLEY
IV AND II CORPS
14–21 April 1945

FRONT LINE, 14 APR
AXIS OF ADVANCE
FORWARD POSITIONS, MORNING 21 APR
ELEVATIONS IN METERS

800 AND ABOVE

0   200   400   600

1   0   1   2   3   4 MILES

1   0   1   2   3   4 KILOMETERS

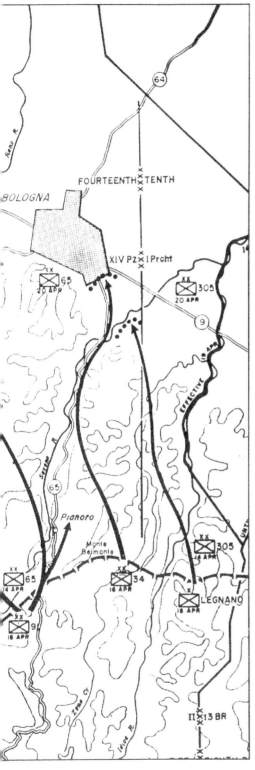

postponed his plans until the 14th. By 0645 fog still blanketed the front. At 0800 the cover began to dissipate and General Truscott told his staff, "We attack at 0830!" The 10th Mountain took off with two regiments abreast, followed by the 1st Armored Division.

The campaign for the valley of the Po was under way.

The enemy had been introduced to the 10th Mountain seven weeks earlier, he had known the 85th, 88th and 91st for many months and the 34th and 1st Armored for a very long time but that acquaintance would end in just nineteen days.

On 15 April General Livesay announced 0300, 16 April, as the time of the 91st's attack north. From 1800, 15 April, to 1800, 16 April, the Division Artillery and its attached units fired 1,823,400 pounds of ammunition.

The 361st Infantry had the unenviable task of taking Monte Adone, Monte dei Frati and Monte Castellazzo. The 363rd Infantry was given the job of attacking up and clearing the highway, the only supply route forward, and also capturing Monte Arnigo. The 362nd Infantry was handed the enviable chore of Division reserve.

At 0200, H minus one, 16 April, the four artillery battalions began a tremendous barrage. All ammunition rationing was lifted and within an hour 3,911 rounds had gone whining through the air and onto Jerry positions. On the left the 361st Infantry jumped off with two battalions abreast. On the right the 363rd moved out under a sky lit with thousands of tracers that streaked across the jet-black firmament.

The 363rd Regimental History for April, 1944 describes the regiment's "going over the top":

It was H hour.

The riflemen wet their lips, looked at one another in the dark, and moved forward across the Regimental front. To the left the 361st Infantry and to the right the 168th Infantry, 34th Division, crossed the line of departure at the same time. The 363rd Infantry's Companies E and G along the highway and Companies L and I to the east of the highway were met by strong enemy fire and minefields as they began the advance. Company L, on the left of the 3rd Battalion zone, lost its 1st platoon leader before it had advanced a hundred yards. Lieutenant Robert L. Quiesser, III, stepped on a *Schu* mine after his platoon had passed through elements of Company K near Barchetta. At the same time Lieutenant Queisser's platoon sergeant, Joseph Cook, was injured and Lieutenant Fleming K. Hurley, Company M mortar observer with the platoon assumed command. Company I on the right of Company L, was also moving slowly towards the ridge top and Hill 377 when the 3rd Platoon hit a

Shattered houses in the Monte Adone area. At 0300, 16 April, the Division jumped off for the distant hills.

mine field. After painstakingly probing through mines with bayonets and trench knives under machinegun fire from the enemy held hill and nearby Zula, a process taking an hour and a half, the company gained another 150 yards up the slope towards the houses of C. il Monte on the side of the ridge. Some self-propelled gun fire was received from Zula and also a counterattack in small numbers just after dawn, but the company held its ground and threw the enemy back. Captain Frank T. Hyland, commanding the company, ordered the 1st and 2nd Platoons around to the right under supporting fire from the 3rd Platoon which also kept moving forward. Under the enemy fire the two flanking platoons moved up to a single house north of C. il Monte by way of a draw. They then paused to reorganize.

Meanwhile Lieutenant Stanley D. Dosey of Company C, 316th Engineers climbed on a bulldozer near an uncompleted bridge site that had been left unfinished the night before, and though he was working less than 300 yards from the front line, he finished the bridge by-pass under the cover of a smoke screen.

By 1130 the first tank was ready to try the new fill to see whether it would hold up or not. If it didn't there would be no armor support and the fight would be that much tougher. The first tank stalled in the middle of the fill. If the tank were improperly handled it might tear the fill, rendering it useless. The motor started and the driver eased the tank carefully over the soft dirt and out onto the hard lateral road. The remaining four tanks in the platoon followed without difficulty.

The first objective of Company G, attacking in the 2nd Battalion zone along the right side of the highway toward Pianoro, was the houses at C. Canovetta. These houses were located on the highway where it passed Hill 367 and ran along the eastern slope of the ridge line from which much of the enemy fire had been received in the battle for the escarpment in October, and had been the scene of many hot patrol actions during the winter months. The houses Osteria Nuova and C. Casella were spaced at 400 yard intervals north of Canovetta along the highway leading to Hill 357 (see 363rd map) with the tiny hamlet of Zula just behind, an equal distance farther north at the junction of the lateral road. Company G, attacking with its 2nd Platoon leading, took Canovetta without firing a shot, the enemy having abandoned it, but immediately came under a mortar barrage and suffered several casualties within an hour and a half of the jump-off time. The 1st Platoon prepared to move through the 2nd Platoon and push on to Osteria Nuova. Meanwhile, Company E, attacking simultaneously along the ridge line across the highway, advanced slowly behind supporting artillery and tanks which had come up the highway to aid in the push. The tremendous shelling had set Hill 367, the company's first objective, aflame and the grass and brush on the hill burned brightly through the early morning darkness. One rifle platoon was deployed on the west side of the hill and another on the east. One of the tanks slowly drove up to the top of the hill but was forced back because the grass fires threatened to set it afire also. As the flames burned out, the troops and tanks again moved forward, this time around the hill to a smaller knob on the northern slope. By 0545 Objective 1 had been taken. With the coming of daylight the exposed left flank of Company E began to receive heavy enemy fire and and troops found they were unable to move forward beyond the hill they had taken in the hours before dawn.

As it approached Osteria Nuova, the 1st Platoon of Company G, commanded by Lieutenant Charles W. Flesher, crossed one minefield safely, then it hit a pillbox whose approaches were mined. Two men were killed instantly—one blown in half, the other's legs off clear to the hips—and several were wounded including Lieutenant Flesher. German grenades, lobbed from the aperture on the lower left side of the highway, wounded nine more Company G men. Trenches zigzagged down under the road and connected to a large room about 15 feet square dug inside the hill. Osteria Nuova was 200 yards north. Staff Sergeant Imler Hiatt, Staff Sergeant James L. McDermott, Staff Sergeant Wayne A. Rosenberry and Private First Class Glen N. Rudy charged the pillbox. They threw four grenades and pumped twenty-four shots into the apertures, killing all four Germans inside. There was a machinegun in the pillbox which never got a chance to fire.

After Technician Third Grade Dennis Plummer, company medic who had run to the first man hit while the grenades were still falling, had fixed up the wounded, the platoon pushed on towards Osteria Nuova. As the advance elements approached the shattered house they were met by a burst of rifle grenades, then fire from panzerfausts. The pockmarked area around the house was mined and fortified with barbed wire and the infantrymen had to jump from shellhole to shellhole to get close. A German opened up with a machinegun just above the group of Company G men.

Said McDermott, 'I could hear the son of a bitch work the bolt—it jammed!.'

The sergeant tossed a grenade up and over. The German took off and was shot. Two more Krauts tried to run down from the house to get the machinegun back into action again. McDermott shot one in the stomach and the other in the arm. Both escaped back to the house. When it was nearly daylight the platoon was able to see that a trench with overhead cover surrounded the house. Apertures for firing were in the top. One German stuck his head up and fired several burps from a machine pistol. The riflemen opened up on him but

ll Corps sector, 28 March 1945. The devastated countryside at the foot of Monte Adone.

he ducked down again, then several flares were fired from the same hole and even a bazooka failed to rout the Jerry.

Daylight came and the German, who proved to be an officer, would bob up and fire or throw a potato-masher. McDermott waited for him to try it once more and as the German raised up to throw another grenade McDermott shot him between the eyes with a captured Luger.

Meanwhile, the 3rd Platoon of Company G came up and was committed around the right of the house in a flanking maneuver, whereupon the remaining Germans in the house gave up. Fourteen prisoners were taken, including the two who had attempted to get to the machinegun. Five more who had gone back and reoccupied the pillbox came in with a white flag after the house was taken. Another two came down the highway from Bologna driving a ration cart pulled by two horses. Private First Class Clyde M. Hendrickson shot one of the horses, upsetting the wagon and spilling the rations all over the road. The two Germans then surrendered. At 1000 three more were flushed out of an adjoining pillbox. The prisoners were from the 145th Regiment, 65th Division.

During the winter months the cellar of the destroyed Osteria Nuova had come to be known as the 'wine cellar'. While the remainder of the house had been reduced to a pile of rubble, the underground portion was intact and was used as a bunker under which the Germans had dug another series of rooms. In the wine cellar the men of Company G found enemy maps—Osteria Nuova was used as an artillery observation post—incidently, the exact type maps that Company G and the rest of the Regiment were using. They may have been run off on the same press. The maps had all the 363rd Infantry former positions charted, including the assembly from which Company G jumped off in the attack. The 3rd Platoon, Company G, after assisting in the capture of Osteria Nuova, pushed on to the third house, C. Casella, 400 yards further up the highway. The 2nd Platoon, now under Sergeant McDermott, occupied the high ground just south of Casella.

Company F, initially in reserve for the 2nd Battalion, moved up between Companies E and G; however, by 1300 all forward movement had stopped because of the heavy enemy artillery and mortar fire and because the two attacking companies had run out of ammunition.

Now that the tanks had crossed the fill at Barchetta and could support the attack with fire and movement, two platoons of Company L formed for another attack to capture Hill 377. One of the tanks, accompanying the infantry, started up the highway toward a harassing machinegun emplaced near Zula, but it hit a mine on the shoulder of the road, threw a track and overturned. A second tank cut off to the right side of the highway to avoid a similar fate. As the two platoons assaulted the alfalfa-covered hill the German increased their machinegun and artillery fire from the ridge. A Jerry bazookaman, in a foxhole on the forward slope of the

This photograph illustrated the complexities of Monte Adone and shows the difficult cliffs and the routes of approach.

hill, spotted one of the tanks as it approached and hit it from 50 yards. The tank burst into flame. Two of the tankers scrambled out, then tried to help a sergeant who was still trapped inside. The commander of the tank company ran over to help but was cut down by the German machinegun fire from Zula. The other crew members were taken prisoner before they could help the doomed sergeant who burned to death in the wreckage.

Company I, reorganizing near C. il Monte, was also joined by tanks and resumed the attack toward Hill 407. Moving swiftly across the open slope the tank-infantry teams had, by 1430, nearly reached the crest of the ridge. One tank was knocked out by enemy fire, and the friendly artillery, not realizing the attackers were so far forward, covered the hill with concentrations. Before the fire could be stopped Company I and the tanks were forced to move back down the slope to C. il Monte to avoid additional casualties on the naked hillside. When the shelling finally raised, Captain Hyland advanced one platoon most of the way up the slope to the two demolished houses, C. Nova di Sopra, then put the remainder of the company in a draw just south of the houses. Here, at 1800, on the slope of the hill, Captain Hyland was mortally wounded.

In the attack on the hill the 2nd Platoon, commanded by Lieutenant James J. Kasney, was among the assault units. Six men—Sergeant Irving Diner, Private First Class Melvin S. Pearson, Adolph A. Herr, Michael D. Pope, Joe C. Davis and Charlie C. McLean—were with Kasney as they approached a communications trench approximately 100 yards along with connecting trenches branching out at 10 yard intervals. After dashing up the hill under intense mortar, artillery and small arms fire, the seven men dove into the trenches for cover only to find them occupied by Jerries. In the free-for-all that followed, the Germans in the main trench opened fire with machine pistols at the same time an artillery shell exploded within ten yards of the group, seriously wounding Lieutenant Kasney. After killing two Germans Sergeant Diner and Private First Class McLean ran out into the fire-swept main trench and carried the bleeding officer to the safety of a branch trench. Here they continued the fire fight, killing one more German, capturing one and driving the rest from the trench. The men realized the condition of the wounded officer was extremely serious, he was losing a lot of blood, and all litter teams were busy taking care of other casualties. They set to work and improvised a litter with a shelter half and two small trees which were growing near the trench, then carried Kasney back to the battalion aid station 1,000 yards to the rear before rejoining the company. Sergeant Diner was killed two days later.

Darkness fell on the first day of the push with very little gain against stubborn resistance and strong enemy defenses. Casualties were extremely high and only one of the objectives larger than company size had fallen. Objective 1 fell within a half hour of the jumpoff. Plans were made that night for Companies E and F to launch a simultaneous attack at 2300 against Hill 367 and 387, respectively, to extend the line across the highway north of Osteria Nuova, then to continue the attack along the ridge.[1]

A 363ster made the initial jump off with Company E:

"On the night of 9-10 April we relieved the 362nd in positions just north of Livergnano. This was about six days before the early morning departure for the valley of the Po. It was 'old home week' for all of us because we took over the infamous 'wine cellar' at La Fahbrica. We had occupied the same sector five months before. Having been shelled, mortared, bombed and raked with all kinds of small arms fire during the last long period, the place was a vast region of utter devastation. Just about every company of all three regiments had, at one time or another, spent some days in the wine cellar since the previous autumn when Company G, 362nd attacked Hill 367. It was as far north as the division got during the drive up Sixty-five.

"The first couple of nights we were in the cellar we sent out a number of patrols to probe the Kraut positions. The rest of the time we just stood guard outside the ruined house. It was terrifying duty. Each night

Conquerors at last! Men of the 361st Infantry pose for a photographer after planting the Stars and Stripes on the top of a fire-blackened Adone.

*Th infamous "Burp Gun." The German **MP Maschinenpistol**. Also known as the "Zipper Pistol." The sound of its high cyclic rate — brrrrrrrttttttt — would send a man to the dirt in one-hundredth of a second!*

the Germans sent over strange flares. They weren't so much flares as they were some type of fireworks. Well, I don't know what the hell they were! They'd pop in the air and shower us with red flecks which instantly disappeared. If they were meant to make us nervous, they damned sure succeeded. The nights were black. Pitch black. Total darkness. Tracers streaked across the sky in long, red lines that snuffed out at the ridge of the horizon, just like so many falling stars except the tracers were much lower and they crossed the sky in horizontal ribbons. They were beautiful to watch and they took our minds off the horror around us.

"The night we jumped off was something to behold! It was as if all the artillery pieces in the world were back of us, pumping rounds into the Jerries. The noise was deafening! We left the cellar, accompanied by two tanks, and began moving up Hill 367. I can't find the words to describe what it was like, the unbelievable racket of the attack. An absolute crescendo of the sounds of artillery blasts, mortars, rockets and rifle fire that reverberated through the mountains, swelling and crashing, swelling and crashing, thundering and booming. We got about halfway up the hill and were stopped cold by some of the heaviest fire we had ever encountered, even on Monticelli. Machineguns caught the tanks and you could hear the sounds of the bullets hitting the metal, ponk-ponk-ponk-ponk-ponk-ponk. I can imagine how those poor bastards inside the tanks must have felt. And mines? There were thousands of them! The engineers had done their best in trying to place white tape along the fields, but to locate them all were virtually impossible. So the first thing you heard, above the roar of the guns, were the screams of men who had stepped on some type of mine. The <u>Schu</u> mines were the deadliest and we had any number of men who lost their legs.

"We fought all morning for that damned hill and we were still there when darkness fell.

"I've been back to La Fahbrica several times. There's nothing there now but a large clump of trees. When I was there the entire area was a huge field of wheat. A new house has been built a few yards northeast of the old wine cellar. A woman in Livergnano told me it took more than a year to remove the hundreds and hundreds of mines that had been sown around the countryside. Even after all those years I was a bit antsy about walking around on the hill."[2]

Lieutenant March Kovas of Company G would later write a graphic description of the 2nd Battalion's struggle along the highway:

"The truck convoy rolled from Barberino to Livergnano up the hairpin curves of Highway 65 through Futa Pass under cover of darkness and halted just north of Livergnano where we dismounted and marched the rest of the way. The truck drivers gunned the motors in the turn around. We worried the noise would attract enemy artillery. The infantry shouldered its gear and plodded toward the foxhole line.

"The sector George Company was to occupy was astride the highway just beyond Livergnano which we called 'Little Cassino'. It was a typical war shattered area. Dead mules that stunk, knocked-out vehicles,

Colonel Milton H. Mater. 1989.

Fifth Army tanks pass through the completely destroyed town of Pianoro.

227

A 361st BARman escorts some German prisoners to the rear in the vicinity of Highway 65.

countless strands of broken communications wire and devastated buildings testified to the ferocity of the battle there.

"George Company CP was in a roofless artillery-battered stone barn on the right side of Sixty-five about 900 yards to the rear of the foxhole line beyond the area. The site was designated Di Sopra on our maps. Down at the foxhole line platoons moved into position on the reverse slopes of hills and were settled by daylight. Lieutenant Carl Blum's 3rd Platoon was in dugouts on the left side of the highway as it ran through a cut adjacent to Company E. The platoon had many hand grenade duels with the Krauts. Lieutenant John McKay's 2nd Platoon was on the right of Sixty-five atop a little hill we dubbed the 'Pimple'. Two evergreens grew on the summit. Jerry was opposite McKay in the ruins of a building called Canovetta. On the right was Lieutenant Charles Flesher's platoon on a reverse slope, his right flank marked by a deep draw. The dugouts were sandbagged and five months of static war left the area littered with ammo boxes, ration tins and discharged equipment. The route to the platoon sites from the CP led down the hill, around two curves in the highway, and was only a narrow footpath along the edge of the road. The first ruined structure was Di Sotto, occupied by Lieutenant Ike Notestine's machinegunners of Company H. Farther down on the left was La Fabbrica where Captain Edmund Carberry had his Company E CP. Farther on was the ruins of a structure marked on our maps as K-87, once a highway maintenance station. Blum's CP was in the basement. Two hundred yards farther were the platoon foxholes and dugouts, facing the Tedeschi. The stretch of highway no longer resembled a highway. A kayoed jeep sat at La Fabbrica, also three Sherman tanks, immobilized and a couple of Kraut vehicles, just hulks.

"Our artillery shelling increased in intensity each night. One night a heavy concentration of artillery with the new type of radar fuse that caused bursts above ground was laid down. Captain Edward Conley and I climbed to the second floor of the roofless CP and watched the fireworks. It was a magnificent, terrible sight, the earth trembled.

"We were all on edge in those final days of preparation for the assault, knowing D-Day was near. Jerry also knew it too, and all night sent up hundreds of flares to keep the sector lighted to discover our movements. We sent out patrols. I took one out to look for mine fields and got only a scare when a rustling noise up ahead in the darkness that the scout and I thought was a dog turned out to be a large weed brushing against a rock in the wind.

"The attack was set for 15 April but was later postponed 24 hours, much to our temporary relief. On 12 April, at midnight, while we were in the CP monitoring the progress of a patrol led by Lieutenant Flesher, the telephone rang. Captain Conley answered it, then called, 'Roger, out!' Turning to us, he said, 'Tonight America lost one of its greatest leaders—President Roosevelt died.' A few moments later Flesher, out in no-man's-land, got the news over the wire. Strange as it seems, under the circumstances, the news stunned us.

"Lieutenant McCanna was the executive officer. We had an excess of officers for the moment due to men returned to duty after recovering from wounds, and newly assigned officers. So, for the moment, I was without a platoon. I wondered how long that would last. A tank platoon was attached to Company G, commanded by a Lieutenant Jackson, fresh from overseas. He had never seen combat and he had made elaborate plans for support but as far as I know never fired a shot after the attack began. He got hit the first day.

"There was a flurry of final preparations all day Sunday, the 15th. Final orders were issued. After dusk, the last K rations and ammo were hauled down to the platoons. Captain Conley went down to brief Flesher and McKay, whose platoons would attack the first objectives. McCanna and I stayed behind to clear out the CP and move it down at midnight. All kinds of liaison people were trampling through the candlelit CP in those final hours, just cluttering up the place. They were the lucky ones, we thought, because when we moved out they would remain. In the dim light you could see how they felt about us who in a few hours would be out there under fire. Shortly before Mac and I and the CP personnel left to join Conley at the foxhole line, Doc Maloney moved his battalion aid station from Livergnano into our company CP. His voice was solicitous as he bid us good luck in the darkness before we moved out. 'I hope you people don't send any work my way,' he said. But we all knew those were idle words, we knew only too well that three hours from now Doc would be patching up mangled, torn bodies which at this moment were whole and normal and intact down there in their foxholes. We shoved the thoughts from our minds, parted the blankets that served as a door and moved down the hill.

"An hour rolling barrage was to soften up the Krauts before the assault. To minimize the danger of short rounds to our troops we drew them back on the rear slope some distance to unused foxholes. The officers joined Conley in a large dugout which was Flesher's CP. It was too small for the six of us so my feet protruded outside. There was not much to say. Canovetta, Osti Nuova, Casella were the initial objectives. From maps we knew their exact locations.

"The platoons were to follow the edge of an escarpment on the company right, then cut back left toward the objectives. Highway 65 was heavily mined. At 0200 on our Hamilton watches, right on the minute, our artillery barrage began. Artillery, cannon, mortars and tank fire went roaring and screaming and whistling over our heads towards Jerryland. It was a terrifying sight even though it was meant for the enemy, but there was always the hazard of short rounds. It was one of the largest concentrations of fire in the campaign. Ack-ack guns were firing tracers and cracked a few feet over our heads. Tanks fired flat trajectory screaming shells. The earth trembled with the explosions. Surely the enemy cannot survive this, we thought.

"Soon enemy shelling began, the earth shook under us and the bitter acrid odor of cordite filled the air. We lay quietly smoking in the dugout, no one saying much. We wondered how close the shells were falling to our platoons around us. I recalled the large, deep holes we had dug on Monticelli Ridge the previous September and how many had taken direct hits. Sandbags formed the roofs of our dugout and we knew it would not withstand a direct hit. One hit very close and a bunch of dirt came down on us. 'Pretty close,' someone said. 'Yeah.' Now by flashlight we glanced more and more at our watches, 0300 was inexorably drawing nearer. With shells still falling I half wondered if Conley would delay the assault command, but I knew he would not. Taking a last drag on his cigarette, he said, in a low, slightly strained voice, 'Let's go.'

"I scrambled up first at the door, found my carbine leaning against the dugout outside. Conley said McCanna and I were to remain here at the jump off point initially to help evacuate the wounded and to keep the ammo coming. He would follow behind McKay's attacking platoon. I rounded up men in the pitch dark to help move them out. A few yards away in the gloom I saw a lot of loose dirt about where Lund and Cappiello, the communications men, had foxholes. I called out but got no answer. I was fearful that some dark shapes in the hole were their shell torn bodies but on touching it found it to be an old discarded raincoat. In the inky darkness, all was confusion. Some of the men were immediately wounded by shrapnel. Then

Company G, 363rd Infantry walks past La Fabbrica after being relieved by the 34th Division.

another shelling came roaring in. Some wounded were already on litters bound for the aid station up at Di Sopra. One of our sergeants, Douglas Poteat, whose squad had a special mission, never had a chance to lead them. He was badly hit in the chest. Two bandoleers of ammo were around his neck and constricting him. I cut them off with my trench knife as mortars kept falling. Finally the shelling let up and I chased a litter team out of a cave, chewed their butts and ordered them to take Poteat to the aid station for he needed urgent attention.

"One man, Clarence Taylor, whom I could recognize by his voice in the dark, asked me to feel his back wound. A fragment had ripped open the flesh an inch deep. I withdrew my bloody hand.

"While up forward small arms fire indicated the troops were hitting their objectives, there was still problems of finding the wounded lying around in the darkness at the jump off point. Someone said a trooper was badly hit 'over in that direction' some 200 yards away. I went to look for him, Brown by name, calling his name in the darkness, but could not find him. I rounded up several mortar section men and, spreading out abreast and calling his name, we soon found him. He was conscious but weak and said he had heard me the first time I went by him in the darkness but was unable to speak. He was a big bruiser, his arms pinioned under him.

"Meanwhile, McCanna was in the dugout, on the phone, following the progress of the platoons, but soon the wire was cut, his 536 radio would not pick up Conley, so he came out to lend a hand with the wounded. The medics had accompanied the platoons in the attack. Another wounded was Tech Sergeant Theodore Gilbertson, our best damned platoon sergeant, sprayed with shrapnel. All that training and planning gone to hell. But he would survive. Other wounded lay in the darkness at the jump off point, in utter loneliness, waiting for help.

Pianoro. This lovely old combination restaurant and coffee-house, like all buildings in Pianoro, was totally destroyed during the fighting.

Pianoro. A waterfall on the Savena River, now long gone. The destruction of these old places is all part of the terrible waste of war.

"There were only two litter teams in the company and both were on the way to Doc Maloney's aid station, 1,000 yards back up the hill. Word came of other wounded up near the fighting. Tech Sergeant Kenneth Hubbard was up there. He had caught a burst of machinegun slugs that broke an arm and a leg. It was still dark and absent medics and litter bearers were a problem. So were others. One GI wandered up and said he was lost from his platoon, that it had gone off without him. I knew him to be a malingerer who had been AWOL from combat once before. I suspected he deliberately stayed behind. Another came out of the dark, a bazooka man whose ammo man was missing, what should he do? I told him to escort the malingerer in the direction of the attacking platoon.

"Over on our left the 'Pimple' was afire. Ammo was burning and exploding and white smoke and flames leaped into the sky casting weird shadows. The highway leading back to the aid station at Di Sopra was taking an artillery pasting. It was the only route our litter teams would be following. I told Mac I was going to see what the hell was keeping our litter teams, so I grabbed my carbine and started out. I got past the 'Pimple' that was aflame and popping and reached la Fahbrica where I understood there was a relay station, but peering at the rubble I could see no opening. It was there but I failed to see the tunnel in the darkness, so I moved on past the

The 362nd Infantry crosses the Adige River at Legnano.

knocked out tank and the jeep. Suddenly the whiz bang of four shells fell near me before I could hardly hit the dirt. I sweated out a few more rounds as dawn broke. I returned to McCanna at the jump off point where he said the litter teams were still missing. This time, now sweating like a horse and mad as hell at the litter teams, I reached the aid station at Di Sopra. Captain Maloney assured me there was a relay team at La Fahbrica somewhere because Lieutenant Smith was down there with them. Back I went, down the curving hill. In the daylight now I found the entrance to the rubble and in a tunnel were the litter teams sitting on their asses. I used some pretty hot words. They said they could not move due to the artillery falling. I said I made it past their safe haven three times, artillery or no. I guess I called them some names because they got right up and followed me on the double down to the jump off point where the wounded waited.

"We turned our attention to the fighting up ahead but knew little. There still was no telephone line. Conley had a 300 radio which let him communicate with battalion. Battle sounds were everywhere: artillery, mortars, tanks, machineguns. We were all tired, some of the crew in the CP dozed but my adrenaline was still flowing and I suggested that I go up front to Captain Conley. McCanna said Conley would let us know when he wanted us. I let it go at that.

"A litter team carrying a GI came by. I could see he was dead or nearly so. His face was unrecognizable. A mine had got him. The flesh had been stripped from one of his legs from the hip down. He had the appearance of a body just dug up from the grave. His face had that familiar yellow pallor. I felt his pulse. He had none. I asked the medic what he thought. He figured the soldier was dead. If he wasn't, he soon would be. So I had them dump him off so they could return for someone else who was wounded. Then I began to have self doubts if I did the right thing. No matter how hopeless the situation looks in combat everything possible is done to preserve life. Again I examined the man closely, bared his chest and placed my ear over his heart, felt his pulse, looked at his half open eyes, touched the pupils. No response. I just stared at the horrendous wounds. So there he lay beside the trail, a mutilated, lifeless body, an American who hours before had been full of life and hope. His name was Elmer V. Bunyard, 34 years old, one of our older soldiers.

"About 1100 our attention was attracted to Company E trying to take Hill 367 about 300 yards to our left across the highway. Through our binoculars we observed a group of GIs crouched low, cautiously moving toward the top. Some were on the right side of the hill, nearest our positions. It was an extremely hazardous situation for them. We knew the Kraut pillboxes and dugouts were just above them. Some of the GIs near the crest got down on their haunches. Suddenly they hit the dirt. In the racket of battle we could not distinguish that a machinegun was firing at them. We watched the drama through our glasses and at that range we could almost see the expressions on their faces. One of them hit the ground and rolled sideways over and

231

over down the hill. I didn't know it then but it was Lieutenant Robert Benckart, one of the toughest in the regiment.

"From the top of the hill a flare went up, bursting into a three star cluster of blue. A moment later a mortar barrage erupted on the hilltop among the assaulting soldiers. They scattered to shelters. A while later I saw one of the few instances of a GI whom I was observing in attack killed by mortar fire. Two Company E men, walking forward up the highway toward the battle line, began to climb the bank to join those trying to take Hill 367. As they reached the top of the bank we watched them closely because we knew they were in great danger from mortars falling above them. And then it happened: as we had them in our glasses two explosions burst right on top of them and momentarily were obscured from the view in the smoke and dust. As the smoke cleared we could see one of the men sliding down the bank, blood streaming from his face and hands. His companion lay in a grotesque heap with his body hanging over the bank, head down. His face was red with blood. A short time later we saw medics casually examine the body on the bank then keep moving.

"It was mid-afternoon now and the battle sounds were easing. We had word from messengers that Company G platoons had taken their objectives. Some of the men began munching on K rations, and though 24 hours had passed since we last ate, most had no appetite for food. Highway 65 remained a target all day for German artillery and all day we watched litter bearers carrying the huge Red Cross flag, dodging shells on the highway. Jerry had zeroed in on that route. About this time I could see a file of infantry coming down toward our area from the rear, avoiding the highway. It was a platoon led by 2nd Lieutenant Russell McKelvey of Company F, one of the roughest rifle platoon leaders in the battalion. He had received a battlefield commission and the Distinguished Service Cross.

"About 1800 came a runner with a written message from Captain Conley that I come forward with three men with ammo, grenades and flares. We moved out following a well worn path where the troops had been tramping and evacuating the wounded. Some distance up I discovered two white objects which, during a night patrol a few days earlier, I had mistaken for rocks in the dark of the alfalfa field. I now saw they were the bodies of two GIs, clothed in their white winter parkas, killed sometime during the winter, a bare 200 yards from their own lines.

"Captain Conley and Sergeant McLeod were in a deep two-man foxhole with the 300 radio lying on the outside edge. McKay's platoon was dug in around the sector and Flesher's and Blum's were in and around Osta Nuova. Just below the buildings a group of fifteen Tedeschi POWs sat on the ground guarded by GIs. Earlier in the afternoon we had noticed a blotch of blue up there and had concluded they were prisoners taken by the attacking platoons. I got in the hole with Conley and he gave me the situation. Two of our men had been killed when they got into a minefield as they attacked Osta Nuova. Bunyard was one of them, the man lying down by the trail with flies on his face. The other was Nando Leoni, a young kid of Italian ancestry. There were numerous wounded, all of whom had been evacuated. Then Ed gave me the attack orders for the night. Blum would take Casella, Hill 357, Company E would try again to take 367, and Fox Company would take Hill 387. It didn't sound good. The men had been on the go for 36 hours and here was another attack coming up. Conley was called back to battalion headquarters and I took over. Shortly, Lieutenant McCanna came forward and we reviewed the situation. Desultory mortar and artillery fire were coming in. Suddenly, over on the left and above us near Osta Nuova, there were several explosions and a lot of frightened shouting in German. I dashed out of my hole and saw Chuck Flesher bringing the prisoners down. He had deliberately brought them through the minefield where two of his men had been killed. The Krauts panicked and began running wildly out of the minefield. More explosions. At last, a terrified bunch of Krauts came down with Chuck prodding them on, swearing at them. Soon five Krauts, with their feet blown off, came crawling out of the minefield by themselves. We made them get down in a bunch while we discussed the situation. Flesher had been hit in the arm earlier in the attack, but remained with his platoon. The mines that had just exploded again nicked him, this time in the legs. In a quiet voice he said he was going back to the aid station. I was next in line to take over his platoon.

"The Krauts carried two of their wounded with them on stretchers. Chuck went with them. Shortly McKay and Blum showed up and I gave them the plans. Blum remarked bitterly that he hoped he got hit so he would not have to continue. He was a mean fighter but there were limits of human endurance.

"The Krauts had been in deep tunnels and caves at Osta Nuova. After a German officer, at the opening of the tunnel, was killed point blank, the remainder gave up. In a large room occupied by Flesher's platoon was found a lot of stuff, a radio, maps and such. While listening to the Kraut radio the men got the surprise of their lives. All our radio calls were being picked up!

"Conley returned about 2200 and got down in the large hole with me and McCanna. While in the hole we underwent one of the most terrifying heavy mortar barrages. Hundreds of shells burst around us. Each whistling shell sounded as if our hole was the target. I was scared, but in a calm sort of way. We would never

347th artillerymen watch as an Italian farmer strips a dead German of his boots.

know if a direct hit got us. I thought of how only three weeks ago we figured we were through with war and death. Then it occurred to me that where we were, three key officers of the company all being wiped out in one hole in the ground. Then who would take over the company? Such odd thoughts occur when death seems imminent. I prayed, without forming the words. I thought, if there's a God, now is the time to make the revelation. Inwardly I reasoned with Him. Conley, McCanna and I were Catholic. Mac was saying the rosary audibly.

"The earth shaking crashes continued for about 20 minutes. Shrapnel filled the air. I do not remember any conversation among us. Just my thoughts. We just pressed ourselves into the bottom of the hole and waited for whatever God had in store for us. Yet, when the barrage lifted and the odor of cordite fouled the air, it was a great relief that we survived, and that only one man was injured. All the shells had fallen just behind us in a draw, or nearby. God had done His part.

"We decided to used the tunnels and caves of Osta Nuova as the CP. We followed the path through the minefield and approached the opening to the pile of rubble that we called the wine cellar. Squarely in front of the opening was the body of the Kraut officer. We stepped over the corpse to enter. Some rubbish cascaded down on the Kraut. We let him lay, a gruesome sight. In a large room were three wounded Krauts. One was a Mongolian who had fought for the Russians and was captured by the Germans. It was funny the way they were captured. After dark the men on guard at Osta Nuova heard a rattling vehicle of some kind approaching from the direction of Zula on the highway, to the north. They thought it was a tank. As it got nearer they fired a bazooka and rifles. It turned out to be two Krauts on a rickety cart hauling up rations not knowing that the position was in our hands. The horse upset the cart and fled in terror, the Krauts shouted kamerad. The fracas netted a five gallon can of rotten kraut, coffee, a sack of hard, black bread that had a sour taste and cans of peas. It was a sorry mess.

"It was now 0100 17 April, Tuesday. Word came that Blum and McKay had taken their objectives. The room was crowded with sleeping troops on the floor. Conley fell asleep. I reported back to battalion on the 300 radio that all was in hand. About 0400 a message crackled over the 300 that was to change my role in the rest of the campaign. It came innocently enough. I was to report to the Battalion CP to see Colonel Angell about some plans. They were plans all right. I grabbed my carbine and leaving the rest of my gear behind, took off down the trail, through the marked minefield. I wasn't sure where the CP was so I stopped at the La Fahbrica aid station where East Company had its CP, to inquire. Captain Ed Carberry was standing at the entrance. I asked him where the colonel was. He replied that Angell was up the highway where Company G's original CP had been. I knew where that was, for sure. Ed had the appearance of an exhausted man. He was mumbling. He always did mumble but now even more so. He mumbled, 'You'll take the first platoon and attack the right side of the hill.' And pointed to Hill 367. I said I did not understand what he was saying. He repeated, 'You'll take your platoon to the right and Lieutenant Eckard will attack on the left side.'

"I was not in his company and it did not make sense to me so I said I did not know what in the hell he was talking about.

"Didn't they tell you?' he said. 'You're in Company E now.'

"It stunned me and a darkness seemed to come over me. I remembered watching the battle of Company E on 367 the day before. Carberry gave me the sad story. Lieutenants Benckart, McKie and Shannon had all been hit. Benckart was the one I had watched through the glasses. That left only Carberry, Eckard and Oswald as officers. Small wonder Carberry was shaken. That's where I came in. As I got the story later, I had been selected to help our Company E because Colonel Angell wanted an 'old timer' he could depend on. I wasn't flattered. I was chosen because I was available.

Suddenly time began to fly. Half an hour to get acquainted with my new platoon and make the plans. I was led by a runner to the platoon in caves some 200 yards from the CP.

I introduced myself to a bearded bunch of weary men. I minced no words. I tried to inject a note of confidence in my voice. Convinced this would be my last attack, I resolved to make the most of it. I had to gain the confidence of these exhausted men. A welcome word came that the attack was set back an hour. More time to get acquainted with the men. I addressed the non-coms. I said we can do it, just follow me. We had a simple plan, we would attack in a skirmish line, abreast. I would lead the first wave, right in the skirmish line. We'd go over together. That, I was to learn later, was what sold Kovas to the platoon.

"I returned to Carberry under the ruins of La Fahbrica, gnawed on a loaf of bread, the first food in 30 hours. I chatted with Eckard who said he would also be in a skirmish line and would give a hand signal when ready. No great tactics, just go in shooting. I half dozed, having two nights without sleep. Our 155 artillery was coming in and I went out to observe it, but was far from satisfied with the hits.

"Anxious glances at our watches. Time was up. Here we go again. We formed skirmish lines. I waved to Eckard on my left, jammed a ground flare pistol to the ground, sending up a red flare and advanced in a crouch. The men hesitated. I shouted at them with all my might. 'Let's go! 'Let's go!' A machinegun was firing off at the left as we reached the crest, still no fire from the enemy. I saw a low fence area. Mines. I stepped gingerly around the spot. Strangely, still no return fire directed at us. I walked through shell holes knowing they would be free of mines. Then I saw a network of trenches and moved forward, firing. No response. A mine exploded to my left, then one directly behind me, showering me with dirt. I glanced back. A GI lay there, his foot blown off. He winced but said nothing. I leaped into a trench torn up by the 155s. More explosions on my left. I fired into entrances to the dugouts. I threw grenades. I was shouting, shouting. We were over the top. I saw three dead Krauts, mutilated by artillery. Now I realized there were no more defenders on the hill. Hill 367 was finally in our hands at the cost of numerous blown off legs of the platoon.

"Litter bearers came to get the man who stepped on a mine behind me. A shred of tendon held his foot which I placed on the stretcher. He was pale but conscious. I tiptoed to the 2nd Platoon area where I discovered Lieutenant Eckard was one of the first to step on a mine. A sergeant carried him out of the minefield, without regard to his own safety. Two of Eckard's men were killed by mines and eight injured. Sergeant James Small stepped on a mine and was thrown up into the air, then came down on another which blew him to pieces. Bits of flesh strewed the area. In a letter from the hospital later Lieutenant Eckard wrote that he was recovering. His foot had been shattered and it was amputated above the ankle. He said a surprise was that he had also been shot in the back just as the attack began. Despite the injury he kept moving ahead in a daze till he stepped on the mine.

"Company E moved over to the east side of Highway 65 into an assembly area at the spot where Company G had jumped off the day before. Monte Adone, towering over us at the left rear, still had not been taken."[3]

II

Adone translates into English as Adonis or beau or dandy. Centuries ago the rugged mountain had been named after the Greek god. The mythological story tells us that Adonis was a beautiful youth who was fought over by Aphrodite, the goddess of love and beauty and Persephone, queen of the underworld. Adonis was killed while hunting a wild boar but was resurrected by Aphrodite. The great god, Zeus, then decreed that Adonis should spend the summer on earth with Aphrodite and winter in the underworld with Persephone, thus symbolizing the cycle of the seasons. The death of Adonis was often commemorated at ancient festivals which celebrated the approach of spring and the coming of winter.

Now, Adone would again be fought over, but not by two beautiful women, but by the determined soldiers of the German 8th Mountain Division and the sweating infantrymen of the 2nd Battalion, 361st Infantry of the American 91st Division. Veterans of the action would agree that Monte Adone was indeed a dandy!

As had the 2nd Battalion, 363rd Infantry, the troops of the 361st jumped off at 0300. The terrain was extremely mountainous and very rugged. On the south side of Adone were sheer rock cliffs with only two winding trails up to Brento and a cart trail skirting the side of Monte Castellazzo. This mountain was a mile east of Adone. Brento was located on a small flat space on the top of the lower escarpment a little over half way to the top of Adone. With the exception of a light mountain shower on the 16th, the weather for the next two days was clear and cool. Due to the nature of the terrain the 2nd Battalion would receive little support from the 3rd Battalion to the right and the 350th Infantry, 88th Division, on the left. For the good work at Monte Adone the 2nd Battalion would be awarded the Distinguished Unit Citation, the third by Division units. The 91st Division was the only 5th Army outfit to receive the award during the Po Valley Campaign. It was a citation that was hard to come by.

The actions of Captain Milton H. Mater's Company F are typical of the 2nd Battalion's struggle for the heavily fortified mountain:

"My first look at the formidable mass of Mount Adone was from the 361st Headquarters at La Guarda in December, 1944. Its vertical face loomed up in front of us like the barrier to our drive to the Po Valley—which it was. It was the key to the German defensive position called the Winter Line.

"The original plan was to jump off on Christmas night in what was known as the 'Pianoro Plan'. Mount Adone and all its approaches were snow covered. It looked like a very tough battle ahead. I remembered that during our Revolutionary War General George Washington made a surprise attack on the Hessian soldiers at Trenton, New Jersey on Christmas night and scored a glorious victory. I had some vague thoughts of telling my men about it as a sort of pep talk before we moved out. However, when I returned from an aerial reconnaissance over the front in an artillery spotter plane on Christmas Eve, I was told the attack on Mount

Several members of the 347th enter the Po Valley. L-R Major Flake McHaney, T/4 David Dong, Pfc. John Neuman, T/4 Regenski and T/4 Alvin Wyriszynski.

Adone had been delayed a few days. Three days later we were told the attack had been called off indefinitely. I think the whole Regiment breathed a sigh of relief.

Finally in April we were back in the same old position. La Guarda was again the regimental headquarters and the mission of the 361st was again to take Mount Adone. This time Company F was to be in reserve with Company G making a frontal attack on the ridge to the right of the Adone escarpment and Company E, under Lieutenant Beal, attacking from still further to the right to come up on top of the ridge. The escarpment face of Mount Adone was thought to be impregnable.

During our previous occupancy of the defensive position, we had detected a path leading up to the right which Companies E and G were to attack and the bulk of Adone itself. Since Company F was in reserve I was able to obtain permission to take out a recon patrol consisting of an officer or platoon sergeant from each platoon to study the escarpment. We went out at night and occupied a shelled out farmhouse in the middle of the field facing Adone. We stayed there all day using our field glasses to study the face of the escarpment and the path. We found that it started from the right, under the ridge, and went to the left at a shallow upward angle close to the low cliff which extended to the saddle. The path kept on to the left for another 300 yards or so until it joined another path which angled steeply to the right, up into the saddle. But just where this second path came to the saddle was one of those nasty German bunkers which we called pillboxes. Where the two paths joined was a bit of shelter in the form of a drop off of about five or six feet to a small piece of sloping ground on which we could set up our mortars and the heavy machineguns which our reinforcing platoon from Company H would carry.

"On our return from the reconnaissance that night I went to Battalion Headquarters and presented my attack plan, with a sketch showing the Mount Adone escarpment and the paths up the face to the pillbox in the saddle, to the Major who was commanding the 2nd Battalion. I said we would have to make a night attack and that we would need artillery fire on the ridge and cliff top and in the saddle to keep the Germans down. When we reached the junction of the two paths, we would set up our mortars and the heavy machineguns and one platoon of riflemen and deliver close-up suppressive fire on the pillbox while two rifle platoons advanced up the steep path to the saddle. When the platoons closed on the pillbox, the platoon leader would fire a red Very pistol flare for the fire to stop; the attacking platoons would then rush the pillbox and wind up in possession of the saddle. The major said that was a hell of a hazardous plan, that we would be exposed in a single line along both paths every foot of the way; that Company E would keep the Germans off-balance with the attack on the right and Company G would walk right over the ridge to occupy the saddle and that he would tell Company F when to move out to follow Company G onto the saddle. Besides, didn't I hea our own artillery? We were having a total barrage all over the ridge, the saddle and Mount Adone and there probably wouldn't be any Germans left when we finally walked up there.

"I remember feeling relieved when I left the Major, skeptical that it would be that easy, though I was also relieved that he hadn't wanted to use my plan. The neck of a rifle company commander is always stuck out, but when he offers an attack plan to hazard his men's lives, it's stuck out too far; what's more, his conscience nags him more than usual.

"The next night, 17-18 April, we jumped off and it was rough. We waited on our side of the Savena River for our turn to follow Company G. But before we jumped off, the wounded were already coming back. I remember one young Company E lieutenant who had been hit in the shoulder. I tried to ask him about the situation on the ridge but all he could say was, 'It's rough!'"

"We finally moved out and climbed partway up toward the ridge before daylight. After daylight it was impossible to move without drawing fire. I remember feeling sorry as hell for Company G up above, leading the attack, and being sneakily glad it wasn't Company F. We heard that 'G' had lost eight killed and eleven or twelve wounded, so far.

"Late in the afternoon, my radioman said Battalion wanted me to get down to the foot of the hill and get on the Battalion telephone which had been stretched across the river. I made my way down, mostly sliding backwards on my stomach. There was a lot of shooting going on but with Company G somewhere up ahead, we had to be careful about shooting back and our artillery had stopped. Somebody said as I slid past him, 'This is no place for a nervous man, Captain.' I agreed with him and told him I hoped he wasn't as nervous as I was!

"The Major was on the other end of the field phone. 'Captain,' he said, 'remember the attack plan you showed me yesterday? Well, regiment wants you to go ahead with it.'

"My premonitions had come true. Company F was going to take that mountain! Due to various high-level arrangements which had to be made we could not move out until 0400. This would not permit us to complete our maneuver that night. The Company F move across the lower path in one long line of about 180 men in the dark of the night, and then clinging to our shallow foxholes all next day, showered by shell fragments and rocks blown out of the face of the cliffs by our own artillery and shelled by German mortars from the top of the cliff, is a saga in itself. One incident stands out:

"Lieutenant Martin, Weapons Platoon commander, was the guide officer, having performed a personal reconnaissance of the path earlier that night with a mine sweeper. He led the company, followed by Lieutenant Bruehl, commanding the leading platoon. Bruehl was followed by his platoon sergeant, a young energetic fellow who showed lots of promise. At a narrow part of the path-cliff face on one side, dropoff on the other, Bruehl stepped on a Schu mine which blew off his heel. Martin, in front of him, got a tail full of rocks and the sergeant behind him got it in the face, temporarily blinding him. In the space of that one explosion, Company F lost three seasoned leaders in the battle for Mount Adone.

"I was in the center when the mine went off. There was so much battle noise we did not hear it. We knew something had happened because the men stopped moving. I went forward to the head of the column—no mean feat with the path just one man wide in most places—to see what had caused the hold up. As I moved forward I found the men facing me as if to go back. I said, in a conversational tone, 'Turn around men. We have a job to do.' There was no hesitation, the men turned around, despite the noise, fragments, dark and confusion, ready to go forward to complete the mission. To me this was the high point of the courage and determination of the American infantrymen and of Company F. I feel a glow of pride to have had the honor and privilege of commanding such men!

"After full dark next night, we resumed our advance along the lower path until we reached the assembly area at the junction of the two paths. The Germans knew we were there but for some reason, probably the continuing attacks from G and E Companies, they had not put any heavy weapons into position to shell us. Maybe they too, thought it was a 'hell of a hazardous plan' and were not prepared to fight us off from this direction. We wasted no time at the junction. We set up the base-of-fire platoon, the mortars and the heavy machineguns. We opened fire and the two assault platoons under Lieutenant Donald Kaiser moved out, up the steep path toward the saddle and the pillbox guarding it. This was one plan that worked. Whether the heavy close-in fire drove the Germans out of the pillbox or killed them, or whether the assault platoon's grenades thrown into the gun slits did it, I don't know to this day. Only one of our men was grazed, almost surely from wild bullets from our own base of fire, on the path to the assault. Remember, it was a dark, black night.

"One incident almost ruined the assault. When Lieutenant Kaiser fired the Very pistol, the shell popped out and didn't flare! Our men in the base of fire were keyed up to look for a red flare as a cease fire signal and wouldn't stop shooting until they saw it or ran out of ammo. Of course, the assault platoons had to stop or run into our own fire. It was a touchy situation in the darkness.

"Luckily, I had my communications sergeant and his two man crew running wire behind the assault platoons with orders to tap into the wire whenever the fighting stopped. His voice came through on the phone. 'Captain, we're stopped! The lieutenant fired his Very pistol and its a dud!' I immediately ran down behind the base-of-fire platoons shouting, 'Cease fire! Cease fire!' The men took up the cry and within seconds all our firing stopped. We heard the assault platoons yelling and firing as they ran up to the pillbox and grenaded it and then on to the few wrecked buildings on the saddle.

"Soon Lieutenant Kaiser's voice came through the phone, 'Captain, we've got Brento.!'

"Yes, the place we fought for so hard and for which the 2nd Battalion had so many men killed or wounded was Brento.

"There are a few postscripts to the Battle of Adone. We captured 26 Germans in and around Brento. When I came up to the saddle after putting the base of fire into position to repel a counterattack in case we were forced out of Brento, several dead were still around, including one staff officer with a load of battle maps and orders.

"Colonel Broedlow radioed to congratulate Company F on taking this tough piece of ground. He also ordered us to send a platoon to the top of Adone and make sure it was clear so that the Regimental Recon men could raise our flag up there for a picture to rival the Marines who had just raised a flag on Mount Surabachi. Unfortunately our flag raising didn't get the publicity that the Marines did. However, our platoon did bring down about a dozen German artillery observers who were waiting in a cave for someone to surrender to."[4]

While the 361st Infantry was battling to scale Monte Adone, the 363rd Infantry still had its hands full driving the Krauts back along Highway 65 and Lieutenant March Kovas was trying to get acquainted with his new platoon:

"About mid-afternoon of the 17th Captain Carberry sent my platoon back on the left side of Sixty-five to occupy Hill 387, opposite Osta Nuova. Now I was the only officer besides the captain and Lieutenant Oswald. My platoon were all strangers to me. We loaded up with ammo and rations. As darkness fell we moved out behind the "Pimple" to the highway, turned north and were led by a guide to our positions on 387. We dug in beside a trail leading down the mountain side to the Savena River. As we lay in our foxholes the familiar sounds of war were all around us. To the rear a blue flash, then the hollow crack of the artillery piece and an instant later the soft rustling sound of the shell passing overhead and then the explosion as it hit. Six rapid, crunching explosions to our left. Mortars.

"About 0230 a column of troops approached from the highway. A voice in the dark spoke. It was the captain of Company B, 361st headed for positions off to our left. He came into my dugout and when he left he inadvertently picked up my carbine outside. A message came that we were moving back to the highway. We were to meet Carberry at Osta Nuova. We arrived but there was no Carberry. I went to the wine cellar and found it occupied by the Battalion CP crew. The corpse of the Kraut officer still lay at the entrance, but a blanket now covered it. Perhaps the Battalion Headquarters staff was not accustomed to such gross sights.

"Later out of the darkness a column approached, led by Captain Carberry, bringing up the remainder of the company. Silent figures shuffled by, halting, moving, shuffling. At last they turned off to the right by some shattered buildings I estimated to be Zula.

"We put our men in empty dugouts and caves. It was now dawn of 18 April. The third day of the assault. So far I had no sleep. I was bone-tired, weary, fatigued. I went to my platoon cramped into an underground dugout. Sounds of snoring led me there. The dugout was so cramped the men slept sitting up. A mentally detached feeling came over me. My mind was slow to grasp thoughts and nothing seemed to matter. I was groping for some spot to lie down when Staff Sergeant Ysbrand Sprik, the radio operator, saw me and led me to the company CP dugout in a narrow passageway that ended with a Kraut bunker with two beds, one above the other. Sprik made room for me on the top bunk. I was too tired to remove my cartridge belt. The canteen and ammo magazines caused me discomfort but I could make no effort to remove them. Even in this exhaustion I could not sleep soundly.

"Carberry wanted me and I detected another mission. I was to take my platoon on a flanking maneuver to the left, cross the Savena River, pick up a platoon of four tanks and lead them to help out Company F which was under attack by tanks somewhere across the river near Pianoro. Carberry gave me the details of the mission. He pointed with a dirty finger to a spot on our map where he thought Captain Crowden's Fox Company was located opposite Pianoro. In this inauspicious manner, with two exhausted infantrymen listlessly examining a soiled map, began one of the strangest odysseys of the war for me. Consulting the map and looking down from our high perch at Zula, we were able to pick out the clusters of buildings marked San Benedetto, C. Nuova, Castiglano and Hill 387. Maggiore where I was to contact the tanks was hidden from view by the mass of Hill 387. I awakened Sergeant Akina and told him to get the platoon ready. We picked up a radio operator from battalion headquarters and a medic, then found the 361st guide who led us to his captain, Company B. I asked the captain if it was him who I oriented the night before. It was. We shook hands. 'How about my carbine?' I asked. 'You picked it up last night in the dark.' He was surprised when he checked his carbine that it was not his. It wasn't mine either. Since taking mine he traded it for still another.

"We descended to the river bed down some Kraut-built wooden stairs, then slid down a steep bank. The river was shallow, and flowed into two rivulets about 200 feet wide each. The streambed of pebbles and stones was about 100 yards wide. We waded across the water and squooshed in our boots.

"No tanks were in sight so I told the platoon to sit tight while a runner and the radio operator accompanied me to search for the tanks. We encountered some GIs at a relay station but they knew nothing of tanks. So taking a runner, a kid named Davis, we went in that direction. We passed two dead GIs, killed by mortars. At the town an officer said he knew nothing of tanks. Time was wasting. Where the goddam hell were those tanks? We trudged back to the platoon. This time I moved forward some 300 yards to San Benedetto, a castle affair. It was the CP of Company G, 361st. The commander said his company was some 1,000 yards up ahead and to the left of the river. He knew nothing about Fox Company. No tanks, no Fox Company and suddenly no communications. We could not contact Jig, the battalion call sign. The Company G commander did have some news. Mount Adone had just been taken.

"Suddenly we heard tanks and looking back down the river we saw them. They were coming boldly down the river bed. I flagged them down. A young 2nd lieutenant poked his head out of the turret.

"'You looking for a Company E patrol?' I asked.

"He was. I told him to stay put while we scouted out the area ahead.

"Finally we got the entire platoon across the river and in the lee of a high bank. Night had long since fallen and God knows where Fox was. I kept sending runners back to the tanks to tell them of our location. We figured we might be nearing Fox Company, but the bank of the left side of the river was sheer precipice and scaling it was out of the question. The 300 radio would not work so we had no help from battalion headquarters. I sent the platoon some distance back around the bend, safe from artillery fire while the radio operator and I tried to contact headquarters. Carrying the back-pack radio of some 40 pounds was no small task, but he went where I went. Much later in the night while I was roaming up and down the river bed and through mine fields, the platoon had bedded down in a cave in the hill that had been a Kraut aid station. Some dead Germans were in the back, dead of wounds. Sergeant Bolzman returned with words he could not find the tanks. I chose one of our best soldiers, Harold Fimple, and we trudged back up the river, found the spot where we had originally met the tanks, but they were not there. Tracks in the river bed indicated they had turned around.

"'Those sons of bitches,' said Fimple bitterly. 'They ran out on us!'

"We returned to the cave. It was now about 0200, the morning of 18 April. Most of the platoon had had little rest. I didn't yet realize that I had a platoon that was on the verge of physical collapse. But we moved out and went on. We climbed some steep paths up to Highway 65 and walked all the way down the road to a point opposite the Pianoro cemetery, but couldn't find the rest of the company. Eventually, a Company G soldier showed me where Carberry was dug in on top of a cliff. Company G had taken Pianoro. Finally, after eighteen hours I found a place to lay my weary head. I awakened a few hours later and we watched the battalion to our right attack Mount Arnigo, a long high hill. We climbed up to the peak of the hill we were on and there below us at our feet lay the Savena River bed where we had roamed. There was Pianoro and the huge ledge we had approached. We'd been within 200 yards of Company F! And another mystery was solved. There in the shadows of the high west bank were the two tanks. They had been disabled by mines.

"Then summoning Sergeant Akina I told him to assemble the squad leaders at once. We were dug in along a trail near Zula. The sergeant formed around me, filthy, black-faced, bearded and exhausted combat soldiers, with tired haunting expressions on their faces. I looked them over silently. I was seething from the frustrations of our eighteen hour ordeal. And then I let loose with everything in the book!

"Later the men confided in me that their first impressions under those trying conditions was that I was crazy and took far too many chances." [5]

The agonizing trials of Lieutenant Kovas and his men were indicative of the costly battles it took to break the German stronghold before Bologna. The 316th Medical Battalion reported that "the taking of Adone resulted in such an intensity of casualties as to necessitate using some of the clerks, technicians and cooks as litter bearers." Of the 770 battle casualties suffered by the Division during the month of April, 432 occurred during the three-day period 16-18 April. On 17 April there were 230 casualties making it the busiest day fo the 316 Medics since the Gothic Line Campaign. The majority—62—of the 95 exhaustion cases evacuatec during the month occurred during the five day period 16-19 April. The patients treated were mostly olc combat soldiers, many of them wearers of the Purple Heart, whose endurance had been worn down as mucl by the strain of prolonged combat duty as by any single operation.

By the end of the day, 18 April, the Division has taken Monte Adone, Mt. dei Frati, Mt. Posigliano, Mt Arnigo and Pianoro. It had been a great day for the 91st!

At 0445, 19 April the 2nd Battalion, 362nd Infantry jumped off without artillery preparation, followec at an interval of four hundred yards by the 1st Battalion. The Regiment was back in the midst of it.

That same night, 18-19 April, the 133rd Infantry, 34th Division, passed through elements of the 363rc along Highway 65 and continued the drive toward Bologna. The men of the 363rd were told that since the 34th was the oldest division in Italy it should have the honor of of being first into Bologna. Whether this wa: true or just another latrine rumor, the troops of the 363rd didn't know and didn't really care.

For the next two days the Division pushed slowly, then more rapidly north. At 0800 21 April, the 2nc Battalion, 361st reached its objective, Hill 286, the last high ground south of Bologna. From the hill our troop: had a panoramic view of the entire city.

Early in the morning of Saturday, 21 April, infantrymen of the 34th Division's 133rd Infantry, ridinc tanks of the 752nd Tank Battalion, rumbled up Highway 65 into Bologna. Elements of the 91st joined the Red Bull Division in mopping up the city while the rest of the Division moved on north past Bologna in the wake of the Krauts, now retreating headlong toward the Po Valley.

Pfc. John Roice was still plodding along with Company G:

"I always thought that some day they would mine Monte Adone for lead and other minerals. Every nigh during the time that the front line was stable, after the fall campaign and the start of spring offensive thousands and thousands of rounds were fired into it.

"Anyway, about the middle of the afternoon of 18 April we unloaded off trucks and started toward the base of Adone. The 361st had pushed on to the top and we relieved them about midnight and pushed on tc our objective. As soon as we had our objective we would be relieved and another company would push on For the next three days we never got any rest. On the morning of the 21st, just at daybreak, we could see a large castle and figured if we could get to it we would have beds to sleep in. We reached it about 1730 bu it turned out to be a monastery. The old man at the door wouldn't let us in but a young nun saw us from ar upstairs window and came down and let us in. From the monastery we could look down upon Bologna. There was a covered stairway from the monastery about eight feet wide all the way down into the edge of the city About halfway down this stairway we halted and walked out on a landing and looked over the whole town We could see tanks flying the Star and Stripes. The lieutenant had a big smile on his face and he said, "Come on, boys!" We secured the first house at the edge of town. Almost every house we went by had people standing at the gate offering a bottle of vino. Our patrol refused the vino because we had a mission to carry out, bu' when we got back to company, it was obvious that everyone hadn't refused the refreshments.

"That night we bivouacked near the airport north of Bologna. All during the spring push the Captair had said, 'When we get to Bologna we'll have beds to sleep in. My answer had always been, 'You may have a bed, but I'll sleep on the floor!' He picked out a room with beds all right, but come bedtime here came the lieutenants and guess who had to sleep on the floor?

"North of Bologna we couldn't walk fast enough to keep up with the retreating Jerries so trucks were brought and we rode in those. Late one afternoon our company was in reserve, which meant we were at the rear of the column. Suddenly, up ahead, a German plane came down the road strafing us. I was sitting in the middle in the back of the jeep with a blanket over me. When the jeep stopped, it seemed to take me forever to get the blanket off. I jumped out and landed on all fours on the pavement. The machinegun bullets were hitting the road a few feet in front of me. There was a drainage ditch on the right side of the road and the plane dropped a bomb in the ditch. It hit the first truck, killing three men and wounding eleven. When things quietec down we drove forward to see why we weren't moving. We'd gone about a mile when the jeep got hot. We found that a bullet had gone through the radiator and had also flattened a tire on our trailer.[6]

Once north of Bologna the Division fanned out in a wide arc and headed northeast. The chief obstacles in the path of the swiftly moving advance were four major rivers—the Panaro, the Po, the Adige and the Brenta. By 2400, 22 April the 91st had reached the south bank of the Panaro, found a crossing and constructec a foot bridge and by 0630 the next morning was moving out on foot toward the Po. At 0800, 24 April the 3rd Battalion, 363rd reached the river at Carbonata. The Po was a formidable obstacle to the Division's advance but it had been an equally formidable barrier to the retreating Germans. The south bank of the Po and the approaches to the river were strewn and clogged with vehicles, guns and equipment. Food supplies had been abandoned. Allied aircraft had caught long columns of enemy trains on the road and trails and left them charred and twisted. Hundreds of horses had been cut loose from the artillery pieces and ammunition wagons and they roamed the countryside. The troops found a large number of vehicles undamaged and after being re-marked with the star of the Allied forces, they were put to use. By 2300, 24 April, all Division units were across the Po and hell bent for the Adige River.

Captain Fred Booth was still commander of Company L, 362nd:

"I can't remember exactly where we were. Somewhere north of the Po. We were in a jeep accompanied by a couple of trucks and four or five tanks. After moving about ten miles during which time we had disarmed hundreds of Germans and sent them to the rear, we reached the crossroads where we had been told to wait for further orders. I recall this day most vividly because this was the day I got "sweet revenge". Back in February of the Winter Line I had gone to Rome on pass. I hadn't had a pass since we jumped off in early July. I had planned on seeing all the glories of Rome but what I did was get drunk. I never got out of the bars except to hit the sack. We all sat around drinking, talking and trying to hide our tears and fears while the band played 'Sentimental Journey' and 'I'll Walk Alone.' When it was time to go back to the front I had a serious

The end of the road. German POWs, accompanied by their horses, assemble in a camp in northern Italy.

hangover and got a late start. We were two hours late checking into Regiment. Someone told me the colonel wanted to see me. There were three of us standing at attention while the colonel chewed us out. You are AWOL. You know what that means? We could put you in jail. On and on. He came close to me, looking up into my face. 'Captain, you're the ranking officer. It's your fault these officers are AWOL'. I wanted to grab him by the neck and shake him. I was thinking, my life has been on the line since July and he carries on like this about being two hours late. Finally, he ordered us to go back to our companies and he turned to his aide and said, 'Make a note that these officers will not be allowed on leave again.' Actually, I was late. I had no excuse. All I could do was stand there and take it. He could have let it pass, but he didn't.

"While we were stopped at the crossroads I was trying hard to get hold of battalion on the radio. Suddenly, up comes an armored car and several jeeps. It was General Livesay. He jumped out of the jeep.

"'Who's in command here?'

" 'I am, sir,' I said.

"'What in the hell are you sitting here for? You ought to be ten miles north.'

"'I was told to come here and wait for orders.

"'Where's your battalion commander?'

"'I don't know, sir. I'm trying to get him on the radio.'

"Just then, up comes another bunch of jeeps. It was Colonel Cotton. And I'm thinking, my God I'm supposed to be up on the front lines and here I am back with generals and colonels. It was embarrassing. Cotton and Livesay met a few feet from me.

"'Goddam it, Cotton,' the general said. 'You've got this operation all screwed up. How come all this firepower is sitting here on its ass?' He looked over at me, then back at Colonel Cotton. 'Now goddam it to hell, get this outfit moving and I mean right now!'

"Cotton stood there not saying a word. I was laughing inside. 'Why aren't you moving?' he asked me. I said, 'If you order me to go north I'll go.' He pointed to the map and said, 'Go there.'"

So we took off after the colonel assured me he would report that order to my battalion. Revenge was mine! Just a minor incident in the total confusion that was the Po Valley. I got a lot of chuckles out of the General chewing out the Colonel."[7]

The 363rd Infantry was the last regiment to cross the Po and the first to reach the Adige. The 2nd Battalion started the move at 1300, 25 April, followed by the 1st at 1630 and the 3rd at 1800. By 0330, 26 April, the 2nd Battalion had contacted elements of the 362nd Infantry and made arrangements to pass through them at the town of Fratta, then continue the advance into the city of Legnago. The Adige River ran directly through downtown Legnago.

For the attack on the city the order called for Company E to clear the town to the left of the highway leading into the city. The 1st Platoon was to seize the bridge across the river while Company F was assigned the task of clearing the town to the right of the highway. As it neared the banks of the river well inside the city the 3rd Platoon surprised a group of fifty Germans attempting to cross the Adige on a barge. Lieutenant John Schreibeis, the platoon commander, called on the automatic riflemen and a light machinegun to fire on the barge as it crept across the broad stream towards the opposite bank. Only four of the Jerries escaped to the opposite bank.

Meanwhile, the 1st Battalion attacked and seized the west bank of the Adige to the north of the 2nd, meeting very little resistance.

Inside Legnago, the 1st Platoon of Company E, was engaged in a fire fight with Germans in a ditch seventy-five yards to its front. Lieutenant March Kovas, now better acquainted with his men who no longer thought he was crazy, divided the leading squad into two groups, giving one the mission of firing and advancing while he took the other half with him around to the left to get on the flank of the enemy and pour fire down the length of the ditch. The little force moved rapidly over the exposed terrain and through the small-arms fire. Lieutenant Kovas stood up and shot two of the Germans, then emptied the rest of two clips at the trench, before shouting for the Krauts to surrender. With no intention of giving up, the Germans replied with a burst of machinegun and rifle fire. Kovas crept toward the ditch, covered by the fire of his half squad. When he was close enough he threw two grenades and repeated his threat. "Come out with your hands up, or be killed!" Ten Germans surrendered.

After two hours of maneuvering through the rubble the city of Legnago was cleared. Amphtracs and DUKWs were brought up for the river crossing. Company G, which had not entered the fight, moved down to the banks of the Adige for the crossing with the leading 1st Platoon, still commanded by Lieutenant McCanna.

As the first men of Company G loaded on the DUKWs enemy machineguns on the far bank raked the levees on the west bank of the river. Despite the fire, the first two amphibious vehicles took to the water under cover of friendly small-arms fire. Midway in the wide stream the first one struck a sand bar and became stranded. It was immediately taken under fire by a German machinegun in a church steeple along the east bank. Two men were wounded. The occupants of the DUKW jumped into the water and crouched behind it as enemy bullets riddled the hull. By this time the second DUKW, commanded by Lieutenant Jack C. Mott, had hit the same sand bar farther down stream. Some of the men in the water swam back to shore. One, Private Leon F. Jolin, swam to the opposite side with everything on but his pack—including boots and helmets—then climbed out on the bank as machinegun bullets spattered into the mud all around him. He wasn't touched, but he was the first man across the Adige.

The feared Po River was crossed without much shouting; however, the crossing of the Adige was a memorable one for the men of the 363rd. Troops of the 316th Engineers, by midafternoon of the 26th, had brought up the ferrying equipment from the Po crossing site and the ferrying of small vehicles continued throughout the night. II Corps engineers moved up heavy bridging materials and started a vehicle bridge. The Powder Rivermen poured across the Adige while enemy artillery ranged over the river with air bursts. Fortunately the Germans were without observation of the crossing and the bursts did not bother the troops working at the river's edge.

By the next mornings, 27 April, the enemy had completely withdrawn to the northeast in almost total confusion.

The 91st moved on.

A division member later looked back at the Po Valley fighting:

"I've always thought the Po Valley Campaign should have been called the Po Valley Slaughter, because that's exactly what it was . . . a slaughter. The Po Valley was a slaughterhouse and the Germans were the hogs. It was absolute butchery. By April, 1945 we had complete air superiority. Well, we'd had it for a long time. Our fighter-bombers roamed northern Italy, at will, shooting the hell out of anything that moved. All along the roads and river banks were hundreds of burned out trucks, vehicles of all kinds, and horses, dead horses so thick you couldn't count them. That's how hard up the Jerries were for transportation. Entire German convoys were wiped out and for mile after mile, along the highways, these littered the shoulders of the road. The destruction was staggering. It was Death on a grand scale.

"Once out of the mountains we went a little loco. When we took prisoners, we stripped them of anything of value. We got their watches, whatever money they had, knives, medals, pistols and what have you. I even saw one guy with a crucifix around his neck. We had men who had wrist watches from their elbows down to their thumbs! On both arms! Some had seven or eight pistols strapped around their waists. Nor did we treat the Germans very kindly. Hell, they'd have done that to us if the shoe had been on the other foot. We showed them no mercy whatsoever. I remember one time we had just taken a break along a fairly decent highway, a hard-surfaced one. We were sitting along the side of the road when, all of a sudden, a German truck came toward us out of nowhere! It was moving rather slowly and there were about six Krauts in the back and one soldier was standing on the running board with a couple of Jerries inside the cab. I'll never forget the surprised look on the face of the soldier on the running board! We could have captured them easily, but instead, we opened fire on the truck. It tipped off the highway and into a ditch. I think the man on the running board died instantly because he pitched face forward down onto the road and rolled over and over for a good twenty yards. We killed every damn one of the Germans! And if we showed any remorse, I don't remember it. That was the Po Valley Slaughter.

"I think it may have been the night of that very same day that something happened which really shook me up. It was close to midnight. The moon was out and it was almost as bright as day. We had been marching for hours and were on a highway headed east. I remember the moon was so bright we cast long bobbing shadows. As we approached this small town we came upon a little Fiat automobile which had stopped directly in the middle of the highway. The body of a priest lay about ten yards from the car and his cassock was drenched with blood. You remember how the doors of the old time cars used to open out forward? One of the doors of the Fiat was swung wide open and the body of a woman was sprawled out on the roads, her legs still inside the car. Our fighters must have caught the car out in the open because one of the woman's arms was nearly severed and her stomach was ripped open, yet she had an almost peaceful look on her face. And she was beautiful! One of the things that still sticks in my mind was that she was wearing bright, red nail polish. Of course, we had seen death in many forms, but this was different. It was hard to comprehend. It was awful, just awful."

The 362nd Infantry remained in positions at the bridge site in Legnago until 1430, 27 April when Task Force George was formed. The force was named after Lieutenant Colonel George W. Richardson and was composed of eight tanks from the 755th Tank Battalion, twelve tank destroyers from the 804th TD Battalion, the 1st Platoon, M8 scout cars, 91st Division Recon Troop, one detachment from the 91st Signal Company and the 3rd Battalion, 362nd. The assigned mission of the force was to proceed to Vicenza.

Task Force George moved out at 0600. Captain Fred Booth and the men of Company L were a part of the force:

"We started at daybreak, riding tanks and trucks as we had since we hit the Po Valley. Every day was pretty much the same, moving fast, rounding up Germans, taking away their weapons, throwing those weapons into a pile and sending the Krauts back to the rear, hoping someone would take care of them. Sometimes we ran into a bunch of the enemy who wanted to fight, but they weren't really sincere about it.

"Our objective that day was Vicenza, but we were told to hold up short of the city and await orders. By noon we were probably a half mile from this strange looking, medieval city. It looked like it once had a wall around it. Now the wall was gone and the city started right where the wall had been. No outskirts, just big, dark stone buildings with narrow, dark streets threading into the city and out of sight. Orders came by radio from battalion headquarters, from God knows where. We were told the Germans had set up defensive positions somewhere in Vicenza and were determined to fight. I was ordered to dismount from the tanks and trucks and take my men and clear the enemy out of Vicenza. We were not to use tanks because the streets were so narrow they would be ineffective and the Germans had anti-tank guns.

"I asked the major on the radio, 'Can we call on artillery?'

"'We have orders not to destroy the city.'

"Why don't we bypass the city and let the Jerries starve?'

"'Captain Booth, you are ordered to clear the enemy out of Vicenza.'

"'Yes, sir.'

"So there we went into the unknown when we knew damn well that the war was all but over. We didn't even have a good map of the city. We went in with two platoons abreast and well spread out. I ordered the other rifle platoon and the weapons platoon to follow after we had gotten well into the city. They would protect our rear and clean up any Germans we might have bypassed. We came under small-arms fire about a hundred yards from the wall of buildings. We hit the ground and tried to figure out where the fire was coming from. We couldn't tell. From prone positions we started to pour rifle fire toward the streets and with simple fire and movement tactics we kept moving until we reached the protection of the buildings. No casualties. What a spooky place. Dark, narrow, curving streets. Big stone buildings looking right down on us. Not a person in sight, but we expected to see a German in every window and every doorway. There seemed to be two important streets. I sent one platoon down one street and I went with the other down the other street. Both seemed to head toward the city center where the poor map I had indicated there might be a square. We stayed close to the buildings on both sides of the street, ready to duck into doorways. We also kept an eye on second story windows and balconies. When nothing seemed to be happening, we gained courage and moved faster. Suddenly, at the head of the platoon, I came around a corner looking down toward a square. I hadn't heard so much small arms fire since Futa Pass. Some big stuff, too. We could hear it exploding down the street. Luckily, we were able to duck back behind the corner building before anyone got hit. Once again, the Germans had opened up too soon, before we gave them many men to shoot at. From a prone position I could look around the corner of the building and could see they had built what looked like a very strong defensive position in a square about two hundred yards down the street. Every time we stuck a helmet on the end of a rifle and put it around the corner, we drew all kinds of fire. Back of us about a half block the street seemed to angle off and I thought it might come in on the flank of the enemy position. so I sent a squad down that street to explore things.

"About that time, a lieutenant from the 91st Recon found us. He had come down the same street. I knew him well, but I hadn't seen him since we took La Guarda back in October. He said he had left his men back on the edge of the city along with the rest of my company. I told him what was going on and that we were waiting for my squad to hit the flank of the Germans in the square up ahead. He said, 'My God, Captain, those Germans won't fight. Let's just go get them!' And, honest to God, he walked around the corner of the building and into the street. Small-arms fire started hard and fast. We could hear the bullets whizzing past the corner of our building.

"The lieutenant did not come back. I said to my men, 'We've got to get him back. Let's get out there and hit the ground firing.' We did. In a few seconds a half dozen of us were out on that street in prone positions firing on that German position. I crawled up to the lieutenant lying there in the street. He was very, very dead.

"Now we had the drop on the Krauts. We kept firing and moving up the street, into doorways, always firing. About then, the squad I sent out, hit the Germans from the flank. The Jerries started to move out, some of them on the run. They ran right into the other platoon of mine that had moved without trouble down an adjacent street. We captured most of them. We had to keep going. I knew someone would pick up the lieutenant. I really didn't have time to think about him until that night. We settled down in the town of Castelfranco, but I couldn't sleep. I couldn't get the lieutenant out of my mind. I thought I could have stopped him some way. It happened so fast. That was a sad, tragic and stupid death. A hell of a guy. I had run into him many times as we attacked along Highway 65. Nearly every day he would contact us, find out where we were, what we planned, then he would head back.

"I saw many tragic deaths in the Italian Campaign, but this was the worst because it was so senseless. I can still see his body lying on that Italian street."[8]

From Vicenza Task Force George stuck out eastward for the city of Treviso, crossed the Brenta River and kept going. It was followed by the 361st's 3rd Battalion which crossed the Brenta on DUKWs in merely twenty minutes. Once across the battalion advanced rapidly on foot and reached Treviso by dusk of 29 April. Treviso was only twelve miles due north of Venice. By 1200, 30 April the entire 361st Infantry had closed in Treviso.

It was at this point that the remnants of the German Fourteenth Army were frantically trying to escape through a narrowing gap between Treviso and the sea. During the afternoon of the 30th the 91st Division and the 6th South African Division linked up with the British 6th Armored Division and closed the trap. The Fourteenth Army, which had fought the Division so long and so hard, was gone!

By now all routes out of Italy had been blocked, and the enemy forces had been rendered utterly ineffective. Only in the north, on the route to the Brenner Pass, did there remain any determined resistance.

"You knew the end was coming," said one veteran, 'you expected it any time, but now that it's come you almost can't believe it. What can you say that makes any sense except maybe a 'thank God'? He's the only one who can really understand how a guy feels."[9]

Grouped in the vicinity of Treviso, the Division went into II Corps reserve to rest and reorganize. The war was all but over and everyone knew it. The three bloody days of fighting to break, inch by inch, through the shell the Germans had built around their positions during the long winter months and the twelve days following when the Division had driven 135 miles from below Bologna to north of Venice and to the foothills of the Alps had broken the back of the German armies in Italy.

Combat for the Powder River Division in the bitter Italian Campaign came to a conclusion at 1900, 2 May. General Livesay announced that all German forces in Italy had surrendered.

"The end of the war," one veteran of the 363rd Infantry recalled, "found us near a tiny village whose name I don't remember. There were no celebrations of any kind and I do not think anyone even muttered, 'Thank God, it's over'. We simply tossed our equipment on the floor of the house we were in, put our heads on our packs and slept the clock around."

On 3 May, 1945 Lieutenant William S. Gavitt of the 91st Signal Company wrote his parents:

Dear Mother and Dad:

The church bells were ringing this morning here for the Victory in Italy Day. It is quite cool out and big, black clouds indicate showers. All is much like the calm after the storm, except for a few wild-eyes Partisans still roaming the streets with their red, white and green banners and slung rifles, and some Italians anxious to have us move out of the houses they vacated to escape the bombings. Events have moved so fast since the middle of April you must appreciate that letter writing has just been out. The hanging of Mussolini, the death of Hitler and yesterday the unconditional surrender of the Germans in Italy seems to just about bring things to a climax, and I hope by the time this reaches you the whole mess will have come to an end.

I hardly know where to begin to tell you the whole story of what took place after the middle of April. The attack on the well-dug-in positions of the Germans across the northern slopes of the Apennines was not at all easy. Monte Adone was one of the big prizes taken by our infantry. I was up there the afternoon it was taken and saw many dead Krauts and doughboys sprawled in the gutters and around the entrances to the caves and pillboxes. It is just unbelievable how our men could have taken that peak.

The Po Valley is as flat as a pancake, but a pleasant change from the mountains. Long, flat fields of grain stretch out between the many canals and ditches.

Sometimes, during the push, we established two or three CPs a day. I moved in what we called the command group. The main CP was just too large to keep up with our pace and twice we didn't see them for two days. We were up at dawn and moving and it was around ten at night before we settled down. We cooked our own rations. Fresh green onions were plentiful and we helped ourselves to the farmers gardens. More than once we hit the ditches at the crack of enemy sniper fire. Great pockets of the enemy were bypassed, so we had to be constantly on the alert.

Just south of the Po River we entered an area where the Krauts had time to burn only about half their vehicles and everyone that night was riding around in Kraut wagons. Dead horses, Jerries, burned trucks and equipment lay strewn all over the area. We found one signal service truck with the dome light still on.

One night just after the CP had settled in a park of a small city and we were standing in the chow line, the Germans who were still across the river on the other side of the town, threw in a terrific barrage of mortar fire. I was in the Crypto truck and literally flew out to hit the ground nearby. As you lay there with the shells bursting, branches falling and shrapnel singing through the air, you have just about the most helpless feeling in the world and there isn't a thing you can do about it.

At another town the major and I went into the Partisan headquarters where the Tedeschi had been the night before. We had fried eggs, Italian bread and vino, which was a real treat. I never saw such a room full of tough-looking characters. The Partisans roam the streets rounding up stray Krauts with great delight. Many of them are just kids and you can't help but think they are out having a good time playing cops and robbers.

Now the question is: where do we go next? We may occupy for a time. It seems like a trip to CBI is not just a possibility but a probability if the war lasts that long. Well, the war isn't over and I signed up this morning to stay in for the emergency—not that I have much choice in the matter.

Give my love to all,
Bill

Endnotes for Chapter Eleven

1 . 363rd Infantry History. April, 1945. Reprinted in *The Powder River Journal*. January , 1982. pp. 10-14.
2 . Letter to the author. August, 1993
3 . Lieutenant Kovas wrote this account during the occupation days near the village of Merna while the events were still fresh in his mind. "I found a typewriter," he told the author, "and wrote as fast as I could whenever I had the time."
4 . *Thunder in the Apennines*. pp 329-32.
5 . Kovas account.
6 . World War II Memories. pp, 27-31
7 . Letter to the author. June 22, 1993
8 . Letter to the author. March 1, 1994.
9 . *19 Days from the Apennines to the Alps*. Fifth Army Historical Section. p. 85.

CHAPTER 12 — OCCUPATION

"The 91st Division has been one of the backbone divisions of Fifth Army. There is no use my telling you, you already know it. You have done the unbelievable and you have made a great contribution to the big Allied picture."

Lt. Gen. Mark W. Clark. December 13, 1944

"I came back from the war much changed. To this day when I see an open field I think, How are we going to get across that?"

Louis Simpson. 101st Airborne Division.

I

On the very day peace came to Italy General Livesay announced to the Division that it had been selected for a mission that would require the utmost diplomacy: the 91st was to occupy the western part of the province of Venezia-Giulia, including the great port of Trieste and the city of Gorizia. During the long haul up the boot of Italy, as the Fifth and Eighth Armies pushed the Germans northward toward the Alps, the Yugoslavian Partisans under Marshal Joseph Broz (Tito) had fought the Germans in their own country. By the end of April, as the Germans made their final disorderly retreat before the Allied onslaught, the Yugoslavian forces had advanced to the Italian border. As the Germans withdrew from Gorizia and the surrounding area under pressure from the rapidly advancing Allied troops, the Yugoslav Partisans entered the city and cleared it of the remaining Germans. Immediately, a territorial boundary dispute developed between the Slavs and Italians. The Yugoslavian government felt the territory should be theirs by conquest, while the Italians desired that the final settlement might be solved by the Allied parties to whom they had previously surrendered.

All this was an obvious worry to General Mark W. Clark, the commander of the 15th Army Group. After a meeting of commanders, General Clark decided to make a show of force by sending the 91st Division into Trieste and Gorizia and moving the British 56th Division eastward to the Isonzo River. The 361st Infantry would occupy Gorizia while the 363rd went into Trieste. The 362nd was to remain in the area of Treviso. Small squads of men were to make modest reconnaissance patrols and were to be prepared in case any conflict broke out between the Slavs and Italians or the Slavs and Anglo-American troops.

At 0730, 5 May, the 361st Regimental Combat Team, with its colors and guidons flying, began the move into Gorizia. All along the route, the Yugoslavian flag, with its blue, white and red horizontal stripes and a large red star in the center, could be

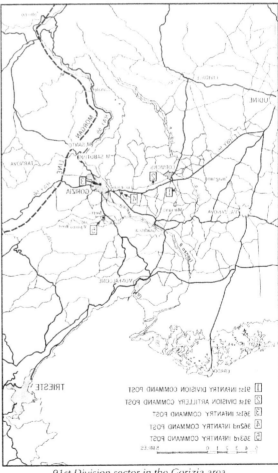

91st INFANTRY DIVISION COMMAND POST	1
91st DIVISION ARTILLERY COMMAND POST	2
361st INFANTRY COMMAND POST	3
362nd INFANTRY COMMAND POST	4
363rd INFANTRY COMMAND POST	5

91st Division sector in the Gorizia area.

247

Civilians of Trieste welcome GIs of the 1st Battalion, 363rd.

seen hanging from the windows of many houses. There was also an ample supply of red, white and green flags of Italy. By 2000 the troops were settled in Gorizia.

On 3 May, the next day after the war had ended, the British Eighth Army entered Gorizia and the other disputed territory claimed by both Yugoslavia and Italy until settlements could be made.

And so, with Yugoslavian partisans under Marshal Tito in command of the city of Gorizia and with Italian factors still seeking to maintain control of the area and with elements of the Eighth Army already in the city, the 361st Infantry, as a combat team, moved out from its positions near Musano at 0740, and entered Gorizia where it relieved the 167th Brigade, British 56th Division.

On the morning of 4 May the soldiers of Company B, 363rd Infantry were alerted to be ready for movement into Trieste. They would go fully armed and ready to fight. This was a stunning turn-around only two days after the end of the war. Those soldiers who thought peace would bring long, lazy days of rest and relaxation were now faced with a confusing mission, one that would again place them in harm's way.

The men of the 2nd Platoon were called over by platoon leader Frank Drazkowski and Tech Sergeant Warren Herbert and given fresh, new boxes of machine gun ammunition.

"Lieutenant," asked one of the men, "who the hell is Tito and exactly where is Trieste?"

Having been occupied for the past ten months in a shooting war of their own, the lieutenant and tech sergeant were hardly up on current geography. The American press had printed little about the war in Italy that had just been fought and won and next to nothing about the partisans of Marshal Tito.

"I don't know the answer," Lieutenant Drazkowski said. "I do know we have orders to go immediately into the city of Trieste and we are going fully armed and ready to fight. War over or no war over, we'll carry out our mission as we always have."

The order for Company B to move had come so suddenly the bitching had not yet started. The men cleaned their weapons, filled their rifle belts, removed grenades from the familiar containers and waited for the six-by trucks that were to take them into Trieste. The company jeeps, with loaded trailers and many carrying mounted light machine guns, were parked and ready to join the head of the truck convoy.

The long column of vehicles moved out, led by a major from Division Headquarters. The ride into Trieste was slow. At nearly every intersection stern-faced troops of the 2nd New Zealand Division, who had gone into the city as part of the British Eighth Army, manned tanks, SP artillery, anti-tank and small field guns. Bren gun carriers and automatic weapons were everywhere.

Company B's brief tour of downtown Trieste, while strained and uneventful, came off without a hitch. Many Italian citizens lined the streets but offered the men of Company B nothing more than faint smiles. No

Having a spot of tea in downtown Trieste. Americans of the 91st Division discuss the situation with New Zealanders of the 2nd New Zealand Division.

vino rosso. No bianco. No kisses. The Powder Rivermen got the impression they weren't exactly welcome.

The 363rd soldiers, fully armed, were sent out in two man teams for two hour periods.

Their orders were clear: shoot back if fired upon. Several hours later the Company supply sergeant assembled the men and told them, "I've got a three story building set up with cots, mattresses and blankets. It ain't the Ritz but it's all we could get on such short notice. You guys are to be 'ambassadors of good will' with Tito's troops. I warn you, stay away from the Yugo women soldiers. Some these cuties carry up to thirty notches on their burp guns. If any of you need any more ammo or grenades help yourself to what's on that truck over there."

Company B was in Trieste to stay.[1]

While the 363rd's 1st Battalion settled itself into its billets in Trieste, the remainder of the regiment took up new positions south of Gorizia in the vicinity of Merna and Scariano.

On 6 May twelve Partisan Brigades, composed of one hundred men each, formally surrendered to the 362nd Infantry in a ceremony held near Treviso. Colonel Cotton, acting for General Livesay, accepted the arms and in a short speech commended the Partisans for their efforts and accomplishments in helping defeat the German armies in Italy. After the colonel's speech and one by the head of the Italian Committee of Liberation, the Brigades passed in review.

On 8 May the 362nd Infantry moved to the area lying east of Palmanova, with the regimental command post established at Trivignano.

By 10 May the Division was in place.

II

Gorizia is located along the Isonzo River twenty-five miles north of Trieste and eighty miles west of the Yugoslav border. In 1945 it covered an area approximately six miles square and had a population of between forty and fifty thousand. It was originally built as a Roman fortress in the 3rd Century, only to be conquered by Attila the Hun in 375 A.D., and in the year 1000 it became part of the Republic of Venice. During World War I the Venezia-Guilia region was a bloody battlefield fought over by Italy and Austria and some portions of Gorizia were destroyed. The struggle has been graphically described by Ernest Hemingway in his novel, A Farewell to Arms.

All during the month of May the situation remained tense between the Yugoslav and Allied troops. On the night of 13 May Yugoslav forces, without any warning, threw up roadblocks around Gorizia and refused to allow British or American vehicles to pass. Colonel Broedlow immediately ordered a general alert for the

91st Division MPs and 91st Signal Company.

361st and only after an all night conference with the Yugoslav authorities did Division officers succeed in getting the alert terminated.

On the 19th, negotiations with Marshal Tito broke down completely. This resulted in some rather nervous times for the men along the Division front. Pfc. Anthony R. Brandano served with the I and R Platoon, 361st:

"We had orders to be armed and ready to defend ourselves if attacked by hostile forces while on pass, but our weapons were to be fired only as a last resort. On 19 May I was detained twice by Yugoslavian partisan soldiers as I was walking along down the center of a desolate Gorizia street. The incidents occurred while I was returning from a brief visit to a civilian family that lived on Via Alviano in the eastern suburb of the city. Usually, whenever an opportunity presented itself, I would casually chat in Italian with interesting women in the area. One attractive young Italian girl, with whom I had spoken to several times in the street near the I & R station, was Rosa. She had obtained her parents consent for me to visit her and meet her family at about 5:00 that afternoon.

"I arrived at Rosa's residence which was the last house on the edge of town. She introduced me to her parents and we all made small talk. They indicated some concern about reprisals, by the partisans, against local women who were considered to be fraternizing with American soldiers. I sympathized with them, and I wanted to avoid a situation that could potentially place them in jeopardy. Eventually, I was able to spend a few minutes talking along with Rosa. An hour slipped by very quickly, and I decided that it was time to leave. My first encounter, with the enemy forces, was not at a road block where they had set up barricades of barbed wire and sand bagged machine gun positions, but with a group of eight partisan soldiers. I was walking down the center of the road and they were standing in front of a large building on the corner of an intersecting street. As I approached them, I continued walking down the street, minding my own business. They didn't appear to be belligerent; they could have been a group of guys just standing on the corner, passing the time of day; just a friendly group of armed soldiers in grey uniforms. My eyes reconnoitered the area for protection and an escape route.

I was carrying a tommy gun and I also had a captured German P-38 pistol hidden under my field jacket. I continued at a steady pace, to within thirty yards of the troops, when they greeted me, and I returned the friendly greeting. I thought, 'That's it! Just let me go by.' But that wasn't it; they signaled for me to stop. I

A Red Cross worker offers doughnuts to Division infantrymen who are getting ready to board ship at the Naples docks.

was asked if I understood Italian and I said I did. I told them I was an American soldier. They asked many innocent questions as though they were trying to satisfy their curiosity about Americans. Then I was asked why I was so heavily armed. I explained that we had orders to carry loaded weapons wherever we went, to defend ourselves in the event we were attacked by hostile forces.

"The sun had set over the horizon and we were already in the twilight of the evening. Soon it would be dark. I politely excused myself and told them I had to hurry on my way because I was going to be late. They acknowledged that they understood, but I was told that their commanding officer would like to see me for just a couple of minutes.

"I decided to go along with them to their company command post. When we arrived at their headquarters I was confronted with about thirty more soldiers. I didn't have to go inside the building because they all came out to the sidewalk where I was. They did not show any signs of hostility, but I kept the weapon under my jacket ready if I was attacked. Their commander, who was a lieutenant, greeted me in English, but it was not a friendly gesture.

He conversed with me for nearly an hour. The questions didn't seemed to have any current military significance. The conversation finally drifted to the weapon I had slung over my left shoulder. He asked if he could have a look it. I kept my eyes on the lieutenant, while my left hand yanked the tommygun off my left shoulder. He casually examined the weapon and said, 'It is not a very good weapon. The Bren guns the British dropped to us are much better than these.' He handed the gun back to me and said, 'We won't detain you any longer, you can leave now.'

"I remained very alert as I continued on my way towards my station. At a city square I ran into a Yugoslavian road block. I could see sand bagged machinegun positions and concertina wire covering part of the square. I was halted by the shouts of foreign soldiers manning the position. I didn't understand the language, but I knew what they meant to do. It was the most frightful experience that I had that evening as they threatened to shoot me down. For several minutes we shouted at each other in language that none of us could understand. I kept shouting, 'I'm an American!', but they either did not understand or they didn't care. I had to stand there while they brought up an interpreter to interrogate me. When the interpreter arrived, I was allowed to advance through the barbed wire to their position. I was not disarmed. The interpreter spoke

Italian and I was able to convince him I was an American soldier. I was scolded for trespassing into their territory, but they let me continue on my way.

"I arrived safely at my quarters at about 9:00 PM. It was a great relief to be back, and incidentally, I never returned to visit Rosa again."[2]

As the days of May slowly passed, the tension among the Slavs, Italians and Allied troops gradually ceased. On the 22nd, General Livesay had again repeated his order, "The only case in which any American officer or enlisted man will fire a shot is for the preservation of his life or of the lives of his comrades." The weather was clear and cool and the days were warming with the coming of summer. The men of the Division quietly manned their outposts and road blocks. Shortly after noon on the 22nd, the 1st Battalion, 362nd Inf. moved north of Gorizia and west of the Isonzo River into a number of old trenches that had been used in World War I. Corporal Walter Pulliam, a correspondent with The Stars and Stripes, went along with the troops. He filed the following report:

WITH THE U.S. 91ST DIVISION NEAR TRIESTE, May 29 —
Gun positions and trenches dug during the first World War are being held today by the 91st Division along the Isonzo River, near Trieste. They are positions from which some of the biggest battle of World War I were fought, the battles between the Italians and Austrians in the years 1915-1918. The 91st moved into these positions in the redeployment which brought U.S. and British forces eastward to certain strategic peaks and localities west of the Isonzo not occupied by Marshal Tito's Partisans. A spokesman at division headquarters said the 91st's movements in the Venezia Guilia area had been accomplished without any clashes, and that the division's relationship to Yugoslav units in the area has had no semblance to conflict.

Men of the 91st were spending much of their time talking bout the historical terrain on which they were deployed. Atop 1,900-foot Mt. Sabotino, men of the 1st Battalion of the 362nd Infantry, believe they have one of the most interesting and historical peaks in the Venezia area. The peak, overlooking the west banks of the Isonzo, was an Austrian strongpoint in World War I. Around its top are dozens of caves and tunnels, in the mouths of which the Austrians mounted guns. Around its sides are numerous trenches dug out of rock, many of them still in good condition. There is even a cable car to bring up supplies from the east, or old Austria-Hungary, side. 2nd Lt. Lloyd B. Collins, Tahlequah, Okla., said the men found at least 30 World War

Castello di Spessa. Headquarters for the 91st Division Artillery in the Gorizia area.

I guns that had been on the peak since 1918. Pfc. Thomas Preski, St. Paul, Minn., said that he had counted 17 caves and that there were many more. The men set up living quarters in the caves—until the rains came and water started dripping through. There is a flat spot near the top and T-5 Anthony Gruts, Dubuque, Iowa, said the men play volley ball and have movies there on off-duty hours. Many of the men say they enjoy the panoramic view from the top of the mountain and find the old war weapons interesting. Enroute to the mountain, the 91st men pass an elaborate memorial to the Italian dead of the first war. They also pass through many cherry orchards and Italian and Slovene civilians along the route wave greetings to the jeep-loads of GIs that pass by.

The troops of the Division rapidly settled into the daily routine of occupation. All units followed a planned schedule with military training in the morning and recreation during the afternoon. Nearly all companies had ball teams, hard and soft. There were also other teams: boxing, swimming, track, tennis and volley ball. Anti-tank Company, 361st won the Divisional soft ball title and the 91st captured the Mediterranean Theater baseball title, beating all the other divisions, the II and IV Corps and the 12th and 15th Air Forces. It was a crackerjack of a team including a number of former major leaguers.

The weeks of occupation dragged on into July and for most of the men it was very good duty indeed. The 2nd Battalion, 363rd was billeted in the small village of Merna, south of the Gorizia airfield. One member recalled the place rather fondly:

"There was a quiet little river called the Vipacco which ran just outside the town and during the long afternoons we used to go down there and swim. We built a diving board and made the area into one hell of a nice place. There was a deep hole right in the middle of the river and you could jump off the board and just keep going down and down. It was hot during July and went down to the river as often as we could. The coolness of the water, which was clear as crystal, was pretty inviting. The house my platoon occupied was

General Lucien K. Truscott, Fifth Army commander, decorates two battalions at a Division ceremony at the

254

an agreeable place with huge windows that rolled out to the mountains. There was a large yard with a patio and vines on a trellis and a covered well with a windlass. We kept beer in a bucket down at the bottom of the well. Things were pretty relaxed and we enjoyed that; however, sometimes in the morning we could hear the sounds of another platoon, billeted up the street from us, going through bayonet drill which seemed pretty silly. 'Long thrust! Short thrust! Butt stroke!'

"One evening after we had accumulated a lot of beer rations, we held a party in the yard. I remember an English soldier drove up in his truck and joined the party. The British seldom passed up an opportunity to have a drink. Things got a little wild. We all joined the Englishman in singing, 'Bless 'em all', then the Englishman joined us in 'Pistol Packin' Mama', then we all sang, 'Roll out the Barrel'. Someone found an empty marmalade can and we started playing soccer, using the can as a ball. I seem to remember the Englishman passing out in the yard.

"The next morning at chow, here comes the Englishman, walking up and down the street. He had lost his truck! I don't know if he ever found it. I remember someone yelling, 'Hey, Limey, how can you lose something as big as a truck?'

"We had a lot of fun that summer. I guess it was fun, or perhaps after all these years, it's just nostalgia."[3]

On 23 July, in a review at the Gorizia airport, the Division was honored by a visit from the commander of the British Eighth Army, Lieutenant General Richard L. McCreery. Two days later, in ceremonies again at the airport, General Mark W. Clark awarded the Medal of Honor to Sergeant Oscar G. Johnson for his actions at Monticelli. One of the most impressive and colorful military formations of the period occurred on 27 July when a Division review was held with General Truscott as reviewing officer. The 3rd Battalion, 363rd Infantry and the 3rd Battalion, 361st Infantry received the Distinguished Unit Citation for their achievements in battle—the 363rd for its gallant fight for Monticelli and control of il Giogo Pass in the Gothic Line, and

Gorizia airport.

255

Members of Company K, 363rd, duffle bags at the ready, wait for the trucks to take them to Naples harbor.

The Volturno Express on the way from Udine to the Redeployment Training Area.

The Volturno Redeployment Training Area. The Fifth Army's final staging area.

the 361st's 3rd Battalion for its battle through the Livergnano escarpment.

The biggest thing on the minds of the men of the Division was the question, "When are we going home?" Through the point system the men who had been overseas longest (one point per month), in the Army longest (one point per month), had the most awards (five points for each Battle Star or combat decoration) or were fathers (twelve points for each child under eighteen) were put at the top of the list to go home and be discharged. All men with high scores were transferred out of the Division and into other units which were scheduled to return to the States.

Then, suddenly, the Big Question was finally answered by an order on 21 July: the 91st would begin movement to the Volturno Redeployment Training area. The journey to the south of Italy began on 2 August and on the 9th the last unit of the Division bid farewell to Venezia Giulia and started the 635 mile trip to the VRTA near Caserta, where the men of the 361st Infantry had shoved off for their long trek north some fourteen months earlier. Part of the Division travelled by train, the rest by truck convoy. The last unit closed in at Volturno on 13 August.

Pfc. John Roice made the journey by train:

"Early in August we loaded into box cars at Udine for the trip to Naples. We were in Bologna about noon of the next day. I bought some melons to go with our 'K' rations, but they were green. Just south of Bologna we hit an eleven mile tunnel. The track had just been fixed and it seemed that you could get out and walk and still keep up with the train. It took a long time to go through the tunnel. We had flashlights and we could look out the boxcar door and see places here the Germans had dug out caves, or at least small rooms. We were just a few miles from this tunnel when we made the spring jump off. As we passed through I couldn't help but think how lucky we were that we didn't have to clear the tunnel of Jerries.

"In Florence, there must have been at least eighty acres of rail yard. The Germans had some kind of machine that would go along the track and place a charge about every twenty feet. Twisted rails from these charges were all over the place. We passed the Leaning Tower of Pisa sometime in the night, so we missed a chance to see that famous place. The next evening we ate supper in the rail yards of Rome. We passed the Coliseum and the remnants of the old aqueducts and then the Eternal City disappeared behind us.

"The next morning we unloaded at Naples and were trucked out to the Volturno Staging area which had formerly been Count Ciano's dairy farm. When I first got overseas I had spent some time at this place when it was a replacement depot."[4]

The first homeward movement of the 91st began on 14 August when the Kingston Victory and the Pauchaug Victory left Naples with elements of the 361st and the 363rd Infantry and the 91st Signal on board.

Meanwhile, spectacular events were taking place in the Pacific Theatre. Japan was brought to her knees by daily raids of 2000 fighter and bombers based on close-by Okinawa and Iwo Jima. The first nuclear bomb devastated Hiroshima on 6 August and the second leveled the city of Nagasaki, two days later. On 10 August Japan was ready to accept the terms of the Potsdam Agreement. The war was over 14 August, 1945. The news was celebrated by the jubilant warriors of the Division for it meant the shooting war was over. Now it was "Home Alive in Forty-five."

On 1 September, the last units of the 91st left Naples on the SS Mount Vernon. Corporal John Lawler, a correspondent for The Stars and Stripes, bid the Division arrivederci:

The Southbound Limited complete with air-conditioning and southern exposure.

NAPLES. Sept. 1—Troops of the 91st "Powder River" Division, veterans of many action-packed days in the Italian Campaign, sailed for the United States late this afternoon after farewell exercises at the port of Naples in which theatre officials, headed by General Joseph T. McNarney, deputy supreme Allied commander, MTO, participated. Credited with knifing hundreds of miles across mountains, rivers and plains while playing a major role in the destruction of German armies on the peninsula, the "Powder River" men, numbering 6,000 aboard the U.S. Navy transport Mt. Vernon, were first lauded in a message from Field Marshal Sir Harold R.L.G. Alexander, Supreme Allied Commander, MTO, which said:

"It is with feelings of extreme regret that this message is one of farewell. This famous division has done a wonderful battle fighting job in Italy and will carry away the gratitude, admiration and respect of friends in this command."

Commending the operations of the 91st Division in this theater, General McNarney said:

"I have come here today to express my admiration for a fine fighting division and to say goodbye to you on behalf of this theater. You deserve a sincere tribute. In your many days of combat, you performed magnificently. You played a vital role in the complete defeat of the enemy in Italy. The 'Powder River' Division saw some of the toughest fighting in Italy. Your 361st Infantry fought as a separate regimental combat team with the 5th Army before the division was committed. The entire division jumped off 12 July and was the first American unit to reach the Arno River. A task force of the 91st executed the end around play which resulted in the capture of Leghorn. One after another German mountain strongholds were captured by 'Powder River' men. The 363rd knocked out Monticelli, key to central defenses and received a Distinguished Unit Citation for its heroic fight. The 362nd captured Futa Pass. Those words are synonymous with the Gothic Line. The 3rd Battalion 361st got its DUC fighting through the rugged escarpment at Livergnano and the 2nd Battalion of that regiment received it DUC for its capture of Monte Adone which opened the way into the Po Valley. The record of your division is second to none.

So we bid farewell to a great fighting division. Good luck and God speed."

With the exception of the La Crosse Victory and the SS Wakefield all ships transporting Division personnel docked at the Hampton Roads Port of Debarkation between 25 August and 10 September. From

25 June, 1945. Gorizia airport. Sergeant Oscar Johnson is congratulated by Col. George Fisher after being awarded the Medal of Honor. General Livesay at left. General Mark Clak, center.

there the troops were transported to Camp Patrick Henry, Virginia—back home again at "Swamp Patrick" The combat history of the 346th Field Artillery describes the return of that battalion:

Finally on 27 August, the <u>La Crosse Victory</u> anchored in Naples Bay and things began to move fast From the start the ship appeared jinxed due to a burned-out generator. This caused a two day delay, but the baggage was loaded and finally on the morning of the 30th the advance detail went aboard to clean the ship At 1300 on the 30th, the rest of the battalion left the VRTA and headed for the docks of Naples. At 1700 all personnel were on board and within an hour, the ship was slipping away from the dock through the dirty wa torn harbor into Naples. Then as the men turned and looked over the bow at the setting sun, they realized that at last, they were on their way home. The ship was crowded but clean, and the weather excellent. These factor combined to make the trip bearable. The food was good even though it was necessary for the men to wa

Champions. The 91st Division baseball team. Winners of the MTO title.

in long lines. Despite these lines few men missed a meal. The ship rocked and pitched for several days and many men ran for the head. Gibraltar was passed in daylight and at night there were no black out restrictions. Many men slept on deck on cots due to the crowded conditions below. Movies were shown every night and the Div. Arty. orchestra played often. The talented personnel of the 346th, under the direction of Lt. Johnson, put on several shows for the entire ship. The Delta Music Shop and One Touch of Vino, starring Alex Weille as master of ceremonies, were both widely acclaimed.

On 10 September, about noon, the La Crosse Victory plowed through a heavy fog into the sunlight surrounding Boston Harbor and we were greeted by whistles, horns and a boat load of WACs as the ship slipped into a berth at Commonwealth Pier. The men unloaded, boarded trains and sped through the New England countryside to Camp Miles Standish and the control of the battalion passed to the staging area personnel. We were all given furloughs and enjoyed a long stay at home. About the 1st of November the few remaining men, about 67, began to straggle into Camp Rucker, AL. The battalion was scheduled to be inactivated 1 December, so it became apparent that the close comradeship existing between the men of the battalion during the three and one half years of life would soon be a thing of the past.[5]

A member of the 2nd Bn., 362nd remembered the debarkation:[6]

"Walking down the gang plank on the tenth of September at Newport News, Virginia, we had to clean up our act and our language, because there were a group of ladies passing out donuts and coffee. After a few minutes they quit passing them out because we were eating too many of them. They told us they didn't want to spoil our welcome home dinner. Of course, we didn't believe there was going to be any dinner, but sure enough, at the orientation lecture where we were told the procedure of our trip home, we were given pink slips, good for one 'welcome home' dinner. And what a dinner it was! We had steaks and if yours wasn't cooked to please you, it could be sent back to the kitchen and cooked to your specifications, but I didn't see anyone send anything back! They were better than anything we had had in a long time. Mashed potatoes, fresh vegetables, fresh milk and other drinks, and you could go back as many times as you wished. I've said it was the best meal I've ever had, but I know it was the best meal I'd had since leaving home.

Merna. June, 1945. The fighting days are over for the 3rd Platoon, Company E, 363rd Infantry. Sergeant James E. Pfau extreme right. The author leans on his rifle under the checkmark.

Arrivederci Italia! The Powder River Division prepares to board the USS Mount Vernon to return to the good old U.S.A. 1 September 1945.

"That night we went to the PX and one guy in our group asked a pretty young clerk. 'Quanta costa?', and got his face slapped rather sharply! She must have been an Italian because all the poor GI wanted to know was how much the article he was looking at cost."[6]

Since the major portion of the Division was separated at the reception centers, only a skeleton force remained at Camp Rucker, Alabama and many a familiar face was missing. On 7 November, General Livesay was transferred to Fort Leavenworth, Kansas. Before he left he gathered his officers together and told them commanding the 91st Infantry Division was "the greatest honor that has ever come to me."

The inactivation of the Division was accomplished by inactivating the units individually as early as their records could be completed and closed. Between 13 November and 29 Novembers, all division units had been deactivated and their colors furled. The Division itself was inactivated on 1 December, 1945.

The gallant record of the Powder River Division in World War II passed into history.

During its combat days in Italy the 91st saw 334 days of war. It spent 271 days on line, 44 days in reserve, 19 days in training, but had not one day of rest! In two World Wars it fought through six campaigns: Lorraine, Meuse-Argonne, Ypres-Lys, Rome-Arno, North Appenines, and the Po Valley. It was awarded six Medals of Honor, three Presidential Unit Citations, 183 Distinguished Service Crosses and thousands of lesser awards and suffered a total of 14,852 battle casualties.[7]

On 14 December 1946, the 91st Infantry Division was activated at the Presidio of San Francisco and for nearly fifty years has been an active part of the United States Army Reserve stationed at Fort Baker, thus continuing the Western traditions of a great division.

Endnotes for Chapter Twelve

1. The Company B actions in Trieste were written by James E. Bell, February, 1994.
2. Brandano, Anthony R. *Burden of Battle*. Herkimer, N.Y. Copyright, 1992. #TXU 548 940. pp, 266-79.
3. *The Powder River Journal*. June, 1982. p, 23.
4. Roice, John *World War II Army Memories*. pp, 36-7.
5. Barry, Calvin E. *Unit Combat History*. The 346th Field Artillery Battalion. 1949. pp, 50.
6. Pfc. John Roice.
7. World War I casualties: 1,454 Killed in Action. 4,654 Wounded or Died of Wounds. World War II: 1400 Killed in Action. 7,344 Wounded or Died of Wounds.

CHAPTER THIRTEEN —
AFTER 50 YEARS

"On the wall we have put a tablet commemorating the fallen, and we have put the names, without making distinctions, of soldiers and civilians, adults and children, avoiding the words 'combatant' or 'enemy.' The inscription says simply, 'You who pass by and look at the peace of this valley, stop a while and remember our dead.'"

An Italian woman of the Resistance

Camp White today. This site was the location of Division Headquarters. Under the fir trees sits a rock monument which marks the entrance to the camp. A bronze plaque was once attached to the rock but was stolen years ago.

91st Division Headquarters. Fort Baker, California. Baker is one of the most beautiful military installations in the United States. Situated at the foot of the Golden Gate Bridge, it is often shrouded in fog and the sea breezes blow over the fort stirring the Division flag. On 14 August, 1993 a ceremony was held on the parade grounds honoring the World War II veterans. The six battle streamers were commemorated in a moving tribute. Afterwards, the 91st Bagpipes played a touching rendition of "Amazing Grace."

Livergnano, June 21, 1992. At eight-thirty in the morning of 21 June, 1992, the bells of the Church of St. John the Baptist began to ring out over the village of Livergnano and over the hills and mountains of the Savena and Idice River Valleys. The bells were rung by several citizens, each swinging a bell by a rope. The campanile of the church had been destroyed during the war so the bells, fastened to sturdy timbers, now sat on the ground several yards from the caretaker's house. As the plaintive, yet joyous, sounds reverberated through the ravines of the peaceful Italian countryside, a large crowd gathered on the flat table-top of Hill 554 for services in the church and for a dinner to be held afterwards. Some sixty veterans of the 91st Division had come to Livergnano as guests of the townspeople to honor the memory of those Americans and Italians who died during the battle for the village. Huge dining tents had been set up under the flags of the two countries: the Stars and Stripes and the Italian Tri-Color. After the dinner, the crow gathered in the town square and were entertained by a choir from Pianoro and Livergnano. The final song was a wonderful and harmonious version of "Amazing Grace."

The last resting place for 537 Powder Rivermen.

"They faced the foe as they drew near him in the stretch of their own manhood, and when the shock of battle came, they in a moment of time at the climax of their lives, were rapt away from a world filled for their dying eyes not with terror but with glory. Such were the men who lie here. They received each for his own memory praise that will never die and with it the grandest of all sepulchures, a home in the mind of men. Their bodies are buried in peace, their names liveth forever. O Lord, support us all the day long until the shandows lengthen and the evening comes and the fever of life is over and our work is done, then in Thy mercy grant us a safe lodging and a holy rest and peace at last."

Top: The United States Military Cemetery at Florence, Italy. Above: The cross of Sgt. Roy Harmon (Co. C, 362nd) who was awarded the Medal of Honor. He died on his first day of combat. Opposite top: The cross of Sgt. Alfred Akers (Co. E, 363rd). He was awarded the Silver Star, Purple Heart with Cluster and the Bronze Star.

These words are on the panels of the cemetery's memorial.

265

The 91st Division Monument was dedicated on a sunny Sunday morning in June. Shortly before ten o'clock groups from around the various communes assembled with their colorful flags representing Marzbotto, Monzuno, Livergnano, Vergato and Pianoro. A band, composed of high school students, and dressed in white blouses and black trousers, supplied the music. A platoon from the Italian Army and a color guard from the U.S. Army base at Vicenza were the military units.

The message on the monument is brief and simple, "To the veterans of the 91st Infantry Division, United States of America, and to the people of Loiano who shared a common bond during that terrible autumn of 1944."

Loiano, Sunday, 12 June, 1988.

A snowy day in February, 1990. The monument is located in a beautiful park on the Via Marconi. Tourist are directed to the memorial by signs placed at the entrance to the village.

267

The three mannikins were dressed by Claudio Coliva of Bologna who used material gathered from the old battlefields along Highway 65. The mannikin to the left is complete with steel helmet, M1 rifle, bayonet, pack canteen, wire cutters and Fir Tree patch. He wears the dogtags of Phillip Scaglia, 2nd Bn Hqs, 361st. The GI in the overcoat holds a pack of Chesterfield cigarettes and wears a cartridge belt. Claudio stands by a replica of the orginal 361st monument which he constructed with the help of his wife, Silvia.

A German bunker at St. Lucia near Futa Pass. The pass was the most heavily fortified position in the Gothic Line. It was captured by the 3rd Battalion, 362nd Infantry, 22 September. Time and the weather have worn off some of the concrete, but it still remains a formidable structure.

The ancient house of La Fortuna on Highway 65 leading into Livergnano. On 8 October, 1944 Captain Chris Hald and his men of Company I, 361st fought an all night battle for the house. The company prevailed;

however, the enemy fell back to Livergnano and Hill 603 where the fighting raged for four days. Since the war the highway has been elevated some five or six feet above the old ground level.

Purple Heart Corner in Livergnano. This spot was constantly pounded by artillery fire. The house in the upper left corner was used as a Division OP.

The same corner fifty years later. The former OP has been rebuilt and Hill 585 is now covered with a growth of new timer. The 91st Division museum is located in the building at right.

Livergnano Rock.

Aconella. All during the months of the Winter Line Division troops were billeted in this building which is now a restaurant. Several yards up the street is the village church where movies were shown. Up the hill from the restaurant

is the cave where the townspeople sheltered themselves from the German and Allied artillery. The wooden door is still there and so are the names of the Division troops who carved them there during the winter of 1944 - 1945.

During the battle for Livergnano ten men from Company K, 361st, hid in this cave to escape the tremendous volley of fire thrown at them from the Germans hidden on Hill 603. These men were the only survivors of the battle, all others were either killed or captured.

The German Cemetery at Futa Pass.

Interior of the Cemetery.

281

Infamous Hill 367 as seen from the north. It was the farthest point reached by the Division along Highway 65. The hill is much higher than it appears in the photograph. Company G, 362nd originally seized the hill in

October, but it was later abandoned and the Germans occupied it from November, 1944 until the jump off for the valley of the Po.

Hill 367, La Fabbrica Ridge, as seen from the south. At 0300, April 16, 1945, Company E, 363rd, accompanied by tanks, charged up the hill. In some of the most bitter fighting of the campaign, the Regiment's 2nd Battalion finally conquered the ridge and drove north up Highway 65 and into Pianoro.

A lonely GI sculpted this female torso near Livergnano.

The 363rd Infantry Monument at the top of Il Giogo Pass. Monte Altuzzo is the high peak in the background. Monticelli is to the extreme left.

The old palace at Pietramala. The word translates into English as "bad stone" or "bad rock." The village was taken 28 September, 1944 by the 361st Infantry. After the war, division veterans joked about it being a "Bad Day at Black Rock" which was the title of a post-war movie. The palace served as division headquarters during the drive up Highway 65.

All that remains of La Fabbrica or the "Wine Cellar." During the Middle Ages it served as a post for the horse-drawn carriages and wagons that traveled the highway. Countless patrols were run from the destroyed house and out into no man's land. Ironically, the sign on the tree reads: "Hunting Prohibited."

During the winter and spring on 1944 - 1945 this area was a wasteland of craters, minefields, trenches and foxholes. The house at upper right is Osteria Nuova. It was along these ridges that Lieutenant March Kovas

and his beleaguered 1st Platoon endured their travails. Over the years the hills have been restored to productivity. Note the neatly terraced vineyard at top-center.

The crest of Monticelli in the 2nd Battalion, 363rd sector. The tower at the right is used to locate forest fires.

An old German trench at the summit of Monticelli. From here the enemy could observe the movement of division troops for miles.

Monte Adone and the road from Monzuno and Monterumici south to Brento. (Courtesy of Claudio Coliva)

FROM S

M. Adone

A rebuilt Brento sits between Adone and Monte Castellazzo to the right. (Courtesy of Claudio Coliva)

APPENDIX A

INDIVIDUAL AWARDS

MEDAL OF HONOR
Harmon, Roy W.
Johnson, Oscar G.

DISTINGUISHED SERVICE CROSS
Ambrose, Francis G.
Anderson, John W.
Bastron, LeRoy A.
Brown, Harry L.
Carlson, Franklin
Conley, Edward J.
Czinki, John
Darragh, Ralph F.
Douglass, Harry W.
Dullum, Roy H.
Eggers, Carroll D.
Fulton, William B.
Gibson, Thomas
Green, Jack E.
Greig, Alexander M.
Hamilton, Harry E.
Hutson, Robert J.
Kaich, Elmer W.
Lake, Johnny D.
Lerma, Rosario V.
Lloyd, Clyde W.
Loe, Joseph D.
Martin, Kenneth E.
Montooth, William A.
McKelvey, Russell M.
Rexall, Teddie B.
Sheff, Bertram N.
Thompson, Robert C.

Turner, Bruce K.
Van Osdol, Joseph O.
Weaver, Howard E.
Westfall, Welton C.
Wilson, George G.

OAK LEAF CLUSTER TO SILVER STAR
Christopher, James L.
Cohea, Jesse L.
Doornhaag, Arnold
Drazkowski, Frank A.
Fox, Raymond W.
Gnemi, Martin L.
Jewkes, Rex W.
Krieger, Mervin
Little, Ralph V.
Meyer, Frank J.
McDermott, James L.
Pope, David E.
Turner, William H.
Van Scoyk, Reed A.

SILVER STAR
Abrego, Manuel B.
Ace, Paul A.
Adams, Dewane J.
Adams, Samuel A.
Akers, Alfred
Allen, Lee D.
Allen, Vaughn E.
Anders, James D.
Anderson, Cletus O.
Anderson, Robert C.

Anstaett, Robert L.
Arquette, William Pfc.
Aubrey, Sam B.
Bacciglieri, Louis T.
Bacheliar, Clifford J.
Bahr, George R.
Bailey, Douglas R.
Baird, Clare W.
Baker, Beryl H.
Ball, Walter G.
Ballard, James O.
Baptista, David
Bargsten, Klaus W.
Beall, Edward C.
Beck, James M.
Benckart, Robert G. Jr.
Berg, Frederick W.
Berry, Eugene A.
Biye, Charles T.
Black, Eli, Capt.
Blakeney, James B.
Bleelie, Carl
Blood, Everett G.
Bloom, Eugene H.
Blum, Carl L.
Blunt, Robert W.
Bodle, Dale
Boecheler, Andrew J.
Boling, Ferdinand A.
Boone, Jay D.
Booth, Frederick W.
Borba, William A.
Bothman, Stanley F.
Bowen, Grover E.
Bowles, Edward L., pfc.
Bramlett, Thomas D.
Branch, Aldert D.
Brigham, Horace D.
Brockmiller, Leonard C., T/4
Broedlow, Rudolph W., Col.

Brooks, Billy M.
Brooks, James C.
Brooks, James F.
Brott, Kenneth C.
Brown, Arthur W.
Brown, David A.
Brown, L.D.
Brozenich, Edward S.
Bruehl, George J.
Bryant, Bert L.
Buchanan, Bennie D.
Bryant, Miller J.
Buchanan, Jack E.
Buie, Herman F.
Bunnell, George D. Jr.
Bunte, Albert G.
Burgess, Leo J.
Burnett, Marion R.
Byars, Hilma L.
Byington, Vernon H.
Callaghan, John E.
Campbell, Hiram E.
Carlin, Thomas A.
Carr, Robert D.
Carron, John J.
Carroum, Omer D.
Caruso, Carmel
Castillo, Ines G.
Castro, Leland G.
Chacon, Ezequiel Jr.
Chaffin, Lon D.
Chambers, George K.
Chappelle, Fred J.
Chastain, William R.
Christopher, James L.
Cioci, Richard A.
Clark, James W.
Clayton, Arvil O.
Clift, Frank W., Jr. Pfc.
Coady, Thomas A.

Cobb, James C.
Cochran, John V.
Cofield, Rudolph
Cohea, Jesse L., Jr.
Cohen, Albert
Collins, Lloyd B.
Colquitt, Newell
Conn, Earl R.
Connelly, Robert J.
Cook, Roy H.
Cortez, Alfred L.
Couch, Malba H.
Cousino, Edsol J.
Cox, Louis A.
Coz, Eifren G.
Cozine, Alfred H.
Crawford, Enos V.
Crawford, Raymond R.
Crayton, Clinton N.
Crego, Russell F.
Crews, Robert F.
Cross, Millard
Cullar, Lewis B.
Cummings, Herbert D.
Curtiss, Stanley M.
Cuthrell, Amos O.
Dano, Maxwell E.
Daughtry, John P.
Davenport, Perry F.
Davis, Joe L.
Dawson, Andrew J.
Dean, Riter H.
Derouen, David P., Jr.
Dewart, Lloyd J.
Diamond, Seymour
Dickens, Loman R.
Dill, Kenneth B.
Diner, Irving
Donadio, Carl J.
Donahue, Thomas F., III

Doornhaag, Arnold
Dougherty, Charles E.
Draper, Charles P.
Drazhkowski, Frank A., Jr.
Duke, George E.
Dugger, Peter
Dunblazier, Max M.
Dunham, Gerald L.
Duran, Johnny S.
Eckard, Chester R.
Eckroat, Virgil O.
Edwards, Delbert L.
Edwards, Theodore F.
Eisfeldt, Henry A.
Elder, Inue E.
Elliott, Leslie H.
Ellis, Ernest M.
Emmert, John W.
England, Marvin D.
Enlow, Roy
Evans, Joe M. Jr.
Eyherabide, Stephen P.
Fayant, Adolphlis J.
Fellows, Albert E.
Fernandes, Joseph R.
Fieberling, Ernest L.
Finnell, Louis C.
Fitzgerald, John J.
Fitzsimmons, Clifford E.
Flesher, Charles W.
Fletcher, James J.
Flores, Simon
Flory, Harold E.
Foley, Thomas P.
Foote, Gordon H.
Foster, John P.
Foster, Marion B.
Fox, Raymond W.
Fraser, Bruce H.
Frederick, Alvin P.

Freggiaro, Joseph R.
Fries, Robert E.
Frye, Robert M.
Gallopo, Salvatore P.
Galyon, Charles A.
Gann, Williard C.
Garcia, Fernando C.
Garner, Alonza J.
Garretson, Richard T.
Gaultney, John O.
Geisen, Fred H.
Gendusa, Joseph F.
Genschaw, Walter W.
Georgopulos, Nick
Gibson, Matthew E.
Giddings, Carl R.
Gifford, Harry F.
Gilbert, William J.
Ginocchio, Joseph B.
Glee, Paul W.
Gloor, Alton V.
Gnemi, Martin L.
Goar, Charles L.
Godfrey, Arthur L.
Goe, Ralph H.
Gonzales, Henry G.
Goodwin, Ernest L.
Goolsbee, Rolland G.
Graham, Lawrence P.
Greczek, Alex S.
Green, James M.
Green, John T.
Greenberg, Morris
Gregory, Joe H.
Grobe, Robert P.
Hahn, Lowell R.
Hale, Warren C.
Hall, David A.
Hall, Donnie B.
Halpern, Jerome B.

Hambrick, William R.
Hammons, John H.
Hanger, Everette W.
Hanley, Jean D.
Hanson, Sherman R.
Harding, James J.
Harlin, Clarence R.
Harmon, Paul B.
Harnden, Donald W.
Harriman, Merwin T.
Harrison, James D.
Hartman, John H.
Harvey, William R.
Harze, Charles H.
Hatfield, Herman W.
Hawkins, Richard I.
Hayes, Preston C.
Heisinger, Ralph W.
Hernandez, Ralph
Hewitt, William R.
Hickman, Ray E.
Higdon, Joseph D. Jr.
Hines, Robert B.
Hixson, Walter G.
Hockreiter, Francis
Holland, George W.
Holscher, Paul F. Jr.
Honstedt, Jack K.
Horne, Aaron R. Jr.
Horne, Richard C.
Hospital, Ralph
Hrelec, William J.
Hughes, Leon
Hunter, Howard M. Jr.
Hurst, Berdon C.
Huter, Theodore F.
Hyland, Frank T.
Hyland, Kenneth L.
Inman, Lloyd J.
Irvin, C.B.

Jasper, George J.
Jenkins, Horace B.
Jenkins, Kelly R.
Jenkins, Newell N.
Jennings, Bert H.
Jewkes, Rex W.
Johnson, Donald V.
Johnson, Howard T.
Johnson, John W.
Johnson, Kenneth A.
Johnston, George
Jones, Clyde E.
Jones, Robert L.
Jones, Vernon F.
Jopke, Henry C.
Karl, Frank Jr.
Kasney, James J.
Katz, Norman P.
Kearney, Philip J.
Keeling, Cleo
Kelch, Clarence J.
Keller, Forrest E.
Kenny, James F.
Kern, Benjamin
Kettman, Julius C.
Keys, William
King, Martin Jr.
Kline, John H.
Klippert, Edward
Kloeb, William C.
Kopelov, Jerome H.
Kovas, March P.
Kracht, Gerald W.
Kreuser, Joseph H.
Krieger, Mervin
Kubasinski, Harry M.
Kunicki, Casmer B.
Lancaster, Edwin H.
Land, Larry L.
Lane, Earl L.

Laninga, Clarence
Lassiter, Buford
Lausten, Raymond L.
Lay, Forest A.
Leath, Don C.
Lentz, William A.
Lerma, Rosario V.
Lester, Robert G.
Levin, Malcolm H.
Lewis, Dilmus L.
Lewis, Kenneth M.
Lewis, Ray G.
Lien, Floyd L.
Lierman, Herbert G.
Lile, Edward F.
Little, Ralph V.
Locklear, William H.
Long, Glen C.
Ludwig, Robert M.
Lusk, Stewart R.
Lynn, Thomas L.
Malee, Frank J.
Mann, Ray H. Jr.
Marcum, Wade H.
Martin, Eugene C.
Martin, Warren H.
Martin, William R.
Martinez, Alfred G.
Martinez, Joe S.
Mason, Jesse
Massey, Alan
Matthews, Claude E.
Matthews, Norman P.
Maxson, Kenneth Richard
Maxwell, Ralph A.
May, John L.
Mayfield, William R.
Meadows, Walter T.
Meek, William I.
Melcher, Donald R.

Menchaca, Rudy
Mesa, Tony
Metheny, Ralph J.
Meyer, Frank J.
Meyners, Ferdinand H.
Michael, Francis M.
Miller, Rex D.
Mink, Eugene M.
Mitchell, Thomas J.
Mitrano, Daniel C.
Mizerski, Walter W.
Mohler, Charles L.
Montalvo, George A.
Moore, Byrel A.
Moore, Daniel M.
Moore, Thomas K.
Morrison, James J.
Morton, Thomas C.
Mudd, Elbert S.
Muller, Robert F.
Mungle, Juvin J.
Murdoch, Craig J.
Murphy, Charles J.
Murray, Warren D.
Myers, Huston O.
McCarthy, Daniel T.
McCormick, French H.
McDermott, James L.
McDonald, Stanley W.
McGowen, Jess Jr.
McIlhargey, James D.
McLane, Walter L.
McLaren, Hugh D.
McLean, Richard C.
McNabb, Dale M.
Nanneman, Aloysius A.
Nash, William J.
Nelson, Earl T.
Nethig, Victor A.
Newell, Lester G.

Nisson, Ivan G.
Noakes, Ray W.
Notaro, Ross A.
Ocasio, Ferminy
Odell, Fred H. Jr.
Ogden, Jesse A.
Olson, Lyle L.
Osenbaugh, Walter M.
Owens, John W.
Palesky, Daniel
Palmer, Crafton A.
Parcells, Frank M. Jr.
Parinella, Joseph J.
Paris, Francis R.
Pastore, Leonard W.
Pate, Alvin J.
Paz, John
Pelletier, Ulysse R.
Pendergrass, Earl
Perles, Albert J.
Peter, George L.
Peterson, Arthur D.
Peterson, Harry
Petroff, Stoian V.
Pickle, Coy R.
Pigg, H.S.
Pioch, Richard G.
Plata, Natalie
Platt, Hancel D.
Platt, Matthew J.
Plummer, Dennis M.
Poland, Lawrence H.
Pope, David E.
Pope, Ernest R.
Popoff, Max J.
Porter, Clifford
Porter, Joe S.
Prall, Robert W.
Prieto, Ines G.
Prior, Earl B.

Pyle, John E., Jr.
Pyle, Woodrow W.
Quale, Clayton J.
Quinn, James F.
Radicella, Anthony J.
Randall, James T.
Rawls, Niles E.
Ray, William G.
Reavis, Isham
Reels, Haskel M.
Regner, William J.
Repass, Heber
Ressiguie, Leo H.
Restifo, Frank P.
Reynolds, Fred R.
Rice, Perry H.
Richard, Willie J.
Richardson, George C.
Richardson, William H.
Riede, Edwin P.
Riesgo, Joe B.
Ritter, Crum M.
Robbins, Robert A.
Roberts, Roy R.
Robertson, Oscar
Robinson, Howard N.
Rodgers, George T.
Romagnoli, Albert
Roquet, Corwin E.
Rosellini, Bruno R.
Rothracker, Robert E.
Rowell, Fred G.
Rowzee, Oscar B., Jr.
Roy, Ferris G.
Ruggles, Robert S.
Russell, Wade F.
Samaniego, Augustine M.
Sanchez, David L.
Sanders, Howard F.
Sansom, William T.

Santos, Jacinto
Sarle, John L.
Sawyer, Charlie R.
Saylor, Daniel D.
Senn, Charles A., Jr.
Schreiner, Elmer
Schuck, Joseph A.
Schwartz, William H.
Scott, Claude J.
Scott, Robert E., Jr.
Scott, Russell E.
Scudder, James H.
Sear, David M.
Sears, John R.
Sheppard, William K.
Sheridan, Thomas E.
Shipman, D.C.
Shishkowsky, John J.
Silva, Raymond A.
Simmons, Chester B.
Simon, Dalferes J.
Skelton, Oscar, Jr.
Skipper, Everette H.
Sladeski, Joseph C.
Smart, Relphard E.
Smith, Cecil L.
Smith, Marcellus
Smith, Stanley L.
Smith, Zeb H.
Smolin, Gustave
Snyder, Hope
Solberg, Granville O.
Solomon, Max R.
Sorensen, Vernon S.
Sowards, Windel A.
Spatz, Ralph R.
Specht, Eugene B.
Spencer, Donald F.
Spencer, Elmer G.
Spooner, William A.

Sprik, Ysbrand
Stanchowicz, Stanley
Stanislav, Herman R.
Starr, John C.
Steele, Charles R.
Stein, Nick
Steinman, David C.
Steinberg, Julius D.
Stewart, Thomas W.
Stockton, Lloyd D.
Stolp, Merrill G.
Stone, Thomas W.
Storosko, Theodore
Swanton, George E., Jr.
Sweeten, Kenneth W.
Sympson, Decil E.
Szaflarski, Stanley A.
Tanksley, Jeptha C.
Taylor, Jack L.
Taylor, Jesse L.
Teter, Herman F.
Tharp, Charles D.
Thompson, Archie M.
Thompson, Donald S.
Thompson, Theodore R.
Tomblin, Clifford C.
Trusheim, James C.
Turkowitch, Jacob J.
Turner, William H.
Valine, Eugene L.
Van Matre, John R.
Van Oss, Orval R.
Van Scoyk, Reed A.
Verkovich, Joe J.
Vittolino, George
Voran, Bruce H.
Waesche, Thomas L.
Waggoner, Raymond L.
Wahl, George H.
Waite, Samuel A.

Walker, Walter C.
Wall, William A.
Walraven, Johnnie E.
Walrond, Darrel E.
Walsh, George D.
Walsh, Robert J.
Watson, George B.
Weitzel, William C.
Wendt, Henry H.F.
Wessendorff, Joseph C.
Wheetley, Earl B.
White, Cecil G., Jr.
Whitman, Willie L.
Whittenton, Ralph M.
Wiechel, Robert K.
Wilkinson, Robert R.
Williams, Tom E.
Williamson, Edgar S.
Williamson, Raymond E.S.
Willis, Albert J., Jr.
Willis, James H.
Wilson, John L.
Wilson, Leoance E.
Wireman, Charles E.
Wisner, Albert F.
Wondrak, Henry J.
Wood, Emmet L.
Woods, R.N.
Wright, William V.
Wynn, Clair C.
Yepez, Gildo R.
Yoquelet, Ray A.
Young, Fred D.
Zuzga, Walter L.

LEGION OF MERIT
Alexander, Thomas L., Jr.
Ambo, Walter J.
Anderson, Tyndall R.
Antinone, Rinaldo J.

Bair, Gordon L.
Barry, Calvin E.
Blass, Carel S.
Broedlow, Rudolph W.
Burtch, Anthel D.
Caster, Orville O.
Coleman, Charlie C.
Collier, Robert B.
Cotton, John W.
Cowin, Earl A.
Donnovin, Joseph P.
Driessen, Harvey T.
Faries, Robert B.
Ferguson, Raymond A.
Fletcher, George E.
Gele, Louis N., Jr.
Gibson, Gerald F.
Griffith, Richard
Grover, Lionel F.
Hospital, Ralph
Hawkinson, David F.
Heinze, Leon W.
Holley, William C.
Jackson, Paul E.
Jernigan, Curtis D.
Ketchum, Harry T.
Kirschenman, Aaron
Kleinert, Harry R.
Land, Ernest H.
Lawson, Willie R.
Loesch, Edward

Lynch, David
Lynn, Woodrow L.
Magill, W. Fulton, Jr.
Millard, Duane F.
Montgomery, Marvin D.
McCleskey, Earnest C.
McHaney, Flake
Neeley, William G.
Newman, Campbell W.
Oldfield, Ados M.
Oshlo, Richard C.
Patsko, John
Patterson, James H.
Pinnick, Floyd V.
Pittman, Beuford A.
Reid, George
Reibe, Francis A.
Stapleton, Herbert T.
Sanden, James
Sargent, Wilburn F.
Scarborough, Richard
Shaw, James E., Jr.
Smith, Stanley L.
Thomson, Edwin K.
Warren, Victor C.
Weekstein, Leon
White, Vander
Wilder, Alvin D., Jr.
Wood, Hollis O.
Woods, Ralph N.

DISTINGUISHED UNIT CITATIONS

WAR DEPARTMENT
Washington 25, D.C., 19 July 1945
GENERAL ORDERS
NO. 58

BATTLE HONORS.—As authorized by Executive Order 9396 (sec. I, WD Bul. 22, 1943), superseding Executive Order 9075 (sec. III, WD Bul. 11, 1942), citations of the following units in the general orders indicated are confirmed under the provisions of section IV, WD Circular 333, 1943, in the name of the President of the United States as public evidence of deserved honor and distinction:

* * *

The *3d Battalion, 361st Infantry Regiment,* is cited for outstanding performance of duty in action, from 7 to 14 October 1944, near Livergnano, Italy. Committed to attack along Highway 65 in the drive beyond the enemy Gothic Line, the *3d Battalion* in 7 days of continuous fighting over rough mountainous terrain, ideally suited for defense, decisively defeated elements of three German divisions and captured the town of Livergnano, the key position in the enemy's prepared line of defense. Unable to use supporting armor because of the terrain and enemy demolitions on the highway, the *3d Battalion* successfully repelled several strong enemy counterattacks, inflicting heavy losses on the enemy, and advanced continuously through the heaviest type of enemy mortar and artillery fire. In a skillful maneuver, one company knifed 1,700 yards through German lines, cutting the enemy's main line of communication and forcing the withdrawal of 300 enemy and six tanks, which had been counterattacking other elements of this battalion. This small force of only 80 men gallantly repelled fanatical, tank-supported enemy counterattacks for 8 hours, even after every machine gun had been destroyed by the terrific enemy fire and ammunition had been all but exhausted. Members of another company, attempted to take Livergnano, fought into the outskirts of the town and resisted enemy counterattacks until the buildings they were defending crumbled as a result of terrific incessant fire from enemy self-propelled guns, tanks, and mortars. Advancing under direct enemy observation against numerically superior enemy forces over rough mountainous terrain, which made it necessary to hand-carry supplies forward and made evacuation of the wounded a difficult and exhausting task, the men of the *3d Battalion* overcame every natural obstacle and each fiercely defended enemy strongpoint. Thus, the courageous infantrymen of the *3d Battalion* succeeded in seizing Livergnano, the keypoint in the enemy's "Caesar Line." By spearheading the Fifth Army's drive, the battalion penetrated the German line at one of its strongest points, thereby rendering the entire line untenable. The indomitable courage and fighting spirit displayed by the men of the *3d Battalion, 361st Infantry Regiment,* in the face of great odds and extreme personal danger, are a credit and inspiration to the armed forces of the United States. (General Orders 70, Headquarters Fifth Army, 10 June 1945, as approved by Commanding General, United States Army Forces, Mediterranean Theater of Operations.)

DIVISION CITATIONS

HEADQUARTERS 91ST INFANTRY DIVISION
UNITED STATES ARMY
APO 91

2 July 1945

GENERAL ORDERS
NO. 84

COMMENDATION OF UNIT.—Under the provisions of Army Regulations 600-55, the following named organization is commended:

Company B, 361st Infantry Regiment, 91st Infantry Division, is hereby commended for outstanding accomplishment in combat. During the period 11 October 1944 to 14 October 1944, near Livergnano, Italy, *Company B, 361st Infantry,* was given the mission of securing from the determined enemy the steep, bare hill that was the key terrain feature in the enemy's prepared line of defense. The enemy positions, deeply entrenched and blasted into solid rock, withstood days of continuous bombing and heavy concentrations of artillery and mortar fire. On 11 October, *Company B* attacked the heavily defended hill. Repulsed after several attempts to advance by withering enemy mortar and machine-gun fire, the Company withdrew to positions at the base of the hill. Early in the morning of 12 October, a second attack was launched. Advancing slowly in the face of intense mortar and machine-gun fire, the men of *Company B,* by skillful and daring maneuvering, succeeded in assaulting and capturing the main enemy cave positions, taking nineteen prisoners and three machine guns. That night, supported by machine guns, rifles, grenades and flame throwers, the enemy counterattacked in force. Although some of the enemy reached positions on the cliff directly above and threw grenades on them, *Company B* gallantly withstood the attack, driving off the enemy and inflicting heavy casualties with accurate concentrated fire. On the morning of 13 October, after a night of ceaseless enemy mortar and machine-gun fire, the Company attacked again. After a fierce fire fight, the men advanced in the face of severe enemy machine-gun cross-fire, courageously assaulting and reducing each enemy strongpoint, driving the routed enemy from the crest of the hill. In the engagement, thirty enemy were killed or wounded, fifty captured, and six machine guns taken. With the loss of this key position, the enemy was forced to abandon the entire line of prepared defenses hinged on Livergnano. The aggressive fighting spirit and unwavering devotion to duty displayed by members of *Company B* reflect the finest traditions of the armed forces of the United States.

BY COMMAND OF MAJOR GENERAL LIVESAY:

RALPH N. WOODS

Lt. Col., Inf.

Actg. Chief of Staff

DISTINGUISHED UNIT CITATION

DEPARTMENT OF THE ARMY
Washington 25, D.C., 8 October 1947

GENERAL ORDERS
NO. 6

BATTLE HONORS. As authorized by Executive Order 9396 (sec. I, WD Bul. 22, 1943), superseding Executive Order 9075 (sec. III, WD Bul. 11, 1942), the following unit is cited under the provisions of AR 260-15 in the name of the President of the United States as public evidence of deserved honor and distinction. The citation reads as follows:

The *363d Infantry Regiment* is cited for outstanding performance of duty in action from 12 to 19 September 1944 in the assault upon the German Gothic Line near Monticelli, Italy. Chosen to make the main effort to penetrate the Gothic Line in the area of Il Giogo Pass, in order that the divisions of the American II Corps could debouch into the Po Valley and outflank the vaunted Futa Pass positions along the Florence-Bologna highway, the *363d Infantry Regiment* stormed the bastion of Monticelli. The strongly prepared defenses on this rocky, rugged, and steep mountain feature guarding the pass were manned by the elite German 4th Paratroop Division. Supported by air bombing and intense artillery concentrations, two battalions struck initially without dislodging the enemy from their deeply dug, fortified positions. Small units began the slow, tedious process of working around one enemy position after another to gain a foothold. The 1st Battalion made the initial penetration and held out against strong counterattacks. Despite the fanatical defense, the enemy was driven back as elements of the division maintained constant pressure and cracked one strongpoint after another. With all battalions in the line, the *363d Infantry Regiment* withstood the intense enemy fires and counterattacks. As the mountain mass of Monticelli, fell to the *363d Infantry Regiment* and the companion Mt. Altuzzo capitulated to units of a neighboring regiment, all enemy resistance in this portion of the Gothic Line collapsed and the road to the north was open. In gaining the vital objective, the *363d Infantry Regiment* displayed heroism, endurance, and teamwork in keeping with the highest traditions of the Army of the United States. (This citation supersedes the citation of the *3d Battalion, 363d Infantry Regiment*, as published in General Orders 89, Headquarters Fifth Army, 10 July 1945, as approved by the Commanding General, United States Army Forces, Mediterranean Theater. Par. 3, WD General Orders 123, 1945, pertaining to the citation of the *3d Battalion, 363d Infantry Regiment*, is rescinded.)

BY ORDER OF THE SECRETARY OF WAR:

G.C. MARSHALL
Chief of Staff

OFFICIAL:
EDWARD F. WITSELL
Major General
Acting The Adjutant General

WAR DEPARTMENT
Washington 25, D.C., 20
October 1945
GENERAL ORDERS
NO. 90

BATTLE HONORS.—As authorized by Executive Order 9396 (sec. I, WD Bul. 22, 1943), superseding Executive Order 9075 (sec. III, WD Bul. 11, 1942), citations of the following units in the general orders indicated are confirmed under the provisions of section IV, WD Circular 333, 1943, in the name of the President of the United States as public evidence of deserved honor and distinction. The citations read as follows:

The *2d Battalion, 361st Infantry Regiment,* is cited for outstanding performance of duty in action from 16 to 18 April 1945, in the vicinity of Mount Adone, Italy. During the 3-day battle to drive the Germans from their heavily fortified positions forming the defense line before Bologna, the *2d Battalion* decisively defeated an advantageously entrenched foe and successfully accomplished its mission. At first all attacks were frustrated by intense enemy resistance as the *2d Battalion* sought to advance through numerous mine fields and over confining routes which led to the objective. The enemy, enjoying clear and full observation, opened automatic, rifle, and mortar fire upon the troops attempting to advance through the mountainous terrain. The assaults were repulsed, and the *2d Battalion,* entrenched under fire at the foot of their objective, evacuated casualties, and hand-carried supplies over the difficult terrain. The next day, having reorganized, the *2d Battalion* attacked frontally and from the flanks, but so heavy was the German resistance that all assaults were stopped and severe casualties suffered.

Attacking again and again, the Americans sought to ascend the mountain and reach the enemy, but the Germans repulsed each effort, using their well dug-in positions to the fullest advantage. On the third day, a coordinated assault again was launched, and the *2d Battalion* moved forward, determined to wrest its objective from the foe. Onward and upward, the men advanced into the face of enemy machine-gun fire, skillfully maneuvering through rugged terrain and mine fields, and closed with the Germans. As a result of the ensuing victory, the defense belt before Northern Italy was broken. The intrepid courage and aggressive determination of the men of the *2d Battalion, 361st Infantry Regiment,* in the face of great odds, are a notable tribute and inspiration to the armed forces of the United States. (General Orders 95, Headquarters Fifth Army, 4 August 1945, as approved by the Commanding General, United States Army Forces, European Theater.)

OFFICIAL:
    FAUSTIN F. JEHLE
    Major, A.G.D.
    Actg. Adj. Gen.

HEADQUARTERS 91ST INFANTRY DIVISION
UNITED STATES ARMY
APO 91

2 July 1945

GENERAL ORDERS
NO. 83

COMMENDATION OF UNIT.—Under the provisions of Army Regulations 600-55, the following named organization is commended: *Company I, 362d Infantry Regiment, 91st Infantry Division,* is hereby commended for outstanding accomplishment in combat. On 19 September 1944, near Poggio, Italy, *Company I, 362d Infantry,* was given the mission of taking the town of Poggio, situated on the crest of a knoll, guarding the approaches to Mt. Gazzaro. The objective, Mount Gazzaro, was guarded on three sides by steep impassable mountains, making it necessary to occupy Poggio in order to secure it, the highest ground in the sector. The enemy was well entrenched behind barbed wire entanglements, supported by machine-gun cross-fire covering every approach to the town, and by mines tactically laid to prevent any infiltration of their defenses. Intense artillery and air bombardments could not penetrate the individual positions that the enemy had selected. It was evident to the men of the company that in order to occupy the town they would have to engage the enemy in hand-to-hand combat. The first attack was launched but resulted in failure although many individual acts of heroism were displayed by the men of *Company I.* In the action many casualties had been inflicted on the fanatic enemy and the company suffered the loss of several officers and men. New plans for a second assault were made immediately. Minute details were warranted with the artillery for the company to attack under cover of a rolling barrage. During the second attack, as the barrage moved forward, the infantry followed closely and was able to over-run completely the enemy's defensive positions. Poggio was entered and fierce hand-to-hand fighting took place within the town. From emplacements on the reverse slope of the hill, machine guns harassed the troops. These emplacements were so well entrenched that they had to be blown open by bazooka fire. Although the company suffered heavy casualties, Poggio was captured. Sixty prisoners were taken along with a large amount of material. This action, and the display of determination and courage by *Company I*, made possible the advance of the entire 362d Infantry which would otherwise have been impossible. The action reflects the highest traditions of the Division and the United States Army.

BY COMMAND OF MAJOR GENERAL LIVESAY:

RALPH N. WOODS
Lt. Col, Inf.
Actg. Chief of Staff

OFFICIAL:
FAUSTIN F. JEHLE
Major, A.G.D.
Actg. Adj. Gen.

KILLED IN ACTION

361ST INFANTRY

Adams, Dalvin J.
Ace, Paul A.
Adkins, Clarence
Alagna, August T.
Albert, Frank E.
Alexander, Thomas D.
Alexis, Oscar H.
Alanzo, Marin
Allen, Smith
Alvarez, Cesario
Anderson, Einar C.
Anderson, John W.
Andrews, Samuel L.
Anthony, William F.
Antoniello, Pasquale J.
Ardoin, Dominic
Armstrong, Oscar E.
Arroyo, Raymond
Ayers, L.D.
Balanda, Clarence A.
Barker, Grady H.
Barker, Joseph
Barnett, Guy V.
Bass, Arthur E.
Bauer, Robert J.
Beach, August T.
Beardempl, Cecil
Beckford, Joshua J.
Behnke, Elson E.
Bell, Joseph, Jr.
Bennett, Clyde E.
Benscotter, James
Bergdale, Arvid J.
Bergstrom, Leroy
Bertagna, John H.
Bertao, Anthony

Bertsch, Virgil
Best, Stanley A.
Bevill, John T.
Bible, Ollie
Biehl, Vincent E.
Birchfield, James
Bitica, Konstantinos
Blaisdell, Joseph
Blake, Constantine
Bolick, Bealer A.
Bolliger, Frederick C.
Bowen, Grover E.
Breeden, James H.
Brewer, Paul
Brindock, John
Brinson, James W.
Broadrick, William
Brodlo, Rudolph
Brosmer, Frank R.
Brown, Harold R.
Brown, James C.
Buchanan, Bennie D.
Bugaj, Joseph J.
Bunch, Charles H.
Burk, Woodrow W.
Burke, James J.
Burrows, Leroy
Burton, Harvey
Byron, Jack E.
Bytner, John L.
Caristi, James J.
Carlson, Edwin C.
Carlson, Erik O.
Carpenter, Israel R.
Carpenter, Luther C.
Carter, James B.
Carver, Edmund T.

Cassidy, John J.
Caudill, Kenneth
Celiga, Steve A.
Cepull, August
Chambers, Ben J.
Chernko, John
Chiapusio, John
Churchich, Milan
Cioban, Walter S.
Clark, King
Clarke, Donald
Coble, Guy E.
Cockrell, Forrest
Coffman, Franklin
Cole, John W.
Colina, Kenneth B.
Collins, Chester
Connell, James M.
Conrude, Raymond H.
Constantinople, Tommy
Cooley, Malcolm V.
Cooper, Archie B.
Copeland, Glen
Corlin, Robert
Corta, James
Crego, Russell F.
Crook, William D.
Crosby, Jack M.
Cross, Millard
Cruz, Candido F.
Cukerman, Abram
Curole, Louis J.
Curran, Richard
Currier, Donald V.
Curchet, Francis
Czubak, Leo J.
Czubek, Raymond
Dalies, Carl J.
D'Amico, Phillip P.
Darragh, Ralph F.

Davis, Glen C.
Davis, Robert G.
Davis, Willie L.
Dawe, George R.
Deal, Bernice L.
Decareaux, Leo A.
DeCarlo, Charles
Delgado, Santiago
Dellinger, Charles
Demas, George
DePuglio, Frank A.
Derickson, Robert
Derouen, David P.
Diamond, Seymour
Dixon, James
Donahue, Raymond L.
Done, Cyril W.
Dougan, Jack
Drake, William L.
Dufore, Harold L.
Dugger, Peter
Dukes, Franklin
Dunch, Victor J.
Elbert, George H.
Edd, Jess A.
Edwards, Delbert L.
Eisensmith, Murray
Elliott, Ray O.
Eng, Glen
Erickson, Emmett
Espinoza, Jesus P.
Faircloth, Fred J.
Fanchin, Lino J.
Fasanella, Thomas J.
Fayant, Adolphus
Felich, Christopher J.
Feneis, Ernest J.
Ferrill, Richard W.
Fickel, Curtis J.
Fieberling, Ernest

Findlay, David
Fischer, Paul N.
Fisher, Leon
Fitzgerald, Russell E.
Fitzsimmons, Clifford
Fletcher, James J.
Foisy, Thomas
Fonaas, Vernon
Frankovsky, George
Franks, Harley
Frazier, Clyde
Frazier, George N.
Froelich, Leonard
Fykson, Robert
Galea, Elmer L.
Gallo, Joseph M.
Galm, Lawrence W.
Garcia, Transcita
Garmon, Kelley
Garven, Clarence T.
Gass, Clifton B.
Gathwright, Robert
Gellert, Jack H.
Gentry, William E.
Giantomasi, Gelard
Gilton, Elwood N.
Girvan, Thomas
Givens, John M.
Glee, Paul W.
Glidewell, Leo
Goelz, Robert A.
Goldberg, Avery
Goldstein, Albert
Gomez, Frank
Gonzales, Benjamin
Gonzales, Carmil
Gonzales, Jose
Goodkin, Bernard
Grandbois, Zenophile
Granger, Donald

Grant, Frank D., Jr.
Grassano, Nicholas
Green, Clyde
Greer, Cecil
Gressman, Herbert
Groves, Kenneth
Gruby, Charles
Gaidros, Adam
Gulgas, Paul
Gurule, Frank
Gutierrez, Jesus J.
Haag, Joseph H.
Hagins, Jack P.
Haley, Bradley E.
Hall, Harold J.
Hamilton, James
Hamm, Fred E.
Hammon, Herbert L.
Hammons, John H.
Hanks, Charlie W.
Hanna, Lee A.
Hargrove, Douglas
Hari, Ben R.
Harrison, Theron
Harrison, Tyrus H.
Hassler, Clarence W.
Hatfield, Herman
Haukvik, Floyd
Haworth, Albert
Hayes, Rhuel
Hayes, Robert L.
Haynes, Willie L.
Hearn, Roy G.
Hegel, Harold
Heidt, Roy
Heiss, Clarence
Hernandez, John Y.
Hernandez, Salvador T.
Hickey, Gaylord O.
Hill, Thomas E.

Hobson, Dixon
Hoffman, Leo E.J.
Holman, Eather J.
Honeycut, James
Hood, Willa
Hopkins, William B.
Howe, Earl B.
Huber, Arthur J.
Huchette, Leon
Huckle, Ivan B.B.
Hughes, Teal F.
Hull, James
Humphrey, Donald
Hurley, Robert E.
Hurry, Obie
Hurt, Deaain E.
Hutzell, Delbert
Idzikowski, George A.
Janiec, Walter
Jarman, Ervin T.
Jefcoat, Billie D.
Jennings, Alvin J.
Jocelyn, Edward J.
Johnson, Charles
Johnson, George L.
Johnson, Theodore
Johnson, Carless
Jolly, Ross
Jones, Samuel
Joseph, Cyrus
Joss, Robert O.
Julien, George J.
Justice, Carol
Kalina, Robert J.
Karwoski, Theodore A.
Kaucic, Ladmer
Keegan, John F.
Kelleher, Joseph D.
Kelly, Delmer P.
Kennedy, James S.

Kenney, Wilmer C.
Keyes, John L.
Kiltles, John H.
King, Ralph T.
Kirscher, Frank
Klase, John E.
Klein, Walter O.
Kmets, Frank
Knaus, Albin
Knuckles, Theodore
Koballa, Charles W.
Kracht, Gerald W.
Krotz, Ernest L.
Kuczynski, Theodore J.
Kudasz, Joseph L.
LaBarge, Francis M.
Lackey, William J.
LaCrosse, Carl E.
Ladenforf, William C.
LaFace, Floren
Lamp, Henry
Lanigan, Edward T.
Laslie, Jefferson
Latham, Horace E.
Laube, Elmer C.
Leary, Joseph E.
Leathers, Leo C.
Lentz, William A.
Levinson, Lewis M.
Lenz, Carl H.
Lewis, Dilmus L.
Lex, Weinard E.
Lindsay, Melvin H.
Livas, Santos
Livingston, George D.
Loden, Nim R.
Loe, Joseph D.
Loeb, Harold S.
Long, Richard E.
Lonzetta, Michael

Lopez, Jesus C.
Lound, Ray S.
Lourick, Nick
Lowrie, Brannon E.
Ludovina, Frank S.
Lulas, Andres G.
Lundy, Wayne L.
Lynwood, Philip A.
Lyth, Robert W.
Mabe, Boyd B.
Macias, Samuel
Mack, Harry S.
Malisch, Howard J.
Malszycki, John J.
Marinko, Jack J.
Marquez, Julio
Martin, Forest E.
Martin, George D.
Matthews, Milton R.
Meyer, Walter A.
Miller, Richard P.
Miller, Thomas A.
Morris, Everett C.
Mowry, Chas. A.
Mulitsch, Harry F.
McTiernan, John J.
Newell, Lester G.
Norris, Warren A.
Olson, Earl W.
Oppenheimer, Eugene
Palonen, Jorma
Parker, Orbie
Pergler, Charles
Plata, Natalie
Polzin, Ralph M.
Porter, Raymond A.
Prokopia, George W.
Salyards, Douglas W.
Sander, Vernon R.
Taylor, Milton

Tucker, Clarence T.
Verke, Clayton E.
Verner, Abraham S.
Vernon, George R.
Vires, Roscoe
Wahlbrink, Karl R.
Walka, Harold C.
Walker, Robert C.
Walker, Wayne K.
Warran, John
Wanholm, Alvin H.
Way, Clifford L.
Wayman, Marcus C.
Weaver, John C.
Wehlan, Paul N.
Welsh, Donald M.
White, Robert W.
Whitman, Willie L.
Wilder, James D.
Williams, Billy C.
Williams, Charles R.
Williams, Marion R.
Williams, Stephen R.
Wilson, George G.
Wilson, Raymond L.
Winkles, Joseph N.
Winstead, Kermit M.
Winter, Gerald H.
Wolf, Kenneth D.
Wood, Earl F.
Yanowski, Joseph J.
Yarborough, Fred T.
Yarbrough, Wiley W.
Yates, Oda A.
Zachrisson, Arthur N.
Zaffuto, Anthony P.
Zamora, Ventura J.
Zamores, Andres V.
Zielinski, Andrew

362ND INFANTRY

Acuna, Raymond M.
Adkins, Willie L.
Alvarado, Reyes R.
Ambrose, Francis G.
Anderson, Varges
Arismendiz, Felix
Armstrong, Earl
Baker, Harold F.
Barker, James T., Jr.
Barger, Vernon G.
Barton, Andrew J.
Beers, Leonard A.
Bell, Kenneth C.
Berry, James A.
Bertino, Frank J.
Blakeman, Francis J.
Bleclic, Carl
Bogenschutz, Arnold G.
Boren, Oscar V.
Borseth, Alvin M.
Borst, Donald F.
Bradshaw, Claude H.
Breitling, Vernon D.
Brieseacher, Harold G.
Brockway, Frederick
Brott, Kenneth C.
Brown, L.D.
Brown, David S.
Brown, George W.
Bruno, James L.
Bruns, Bloyce L.
Bryant, Leon
Buchanan, Eugene L.
Buchanan, Vernon L.
Buckley, Wadie
Burgess, Roy
Burnett, Marion R.
Caballero, Marcelo F.
Caccia, Edward

Calabria, Carlo
Cambell, Robert
Campbell, Franklin D.
Cannon, John R.
Carter, Earl
Carlson, Franklin E.
Carter, Walter D.
Castaneda, Caralampio
Castro, Frank J., M/Sgt.
Cavallaro, Bernard J.
Chacon, Ezequiel
Chandler, Lonnie
Christie, Calvin C.
Cieslik, Julius H.
Clark, Archie T.
Coates, Robert E.
Coe, Joseph B., Jr.
Cofield, Rudolph
Collins, Thomas Jr.
Columbus, Ernest H.
Connelly, Jack J.
Contreras, Harvey J.
Conway, John A.
Cornwell, Lester H.
Courtright, Lewis M.
Czinki, John
Dale, James M.
Dalke, Emil U.
Daniels, John
Danna, Jesse P.
Dano, Maxwell E.
Daugherty, Leon
Dawson, Wallace
Dechiara, Donald D.
De John, Frank
Del Vicario, Joseph A.
Detmer, James A.
Devlin, Gerald J.
Diefendorf, Lewis E.
Di Giovanna, Kelly C.

Dollar, Raymond
Dominquez, Joaquin R.
Downing, Robert D.
Drake, Dale I.
Drawyer, Delbert E.
Duncan, Donald A.
Dunn, Hollis E.
Eagon, Willard
Edwards, Jack
Eggers, Carroll D.
Ekis, Archie R.
Elder, Inue E.
Eldridge, Wallace K.
Elliott, Leslie H.
Ellis, Bert R.
Enlow, Roy
Farr, Woodrow
Faunt, George L.
Fawver, Forest B.
Finn, Sheldon
Firsty, Morris
Foley, Thomas P.
Forpanek, James W.
Foster, Chester M.
Francis, Simon A.
Frank, Stanley, Lt.
Franks, Rupert A.
French, Hugh S.
Futch, Merle H.
Galaviz, Fidencio C.
Galimore, Weldon
Garcia, Alfonzo
George, Lloyd J.
Gerber, Emil E.
Gerety, William P.
Gerhardt, Richard H.
Gerry, Frank C.
Gette, John T.
Gibbs, Lloyd F.
Gifford, Hughie D.

Gilbert, Joseph M.
Gilbert, William J., T/3
Gillett, David L.
Ginsberg, Isidore
Glasser, Joseph S.
Goldblum, Leon
Gomez, Jesus M.
Gonzales, Esiquio
Goodbird, Stanley
Goreham, Vernon W.
Goren, Isadore W.
Gorkowski, Lewis G.
Gower, James H.
Grant, Horace G.
Grant, Jack
Graves, Clarence C.
Gray, Earl D.
Greczek, Alex S.
Green, John T.
Griffin, Willie R.
Groe, Orin T.
Gruen, John H.
Guiliano, Vincent
Gulley, Willard C.
Gussler, Milton M.
Guzinski, Sylvester T.
Haimes, Henry D.
Hajduk, Alfred M.
Hale, Elbert S.
Halpern, Jerome B.
Hancock, Hubert V.
Hanley, Jean D.
Hansen, Bernard J.
Harmon, Paul B.
Harmon, Roy W.
Harper, Cecil R.
Harris, Elmer L.
Harris, James L., Pfc
Having, Lawrence H.
Heisinger, Ralph W.

Henning, Harold
Henson, Howard L.
Hernandez, Santos C.
Herrera, Benjamin W.
Hibben, Mike
Hickman, Clifford E.
Hicks, Houston G.
Higgins, Burl S.
Hinkel, Raymond F.
Hodge, Otto
Hoffman, Oakleigh M.
Holcomb, Rupert R., Jr.
Holland, Arthur N.
Holmes, Willie
Hoover, Samuel V., Jr.
Howdy, Mervin T.
Hughes, Lamer L., pfc.
Hughes, Orville L.
Hulett, David E., pfc.
Hunting, Edmond V.
Huter, Theodore F., T/4
Hyland, Kenneth L.
Ilaszcat, William
Imboden, Guy V.
Imondi, Basil
Jackaway, Lester B.
James, Cecil
Jarzambowski, Donald P.
Jenkins, Benjamin H.
Jerpbak, Jas. E.
Johnson, Buck
Jones, Albert A.
Jones, Maurice E.
Karna, Wesley
Kemp, Benjamin F., Jr.
King, Fred M.
Kirstine, Andrew N.
Klaphaak, John R.
Klein, Aaron
Knaus, Henry R.

Knight, Wendell A.
Koch, Earl G.
Koch, Paul W.
Kolak, Rad J.
Koogler, Jack R.
Kunkel, Howard R.
Kunz, Joseph C.
Ladd, James E.
Lager, John R.
Lalonde, Roland A.
Lamb, Carlton A., Jr.
Land, Alvis B.
Landreth, Earl E.
Landry, Lawrence
Lanier, Haines H.
Lara, Jesus R.
Lavendoski, Gerald P.
Lewis, Norman, Lt.
Levitt, George M.
Lindberg, George R.
Lines, Howard S.
Linstedt, Fred G., Jr.
Lucas, Russell S.
Lumpkin, Chester T., Jr.
Lynes, Floyd W.
Lux, Alfred E.
Lyons, Richard L.
Macchio, Andrew A.
Maciolek, John A.
MacDonald, George M.
Mahoney, Wade E.
Mann, William F.
Mansor, Mansor J.
Marcille, Adelard A.
Marcyan, Edward J.
Maret, George H.
Marker, Watson
Martineau, Gerard A.
Martinez, Ernest
Masso, Louis A.

Masters, Harry, S/Sgt
Mathis, T.W.
Medran, Joseph R.
Melott, Theo. J.
Merritt, Thos. D.
Merritt, Wm. H., Jr.
Meyer, Lawrence E.
Meyerhoefer, LaVerne L.
Miller, Robt. P.
Miller, Theodore R.
Milligan, Verl J.
Mills, Leonard D.
Milstead, Amos A.
Mitchell, James L.
Modrak, Michael
Monahan, Thomas F.
Moor, John F.
Moore, Ellis W.
Moore, Mervin B.
Moraine, Russel E., Jr.
Murry, Samuel D.
Murry, Warren D.
McCarthy, Edward A.
McClure, William N.
McCusker, Robert E.
McDonald, Donald
McEldowney, Charles T.
McGee, John R.
McIntosh, Earl N.
McNamara, Patrick J.
McNichols, Murrel E.
McQuage, Arthur C.
Nance, Frances D.
Nanneman, Aloysius
Neide, George R.
Nelson, Frank
New, Orville F.
Nicholson, George A.
Nielson, Russel A.
Norton, Leroy F.

Nunez, Antonio
O'Brien, Nelson E.
Ochal, Joseph
O'Donnell, Charles W.
O'Donnell, James J.
Oelerg, Andrew J.
Ohman, Roy C.
Ojeda, Richard M.
Olsen, Eldon A.
Orr, George C.
Orsak, Alfons J.
Osgood, Richard E.
Ostaszewski, Stanley
Parodi, Arthur
Parrish, Doyle M.
Passarino, Samotor
Paulson, Chester S.
Pearson, James L.
Pease, William H.
Pelletier, Romeal A.
Pemberton, George E.
Perry, James J.
Perry, Mason
Petersen, Billy E.
Peterson, Harry L.
Peterson, Orville H.
Petrick, Elmer M.
Pickle, Henry
Pierce, James V.
Pincus, Max
Pineda, Felipe
Piscitelli, Mario A.
Pitcher, Harry B.
Plate, Arthur
Plona, Casimer
Poley, Henry A.
Pool, James W.
Porter, Charles W.
Porter, Joseph S.
Poulopoulos, Peter

Powell, Harvey L.
Prall, Robert W.
Prawdzik, Melvin A.
Prebonich, Frank J.
Price, Earnest C.
Price, Glenn
Proffer, Lloyd E.
Provencio, Raymond T.
Pyle, Woodrow W.
Quinton, Levi
Radin, Samuel
Ramirez, Inez
Ramirez, Lupe R.
Ramp, Francis E.
Raney, John L.
Red Eagle, Moses M.
Reinhardt, August L.
Regier, Henry H.
Renfro, Orvel R.
Renda, Michael
Reyes, John G.
Richardson, Bruce A.
Rickabaugh, Everett E.
Rico, Louis J.
Ristine, Tyrus C.
Robinson, Warren
Robinson, Wilbur H.
Roeser, Clifford R.
Rogers, Charles E.
Romano, Mario U.
Rowzee, Oscar B., Jr.
Roy, Ferris G.
Rykena, Albert C., Jr.
Saenz, Humberto
Salisbury, Patrick H.
Salomon, Ernest F.
Sanchez, Antonio F.
Sarle, John L.
Sauter, Byron
Savage, Patrick J.

Schaeffer, Arlan M.
Schreir, William A.
Schuettpelz, Burton W.
Schultz, Kedrick W.
Scott, Roy E.
Selinsky, George J.
Sipes, Charles B.
Skipper, Andrew J.
Smiley, Richard E.
Smith, Archie C.
Smith, Dorvin L.
Smith, J.T.
Smith, John G.
Smith, Moses L.
Smith, Omer L.
Smith, Robert D.
Smith, William A.
Smith, William C.
Soujak, Joseph, Jr.
Sousa, Wesley J.
Southern, Lowell E.
Spatz, Ralph R.
Spence, George K.
Stahosky, Deval B.
Starling, Paul R.
Steckling, Howard W.
Steele, Charles R.
Steele, Jack C.
Stirewalt, Ernest B.
Stock, George C.
Stocklos, Stacey F.
Striefer, Louis
Stubbs, Gene M.
Suey, Michael
Suttle, John D.
Swift, Howard W.
Tank, Arthur J.
Thomas, Tyree C., Jr.
Throne, John H.
Trawick, Thomas E.

True, Luther L.
Turner, Honor R., Jr.
Utley, William R.
Van Der Vaart, Edwin F.
Van Lierop, Carolus P.
Van Osdol, Joseph O.
Vaughan, Joseph B.
Villalogos, John H.
Vincent, Homer R.
Visintainer, Rudolph
Waechter, Harry H.
Walker, Eura I.
Wall, Elbie W.
Walsh, Robert J.
Wamsley, Carl D.
Webb, Sydner J.
Weldon, Raymond O.
Wendt, Edwin O.
Wertz, Edward R.
Wetzel, Raymond A.
White, Jacob A.
Whiteley, Arther J.
Whittington, Virgil J.
Whitworth, Hector J.
Wickman, Chester H.
Wight, Harry W.
Wilk, Stanley
Wilkof, Sanford
Wilson, John L.
Wishow, Clifford A.
Witherspoon, James C.
Wood, Clarence E.
Wood, Emmet L.
Worley, William C.
Wray, Rufus R.
Wright, Jewel D.
Young, Waldron D.
Zarunski, John J.
Zenty, Emeryk V.
Zimmer, Arthur P.

363D INFANTRY

Abowitz, Herbert M.
Ackley, Richard W.
Acosta, George C.
Acosta, Tony M.
Adams, Jay W.
Akers, Alfred
Alvarez, Julian T.
Anderson, George A.
Anderson, Robert F.
Anderson, Robert W.
Antill, Wayne H.
Arendt, Anthony J.
Arthur, Orbin L.
Ashmore, James L.
Bacciglieri, Louis T.
Bahner, Leo O.
Baitz, Anthony M.
Baker, William N.
Bakowski, Felix J.
Banks, Mathew V.
Barber, Lenzly R.
Barbiero, Fausto
Barlow, Graham J.
Barnes, Clarence L., Jr.
Barnes, Cletus
Barrios, Stanley T.
Bauer, Wm. D.
Baum, John S.
Bazidlo, Peter E.
Beal, Charles E.
Beer, Paul L.
Beland, George L.
Beltran, Jose D.
Bender, George C.
Benge, Herman E.
Benshoff, Alvin W.
Bixler, Henry H.
Bloedorn, Elroy H.
Blunt, Roger W.

Bonvicino, John
Booth, Coy
Bourey, Donald J.
Boyles, Alfred J.
Brannon, Cleo
Braun, Robert C.
Brookman, Edward H.
Brown, Charles E.
Brown, Jessie W.
Brown, Raymond A.
Brown, Warren E.
Bryan, James O.
Bryant, Miller J.
Brzozowski, Stanley J.
Buchanan, Jack E.
Buie, Duie E.
Bunce, Leon M., Jr.
Bunker, John W.
Bunyard, Elmer V.
Burkhalter, Ralph H.
Burklow, John R.
Byars, Ralph J.
Byrd, Calvin L.
Cain, Gaither H.
Campbell, Robert L.
Canavan, Austin P.
Carlos, Ventura B.
Carneal, Patrick H.
Carter, Morrill L.
Caruso, Frank S.
Case, Ulysses
Catt, Clyde B.
Caywood, Theodore C.
Cervini, Joseph P.
Chavez, Raul A.
Cheatham, Ermy W., Jr.
Chittick, Robert V.
Christiano, Vincent P.
Choff, Ralph M.
Cobb, Murl L.

Coberly, Hayden E.
Cole, Alvin C.
Collins, Edward S.
Collins, Vernon J.
Colunga, Felipe B.
Connelly, James P.
Cook, Elmer L.
Cooley, James E.
Corton, Edwin E.
Couch, George W.
Cozad, Karl W.
Craig, Edwin E.
Crews, Robert F.
Criner, Quention
Cullar, Lewis B.
Curto, Charles C.
Cvijanovich, Sam L.
Daniels, Claude
Davis, Robert R.
DeBord, Charles B., Jr.
Degerlomoe, Tony
Dell, Franklin
Depew, Clair H.
Des Rosiers, Aime J.
Diner, Irving
Doble, Harry A.
Dodd, Denver H.
Dover, Robert A.
Driscoll, Thomas L.
Dubla, Carl D.
Dugas, Alfred H.
Duncan, Howard E.
Duncan, Marvin M.
Dunne, Thomas L.
Durham, Floyd
Dzik, Casimir J.
Eberhart, Raymond A.
Eberle, William, Jr.
Eells, Edwin C.
Egert, Frey D.

Eggert, Albert A.
Elliott, John J.
Elser, Earl H.
Elwood, Harry R.
Emig, Robert E.
Emlinger, Henry C.
Eschallier, Jean M.
Esquibel, Daniel, Jr.
Fain, Alvis M.
Farnham, Gerald E.
Fast, Walter V.
Feilbach, Paul T.
Ferrimani, Vincent D.
Figueroa, Damen S.
Fisher, Phillip
Fleharty, Lester C.
Flores, Joaquin C.
Flud, Haldeman J.
Forrest, Byron
Fortune, Ernest L.
Franciskovich, William
Franklin, Harley E.
Fratarcangeli, Joseph G.
Friedrich, Joseph F.
Fullwood, Stanley A.
Gabhart, Marvin D.
Gallegos, Herman
Gallo, Alfred
Gallus, Lester A.
Ganner, Allan B.
Garcia, Marcelo M., Jr.
Garner, Clarence C.
Garrett, Paul H.
Garrison, Robert F.
Gayhart, Claude W.
Giallombardo, Frank J.
Giddings, Carl R.
Gifford, Harry F.
Gilhooley, Thomas A.
Gilliland, Lee M.

Gleason, Edmund M.
Goldsmith, Sidney W.
Gomez, John C.
Gonzalez, Claudio
Gorath, Richard
Gordner, William A.
Graham, Keith B.
Grecsek, Edward R.
Grandokken, Andrew
Green, Oscar W.
Greig, Alexander M.
Grimes, Wilbur E.
Grittini, Joseph J.
Grodt, Earl K.
Grossman, Abraham
Grosso, Michael A.
Gutches, Ralph J.
Hageman, Robert W.
Hamann, Leo E.
Hanke, Laverne G.
Harder, Albert E.
Harris, Harold T.
Harrison, Louie D.
Hatcher, Robert C.
Hartline, Roy C.
Heeg, Joseph T.
Hemphill, Harvey L.
Hertel, Norbert F.
Hester, William E.
Higdon, Joseph D., Jr.
Higgins, Berlyn
Himmelstein, Saul S.
Holan, Charles W.
Hollinghead, Ernest I.
Hoober, Bertram E.
Hood, George C.
Hopkins, Pharoah I.
Houltram, John
Howell, Claude H.
Hubbard, Vernon

Hughes, Ottis D.
Hulsizer, Harold L.
Hunter, Garland M.
Hurlbert, Robert L.
Hutchinson, Henry A.
Hyland, Frank T.
Ide, Walter J.
Jagodzinski, Frederick J.
Jasie, Milton
Jeffrie, Harvey H.
Johnson, Elvin
Johnson, George A.
Johnson, Gerald L.
Johnson, Herbert C.
Johnsen, Russell J.
Jolley, William, Jr.
Jones, George C.
Jones, Lonnie M.
Jones, Rosco E.
Jopke, Henry C.
Judd, Lloyd
Kalck, Lawrence W., Jr.
Keahne, Frank
Kelch, Clarence J.
Kentner, Lewis K.
Keyes, Charles M.
Kimrey, Boyd R.
Kjellerson, Ernest W.
Kleinert, Frederik C.
Kline, Hugh D.
Klos, Nicholas J.
Knight, Jack H.
Kohler, Telford C.
Koivisto, Edwin R.
Kor, Warren H.
Koranda, Joseph W.
Koski, Toivo W.
Kozinski, Edward P.
Kozlowski, Bernard E.
Krajenta, Wallace

Kramer, William
Kriens, Roy N.
Kulakowski, William W.
Kwiatkowski, Edwin
LaFranchi, Clarence A.
Laganowski, Frank A.
Lambrix, Irving R.
Lampi, Reino W.
Land, Larry J.
Layland, Gerald I.
Leath, Don C.
Lee, Fred W.
Leehman, Walter H.
Lennox, Sidney A.
Leonard, Harold E.
Leoni, Nando D.
Leos, Porfirio V.
Leslie, Edward A.
Levy, Albert M.
Likins, George A.
Lohmeyer, Edgar G.
Lomonaco, Vincent A.
Long, Edgar
Lowry, Clifford A.
Lukowitz, George M.
Lucas, Samuel E.
Luna, Rito
Lunders, Howard E.
Ludwig, James A.
Lynch, Claude A.
Mackowey, Arthur W.
Mahaffey, James C.
Malone, Cleve T.
Malone, Savadore J.
Marano, Anthony
Marcum, Wade H.
Marshall, Max M.
Martin, Harold
Martin, William R.
Martinez, Domingo R.

Martinez, Pete A.
Mason, Thomas W.
Massetti, Marino
Mathes, Edwin M.
Meir, Vernon A.
Meinardus, Edward E.
Melchiori, Clarence
Mendez, Frank
Merx, Wilbert I.
Metzger, Edward F.
Meyners, Ferdinand H.
Miles, Clifford E.
Miller, Bernard W.
Miller, Charles H.
Miller, John J.
Miller, Robert E.
Mitchell, Jack
Moles, Floyd H.
Moore, Thomas K.
Moore, William T.
Moreno, James P.
Morris, William L.
Mosbeck, Vernon E.
Muckerheide, Lowell J.
Mullen, Chester L.
Mullen, Edward T.
Mumford, Geddes
Murphy, Travis J.
Murray, James M.
Myers, Oscar M.
McAllister, William V.
McBurnett, James B.
McCarley, Jack C.
McCauley, Delbert A.
McClendon, J.W.
McComas, Jennings H.
McCormick, John W.
McDonald, William B.
McElravy, Clardean L.
McGinn, William P.

McIlhargey, James D.
McKinney, Richard C.
McLaughlin, John J.
Nagel, Clifford V.
Nanos, John
Neal, Eugene B.
Nehoitewa, Owen R.
Neider, Charles R.
Nelson, Edwin R.
Niemiste, Emanuel E., Jr.
Nix, James F.
Norris, Lloyd O.
Norton, Sylvester
Nye, Robert D.
Ochoa, Arthur O.
O'Leary, Gerard E.
Olmstead, Clifton B.
Olson, Walter A.
Olszewski, Joseph, Jr.
Ona, Arthur
O'Rear, Levi W., Jr.
Ortega, Juan J., Jr.
Owen, Ralph L.
Palola, George E.
Parinella, Joseph J.
Pearce, Oscar E.
Pederson, Peter
Penning, Wm. J.
Pereau, William P.
Perez, Florenzo
Peterson, Waldo
Petter, Alfons F.
Petty, Gene W.
Phillips, Lee E.
Phillips, Newell E.
Pierce, James T.
Piller, Frank J.
Pillow, Clyde E.
Pizzati, John
Pojanowski, Raymond T.

Pokorni, Herbert A.
Post, Gerald D.
Provencher, Wm. H.
Ptomey, Jas. E.
Purcell, Walter L.
Raine, Thomas W.
Ray, William G.
Redmond, Cecil R.
Reece, Charles L., Jr.
Reed, Jim N.
Reed, Ollie W., Jr.
Rempel, Dietrich B.
Reyes, Samuel G.
Reynolds, Fred R.
Rhiner, Gilbert F.
Rice, John W.
Richter, Frederick M., Jr.
Riley, Arthur E.
Riley, Kenneth
Roberts, James E.
Robinson, John B.
Rodriguez, Alonzo
Rogers, Victor M.
Rosellini, Bruno R.
Royster, James C.
Rubinstein, Isidore
Ruccio, George W.
Russell, Howard M.
Russomano, Arthur
Sadler, Bertram H.
Sams, Lyle J.
Sanchez, Luciano
Sanford, Albert L.
Sansing, David L.
Saponiere, Wm.
Saxon, William B.
Saylor, Daniel D.
Schank, Orland W.
Schaper, Vernon W.
Scheiner, Henry

Schiano, Thomas L.
Schirmer, Walter H.
Schmidt, Loren F.
Schneider, Robt. E.
Schronce, William H.
Scott, Herbert
Shaffer, Arnold D.
Shaffer, Henry P.
Shaffer, Leo E.
Shain, Lewis E.
Sheedy, James G.
Shelton, Morris M.
Sherrill, William T.
Shimer, Leland C.
Shook, John E.
Sievers, Edward L.
Simko, Francis J.
Simmons, Carl M.
Simpson, Hubert S.
Six, Ralph
Small, James D.
Smelcer, John R.
Smith, Cecil L.
Smith, John D.
Smith, Richard R.
Smith, Robert M.
Smyth, Harry A.
Snead, Walter R.
Snider, Elmer
Solganick, Isadore
Solsman, Wm. R.
Spears, Barney F.
Spiewak, Edward J.
Spirito, Nicholas D.
Split, John E.
Staples, Leroy E.
Stark, Junior G.
Starr, John C.
Stephens, Charles P., Jr.
Stephens, John A.

Stern, Alvin J.

Stoll, Theron E.

Strange, James E.

Strobel, Charles D.

Strubbe, Clarence C.

Sylvester, Ralph, Jr.

Szczombrowski, Henry J.

Tamker, John F.

Taylor, Joseph L.

Taylor, Wm. B.

Tedford, Johnnie T.

Thomas, Cletus W.

Thomas, George R.

Thomas, Harry D.

Thomas, John E.

Thomas, Roy H., Jr.

Thompson, John E.

Thornburgh, Wilbur C.

Thornhill, Theo T.

Thornton, Emory G.

Thums, Daniel J.

Tice, Gary P.

Tidwell, James H.

Trotta, Dominic P.

Tucker, Jim

Turner, Arlyn R.

Turner, Lucius L.

Tyson, Lynn E.

Urban, Arnold A.

Vaca, Charles R.

Vaca, David L.

Valdez, Albert C.

Vana, Alex R.

Vasques, Frank

Vaughan, Henry S.

Vinovich, Daniel D.

Vitagliano, John

Waggoner, Samuel R.

Walker, William H.

Walters, Simon A.

Warner, Benjamin J.

Warren, Arthur

Warthen, Gerald L.

Waters, Charles W.

Watson, George E.

Weaver, W.J.

Wesseler, Bernard H.

Wesson, Clint A.

West, Arbie J.

Wheeler, Raymond R.

White, William C.

Whitefield, Ralph H.

Weiland, Harold W.

Wilson, Leonce L.

Winfrey, Wiley J.

Wixon, James R.

Wolf, Albert

Wolf, Francis N.

Wolfe, Lloyd A.

Wolkenfelt, Alexander J.

Wood, Paul E.

Woodland, Ward C.

Woody, John C.

Wright, Charles L.

Wroten, Alfred I.

Yanocha, Matthew J.

Yeazel, Samuel L.

Yonkers, Russell W.

Yontz, Billy S.

Young, Arch B., Jr.

Zapf, Newell P.

Zivicki, Hubert D.

91ST SIGNAL COMPANY
Erickson, Lloyd R.
Messinger, John W.
Schrader, Robert L.

91ST QUARTERMASTER COMPANY
Farnell, Lloyd D.
Johnson, Harris, Jr.
Lynch, William P.
McCoy, Raymond I.
Ward, Vance J.

791ST ORDNANCE COMPANY
Friar, Howard W.
Gorius, Wilfred F.
Gray, Lynn R.
Jagielski, Norbert B.
Sorrells, Clyd H.

DIVISION ARTILLERY
Clark, Paul F., Jr.
Howell, Madison L.

916TH FIELD ARTILLERY BATTALION
Adgeoff, Theodore
Allen, Erastus
Burton, John W.
Dalziel, William
Davis, Robert P.
Hand, Delmar L.
Higgins, Roy
Horton, Fred L.
Hughes, Leonard
Hunter, Howard M., Jr.
Gailey, Newton C.
Gurr, Howard A.
Koenig, Arthur M.

Lyons, Shelly R.
Moore, Carl F.
Nichrasz, Anthony
Nort, Elroy A.
Nunn, Robert E.
Richardson, Connor W.
Royce, Frederick O.
Rybicki, Stanley F.
Spooner, William A.
Tekell, James L.

346TH FIELD ARTILLERY BATTALION
Birk, Richard O.
Bonds, Clyde R.
Kunesh, Emanuel J.
Walker, Hubert G.

347TH FIELD ARTILLERY BATTALION
Atwell, Louis E.
Bonham, Carl T.
Bush, Oscar J.
Gillies, William J.
Jurgens, Lorance H.
Murphy, Albert L.
Neumann, Milton A.
Oswald, Edgar H.
Smith, Ernest L.

348TH FIELD ARTILLERY BATTALION
Dziedzic, Walter
Polinick, Edward

316TH ENGINEER BATTALION
Barton, Francis C.
Bostic, Paul W.
Ellione, Felix E.

Gardner, Francis E.
Golubic, John J.
Gonzales, John H.
Holloway, Ollie J.
Iwers, Joseph H.
Lane, Robert R.
Marling, Ross P.
Motley, John J.
Nevils, Alvin F.
Pollis, Joseph
Ray, Loyd C.
Smiderle, Ralph
Smith, Earnest B.
Southern, Dean H.

316TH MEDICAL BATTALION
Birchfield, James S.
Cullen, Phillip B.

Farber, Donald A.
Garrels, William C.
Gil, Gilberto
Gonsowski, Thomas J.
Nerbas, Arthur H.
Roberts, Harold D.
Stewart, Lloyd H.

91ST CAVALRY RECONNAISSANCE TROOP
Dessen, Donald I.
Farmer, William C.
Gaskins, Henry H.
Hall, Leo L.
Riede, Edwin P.
Seeddorff, Clifton L.
Wisz, Henry

APPENDIX B

Headquarters 316th Medical Battalion
United States Army
A.P.O. #91

10 November 1944

Subject: Unit History
To: Commanding General, 91st Infantry Division, APO #91, U.S. Army
(Attn: AC of S, G-2)

1. The 316th Medical Battalion continued to do its part in providing care, treatment, and evacuation of the casualties of the bucking 91st Division and quite often, casualties of other nearby U.S. Military installations, Allied Units, Prisoners of War, and Italian Civilians. The Medical Battalion had followed the fighting men through the battle over the Gothic Line, and at the start of October the fighting men were mopping up the remaining Gothic Line mountains and were battling toward Bologna and the Po Valley. However, the fighting during October has been as severe, bitter, and tiring as any yet experienced by the 91st Division. The Germans have determined to stop the push toward Bologna and have succeeded in stopping the troops to the point where its advances are measured in yards rather than miles; and at times by fierce counter-attacks causing temporary withdrawals. Rain and mud have been obstacles to military progress and especially have they been factors of personal discomfort and misery to the fighting men. Despite the hampering effects of weather and terrain, the essential factors of the generally static front have been especially fanatical, do-or-die Kraut fighting with a surprisingly large supply of ammunition, generally matching our artillery shell for shell. The troops toward the middle of October have been marked as ten miles from Bologna and at the month's end there was still eight miles to go.

In view of the tough, stubborn resistance of the Germans, and the consequent slow, grim march toward Bologna, the Medical Battalion has not made as many moves as has been customary in previous months. The life and movement of the Medical Battalion has been along the crucial, strategic Florence to Bologna Highway #65. The weather for the month as a whole has been a source of much inconvenience and discomfort. Except for a few clear days, rain has predominated as the villain, and with the rain came the inevitable and notorious Italian mud — thick, slippery, sticky; bad for both man and machine. However, to combat the approach of unmistakable cold weather, winter equipment has been issued to the men, and good use has been made of it. Sweaters, wool socks, new type field jackets, and shoe pacs were distributed. The piece of equipment which featured these new issues was the sleeping bag, designed to utilize man's body heat. Stoves burning oil were also used for the comfort of patients. In conjunction with the issue of the winter equipment and the cooling weather, Medical Officers of the Battalion spoke to the men about Trench Foot — its characteristics, causes, and treatments, and the basic importance of foot hygiene.

Ranking with the mud and rain as a damper on the men's morale was the pitiful small quantity of mail; except for a few big happy days, the mail has been meager and scanty, at times practically non-existent.

There have been some grim notes for the Battalion. The Geneva Cross is no guarantee of complete safety and security. At some time during the month all the component parts of the Battalion have experienced the dread and fright of enemy artillery fire. Many of the men when no occupying a building had dug slit trenches, particularly after the unmistakable whine of an incoming shell or two was heard. A few of the men were killed; a few were injured; and the great majority experienced the tension, the shivers, and the frightening phantasies of the imagination regarding what a speeding shell or fragment could do to our mortal bodies. Often the enemy fire was not aimed directly at the Red Cross of a tent, building, or vehicle, but at times the shells did come close enough to sober the men and raise their sympathies for the front-line men whose job it is to be in the midst of the hell of body-ripping shells, fragments, and bullets.

To mitigate much of the drab routine and occasional grimness of our work, there have been several factors of positive morale value. A PX, featuring candy and beer was distributed at low coast twice during the month. Throughout the month the Battalion had a quota of men going into Renaissance-famed Florence for a four day rest; names were drawn from the hat and each man was full of hope every four days. Some of the men were driven into Florence to see Apollo-staged, "The Barretts of Wimpole Street" starring Katherine Cornell and Brian Aherne; the play was generally enjoyed. Movies were shown in a room or tent several times toward the end of the month, and were widely appreciated for their value as entertainment and diversion. October 12th marked the Battalion's six-month anniversary overseas so the men were duly presented with overseas stripes. Throughout the Battalion, men were grouped one evening to hear a reading of choice portions of the Articles of War.

Especially appealing outside affairs were the invasion of the Philippines and the great U.S. Naval victory over the Japs, and the St. Louis Browns — St.

Louis Cardinals World Series. Many of the men voted by war ballot but there was no noteworthy display of excitement or animated discussion on the approaching presidential election. The main interest and concern has been with daily activities and personal interest and occupations; a quick end to the war and a return to the States would please the men more than anything else. Highly hopeful and widespread predications of German defeat by November have flopped, and are for the most part forgotten. There is no longer talk of home before this Christmas; a winter stay here is more or less expected.

The month ended for the Battalion as a whole with Uncle Sam being as punctual as usual, and the men received their wages in the customary Allied Lire.

2. The beginning of the month of October found Headquarters and Headquarters Detachment near La Mazzetta. In this area of rain and mud, the men were issued much of their winter equipment — wool socks, shoe pacs, stoves, combat jackets. M/Sgt Matthew J. Gress was pleasantly, and completely surprised by a visit from his brother, Pvt Paul Gress of the 12 TAC; the brothers enjoyed a few days together at the Detachment and then left for a four-day rest in Florence. After nearly two weeks near La Mazzetta, the Detachment rode Highway 65 traffic to a side of a hill a short distance from war-torn Loiano. Men were issued sleeping bags here. Reassigned to the Detachment was verbose, jovial Pfc Joseph Singer, proudly left-breasting a Purple Heart for a leg wound caused by a bit of shrapnel from a stray shell in the Rear Echelon in September. It was learned that Pvt Leslie R. Helms, Jr. formerly a member of the supply section of the Detachment, later assigned to Company "A" as a liaison man, was put into Class "B" for medical reasons and is now assigned to lighter duty elsewhere. But the feature of the encampment at Loiano was the heavy shelling of our area; the German target was the 1st Armored Division tanks below us. However, enough shells landed near enough and around us to give the men their worst fright since being overseas; slit-trench digging was at its all-time peak for the Detachment. In fact, the shelling of the tanks was believed too near for our own security, so it was judged prudent to move back. In its first and only withdrawal, the Detachment moved back a few miles to a side of a hill near Roncastalto. The retreat proved to be a wise one since a short time later many enemy shells dropped into our recently-abandoned area; casualties very probably would have resulted had we still been there. A sense of security and safety prevailed at the new area; no slit-trench digging was in evidence. However, the rains really came and stayed near Roncastalto; and the inevitable mud was everywhere. It was the worst area yet for the Detachment in regard

to mud and its obstructive and discomforting qualities for man and vehicle. As a matter of fact the vehicles slid and gripped their way from the area up the mudroad onto Highway 65 only with a great deal of difficulty and delay, calling upon the drivers and vehicles utmost output. It was in this field of mud near Roncastalto that the Detachment spent the last days of October.

3. The Clearing Station, Company "D," was fairly busy throughout the month evacuating the injured, wounded, and diseased; the peak activity of late September when the Gothic Line was being broken, was not reached however. At the month's start, Company "D" was just off Highway 65 near La Mazzetta. It was here on a bright moon-lit night that the station experienced the dread of an air attack by a lone German plane. Several anti-personnel and demolition bombs landed fairly close to the station tentage, the nearest bomb exploding about 100 yards away. The next morning amid animated discussion, five respectable-sized craters were inspected. Two of Company "D" men received minor fragment wounds and were evacuated to a hospital. The men at Tec 5 Jim T. Holm and Pfc Lloyd Fleming; they are the first men of their organization to receive the Purple Heart. It was very fortunate for Company "D" that the bombs landed on a slope where the terrain protectively took care of much of the flying, deadly, fragments; casualties may well have been heavier otherwise. Tec 5 Holm has already returned to full duty. Pfc Lloyd Fleming is expected soon. The clearing station was only a short distance from the highway but several days of rain resulted in almost impassable mud, making it necessary to bring in boards and bricks for a crude but negotiable vehicle-path. The Fifth Army Surgeon General, General Martin, and Bebe Daniels, top Hollywood actress some years ago, were at the Clearing Station for material on the handling of the wounded behind the front-liens. Data was obtained and patients were interviewed and eventually the material will be used in a broadcast over the "Purple Heart Hour" back in the states. Red Cross girls were commonly seen serving coffee, dough-nuts and exuding good cheer in the evacuation tent. Stoves burning parts of discarded ammunition cases and later oil, added greatly to the comfort of the tents. On the 14th the 1st Platoon moved forward to a spot just below Loiano, while the 2d Platoon remained in the same area near La Mazzetta. The 1st Platoon near Loiano did not have long to wait before it got its worst dose yet of nearby incoming shells, aimed at tanks several hundred yards below, but being close enough to make the powers that be, decide it wiser to move back. Consequently the 1st Platoon moved a few miles back to an area near Roncastalto. The whole company was together once again as the 2d Platoon moved up from near La Mazzetta. For the first time in several weeks a platoon

of the 33d Field Hospital was next to the Clearing Station. For the Clearing Station this area has proved to be the worst yet for ambulance travel. The area is on a slope of a hill; the road from the station to the highway 65 is merely a dirt path, which was turned by subsequent steady, heavy, rains into a stream of mud, quite beyond the power of the trucks and ambulances. Men and materials and machines had to be called in to construct a less fluid and more tractable road; scores of men, many bricks, a bulldozer, and finally an unraveled roll of wire and steel was used with eventual success. The somewhat improved road made vehicular travel certain enough for a while, but for the men in the area there was still mud to trudge through at the month's end near Roncastalto.

4. Collecting Company "A" was in reserve near Selva at the start of the month; consequently casualties processed were slight in number. On the 4th, the Company moved in Montalbano and two days later they moved into Loiano. It was at Loiano that most of the Company spent the rest of the month, from the 6th on. As a result of this unusually long stay in one locality the men eventually began to call it the "Loiano Rest Center," and themselves, the "Rear Echelon Troops." All was not silent and secure however, for on several days in the 2d week of the month, enemy shells zoomed in and shrapnel flew and whistled. The men were well protected by the sturdy brick of their Italian building, and fortunately no one was injured. Pfc Meyers and Pfc Dickerson received a citation for courageous action under fire; the citation was signed by the 91st Division's Commanding General, Major General Livesay. Several of the men were awarded the Bronze Star Medal for meritorious service in combat on July 2, 1944; the proud men are Tec 5 Cunningham, Tec 4 Harry Martin, Pfc Prince, Pfc Friedman, Pfc Alcocer, Pvt Massa, Pvt Wales, and Pvt Hill. While on duty near the front-liens at Livergnano, Private Dennehy and Private Clarence Collins were slightly injured by shrapnel. Shells dropped into the area on the 21st causing the inevitable fear, the taking of cover, bur fortunately no injuries. One half of a station section that has been operating nearer the front-liens for a week returned to the main body of the Company at Loiano. S/Sgt Pearson, a station platoon sergeant, was commissioned a 2nd lt, MAC, and transferred to Company "B" as a litter-bearer officer. Altogether Company "A" processed 1200 men, and as the month passed by, the company as a whole was still at Loiano, the men's self-styled "Loiano Rest Center."

Company "B" has the month's record for traveling and being in more different localities. The Company's activities area also noteworthy for their work as two stations in two sections. For the most part they worked separately, although they did join a couple of times, especially on their last move of the month which highlights their month's activity. Station Section Number One was at Fretramaia at the beginning of the month; soon it moved to Filigare, then to Monghidoro, then to Loiano, to La Fioretta, back to Loiano, and back again to La Fioretta. Station Section Number Two did not move quite so much. Starting the month at La Posta, it moved to Filagare, and then on the 6th to La Fioretta where it remained for over two weeks. Pfc Theodore Lauer and Pfc Wayne Chappell, ambulance drivers, had a hair-raising time when their ambulance had a few frightening bullet holes. Pvt David C. Bogard and Pvt Harvey S. Blacketer were sent to the Clearing Company C for reclassification due to physical inadequacies.

The highlight of the month occurred on the 25th of the month when the entire company left La Fioretta and traveled for 6 hours and 22 miles over a road of mud, holes, and bumps, finally ending up at Sillaro shortly before midnight. The men slept as well as they could that night, and in no time at all were face to face with quantities of mud and work. The men worked harder than they had in previous weeks. Chow for a while was regarded as inadequate for the appetites that were developed by the work done amid mud-covered conditions. The move into Sillaro marked the beginning of Company "B's" medical support of the 362d Regiment which was attached to the 88th Division. As though the mud, work, and inadequate chow was not enough, enemy shells dropped in on the 30th; but no casualties resulted.

There was still work and mud as Company "B" was still supporting the 362d Regiment attached for the time being, to the 88th Division as the 31st of October ticked away. The Company handled 1374 men during the month.

5. Company "C" had the ill fortune to have the past month highlighted by tragedy. Very early in the month 1st Lt Nerbas and S/Sgt Garrells took an ambulance to a forward aid station to help evacuate the wounded. Shells were dropping in, and as the loaded ambulance was preparing to leave, a direct hit was scored. All seven occupants of the ambulance except on American soldier were killed, including ironically, a wounded German soldier. S/Sgt Garrells was killed instantly, shrapnel piercing his brain. 1st Lt Nerbas died several minutes later from a severe stomach wound. After starting the month at Montalbano, the Company moved into Monghidoro on the 4th. The men again got a bitter taste of shelling that day. Soon tragedy once more hit the company. Sgt Forbes was peep-driving Captain Minella and Captain Shima on a tour of duty when a lone Nazi plane roared down and strafed and bombed them. All three men had jumped out for cover. Only Sgt Forbes was hit, and severely wounded in the head, neck and shoulder. There was hope for his recovery as he was evacuated

to a hospital, but unfortunately his wounds proved to be very serious and Sgt Forbes passed away on 16 October.

Lt Spicer was promoted to 1st Lt becoming Motor Platoon Leader. Tec 3 Nyrop took over the leadership of the Litter-Bearer Platoon and shortly thereafter was commissioned a 2d Lt, MAC; Lt Nyrop is the first man of the Company to be commissioned from the ranks. On the 10th the Company left shell-torn Monghidor and arrived at Monte Bastia where they spent the rest of the month. S/Sgt Cairns, of Canadian birth, journeyed to Rome to become a proud citizen of the U.S. On the 20th the 363d Regiment was taken off the front-line; consequently Company "C's" activities were limited. However, the regiment was concentrated within enemy artillery fire, and firepower is just what the Krauts shot in. Some resulting casualties and especially the daily Regimental Sick-Call kept the Company on the job. For the entire month 1463 admissions of all sorts were handled. Tec 4 Wade "Duck" Hedrick was promoted to Tec 3 and Tec 5 Gerald "Snoring Bush" Hartgenbush was pleased with a promotion to Tec 4. Private Allnut and Private Kryzenski had a narrow escape which temporarily raised their blood pressures and caused a quicker, sharper beating of the heart. As they were speeding along Highway 65, enemy tracer bullets were pursuing the hopefully fleeing ambulance. Bullets kicked up dirt on both sides of the vehicle, but the men and vehicle emerged from the race untouched. Other drivers and vehicles also underwent the tension of close calls. Pfc Reuter, while on liaison duty narrowly missed death or serious injury when a piece of shrapnel hit him in a vital spot; luckily the power and speed of the shrapnel was nearly gone and only a bruise resulted. Company "C's" most tragic month of the war passed into sorrowful history as the men, still in support of the resting 363d Regiment, remained at Monte Bastia.

6. The following statistics of Medical Treatment and Evacuation for the month of October were compiled from records of Units of the 316th Medical Battalion:

   a. Average length of litter hauls: One and one-half (1 1/2) miles.

   b. Average distance from Battalion Aid Stations to Collecting Stations: Two (2) miles.

   c. Average distance from Collecting Stations to Clearing Station: Four (4) miles.

   d. Total number of miles travelled by ambulances of the Battalion during the month: 23,000.

   e. Average time required to evacuate casualties from point of injury to the Clearing Station: Five (5) hours.

   f. Number of cases of Trench Foot treated during the month: 39.

g. Total admissions to the Clearing Station during the month: 4,330.

h. Total Number of men processed by Collecting Companies during the month:

        Company "A" 1,208

        Company "B" 1,374

        Company "C" 1,464

             Total 4,046

i. Total number of admissions to the Clearing Station who were returned directly to duty during the month: 568.

j. Total number of units of Plasma administered by units of the Battalion during the month: 174.

                For the commanding Officer:

                CLIFFORD B. WALRATH

                1st Lt, MAC

                Unit Historian

APPENDIX C

The Advance from Monghidoro to Livergnano
316th Engineer Battalion, October, 1944

The 316th Engineer Combat Battalion encountered two major problems o combat during the bitter fighting along Highway 65 in October. During the first hal of the month, the Engineers were occupied night and day with the job of keeping the highway open to support and supply two infantry regiments. Usually secondary route could not be utilized for third purpose. During the last half of the month, as the fighting grew more bitter and the enemy's resistance became almost fanatical, the Engineer for the first time in their combat experience played a major role in setting up defensive positions.

As the 91st Division continued its northward advance along the vita highway, the Engineers' missions were not new. But adverse weather conditions — steady rain, often for several consecutive days — turned their jobs into ever bigger tasks, and the Battalion was kept exceptionally busy with the added "battle of mud." And it was, at times, a battle. The mud required the extra effort of more fill material for craters, extra maintenance work on by-passes. This battle of mud was most pronounced during the period in early October when the foot troops were advancing toward Monghidoro. Because there was not suitable material close at hand, extra time and effort was required to carry the rubble of shelled buildings from nearby towns to the sites of the road craters. An added strain was put on the Engineers because the infantry was advancing steadily at the time, and more time was required on each road job, due to the mud and rain. Thus, extra efforts were put forth to keep the highway and the poor secondary roads and trails open in pace with the foot troops.

Company A found it necessary to employ two platoons with bull dozers to fill craters on Highway 65 north of Radicosa Pass. The depth of the mud, and lack of base to the ground, was amazing. One enlisted man, losing his footing, sank into a bog up to his arm-pits and had to be pulled out by companions. In one of the craters, it was necessary to pour 75 truckloads of rock and rubble which had been taken from the shelled buildings of Pietramala.

Despite the delays caused by the bad weather, however, the Engineers kept elements of all three line companies on the roads almost constantly, and swept and maintained a total of 80 miles of road during the month. This figure seems surprising when it is remembered that the Division's advance straddled Highway 65; that there were few other roads in the sector; and that the Division's advance was halted in mid-October.

B Company had the main responsibility for Highway 65 as the 362nd Infantry advanced toward Monghidoro and occupied the town. On the left, as the 363rd moved northward to take Montepiano, C Company had the mission of opening small trails in order for the infantry peeps and small vehicles to reach the front line troops. The work in the sector was slow and rough; a poor road was opened to the east of Montepiano. The company also found the obstacles of mines in the sector. The Engineers lifted eight German "S" mines along the road a few hundred years north of Piamaggio. As the 363rd's forward elements moved toward Roncastaldo, the Engineers followed closely, sweeping the secondary road clear of mines.

Extremely handy for the work of filling craters and making by-passes which would stand the heavy traffic in the bad weather was a pile of rock just south of Monghidoro. An estimated 200 truckloads of rock were in the dump, and the Engineers readily put the material to use. Thirty loads were used on the night of 4 October to help fill craters along the highway. A crater 40 feet long, 20 feet wide and 10 feet deep was encountered on the highway some 2,000 yards north of Monghidoro as the 362nd's foot troops moved toward Loiano. Company B used one squad of men to fill the crater with the loose dirt and rock lying at the site.

The enemy's retreat was stubborn. His methods of cratering and mining the routes were systematic, and the obstacles thrown up in the path of our advancing troops were the same type encountered time after time in the past by the Engineers. The enemy's main obstacles along the highway were craters. Along the poor roads on either side of the highway, mines were frequently used. Company C found box mines in the road at La Fratta south of Loiano on the afternoon of 5 October, but the men were unable to remove them during the daylight hours due to close enemy observation from positions around Loiano. After dark on the 5th, however, the mines were cleared away, allowing peep traffic to move closer toward the leading troops of the 363rd, which were then engaged in an attack on positions in the vicinity of Loiano. The company found two more fields of mines which were hindering the movement of the 363rd west of the highway. Mines were cleared from the road west of Bibulano and twenty Italian box mines were removed by two squads south of Loiano.

The enemy apparently did not have the time necessary to do one demolition job which would have created a major Engineering problem. Perhaps the foot troops advanced upon him too quickly. At any rate, after overcoming stiff resistance and capturing Loiano, the infantry pressed the enemy back toward the ridge north of Sabbioni and, as B Company of the Engineers moved along the highway, an uncompleted job of cratering was found. On the section of Highway 65 north from Loiano to a point about half a mile from Sabbioni, the Engineers found cratering charges installed. They removed 60 charges which had not been set off. In thirteen cratering holes were twenty six 170 mm artillery shells, improvised for use as cratering charges. Also along that stretch of road were 200 box mines which had not yet been buried or activated by the Germans. B Company cleared the road and swept the route clear through Sabbioni.

As the 361st Infantry took over the east sector of the 91st Division front, A Company of the 316th Engineers reconnoitered for a lateral road leading from Highway 65 to the villages of Scanello and Onazzano, while B Company made a reconnaissance of the road leading to Casoni.

On the morning of 7 October, one detail from A Company found itself in a "hot" spot on the highway beyond Sabbioni. Tanks which were supporting the 361st were ordered to advance along Highway 65 and take up forward positions for an assault on the enemy, who was occupying high ground beyond Sabbioni. A crater - not a completed job, but still an effective obstacle - had been blown in the road about two miles out of the town, and the tanks were unable to pass it. Lt. Alex B. Crawford of A Company led nine of his men up the road to make the crater passable. The Engineers were subjected to artillery fire before reaching Sabbioni, but continued through the town, parked their peeps behind an embankment on the other side, and walked along the road to the crater. They used only hand tools to fix the crater, because the site was too far forward to risk a dozer. As the men began filling the large hole, artillery and mortar fire was directed at them, and they were forced to take cover several times, But, as the fire let up, they returned to the job and, after several delays caused by the enemy fire, they had filled the crater sufficiently to allow the tanks to pass along the road toward their positions. As the Engineers completed the job and were returning to their vehicles, a German machine gun on the ridge above them opened up and directed fire at the men. After a period of time under cover along the road, the Engineers decided to risk the fire and attempt to move down the road toward their bivouac. Some of the men sneaked down to the cover of bushes along the south side of the highway, and made their way through the field of fire to the town. Several others jumped into the two peeps, directed fire from their own sub-machine guns in the direction of the German gun, and drove swiftly down the road through the field of fire and safely into Sabbioni without casualties.

The risk had been great, but it had been worth it. The road was passable for the tanks now, and the armor moved forward to positions from which they brought effective fire on the enemy.

The Division's advance during the next day was spectacular. Foot troops neared the town of Livergnano, where Highway 65 moves over a "saddle" in a narrow bottleneck between hills and escarpments. To the east, as infantry moved to Barbarolo, the Engineers swept the road running from Casoni to Barbarolo, giving supply vehicles access to the forward elements of the 361st. In the 362nd sector to the west and south of Livergnano, B Company of the Engineer Battalion cleared the road which leads north out of Sabbioni over the ridge to the town of La Guarda. The enemy had blown two craters in the road near La Guarda, but they were filled easily enough in six hours of work.

As the foot troops began their assault on Livergnano, cleared all the area below the town of enemy troops and concentrated their efforts on the "bottleneck," the Engineers quickly improved the roads where craters had been hurriedly filled or by-passed, and made all routes passable to the front lines.

Livergnano was a natural strong point for the enemy. It was a key point, and there was no way of getting around it. The hills and escarpments on either side made the building of trails on the flanks an impossible task. There was no way to get heavy weapons into position. The search for likely places through which guns could pass in order to bring direct fire on enemy armor in the town was fruitless. Foot troops could move into the town, all right, but they could not get the proper support of heavy weapons to combat enemy tanks, and vehicles could not move into the town from the only entrance - Highway 65. The highway just south of the town was built on a shelf on the side of the ridge, and enemy demolitions men had blown it away. It was necessary to fill the road before vehicles could move in to assault Livergnano. And the crater site was under direct observation from enemy forces in the town.

It was a major problem. Reconnaissance on the night of 13 October showed that a bull-dozer was necessary; hand labor would not be able to fill the road. And, so close under enemy guns was the site that it was felt that the noise of a dozer at work would surely bring down fire that would cause casualties, and further delays.

But on the night of 14 October, the mission was given to 1st Lt. Arthur A. Barbata of Company A and his platoon. Just after dusk an Engineer patrol moved to the crater to study the problem. They found a hole in the road 75 feet long and sloping between 45 and 60 degrees.

Because of the concentrated barrage of white phosphorous shells within 150 and 200 yards of the crater - plus several high explosive shells - it wasn't considered safe to employ a bull-dozer or men with picks and shovels to repair the crater. The only solution, it was decided, was the "tank dozer."

Arrangements were made with the 16th Engineers of the 1st Armored Division to use one of their tank dozers. The tankmen looked at the crater at 2300 and declared that the tank dozer was not capable of doing the work. The tank dozer could not operate across the slope because of the possibility of shearing a track. Also, the tank dozer could not dig into the hill and cast the dirt into the fill.

The only alternative was to use a regular bull-dozer, with an angled blade, though it had been decided earlier that use of such an unprotected machine would be unsafe.

Lt. Col. William C. Holley, the commanding officer of the 316th, was present at the site throughout the night's operation. He had arranged that, in addition to the security of foot troops one-fourth of a mile north of the crater, counter-battery and counter-mortar fire would be laid down on call from him. These arrangements had been made with Corps and Division Artillery. When reconnaissance was completed and the dozer was ready to start work on the crater, Colonel Holley called for artillery fire. Working swiftly and expertly, the dozer operator dug dirt from the side of the hill, pushed it into the hole. In less than fifteen minutes, he cut his way through the crater, making it passable one way for tanks and light transportation.

Now the "gate" to Livergnano was opened. Our forces moved in, with supporting fire power this time. The town was occupied during the night of the 14th, and on the 15th the infantry was able to advance north of one of the worst "bottlenecks" that had ever confronted the Division in combat.

The Engineer's Part in Defense

Livergnano was secured. The Division's foot troops moved northward again along Highway 65, slowly, against the most stubborn resistance yet encountered. The enemy artillery and mortar fire was heavy, and the infantry moved forward only with great effort and expense. The advance, in mid-October, slowed down and then came to a halt. A determined, reinforced enemy was facing the Division.

In those days following the occupation of Livergnano, new mission for the Engineers decreased in ratio with the decrease in new ground taken. B Company had swept and cleared the highway to the front lines. Poor lateral roads to either side of the main route in the Division zone were opened for light traffic to units on the flanks. For several days, from 16 October to the 22nd, the Engineer companies found few new roads to maintain. They had more time, men and equipment available for improving the routes which they had already hurriedly opened as the infantry had moved north. Where they had quickly filled craters for one-way traffic, they now returned to widen and improve them for two-way, heavier traffic. Where roads were showing the wear and tear of unaccustomed numbers of supply trucks, they graded and smoothed them.

The advance from Monghidoro through Livergnano had presented a lot of obstacles. During the Division's movements in October - and that meant, in the main part, during the first half of the month - the Engineers had filled 40 road craters, removed three road blocks, installed nine culverts, and constructed thirteen by-passes. Now, with the front lines in a static state, many of these were improved.

One of the front line missions of the Engineers after the fall of Livergnano serves to show clearly the close cooperation between infantry and supporting Engineers in direct action against the enemy. In order to assault the armor which the Germans were employing north of Livergnano, the 363rd Infantry wanted to bring three of its anti-tank guns into good firing positions on the north side of a ridge a short distance northeast of the town. A small trail running due north to the desired position was found by C Company of the Engineers, but it was too narrow to accommodate the .57mm guns. A dozer was set to work to widen the trail, but the work was rough and hampered by bad weather, and the dozer fell off the trail, stuck fast in the mud, with its motor stalled. It blocked all attempts to get the guns past. The Engineers then made a foot reconnaissance of another possible route. They used two peeps, hooked together in order to have sufficient power, to tow the first gun up the ridge over the new route. They managed to get the two peeps and gun almost to the top of the ridge, but the peeps couldn't quite make the remainder of the grade. Again, the Engineers employed a dozer. The dozer widened the trail as it went in order to get to the stalled peeps and gun. The dozer pulled the gun into position, helped the peeps down the ridge, and then returned to tow the other two guns into the desired positions.

Where, during the first part of the month, the Germans had been the main source of Engineer problems, the terrible Fall weather conditions now became the cause of many extra man-hours of road work. The Battalion was not unprepared; it had fought the "battle of mud" earlier in the vicinity of Pietramala, Monghidoro and Loiano. It had learned from experience, and sheer work.

While some elements continued to concentrate on the improvement of the roads in the Sabbioni-La Guarde-Livergnano are to keep supplies moving to the forward troops, others "back-tracked" and handled the jobs that arose in the areas toward the rear.

The slow, steady rain that fell on the curving mountain roads caused, among others, one problem that kept elements of A Company busy for several days. The 91st Division Clearing Station had been set up off Highway 65 south of Loiano. One dirt road led into the area. The rain, plus the heavy amount of traffic which necessarily moved in and out of the area, had made the road almost impassable, and ambulances and other vehicles found it a major problem to get to the Clearing Station. On the 18th, the Engineers put 18 truckloads of rock on the road, and on the 22nd they placed 50 more loads of rock on the road. Still, with the continuing rain, the road remained in very bad condition. There seemed to be no base to the road, and the mud was loose and deep. Sixty truckloads of rock were poured on it on the 28th, and the Engineers returned the next day to drain the road and install a culvert in one place. The rain and the traffic continued to make the roadway almost impassable. The Engineers decided to put their own base down. They obtained chicken wire matting, dumped many truckloads of straw along the road, added rock for more foundation, placed 500 years of the matting on the route and pinned down the matting with long rods which they had taken from artillery shell cartons. A number of Italian civilians who had been hired by the Clearing Station were employed to ditch the road.

On the 22nd, the Engineers' main effort changed. Receiving orders that the Division would take up defensive positions along the present front lines, the Engineers' main mission was diverted from road maintenance to the task of supplying, supervising and installing field fortifications. On the scale planned, this was a new combat experience for the Battalion. But it was work for which the Engineers had long trained. The 135th Infantry of the 34th Division was attached to the 91st Division and given the west sector of the Division zone. Company B of the 316th Engineer Battalion was placed in direct support of the 135th. The 361st Infantry occupied the right sector. The units were ordered to use barbed wire, mines and cratering charges to assist in defending their lines so that only a minimum number of foot troops would be required actually on the line at one time. One purpose was to rest a maximum number of troops.

A few days later the 362nd RCT, with C Company of the Engineers attached, was ordered to move to the 88th Division where it would operate as an attached unit of that Division. The move to the east was accomplished on the 25th, and Captain James C. Coulter, the Engineer company commander, reported later that the roads and bridges in the sector were in need of constant attention. The 88th Division Engineers' main effor was building a road from the town of S. Clemente over N. Grande. C. Company's part in this mission was the leading and hauling of rock. The company also had the responsibility for the MSR from S. Clemente to a point about three miles beyond the town. Captain Coulter reported that the road was a mass of mud and that traffic over the route was heavy, necessitating constant maintenance work.

Upon receipt of orders from Division on the 22nd, the Engineer Battalion set to work immediately on the 91st's defense plans. It knew its mission was to supply all fortification materials to the infantry, and that it would furnish technical supervision for the stringing of barbed wire entanglements and concertinas, and the placing of cratering charges and the laying of mines. Procurement was the initial problem, and it was met on the first afternoon. Contacts were made at once with Army supply authorities. The first supplies were in the Battalion's hands on the next day. By the end of the month, the Engineers had obtained 68 truckloads of fortification materials, most of it from the port of Leghorn, which had been captured in July by a force including units of the 91st. A total of 160,000 yards of barbed wire had procured, along with 106,000 sandbags, thousands of yards of wire concertinas,

2,500 anti-tank and anti-personnel mines, eight tons of demolitions and 100 trip-wire flare devices.

By the end of the month, the Battalion had laid 57 anti-personnel mines, 16 anti-tank mines, placed 3,230 pounds of cratering charges along strategic parts of roads on the Division's front, and 4,985 yards of wire entanglements and concertinas had been strung, either by the Engineers or under their supervision. Thousands of sandbags had been issued for protection of machine-gun and mortar emplacements, dug-outs, and artillery positions. At the end of the month the work to improve the Division's defensive positions was continuing.

Mines were laid by the Engineers on orders from the Infantry Regimental commanders. The sites for mines were selected, or approved, by the infantry commanders. Except for one field of 60 anti-tank mines which were placed on Highway 65 at the MLR by the 362nd Infantry, all mines which were placed in the Division's sector were laid by the Engineers themselves. In almost all cases, only small minefields of eight to twelve mines were laid. Anti-personnel mines were placed along paths, trails and poor roads where it was most probable that an advancing enemy would sent troops. Most of the mines were placed in the sector west of Highway 65 in the vicinity of the MLR, which ran southwest. Six anti-personnel mines were laid on the dirt road leading northwest out of Livergnano. A little farther west of the town, nine more were laid in a path.

The mine-laying, as with most of the other work of installing defensive measures, was necessarily done at night. Enemy observation on many of the sites was excellent, making daylight work highly dangerous. Throughout the period, the Engineers were subjected to artillery and mortar fire, but suffered no casualties during the laying of the mines, placing of cratering charges or stringing of barbed wire.

The highway in the vicinity of Livergnano and the secondary roads around the La Guarda area in the west sector were prepared for demolitions in several places. In almost all cases, 40-pound charges were used. Sixteen of these charges were placed on the road just west of La Guarda, seventeen were installed in the road at Scascoli, ten at La Valle. On Highway 65 ten 40-pound charges were placed on the southern outskirts of Livergnano. Two lots of fifteen charges each were placed on the dirt road running northwest out of the town, and ten charges were placed on the highway on the northern outskirts of Livergnano. None of these cratering charges were to be set off except by Division order.

There was a particularly interesting incident connected with the placing of the cratering charges on the highway north of the town. Only a few days before, when the foot troops were pushing northward clear of Livergnano, the Engineers had filled a crater which had been blown by the retreating Germans. Now; in defensive positions, the Engineers returned and placed their own cratering charges in the same spot.

Wire was laid in abundance, especially in the left sector of the Division zone. On the MLR across Highway 65, concertinas were laid in the road. The 135th Infantry used wire along almost all of its front. The wire was strung in single and double apron strands across paths and trails, in creek beds and draws, and in other low places along the front. The Engineers had supervisory personnel on hand each night to assist the infantry in properly stringing their wire. Below the MLR, in the area west of La Valle, about 1,00 yards of wire was strung to protect the Division's left flank.

At the month's end, the positions had already been strengthened and improved. The defensive mission was being continued.

APPENDIX D

Loose Rein Charlie Gerhardt

Veterans who served under Major General Charles H. Gerhardt will never forget the man who initially took command of the Division upon activation, particularly those officers who were at Camp White during the early training days. Captain Charles E. Brown, commander of C Battery, 346th was one of them.

Loose Rein Charlie Gerhardt
"By God You'd Never Know It"

On 24 July 1942, it had been only three weeks and three days since I had received my commission at Fort Sill. My assignment after commissioning was to the 91st Infantry Division which was in process of being formed near Medford, Oregon, at Camp White. Following the rigors of Officers Candidate School, the new Second Lieutenants were given seven days leave in which to recover. I spent my leave with my parents who were then living in Spencerville, Ohio, and then headed for Oregon by train. As I recall, the train took me to Portland and from there to Medford, Oregon, and Camp White, the trip was by bus.

At that time, July 24th, Camp White was still under construction, and contractors equipment and people could be seen all about the Camp. For what I assumed were security reasons, the bus could not go beyond the Camp Main Gate, so I was left to hike the mile or so from the gate to Division Artillery Headquarters, carrying my well loaded val-pak. It was a hot day on the "Agate Desert" and a loaded val-pak was an awkward burden to carry, so it was not a particularly pleasant walk.

Up to this time I had never heard of Major General Charles H. Gerhardt, and certainly I had no expectation whatsoever of meeting him the way I did. About half way toward my destination I was walking along the newly paved road which had deep ditches on both sides. In what appeared to be a parade ground or at least an open area to my left, I observed an individual riding a bay horse. At that time I was not even certain that it was a member of the military establishment, since this person had on a khaki short sleeve shirt and an army service cap, neither of which at that time was regulation uniform. As it turned out, he also had two silver stars embroidered on each of his epaulets which, of course, could not be seen from ground level. The thought that occurred to me was that this was a Military Policeman patrolling the unfinished camp area to keep out unauthorized personnel. When he wheeled his horse toward me and shouted in a challenging voice, "Lieutenant, are you a member of the Armed Forces of the United States?", I still thought he was only trying to determine if I was authorized to be on the premises, and I simply replied, "Yes, am!" His next comment, however, gave me some reason to reflect that perhaps h had some other role, for it was, "By God you'd never know it! You get you Commanding Officer and report to me!" With that he wheeled his mount to the opposite direction and took off at a full gallop.

I still had no indication of the individual's rank and thought that perhaps I ha been accosted by a First Lieutenant or at most a Captain of Military Police Reflecting on this as I trudged along, I began to have second thoughts. The man imperious bearing and commanding tone of voice pointed to the conclusion tha I had offended someone of somewhat higher rank. Even so, I was not overl concerned at this point. After all, I had official orders to report to this very place and I was sure that this would clear up any misgivings that the man on the hors may have had.

Division Artillery Headquarters was temporarily in a building adjacent t Division Headquarters. I was directed to a room where I was told I would find th Acting Battalion Commander of my unit, the 346th Field Artillery Battalion. Th acting commander was a pleasant young major to whom I reported. He examine my orders and directed me to the BOQ where I would be quartered. At that poin I inquired of him, "Who is the character on the horse?" His face took on a somewha pained expression and his immediate response was, "My God what have yo done?" Whereupon, I explained the incident which had occurred on the way fron the main gate. The Major informed me that I had had a run in with the commandin, general of the 91st Infantry Division, Charles H. Gerhardt. I think the Major an I both concluded at the same moment that perhaps the General was expecting som more formal military recognition than I had given him - such as perhaps a salute The Major told me to go on to my quarters. He would make an appointment wit the General the next day and the two of us would report as ordered.

On the way to the BOQ the potential impact of what had occurred began to sink in. I could visualize gold bars fluttering off in the breeze, and mine being one of the shortest commissions in the history of the United States Army. It seemed the bette part of wisdom to busy myself with preparation of my defense. I disposed of my val-pak in my assigned room and headed out for the scene of the crime. I establishe the proximate positions of myself and the General and paced off the distance from where I was walking, down through the ditch and across the parade ground to where the General had been on his horse. The distance measured well over the thirty pace; which was the distance within which the rules of military courtesy and discipline required saluting a superior officer. I didn't really expect the General to be very much impressed with this, but I did think that perhaps a court-martial would take it into account.

Later that same afternoon, General Edward S. Ott, the Commander of Division Artillery, held an Officer's Call of all the artillery officers who had reported in so far. The meeting was to be held at the end of the temporary Division Artillery Headquarters. There was a small porch or landing at the end of the building and that is where the General chose to address the troops. Just by chance I was in the hallway of that building as the General was preparing to make his appearance. I noticed that he had his overseas cap on backwards, so that the star was in the back instead of in front. Knowing that that would be a source of great embarrassment to the General, I approached him and said, "Pardon me General, but your cap is on backwards." He thanked me very graciously. As he was addressing the assembled officers shortly after, he said, "I want all officers in Division Artillery to be alert and observant at all times, just like the young lieutenant who told me as I was coming out here that I had placed my hat on backwards." This accolade was entirely unexpected. It is not difficult to appreciate the mixed feelings of a young lieutenant who on the one hand felt he was about to be decommissioned, and on the other was being cited as an example of the type of alert officer the Division Artillery commander wanted to have in his unit.

The next day I reported in to my acting battalion commander at the appointed hour in my freshest uniform with insignia and shoes gleaming. The Major thought the saluting distance factor might help, but he wasn't overly optimistic. We reported to the General's aide, and after a short wait were ushered into the General's presence. The Major reported and identified who we were. It seemed to me that at first the General was a bit puzzled as to why we were there, and the Major went on to explain. Not far into the Major's explanation, it was obvious the General's recollection had been refreshed, and he blurted out, "Oh, he's the one!" His tone was such that I was sure I'd had it. He walked over toward me, looked me up and down, and asked me where I'd gone to college, and what my Army experience had been. I answered briefly and to the point. He turned to the Major and with a wave of his arm said, "Put him through his paces! Put him through his paces!" The Major and I did a crisp about-face and marched out, both greatly relieved. That was it.

Loose Rein Charlie Gerhardt
Hell For Leather

Sometime after WWII an article appeared in "Army" magazine about General Gerhardt and his insistence on strict adherence to the rules about segregating the types of garbage at units kitchens. In the story the author referred to the General as "eccentric", using that word to suggest that the General was considerably "off his rocker". The General was anything but eccentric in that sense. A more accurate description would have been "Hell For Leather". His style may have been flamboyant, but in all fairness, it had one central driving theme, and that was to make better soldiers out of all the people who had been assigned to his division. Some cases in point follow.

In reading these accounts about the General, keep in mind that most of what is described took place in the cadre training period. This was the two or two and a half months from the time the officer and non-commissioned officer cadre assembled until the Division began to receive its fillers, who came mostly from the induction centers across the country. This was a time of getting acquainted, getting organized, leadership training and preparing to receive the fillers. The officers and non-coms who came with the cadre from the 1st Cavalry Division were better acquainted with each other than the rest of us. Some of us among the 65 officers assigned to the Division from OCS Class 20 knew other, but usually only people who had been in the same Selection of the Class. Officers assigned from the Reserve Officers Corps were mostly strangers to each other, although a few had been acquainted before assignment to the Division. In effect it was a "shakedown cruise" for the leadership elements of the Division.

The Daily Bulletin

Just as soon as the General had an office set up, he began publication of a Division Daily Bulletin. This was before activation of the Division 15 August 1942, and in the time when the commissioned and noncommissioned cadre was being assembled.

In Daily Bulletin No. 1 the General decreed in very explicit terms that all directives and instructions contained in the Daily Bulletin would be considered standing orders. In the time the General was with the Division, every possible topic that could come up in training a division was published in that bulletin.

The Training Stick

The Division was to have a motto which was, "March, Shoot and Obey!" To assist in the marching part, the General ordered that every officer would carry a training stick. This was to be made of one inch dowel thirty inches long, which was the length of the soldiers step in close order drill. The stick was to be varnished with clear varnish and was to have two white bands, one six inches wide, on one end and one three inches wide on the other end. This was to serve as a graphic reminder to officers and men alike of the swing of the arm in marching, six inches to the front and three inches to the rear.

The Sight Picture

To further advancement of the "shoot" part of the Division motto, the General published the "Sight Picture" in the Daily Bulletin, and ordered that every soldier in the Division was to be able to describe this. The sight picture consisted of a diagram showing the alignment of the rear sight of the rifle, the front sight and the target, as seen by the person firing the rifle. The General would quiz soldiers about this at random, and if they could not adequately describe the sight picture, the soldier's commanding officer had some tall explaining to do.

I can never forget an incident when part of our Battery was on the rifle firing range and a QuarterMaster Unit under the command of a lieutenant took up position on our left flank. It was the lieutenant's misfortune to have the General gallop up on his horse to observe the firing. He singled out one of the Quartermaster soldiers and demanded that he describe the sight picture. Whether because he didn't know the answer or because of sheer fright, he couldn't describe the sight picture. The General wheeled toward the officer and bellowed, "Lieutenant, if this were combat, I'd draw my pistol and blow your brains out!", at the same time laying his hand on his pistol holster as if to dramatize the point. I'm not sure but what the Lieutenant had the feeling his brains were about to be blown out then and there, combat or no combat. With that the General ordered his Aide to get the Lieutenant's name and his unit, wheeled his horse and galloped off.

It was my good fortune that the General had become so excited that he left in the abrupt manner he did. All of the Charlie Battery soldiers knew how to describe the sight picture, but after the General's demonstration I'm not sure any of them could have done it without considerable stammering and stuttering.

Smoke Abatement

With General Gerhardt black smoke coming from a chimney was on an equal level of excitement with the sight picture, suntans, marching and obedience.

It was proclaimed in the Daily Bulletin that with proper education of troops, it was possible to burn our soft coal in the furnaces and hot water heaters of each barracks, BOQ and other buildings without there being any smoke. The proper technique was to push all of the live burning coals toward the back of the furnace and to deposit the new coal in the forward pocket thus created. The theory was that the smoke given off by the charge of new coal would be super heated and burned by the heat from the live coals at the back. Actually, this worked quite well, and came in handy in later civilian life.

Every unit was required to have a smoke abatement officer and a smoke abatement non-commissioned officer. Their mission was to conduct training in how to properly fire a furnace and to enforce the Smoke Abatement rules with the unit. Woe to the commanding officer whose building belched forth black smoke. Time after time the General would catch sight of the telltale black smoke and gallop off like Sheridan riding toward the sound of battle. He would search out the offending commanding officer, who to his own great consternation, would first learn of the offense from an excited Major General on a froth covered horse. Somehow, it seemed the galloping ride only served to spur on the General's excitement and anger.

But the General couldn't be everywhere, and so more often than not, there would be a call from Division Headquarters to the Headquarters of the unit where black smoke was coming out of the chimney. A written reprimand from the General would follow through channels, and the poor offending commanding would have to reply by endorsement. It's laughable now, but it sure kept every commanding officer in the Division in a sweat, along with all the other sweat conditions the General engendered.

Compulsory Sun Tans

The General ordered that every soldier in the Division was to have a suntan, unless excused for medical reasons. To bring this about every individual in the Division would participated in supervised sunbathing. Initially, this would be fifteen minutes only - seven and one-half minutes on one side, seven and one-half minutes on the other. Gradually, this was increased until every individual had the desired shade of tan. After that, most outdoor training was to be conducted with all personnel stripped to the waist, except in the inclement weather.

At times when soldiers were wearing shirts for whatever reason, the General would at random stop a soldier and order, "Take off your shirt soldier." If that soldier did not have the proper shade of tan, the General said nothing further to the soldier, but immediately sought out his commanding officer who had better have a good reason why the particular soldier didn't have the proper tan.

Uniforms

When it came to uniforms the General had quite a creative streak. As mentioned in my story about my first day at Camp White when the General took exception to my not saluting when he was some distance away on his horse.

He was wearing what's called the Garrison Cap. It's the flat top cap with the bill in front. Actually, at that time it had been outlawed for the duration of the war.

In addition the General had on a short sleeve shirt, which at that time was not authorized, and he had on cavalry riding pants and boots.

Of course, Generals have considerable leeway in designing their own uniforms, or at least they used to have, but in this case he projected unauthorized uniform combinations down to the troops. First off, regulations did not permit soldiers to go about stripped to the waist as the General ordered. Also, regulations did not authorize short sleeve shirts at that time, and so none were available through regular supply channels. The way you obtained a short sleeve shirt was to take a perfectly good long sleeve khaki shirt and cut the sleeves off. Of course, you had to have a tailor do it so that it was the proper length and the cut off edge could be properly hemmed.

Garbage

Garbage very quickly became a sore point with mess sergeants and commanding officers. This was not due so much to the wartime necessity for salvaging and recycling or even the mechanics of sorting and handling. The real soreness came from General Gerhardt's method of enforcing the rules and regulations about the manner of handling garbage.

Those rules and regulations as published in the Daily Bulletin were that each mess hall was to have five garbage cans, one for each category of garbage and trash. The first can was for edibles, the second for non-edibles, the third for tin cans, the fourth for glass and the fifth for paper. The last four were relatively easy. The first, the edibles, was by far the most troublesome. By definition the edibles were food scraps from tables in the kitchen which the farmer-contractors hogs would eat. What many of the city boys on KP never really caught onto was that hogs do no like egg shells or coffee grounds in their food, and most certainly, they did not like non-edibles, tin cans, glass and paper. Each day the farmer-contractor would collect the edibles from the mess halls in the Division. If he found any of those four items in the edibles, which his hogs pointed out to him by refusing to eat such items, the farmer would report this to Division Headquarters, and in every instance, this came to the General's attention. To have the offense discovered and reported in this manner was really the easy way out for the mess sergeant and the commanding officer. While it brought a reprimand from the General and a requirement to reply by endorsement as to how this could possibly happen, the pain was not nearly as excruciating as when the General discovered improperly sorted garbage on his daily rounds of inspection. While he was unhappy anytime he found garbage not sorted according to regulations, when he found egg shells or coffee grounds in the edible can, his displeasure bordered on apoplexy.

On such occasions he would immediately have the KP's dump the contents of the edible garbage can on the pavement near the kitchen and would send his aide to Battalion Headquarters to summon the battalion commander. After this happened the first time in the Division, no one had to tell battalion commanders what was next. What was next was that the battalion commander (usually a Lt. Col.) was ordered to sort the egg shells or other inedibles out of the garbage, all while being harangued by the General. All of this in the presence of the General, his aide, the mess sergeant, the KP's and whoever else happened to be around. There were no known cases of repeat offenders.

Curiously enough, the General did not summon the company or battery commander. His point was to make enough of an impression on the battalion commander that that commander would make absolutely certain that nothing of that sort ever happened again in his command. It was pretty drastic medicine!

The classic case of garbage sorting came one day when the General discovered egg shells in the edible can at one of the battery mess halls of the 348th Field Artillery. He would discover these forbidden bits by dipping his training stick into the garbage and stirring it around.

In any event the General's aide went to fetch the battalion commander, who in this case was Lt. Col. Buhl Moore, a big, strapping soldier like figure, very impressive. Now, it happened that Col. Moore's permanent rank in the Army was greater than that of General Gerhardt. (The ranks held by most officers in wartime were temporary ranks. Regular Army officers had permanent ranks to which they were supposed to revert after the war.)

Col. Moore did not take kindly to the summons delivered to him by the General's aide. He instructed the aide to tell the General that he would be there promptly. He went to his quarters and changed into his dress blues, complete with cape and all awards and decorations. As he strode into sight of the General, he was just putting on his dress yellow lisle gloves.

Standing ramrod straight, Col. Buhl Moore gave the General a snappy salute, at the same time declaring, "Lt. Col. Buhl H. Moore reporting to the General as ordered, Sir!" The General's face flushed red as a beet, but still he ordered the Colonel to sort out the egg shells. The Colonel did. Really, it was rather sad.

I do not recall that there was any instance of commanding officers sorting garbage after that.

It always seemed to me that there were better leadership techniques for instilling discipline in a unit. It must be said, however, that the General did succeed in getting across the idea that his orders were to be obeyed.

The Division Battle Cry

In WWI, the soldiers of the 91st Division had been drawn from the states of the northwest as far as Montana and Wyoming. The Powder River originates in eastern Wyoming and flows north through eastern Montana into the Yellowstone. The story goes that before uniforms were issued, one soldier called out to another, "Hey cowboys, where you from?" The response was, "Powder River!" The reply from the first soldier was, "Let'er Buck!" This sort of exchange was repeated at times across Fort Lewis, and so was born the Division battle cry of the 91st Infantry Division, "Powder River Let'er Buck!" It became the official battle cry for the WWI Division throughout its training and its fighting in France.

There is a longer version which goes: "It's a mile wide, an inch deep, too thin to plow, too thick to drink, flows uphill all the way to the sea, Powder River, Let'er Buck!"

At one point early in the game, General Gerhardt gathered all of the officers of the Division on the bleachers behind Division Headquarters. After a speech on some topics I do not remember, he shouted into the microphone, "In WWI this Division had a battle cry. It was Powder River, Let'er Buck! That's gonna be the Division battle cry in this war.! And then out of the blue without any warning, he says, "Now, give the Division battle cry at my command, command!" Now for the most part we considered ourselves educated, mature, even sophisticated people, and to most of us this all seemed a bit juvenile. There was an almost inaudible, "Powder River, Let'er Buck", hardly in unison at that. The General bellowed into the microphone, "Goddammit, that's not loud enough, and you're gonna stay here til it is!" And we did.

It took awhile for Powder River, Let'er Buck to catch on, but it did. It became ingrained in every individual in the Division, even to the point where at times soldiers of a unit would spontaneously cry, "Powder River, Let'er Buck!" especially when the going got tough, whether from weather, physical exertion or pure exhaustion. Even today it stirs strong emotions in any man who wore the fir tree. After training and combat, we had to admit the General knew what he was doing with "Powder River, Let'er Buck!"

The 91 Mile March

Along in early September 1942, really before we had been completely acclimated to Powder River Let'er Buck, the General again assembled all division officers on the bleachers behind Division Headquarters. He went through a list of things he had on his mind and then said, "By God (usually when the General wanted to emphasize a given point, he started it with "By God" or "Goddammit) this is the 91st Division and we're going on a 91 mile march!" By this time we'd been with the General enough to know that that was exactly what we were going to do.

Our real fear was that with his approach to things, we were going to do it in two or three days. If that was his idea, we were fortunate that wiser heads prevailed. Actually, we took six days which made an average of 15 miles a day, which for our age and condition wasn't that bad at all, for most of us. It was extremely hard on some of the senior staff officers and commanders - as with Colonel Virtue, the Division adjutant general (mostly administration and personnel work). He probably had not done a hike of more than two or three miles over the last twenty years, until he met up with General Gerhardt.

The official distances were 10 miles the first day, September 7, 14 miles on the 8th, 16 miles on the 9th, 16 miles on the 10th, 15 miles on the 11th and 20 miles on the 12th. With as a long a column as we made on the road, these distances varied some from unit to unit. For the last day, the Record of Events Section of the Charlie Battery Morning Report reads, "Left Sturgess Mine 0700. Arrived Camp White 1450. Distance marched 22.1 miles. Total distance marched 91.55 miles. Morale-Excellent. Completed march without a casualty."

As a matter of fact, the 346th Field Artillery was the only unit in the Division to complete the march without losing a single man. The Division Daily Bulletin for 12 September announced that, "The 346th Field Artillery Battalion is the only unit in the Division to finish the 91 mile march without dropping out a single individual." (Some claim there was switching of KP's who came out in the Kitchen Trucks.) Four days later the General's father wrote to him, "You are certainly putting them through their paces, and they will either be fit or finished."

In all fairness to the Infantrymen, they carried a heavier total load than other troops in the Division. The Infantry pack weighed in somewhere between forty-five and sixty pounds. Most in non-Infantry units carried a musette bag pack attached to webbing suspenders in turn fastened to the web belt. This contained a days change of clothing, mess kit, toilet articles including towel and other assorted items. Two blankets rolled in a shelter half (one-half of a pup tent) were formed in horseshoe shape over the mussette bag and lashed to it. In the Field Artillery the officers and senior non-coms carried side arms (the Colt .45 semi-automatic pistol) and all others carried the 30 caliber carbine. In the infantry officers and senior non-coms carried either the .45 or the 30 caliber carbine. All others carried the M1 30 caliber semi-automatic rifle, twice the weight of the carbine.

To demonstrate what he considered his superior physical condition, General Gerhardt started out the march carrying a BAR (Browning Automatic rifle) which weighed 19.2 pounds, almost twice the weight of an M1. From time to time the

General's wife would bring their ten year old son to march with the troops. The boy marched the first day and noted with pride that his father was carrying a larger gun than anyone else. When his mother brought him back the second day, he quickly noticed that his father had switched to an ordinary M1 rifle. He blurted out, "Daddy, where's that other gun?" The General quietly tried to hush him up, but with the insistence of a ten year old, his son repeated the question. This question and response sequence went on several times until finally the General said, "Well, to tell you the truth, son, your old man just ain't the man he thought he was." The ten year old had forced an answer that no one in the whole Division could have gotten otherwise.

Most of the fifth day and part of the sixth day, the marching was in rugged mountain terrain. At first it seemed to hit the downhill side after a long steep climb. It wasn't long before we learned what seasoned marchers know, and that is that it's tougher on the knees going downhill on long stretches than it is going up.

Approaching the outskirts of Medford, we must have been a bedraggled looking bunch. As we encountered townspeople out to cheer us on, sagging forms straightened up, the ranks closed and the pace quickened. So far as I can recall, it was the first time we'd ever been in the formation parading for civilians.

Most of the time each battery or company kitchen truck came out for the evening meal and breakfast and with a brown sack lunch for the next days march. Captain Warren, then the C Battery commander, ordered the mess sergeant to have a keg of cold beer waiting for the battery when it marched into the battery area. From Medford to the battery area was about eight miles, but we covered that in record time, something on the order of the old horse headed for the barn. It was a hot sunny day, but the cold beer was waiting for us, as the Captain had ordered, when the footsore troops of Charlie Battery closed into their area. That cold beer was by far the best any of us had ever tasted.

Small wonder that the General's antics and efforts began to attract the attention of the Press. The Daily Bulletin for 26 December 42 quoted Pinkly of United Press, "You are doing a superb job of hardening and toughening up the 91st Division." Not too long after that, Time Magazine did a piece on General Gerhardt and the 91st. It was done as a companion piece to another about a striptease artist. The heading for the duet was, "He Strips to Train, She Strips to Tease!" This harks back to the Suntan and Uniform Stories.

The Decathalon

General Gerhardt's mind was always actively working on different means and methods of toughening his men, building self-confidence and esprit, and in the process, eliminating (as he saw it) the weak and unfit. In the early days we could only believe that he stayed awake nights thinking up new ways to do this.

In one such session, borrowing from his athletic background and the Greeks, he came up with the idea of a military decathlon. Similar to the civilian athletic event, this was to be a series of ten events of military skill, discipline and endurance. As we understand, he first mentioned this to his two aides who showed great enthusiasm for the idea (whether faked or real, we'll never know). In any event, their enthusiasm got them the assignment of laying out the decathlon course.

And a fiendishly good job they did. I'm sure it was every bit as stenuous as the General had originally pictured it in his mind. The course consisted of: (1) a 5 mile hike to the rifle range; (2) firing ten rounds with the rifle; (3) hike back to camp, and in the course of that, performing events 4, 5 and 6; (4) was to stop at the pistol range and fire ten rounds with the .45 semi-automatic pistol; (5) stop at the obstacle course and run the entire course, which was a veritable decathlon all its own; (6) next, stop at the grenade throwing course and attempt to throw three practice grenades through a 4' x 4' frame made of two by fours approximately fifteen feet off the ground; (7) hike 5 miles to the Rogue River; (8) swim the Rogue River with pack and rifle; (9) run up the steep river bank and crawl some distance under low strung barbed wire; (10) run 100 yards wearing a gas mask. All events were carefully scored.

Having laid out the Decathlon as ordered, the aides reported back to General Gerhardt enthused by what they considered to be the good work they had done. To their great short-lived pleasure, the General was equally enthusiastic. To reward his aides for such a fine job, he ordered the two of them to be the first to run the course, with the condition that if they did not have the two highest scores among the officers of the Division, then he would find himself some new aides.

Some further comments are necessary to attempt to recreate the full impact of the Decathlon. First, the event had to be completed within a minimum time frame. Those who failed to do this were required to run the course a second time. Those doing better than the limited time, were given additional points on their total score. The time element meant that all of what are described as "hikes" had to be done about half at marching pace (quick time) and half at double time. Needless to say, this type of exertion did nothing to steady the eye and the rest of the body for firing the rifle and the pistol and even for throwing the grenades. Similarly the hike to the Rogue River, swimming the river and charging up the steep bank left the participant in a virtual state of quivering collapse at the top of the bank. In this state of loose body control, it was difficult to crawl under the low slung barbed wire without being caught on the barbs.

The real coup de grace came, however, on the 100 yard dash wearing the gas mask. The masks were made of rubber and metal and for hours and had been laying on a dark canvas tarp in the hot sun. Every gasp for air brought only a hot blast that seemed to seer every part of your breathing apparatus. What a joy at the end of the 100 yards to rip off the gas mask, take a deep breath of fresh air and feel the cooling effect of the rapidly evaporating water of the Rogue. It was over!

Having anticipated the horrors of having to run that event twice, I was motivated enough to make a passing score the first time around. The General's aides, having even more motivation than the rest of us, also made it the first time around, and furthermore, did have the two highest scores among the officers of the Division. Their jobs were saved, but I'll bet anything that if they ever laid out another military obstacle course, it wasn't as rough as the one at Camp White.

A further note about the Rogue - to speak of a swim across the Rogue River is to speak of more than just a couple of laps across your swimming pool. The Rogue is known for its swift current and cold water. It flows out of the Cascade Mountains where its waters are produced by the melting snows of winter. At the point of the Decathlon crossing, it is about 150 feet across. The swiftest current is in the middle. It took a strong swimmer to make it across without winding up way down the stream.

On a previous occasion, General Gerhardt came close to losing a goodly number of the members of his Division staff and senior unit commanders. It was the General's intent to put on a demonstration for a group of good citizens of Medford. Included in his demonstration group were two Brigadier Generals, a half dozen colonels and lieutenant colonels, and majors in proportion, some in their fifties. All of them had packs, canteens, helmet liners and M1 rifles with fixed bayonets. The demonstration turned into a debacle. The General, his aides and a few others made it to the far shore. Had it not been for the safety rope strung across the river and the goodly number of life guards on hand, the event could have turned into a real tragedy.

The Alerts

During our early days at Camp White, there was a series of incidents in which Japanese submarines shelled the Oregon-Washington coast several times and launched balloons with bombs attached to them to drift inland and explode upon landing. All of this was very much at random and nothing of significance was ever hit by either of the weapons. Most of the balloons landed at widely scattered locations in the pine forests covering the Cascade Mountains. The effect on the U.S. population, however, was electric. There was media speculation as to whether this was a prelude to the invasion of our mainland by the Japanese. While it is doubtful that the military high command felt this was an imminent possibility, for political reasons our government did not dare to ignore it. Defense sectors were organized along the entire western coast, and the 91st became a part of this.

This was indeed grist for General Gerhardt's mill. How much of what followed was ordered by higher headquarters, and how much was the General's own idea we never knew. The General's approach was to treat the situation as though the Japanese might storm ashore at any moment. Keep in mind that the Division still had only its officer and non-commissioned officer cadre.

The General set up a series of Alert exercises to train for ready response at all echelons. No one except the General, and possibly his G3 (operations officer), knew when these Alert exercises were going to occur. As it turned out, most of them took place sometime between 2200 and 0530. The Record of Events Section entry in the Charlie Battery Morning Report for 5 October reads as follows:

"Division Practice Alert. Battery alerted as 0515. Marched to Battalion Headquarters and reported there at 0535. Battery entrucked and pulled one howitzer. Batteries lined up and joined combat team at 362d Infantry Motor Park at 0650. Travelled 2 1/2 miles toward Antelope Range and went into position to protect Camp White from enemy attack from east. Ate breakfast in field and then moved back to camp, arriving in Battery area at 1025. Distance marched 5 miles. Weather-clear and cool. Morale-good."

At other times the Alert would be in the wee hours of the morning and end within an hour or less, when all units reported to Division that they were in formation and ready to move out.

The Alert on 13 November came at 0530 and lasted through the 14th, ending on the 15th at 1115. That's the sort of thing the units had to be prepared for, even on the one hour Alerts which only tested readiness. To fake it was to not be prepared for two or three days in the field.

One Alert that stands out among the rest came at 2200 hours. There was a dance going on at the Division Officers' Club with a good representation of the Division's officers in attendance. Whether by design or coincidence, the route of march out into the range went right by the Officer's Club. In the true spirit of a combat alert, all officers were ordered out of the club to join their respective units as they passed by.

What a sight it was the next morning to see those gentlemen in uniform of "pinks" and greens, wearing low cut dress shoes and overseas caps, rather than G.I. shoes and helmets. By the time they got back to Camp, they and their dress uniforms were a shambles. They were covered with the dust, mud and dead grass and leaves encountered in the maneuver area. While initially none of them were really that pleased about the whole situation, they took it in good spirits, shined their shoes and sent their uniforms off to the cleaners. Somehow it seemed that after such an experience you couldn't join in the final, "Powder River, Let'er Buck!" at the top of your lungs and still be disgruntled. Maybe that's part of what "Powder River, Let'er Buck!" was all about.

If You Can't See It, You Can't Hit It!

Like the rest of us, General Gerhardt learned a few things during the cadre training period. One of the best examples of this grew out of an artillery firing demonstration conducted by Captain Warren.

After the firing the General came up to inspect the piece, in this case a 105 mm howitzer. He looked over different parts and then peered into the gunsight. Keep in mid the head of the gunsight would turn 6400 mils (360 degrees) so as to be able to refer to aiming points or aiming stakes in any direction to control the direction of the tube for firing. In this case the sight head was turned to the right rear. Upon looking through the sight the General exclaimed, "What do I see? I see myself! Goddamit, if you can't see it, you can't hit it! We're going to put these guns on top of hills where we can see what we're shooting at, just like they did in the Civil War."

Even though he had but a short while before been a lieutenant colonel of Cavalry, it was incomprehensible to us that apparently the General had never been introduced to the concept of indirect fire. There had been great changes in artillery tactics, techniques and method of fire since the years of the Civil War. Instead of being able to see what he was shooting at, as in those days, by the time of World War II and even World War I, the cannoneers seldom saw the targets they were shooting at. An observer, usually with the Infantry or in an observation plane, would send down the location of the target in relation to the guns, either by telephone or radio, to a Battalion Fire Direction Center or directly would convert the target location information into fire commands to the guns at the batteries which would tell them what deflection (direction) to set on the sight and what elevation (how far to raise the tube) to set. It was almost always necessary for the observer to make adjustments after the first rounds were fired.

It was our good fortune, and the Division's, to have as Division artillery commander, Brigadier General Edward S. Ott, who was one of the finest officers in the service. Not only did he know his artillery well, he was a soft spoken, thorough-going gentleman. As we all learned, this quality did not mean that he was not firm. We soon found out that when an officer like General Ott made a suggestion, that was an order.

No one said anything to General Gerhardt out in the field about the changes in artillery since the Civil War. General Ott in his very diplomatic manner had a private session with the General in which he explained how modern artillery worked. We never again heard General Gerhardt say anything about putting out guns on hill tops. He was quite content to leave deployment and management of the artillery to General Ott.

What, Then, Is To Be Said Of General Gerhardt?

General Gerhardt left the 91st in July 1943. He had been with the Division just a little short of one year. He was sent to command the 29th Infantry Division which was then in England. The 29th turned out to be one of the assault divisions in the Normandy landings. Though we never saw or heard any authoritative confirmation, we always assumed that he was sent to his new command because of the aggressiveness he displayed in training and assumptions at high levels of command that this quality would carry over into combat - which by all reports it did, in this case.

I had always said while the General commanded the 91st that, "If we fight with this man, we will have a Big Name .... and Big Cemeteries!", and this is just exactly what the 29th had. Of all the one hundred U.S. Divisions, the 29th stood fourth in total number of casualties.

Some of us heard after the war that General Gerhardt was called on the carpet at the Pentagon to explain and justify his heavy casualties at St. Lo. That has always seemed somewhat unfair to me, for it appeared that he was taken from the 91st and sent to the 29th just because of his hell for leather aggressiveness and the desire of the Army to have this type of leader commanding assault landing divisions.

Whether because of high casualties or just by chance, the General was reduced from Major General to his permanent rank of lieutenant colonel. In that rank he served one or more tours as a military attache in South America.

I saw General Gerhardt only one time after the war. That was in the Officers Club at Fort George G. Meade in Maryland in the early 1950's. The General was seated by himself at a table for two when I spotted him. While I did not immediately break out with "Powder River Let'er Buck", I did go over and introduce myself, told him of my outfit and that I had been on the 91 mile march. His immediate response was, "Do your feet still hurt?" We chatted briefly, but long enough to be able to tell that the General enjoyed his days at Camp White with the 91st.

Whatever it might have been like for the 91st to have fought under General Gerhardt in Italy, most Powder River men feel that our training under him was good for us. It was not pleasant and it was rough, just as war itself is unpleasant and rough. It did much to prepare us temperamentally, in state of mind, in physical toughness and in military skills for what we faced in Italy. It drilled into us the prime mission of an infantry division - victory in combat.

In reflecting on the matter during and since the war I have concluded that we in the 91st were fortunate to have General Gerhardt during the most formative months of our training and, perhaps, even more fortunate to have General Livesay lead the Division in corps maneuvers and combat. Like General Ott, General Livesay was firm, steady and gentlemanly. He demanded our best and with his own leadership style and techniques, he got our best. It is my own opinion that the 91st accomplished as much in combat in Italy under General Livesay's firm and considerate leadership as it would have under General Gerhardt's more flamboyant style.

In the time he was with the 91st, General Gerhardt's most glaring fault was his penchant for reprimanding people in the presence of their peers, subordinates and, indeed, all other ranks. Certainly, this was a serious departure from what we were taught in leadership training. In some commands his treatment of Colonel Moore in the garbage incident would have resulted in his having been reprimanded or even more severely disciplined.

The General may have felt that the urgency of the war situation demanded this sort of thing. Commanders at all levels were under great pressure to turn out combat ready divisions in the shortest possible time. Their success in doing this prompted General Erwin Rommel in his memoirs to marvel at the speed with which the U.S. Army turned "raw recruits" into combat ready divisions.

Perhaps the permissibility of the immediate public reprimand is a matter of degree. I recall when Colonel Cotton of the 362nd Infantry Regiment was leading his 3rd Battalion Combat Team across the Po Valley after the 5th Army burst out of the North Appenines. The Germans were in rapid retreat. Colonel Cotton had stopped his command group to do some map reconnaissance about where we were and where we should be heading. I was there as liaison from the artillery. Some of us noticed a small cloud of dust rapidly growing larger. In mere minutes General Livesay's jeep was screeching to a halt alongside Colonel Cotton and his group. The General leaped from his jeep shouting, "Colonel Cotton, Suh, your orders were to keep moving in pursuit of the enemy and not to stop, Suh! You are to move out at once, Suh!" In a flurry of folding maps and a stampede of people to their vehicles, we were off in a flash. As I recall we didn't stop till we hit the banks of the Po River.

I do not recall or know of any other instance of General Livesay's issuing a direct public reprimand in that fashion, although it may have happened. The point is he did it in a much more controlled manner than shouting, "I ought to draw my pistol and blow your brains out!", as General Gerhardt did on the firing range that day. Sooner or later every commander faces a situation were the book rule has to be bent a little bit, but these had better be exceptional situations.

BIBLIOGRAPHY

Appennino Bolognese. civilita ed incanti della nature. L'inchiostroblu. Bologna. 1989.

The Army Almanac. A Book of Facts Concerning the Army of the United States. Washington. 1950.

Blumenson, Martin. Salerno to Cassino. Office of the Chief of Military History. Washington. 1977.

Brandano, Anthony R. Burden of Battle. Unpublished manuscript. 1986.

Brown, John Sloan. Draftee Division. University Press of Kentucky, 1986.

Casella, Luciano. The European War of Liberation. Tuscany and the Gothic Line. La Nova Europa. Firenze. 1983.

Clark, Mark W. Calculated Risk. New York. 1951.

Consalvo, Domenick S. The Eagle That Did Not Fly. Paxton, Ill. 1989.

Delany, John P. The Blue Devils in Italy. Infantry Journal Press. Washington. 1949.

D'Este, Carlo. Fatal Decision. Harper Collins. New York. 1991.

———. World War II in the Mediterranean. Algonquin Books. Chapel Hill, N.C. 1990.

Fifth Army History. Volumes 6-9. Privately printed. 1946.

Fisher, Ernest F. Cassino to the Alps. Center for Military History. Washington. 1977.

From Oasis into Italy. War Poems and Diaries from Africa and Italy. Shepard-Walwyn. London. 1983.

Fry, James C. Combat Soldier. National Press. Washington. 1968.

Graham, Dominick and Bidwell, Shelford. Tug of War. The Battle for Italy. St Martin's Press. New York. 1986.

Hawsey, Wade and Wahlfeldt, Betty Galman. War Journey. BW Enterprises. Cantonment, FL. 1986.

Huebner, Klaus H. Long Walk Through War. Texas A&M. College Station, Texas. 1987.

La Futa. una strada nella storia. Fotografie di Stefano Monetti. Testi de cure di Maurizio Ascari. L'inchiostroblu. Bologna. 1991.

Livengood, Roy. Thunder in the Apennines. The Story of the 361st Infantry in Italy. Waukegan, Il. 1981.

Lombroso, Sylvia. No Time for Silence. Roy Publishers. New York. 1945.

Livergnano, 1944-45. a cura di Sellari, Luigi. La Scarabeo. Bologna. 1992.

Lydick, Jesse with Paula Ruth Moore. One Man's Word. Nightjar Press. Las Cruces, NM. 1990.

Monetti, Stefano. Appennino. armonic di un pasesaggio. L'inchiostroblu. Bologna. 1989.

Montemaggi, Amedeo. Offensiva della linea gotica. Guidicini a Rosa Editori. Imola. 1980.

MacDonald, Charles B. and Mathews, Sidney T. Three Battles: Arnaville, Altuzzo and Schmidt. Center for Military History. Washington. 1952.

Morris, Eric. Circles of Hell. The War in Italy, 1942-1945. Hutchinson. London. 1993.

———. La Guerra Inutile. La campagna d'Italia. Longanesi. Milan 1993.

Morris, George M. The Replacement. Privately printed. 1991.

Orgill, Douglas. The Gothic Line. Zebra Books. New York. 1986.

Puptent Poets. Compiled by Cpl. Charles A. Hogan and Cpl. John Welsh III. The Stars and Stripes. Italy. 1945.

Robbins, Robert A. The 91st Infantry Division in World War II. Infantry Journal Press. Washington. 1947.

Roice, John. Army Memories. Privately printed. No date.

Rosignoli, Guido. The Allied Forces in Italy. 1943-45. Sterling. New York. 1989.

Schultz, Paul L. The 85th Infantry Division in World War II. Infantry Journal Press. Washington. 1949.

Tapert, Annette. Lines of Battle. Letters from American Serviceman, 1941-45. Times Books. New York, 1987.

Truscott, Lucian. Command Missions. New York. 1946.

Villari, Luigi. The Liberation of Italy. C.C. Nelson-Appelton. 1959.

Vitali, Roberto. Pianoro. Storie e immagini di un antico borgo. Cooperative Culturale Charlie Chaplin. Ferrara. 1989.

Wiltse, Charles M. The Medical Department: Medical Service in the Mediterranean and Minor Theaters. Center for Military History. Washington. 1965.

Workers of the Writers Program. WPA. Oregon. End of the Trail. Metropolitan Press. Portland, Oregon. 1940.

ACKNOWLEDGMENTS

This book could never have been written without the cooperation of the veterans of the Powder River Division who sent me their comments and personal narratives. A list of these contributors would require several pages so I'll simply say, "You know who you are." However, there are a few individuals whom I would like to thank personally for one reason or another. They are: James E. Bell, Ennis Beeson, Henry Behringer, Fred W. Booth, Anthony R. Brandano, Charles E. Brown, Charles R. Cawthon, Mel Cotton, Robert Dunning, Lt. General Bill Fulton, Paul Fussell, Martha Gellhorn, Virginia Keys, March Kovas, John Lynch, Jean Mater, Bob Palassou, John Roice, Phil and Georgie Scaglia, Bob Schmieding, Louis Simpson, and my editor Pamela Wood.

Nor could I let this book go to print without mentioning and thanking my many Italian friends for their help, hospitality, love and friendship. They include: Cesare Agostini; Fernando Bettini; Claudio Coliva; Rossano and Claudio Corradetti, Pierluigi Corraro, Domenico and Stella Filelfi, Fernando and Mariella Gemignani, Ardevilla Lelli, Umberto Magnani, Giuseppe Mazzanti, Patrizia Piana, Franco Santi, Luigi Selleri and the townspeople of Loiano and Livergnano.

Lastly, my thanks go to my wife Rita for her steadfastness, loyalty and love.

Gorizia. Smiling members of Company I, 361st. Standing, left to right: J. Arvantes, A. Avila, H. Boynton. Kneeling, left to right: J. Mazurowski and Lt. Roberts.

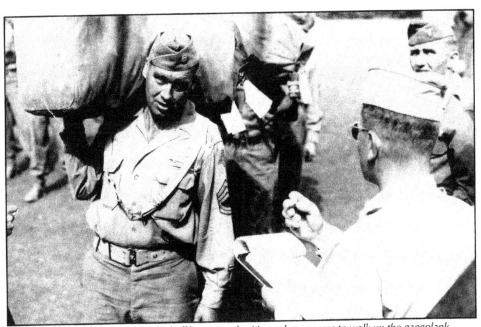

An infantry sergeant is checked off by port authorities as he prepares to walk up the gangplank.

Oregon Days, 3rd Battalion, 363rd Infantry. (Photos from Richard Root.)

Left: T/5 Lawrence J. Foye having a short snort and 1st Sgt. Richard Mosier, with the pistol, demanding a "turn" at the jug. Both of company I, 362nd. Right: T/4 Casper J. Gilles, cook in company I, 362nd.

An exhausted 5th Army infantryman takes ten during the drive north.

91st Division Insignia. Fort Baker, California.

Printed in the USA
CPSIA information can be obtained
at www.ICGtesting.com
JSHW012018140824
68134JS00033B/2765

9 781620 454138